Sound Matters

Biblical Performance Criticism Series
Orality, Memory, Translation, Rhetoric, Discourse

David Rhoads and Kelly R. Iverson, Series Editors

The ancient societies of the Bible were overwhelmingly oral. People originally experienced the traditions now in the Bible as oral performances. Focusing on the ancient performance of biblical traditions enables us to shift academic work on the Bible from the mentality of a modern print culture to that of an oral/scribal culture. Conceived broadly, biblical performance criticism embraces many methods as means to reframe the biblical materials in the context of traditional oral cultures, construct scenarios of ancient performances, learn from contemporary performances of these materials, and reinterpret biblical writings accordingly. The result is a foundational paradigm shift that reconfigures traditional disciplines and employs fresh biblical methodologies such as theater studies, speech-act theory, and performance studies. The emerging research of many scholars in this field of study, the development of working groups in scholarly societies, and the appearance of conferences on orality and literacy make it timely to inaugurate this series. For further information on biblical performance criticism, go to www.biblicalperformancecriticism.org.

Books in the Series

Holly E. Hearon & Philip Ruge-Jones, editors
The Bible in Ancient and Modern Media

James A. Maxey
*From Orality to Orality:
A New Paradigm for Contextual Translation of the Bible*

Antoinette Clark Wire
The Case for Mark Composed in Performance

Robert D. Miller II, SFO
Oral Tradition in Ancient Israel

Pieter J. J. Botha
Orality and Literacy in Early Christianity

James A. Maxey & Ernst R. Wendland, editors
Translating Scripture for Sound and Performance

J. A. (Bobby) Loubser
Oral and Manuscript Culture in the Bible

Joanna Dewey
The Oral Ethos of the Early Church

Richard A. Horsley
Text and Tradition in Performance and Writing

Kelley R. Iverson, editor
*From Text to Performance:
Narrative and Performance Criticisms in Dialogue and Debate*

Annette Weissenrieder & Robert B. Coote, editors
*The Interface of Orality and Writing:
Speaking, Seeing, Writing in the Shaping of New Genres*

Thomas E. Boomershine
*The Messiah of Peace:
A Performance-Criticism Commentary on Mark's Passion-Resurrection Narrative*

Terry Giles & William J. Doan
The Naomi Story—The Book of Ruth From Gender to Politics

Bernhard Oestreich
Performance Criticism of the Pauline Letters

Marcel Jousse
Edgard Sienaert, editor
*Memory, Memorization, and Memorizers
The Galilean Oral-Style Tradition and Its Traditionists*

Sound Matters

New Testament Studies in Sound Mapping

Edited by
MARGARET E. LEE

CASCADE *Books* · Eugene, Oregon

SOUND MATTERS
New Testament Studies in Sound Mapping
Biblical Performance Criticism Series 16

Copyright © 2018 Wipf and Stock Publishers. All rights reserved. Except for brief quotations in critical publications or reviews, no part of this book may be reproduced in any manner without prior written permission from the publisher. Write: Permissions, Wipf and Stock Publishers, 199 W. 8th Ave., Suite 3, Eugene, OR 97401.

Cascade Books
An Imprint of Wipf and Stock Publishers
199 W. 8th Ave., Suite 3
Eugene, OR 97401
www.wipfandstock.com

PAPERBACK ISBN: 978-1-5326-4996-7
HARDCOVER ISBN: 978-1-5326-4997-4
EBOOK ISBN: 978-1-5326-4998-1

Cataloging-in-Publication data:

Names: Lee, Margaret Ellen, 1954-, editor.

Title: Sound matters : New Testament studies in sound mapping / edited by Margaret E. Lee.

Description: Eugene, OR: Cascade Books, 2018. | Biblical Performance Criticism Series 16. | Includes bibliographical references.

Identifiers: ISBN: 978-1-5326-4996-7 (paperback). | ISBN: 978-1-5326-4997-4 (hardcover). | ISBN: 978-1-5326-4998-1 (ebook).

Subjects: LCSH: Voice in literature. | Orality in literature.| Bible—New Testament—Criticism, interpretation, etc.

Classification: BS2361.3 S55 2018 (print). | BS2361.3 (epub).

Manufactured in the U.S.A.   10/29/18

Scripture quotations marked (NRSV) are taken from the New Revised Standard Version Bible, copyright © 1989 National Council of the Churches of Christ in the United States of America. Used by permission. All rights reserved worldwide

Scripture quotations marked (NIV) are taken from the Holy Bible, NEW INTERNATIONAL VERSION®, NIV® Copyright © 1973, 1978, 1984, 2011 by Biblica, Inc.® Used by permission. All rights reserved worldwide.

Scripture quotations marked (WEB) are taken from the World English Bible, which is in the public domain. (https://worldenglishbible.org/)

Contents

Acknowledgments | vii
Contributors | ix
Introduction | 1
—Margaret E. Lee

1. Sound Mapping Reassessed | 8
   —Margaret E. Lee

2. New Adventures in Sound Mapping: A First-Timer's Attempt at a New Methodology | 27
   —Adam G. White

3. Luke's Strategy for Interpreting Parables | 42
   —Bernard Brandon Scott

4. Caves, Cattle, and *Koinonia*: Acoustic Shadows across Textual Walls | 69
   —Jeffrey E. Brickle

5. Investigations into the Sound's Message of Philippians 1:27—2:18 | 84
   —Bernhard Oestreich

6. Underexplored Benefits of Sound Mapping in New Testament Exegesis | 120
   —Dan Nässelqvist

7. Discourse Segmentation, Discourse Structure, and Sound Mapping (Including an Analysis of Mark 15) | 133
   —Frank Scheppers

8 A Sound Map of Revelation 8:7–12 and the Implications for Ancient Hearers | 179
—Kayle B. de Waal

9 Rhythm, Sound, and Persuasion | 193
—Nina E. Livesey

10 The New Testament Soundscape and the Puzzle of Mark 16:8 | 215
—Thomas E. Boomershine

Author Index | 245

Scripture Index | 251

Acknowledgments

Sound Matters owes a debt of gratitude to several program units of the Society of Biblical Literature whose leaders have supported sound mapping from its inception. These include the Matthew Seminar, where sound mapping was first introduced, the Bible in Ancient (and Modern) Media Section and the Performance Criticism of Biblical and Other Ancient Literature Section, which have dedicated programs to sound mapping and encouraged its development over many years. Sustained interest and invaluable support from Joanna Dewey, Holly Hearon, Richard Horsley, and Pieter Botha have proven invaluable in sound mapping's development. David Rhoads first suggested a collection of essays on sound mapping and guided this project to completion. K. C. Hanson welcomed this project at Cascade Books and improved its outcome through his expert support. Because sound mapping captures fleeting qualities of the spoken word, it also strains the boundaries of the print medium. Matthew Wimer and Ian Creeger at Wipf and Stock confronted these challenges with patience and creativity, enabling the contributors to resolve their various typesetting challenges, large and small. Finally, we owe special thanks to Werner Kelber, whose pioneering work opened the door for sound mapping and whose tireless support has sustained our efforts and fueled our creativity.

Contributors

Thomas E. Boomershine, PhD, is Professor of New Testament (1979–2000) and Professor of Christianity and Communications (2004–2006) Emeritus at United Theological Seminary, Dayton, Ohio. Tom founded the Network of Biblical Storytellers, International in 1977 and has lectured and led biblical storytelling workshops around the world. He is also the founder (1982) and past chair (1982–1989) of the Bible in Ancient and Modern Media group in the Society of Biblical Literature. Major monographs include *The Messiah of Peace: a Performance Criticism Commentary on Mark's Passion-Resurrection Narrative* (Cascade Books, 2015) and *Story Journey: An Invitation to the Gospel as Storytelling* (Abingdon, 1988).

Jeffrey E. Brickle, PhD, serves as Professor of Biblical Studies at Urshan Graduate School of Theology, where he has taught in the areas of biblical studies and languages since 2002. Along with numerous published essays focused on ancient media culture, he is the author of *Aural Design and Coherence in the Prologue of First John* (T. & T. Clark, 2012). Brickle holds degrees from Harvard University, Gordon-Conwell Theological Seminary, and Concordia Seminary, St. Louis.

Kayle B. de Waal, PhD, is Senior Lecturer in New Testament and leads the Avondale Seminary at Avondale College of Higher Education in New South Wales, Australia. He has published four books, including *An Aural-Performance Analysis of Revelation 1 and 11* (Lang, 2015) and a number of book chapters and journal articles. He enjoys leading students on mission trips with his family.

Margaret E. Lee, ThD, is retired as Assistant Professor of Humanities at Tulsa Community College, Tulsa, Oklahoma, where she has taught Introduction to the New Testament since 2007. She is the author of "Sound Mapping" in

The Dictionary of the Bible in Ancient Media (Bloomsbury, 2017) and numerous articles on sound mapping. She is coauthor with Bernard Brandon Scott of *Sound Mapping the New Testament* (Polebridge, 2009), and with Scott and others is coauthor of *Reading New Testament Greek: Complete Word Lists and Reader's Guide* (Hendrickson, 1993).

Nina E. Livesey, PhD, is Associate Professor of Religious Studies and Interdisciplinary Studies at the University of Oklahoma. She is author of two monographs, *Galatians and the Rhetoric of Crisis* (Polebridge, 2016) and *Circumcision as a Malleable Symbol* (Mohr/Siebeck, 2010), and numerous articles. Her interests include Pauline studies, early Jewish-Christian relations, Christian origins, and rhetorical analysis of ancient texts, especially those of the New Testament.

Dan Nässelqvist, PhD, is Associate Professor of New Testament exegesis at Lund University, Sweden. He has previously published a monograph on early Christian reading practices and sound analysis (Brill, 2015), as well as a textbook in New Testament Greek (Studentlitteratur, 2014).

Bernhard Oestreich, PhD, is Professor of New Testament at Friedensau Adventist University, Germany. His main research areas are performance criticism, ritualized actions, and metaphoric speech. He is the author of *Performance Criticism of the Pauline Letters* (2016; German original 2012), "Metaphors and Similes for Yahweh in Hosea 14:2–9" (1998), and essays on absurd metaphors in the Gospels and in the book of Hosea, on symbolic language in the book of Revelation, on early Christian rituals, and on strategies of reconciliation in the Pauline letters. He has also published two books on homiletics (2003 and 2015).

Frank Scheppers, PhD, is the author of *The Colon Hypothesis: Word Order, Discourse Segmentation and Discourse Coherence in Ancient Greek* (VUB Press, 2011).

Bernard Brandon Scott, PhD, is Darbeth Distinguished Professor Emeritus of New Testament at the Phillips Theological Seminary, Tulsa, Oklahoma. He is the author and editor of many books, including *The Real Paul* (Polebridge, 2015), *The Trouble with Resurrection* (Polebridge, 2010), *Re-Imagine the World* (Polebridge, 2001), *Hear Then the Parable* (Fortress, 1989), and is coauthor with Margaret E. Lee of *Sound Mapping the New Testament* (Polebridge, 2009). A charter member of the Jesus Seminar, he is co-chair of Westar's newly established Christianity Seminar.

Adam G. White, PhD, is a senior lecturer in New Testament at Alphacrucis College in Sydney, Australia. His main areas of interest are the Pauline letters and their Greco-Roman context. He is the author of *Where Is the Wise Man: Graeco-Roman Education as a Background to the Divisions in 1 Corinthians 1–4* (T. & T. Clark, 2015). His current research is focused on excommunication in the early Christian communities. When he is not trying to corral three young children, he enjoys photography and scale modeling.

Introduction

Margaret E. Lee

Sound matters. Over the past century, orality studies in classics and comparative literature have retrieved the public and performed character of ancient literature. Milman Parry's work on the epithet in Homer in the 1930s and Albert Lord's subsequent exploration of modern sung epics launched sustained exploration in the early twentieth century of ancient media and its role in communication. Its advent urges a transformation of our understanding of the New Testament to restore its living voice.

Media studies of the Greco-Roman world have elucidated a literary environment replete with complex interactions between speech and writing. In the ancient world, literary composition spanned a wide range of activity for different communication purposes. The compositions of the New Testament were neither invented *ex tempore* in the moment of performance nor studiously inscribed in a solitary writer's grate. They emerged as literature from vibrant communities, born in sound and shaped by auditory dynamics. Their εὐαγγέλιον, their announcements of good news, are not silent scriptures but voiced utterances, spoken aloud and heard.

Since the publication in 1982 of Walter Ong's *Orality and Literacy: The Technologizing of the Word* and Werner Kelber's groundbreaking *The Oral and Written Gospel* the following year, entire sub-disciplines have developed in New Testament scholarship and new professional associations and collaborations have formed to bring media studies into conversation with traditional historical criticism. These have been fed and promoted by The Bible in Ancient (and Modern) Media Section and Biblical Performance Criticism Section of the Society of Biblical Literature, among many other efforts. Publication in 2017 of *The Dictionary of The Bible and Ancient Media* (DBAM), edited by Tom Thatcher and others, attests to the rich results of media studies of biblical compositions. DBAM's introduction by Raymond Person and Chris Keith ably chronicles the emergence of this area of inquiry. In view of such pioneering work and the ensuing intellectual ferment, we must now confront New Testament compositions not as mute texts but as a collection of living, spoken events.

New insights require new methods and tools. In 1993, Margaret Ellen Lee and Bernard Brandon Scott began to experiment with a process for analyzing Greek literature as speech. After several exploratory articles and Lee's doctoral dissertation in 2005, Lee and Scott's *Sound Mapping the New Testament* was published in 2009. The book presents the analytical techniques that Lee developed in her dissertation project and tests those techniques on a variety of New Testament passages that have presented problems for the history of interpretation. By demonstrating a procedure for identifying a composition's auditory characteristics and a format for analyzing them, Lee and Scott forged a new analytical tool designed to precede and inform New Testament interpretation.

Lee and Scott have urged that sound mapping's techniques are accessible to anyone who reads Greek and that the results of sound mapping should be replicable and verifiable because sound mapping begins with an empirical database, a written text. This is not to say that sound prescribes interpretation, nor does it deny the crucial roles of creativity and insight in the interpretative endeavor. Yet Lee and Scott have maintained that sound mapping attends to phenomena that inhere in language itself and are rooted in universal dynamics of auditory reception.

The phonetic Greek alphabet encodes speech in the way it occurs, as a linear stream of sound. Sound mapping begins with the artifact of each ancient composition's spoken delivery, a critical edition of the text. A sound map depicts a composition's audible characteristics in graphic form and exhibits them for analysis. It presents a composition according to its auditory units and highlights its audible patterns to uncover that composition's structural skeleton and soundscape. Thus sound mapping's results can be shared, argued, and refined among the New Testament's many interpreters.

This volume invites and pursues such collaboration. In *Sound Matters: New Testament Studies in Sound Mapping*, a community of scholars representing five countries and three continents tests sound mapping's proposals and reevaluates its claims. Their essays refine its insights and raise new problems after a decade of practice from a range of viewpoints, interests, and levels of expertise. The scholars who have contributed to this volume have adopted sound mapping's fundamental assumptions and employed its analytical techniques to enlighten their own areas of scholarly interest and to generate new interpretative insights. Their essays show why sound matters and how the New Testament's sounds shape its message and its meaning.

My own reassessment of sound mapping begins the volume by taking stock of four monographs that incorporate techniques outlined in *Sound Mapping the New Testament* and critique its claims. These important studies have raised questions concerning pronunciation, delineation of the unit for sound analysis, the relevance of ancient reflections on the sounds of ancient Greek and Greek prose style, and other issues. In so doing, these monographs suggest ways to refine sound mapping and they point in new directions. All four authors of the monographs mentioned in my essay have graciously contributed new studies to this volume.

The next two essays illustrate the wide range of sound mapping's utility. Because sound mapping employs technical tools that rely on close examination of Greek literature at the micro-level, its rigors might seem daunting to the neophyte or redundant to a veteran scholar. In the first essay for this volume, Adam White tries his hand as a newcomer to sound mapping. He explores sound mapping's potential as a hermeneutical tool and tests its ease of use for a beginner. In this volume's second essay, Bernard Scott employs sound maps from the vantage of considerable experience. By means of sound maps, Scott uncovers subtle and sophisticated compositional strategies for Luke's incorporation of parables into his gospel. These two essays stand at opposite poles of familiarity with sound mapping and they differ widely in their hermeneutical interests. Nevertheless, both scholars apply sound mapping's techniques with a light hand and an open mind. Neither bogs down in technical detail and both achieve fresh insight as they clarify their interpretative conclusions about material with which they have become intimately familiar. White concludes that sound mapping affirms his insights into Paul's correspondence with the Corinthian community and Scott finds that sound mapping supplies an indispensible key to unlock Luke's persuasive artistry.

In an earlier monograph, Jeffrey Brickle astutely observed that sound mapping allows an interpreter to analyze sounds we can see. He became the first to publish a monograph using sound mapping after exploring this technique in his dissertation project. Brickle's *Aural Design and Coherence in the Prologue of First John* seizes on sound mapping's most fundamental technique: giving graphic expression to audible evidence. In his essay for this volume, Brickle calls sound mapping a "game changer" for hermeneutics and for media studies as he invests in its possibilities and reaps its rewards.

Brickle's 2012 monograph also introduced Greek pronunciation as a thorny issue for sound mapping. If sound matters and if sound maps illustrate how this is true, then surely it also matters how spoken compositions were pronounced. Brickle's *Aural Design* made an important attempt to address the problem of pronunciation in the first centuries CE by sound mapping the same passage according to two different pronunciation schemes: Erasmian pronunciation and the Historical Greek Pronunciation scheme devised by Chrys Caragounis. While Brickle did not attempt to resolve the problem of determining how New Testament compositions were pronounced, he established an important methodological milestone by carefully testing various possibilities. Subsequently, Thomas Boomershine addressed the pronunciation problem somewhat differently in his performance-critical commentary on Mark's passion-resurrection narrative, *The Messiah of Peace*. Acknowledging the limits of our knowledge of Greek pronunciation in the first centuries CE, Boomershine offers a convincing rationale for his use of Erasmian pronunciation in his performances of Mark's Gospel in Greek.

Thus the issue of Greek pronunciation has so far evaded resolution but Bernhard Oestreich tackles the conundrum with fresh vigor in his essay on Phil 1:27—2:18 for *Sound Matters*. Engaging his expertise in ancient rhetoric, Oestreich advances judicious hypotheses about pronunciation at a particular time and place to achieve new insights about Paul's message. Oestreich finds in sound mapping a useful tool to reconstruct a particular composition's actual sounds as articulated in performance. His essay posts important gains on the problem of Greek pronunciation. He concludes with a list of methodological gains that summarizes the importance of sound analysis for interpretation.

Dan Nässelqvist's 2015 monograph, *Public Reading in Early Christianity*, affirms the importance of sound for New Testament literature as he observes how audible features organize a spoken composition. Nässelqvist coined the term, "aural intensity" to characterize ways that sounds can highlight a composition's areas of focus. His contribution to *Sound Matters* summarizes some of the conclusions he developed there. One interesting finding in Nässelqvist's essay confirms the suggestion Lee and Scott advanced in *Sound Mapping the New Testament*: that sound mapping not only identifies a composition's structure and distinctive audible features but it can thereby illuminate text-critical problems that have bedeviled interpretation.

Nässelqvist challenges the notion of performance as applied to New Testament material but he agrees with performance critics about the primacy of vocalization, since New Testament compositions were spoken aloud in antiquity. Because sound mapping figures prominently among the analytical tools Nässelqvist employs in *Public Reading*, his monograph explores ways to refine sound mapping's techniques. Nässelqvist critiques sound mapping's observations about ancient reflections on Greek prose style and he raises questions about the criteria for delineating a sound unit's boundaries. For sound mapping to realize its full potential it must answer such critiques regarding its procedures and its theoretical foundation, especially as they relate to the identification of sound mapping's unit of analysis.

Sound mapping as defined in *Sound Mapping the New Testament* begins by identifying the basic unit of Greek prose, the colon. This starting point derives from the vast literature that survives antiquity concerning the Greek language. In 2011, Frank Scheppers published *The Colon Hypothesis*, a magisterial exploration of the colon as a sound unit in ancient Greek. He pursues this subject by applying analytical tools from contemporary discourse analysis to classical Greek prose. His detailed study sets forth criteria for delineating the boundaries of a colon. Scheppers confirms sound mapping's contention that cola organize speech and coincide with its fundamental units. In his essay for *Sound Matters*, Scheppers develops a sound map for Mark's crucifixion narrative and engages in dialogue with Thomas Boomershine's video performance of this narrative in Greek. Scheppers's contribution to *Sound Matters* brings a unique perspective from outside New Testament studies and connects sound mapping with the vast resources of classical philology and modern linguistics. From the vantage of these ancient and modern viewpoints, Scheppers suggests new directions for honing sound mapping's tools and techniques.

Having established that sound organizes discourse, its impact on literary structure becomes vividly apparent. Kayle B. de Waal investigates an audience's perception of a composition's structure in his 2015 monograph, *A Aural Performance Analysis of Revelation 1 and 11*. His essay for *Sound Matters* pursues this theme, illustrating how sound organizes ideas to make meaning. De Waal's work on the book of Revelation affirms the value of sound analysis for discerning a composition's structure and understanding its meaning.

Ranging beyond compositional structure and informed by her interest in ancient rhetoric, Nina Livesey explores the impact of rhythm for persuasion in her essay for *Sound Matters*. Her essay reminds us that, while Greek prose lacks the rhythmic dimension of poetic meter, it nevertheless relies on rhythmic pacing to engage its audiences. Livesey derives important insights into Paul's rhetoric by mapping the rhythms of his speech as preserved in his letters.

Thomas Boomershine, a pioneer in media studies of the New Testament, employed sound mapping in his 2015 performance commentary on Mark's passion-resurrection narrative, *The Messiah of Peace*. As a result of his commentary and his many performances of the narrative in Greek, Boomershine has argued for the necessity of a major paradigm shift in our understanding of the New Testament. In his essay for *Sound Matters* Boomershine shows how sound mapping facilitates the paradigm shift from mute text to spoken performance. His analysis of Mark 16:8 illustrates how sound mapping serves as an essential tool for accomplishing this shift and letting scripture live and breathe for modern audiences as it once did for ancient ones. Thus it seems fitting that Boomershine's essay should conclude this volume in Cascade Books's Biblical Performance Criticism Series.

Sound matters. This volume's ten studies root sound mapping more deeply in the interpretative endeavor and expand its application to a community of scholars. Sound mapping furnishes crucial analytical tools that support various hermeneutical interests, despite divergent views concerning the dynamics of composition and performance. The contributors to this volume extend sound mapping's reach to encompass every level of professional experience, a wide range of literature, and a broad spectrum of methodological tools. Their explorations of its problems indicate how sound mapping can be improved and refined while their different applications of sound mapping's techniques expand its utility. Sound mapping now belongs to the whole scholarly community and not just to its inventors and early proponents. We hope this volume will encourage still more scholarly collaboration and open new doors to interpretative possibilities that have yet to dawn in our imagination.

Bibliography

Boomershine, Thomas E. *Messiah of Peace: A Performance-Criticism Commentary on Mark's Passion-Resurrection Narrative*. Biblical Performance Criticism Series 12. Eugene, OR: Cascade Books, 2015.

Brickle, Jeffrey E. *Aural Design and Coherence in the Prologue of First John*. Library of New Testament Studies 465. New York: T. & T. Clark, 2012.

De Waal, Kayle B. *An Aural-Performance Analysis of Revelation 1 and 11*. New York: Lang, 2015.

Kelber, Werner H. *The Oral and the Written Gospel: The Hermeneutics of Speaking and Writing in the Synoptic Tradition, Mark, Paul, and Q*. Philadelphia: Fortress, 1983.

Lee, Margaret Ellen, and Bernard Brandon Scott. *Sound Mapping the New Testament*. Salem, OR: Polebridge, 2009.

Nässelqvist, Dan. *Public Reading in Early Christianity: Lectors, Manuscripts, and Sound in the Oral Delivery of John 1–4*. Novum Testamentum Supplements 163. Leiden: Brill, 2015.

Ong, Walter J. *Orality and Literacy: The Technologizing of the Word*. New York: Methuen, 1982.

Person, Raymond F., Jr., and Chris Keith. "Media Studies and Biblical Studies: An Introduction." In *Dictionary of the Bible and Ancient Media*, edited by Tom Thatcher et al., 1–15. New York: Bloomsbury T. & T. Clark, 2017.

Scheppers, Frank. *The Colon Hypothesis: Word Order, Discourse Segmentation and Discourse Coherence in Ancient Greek.* Brussels: VUBPress, 2011.

Thatcher, Tom, et al., eds. *Dictionary of the Bible and Ancient Media.* New York: Bloomsbury T. & T. Clark, 2017.

1

Sound Mapping Reassessed

MARGARET E. LEE

Mapping sounds—the very concept seems strange and its usefulness elusive. Why plot sound on a map? The attempt to capture fleeting sound in a graphic image reflects the need to stabilize and then analyze ephemeral experience. Sound mapping commits to the proposition that sound matters. It places priority on the dynamics of listening and asks how these dynamics influence meaning. This essay traces the history of sound mapping, assesses recent studies that employ sound mapping, and suggests directions for the future.[1]

The Journey toward Listening

The idea of mapping a composition's sounds began as Bernard Brandon Scott's insight. Scott coined the term, "sound mapping" and was the first to perceive important possibilities for analyzing New Testament compositions as speech. Our collaboration began with a paper for the Matthew Seminar

---

1. This essay is a version of a paper I presented at the Society of Biblical Literature (SBL) Annual Meeting in San Antonio, Texas, in November 2016 at the invitation of the Bible in Ancient and Modern Media (BAMM) Section of the SBL. That session launched the plan for this volume of essays. BAMM's enduring interest in sound mapping and the support of the Biblical Performance Criticism Section of the SBL have promoted sound mapping, given it international exposure, and enabled the exploration of its techniques and interpretative potential.

of the Society of Biblical Literature (SBL) in 1993 in which we conducted an experiment with sound mapping using the Sermon on the Mount as a test case.² We chose this passage because it is memorable, framed as a speech, and contains significant material for detailed analysis. Our preliminary investigation convinced us that sound mapping could change how we understand the New Testament.

Encouraged by the initial reception of this experiment, I began to explore ancient discussions of literary composition in Greek to better appreciate their understanding of Greek literature as speech. My early investigations explored Greek grammar as a τέχνη or science of sound. My article, *The Grammar of Sound*, identified the colon and the period as basic sound units and suggested new interpretative horizons for mapping sounds in a Greek composition.³

I then undertook my doctoral dissertation project to develop a theoretics of sound, create a method and vocabulary for sound analysis, and test its power as an analytical tool. In that project I reexamined the Sermon on the Mount using the theoretics I had developed. I expanded, revised, and corrected our original sound map of Matt 5–7 and began to observe similarities between the Sermon's auditory features and other sound signals in Matthew's gospel.⁴ Armed with a more comprehensive foundation for sound analysis, Scott and I then resumed our collaboration in *Sound Mapping the New Testament* to present the process of sound mapping and analysis to a wider audience and apply it to a broader range of New Testament material.⁵

---

2. Scott and Dean, "A Sound Map of the Sermon on the Mount." The paper was subsequently revised and published in *Treasures Old and New: Recent Contributions to Matthean Studies*, edited by David Bauer and Mark Allen Powell, 1996. Several early works on sound mapping appear under Margaret E. Lee's former surname, Margaret E. Dean.

3. Dean, "Grammar of Sound."

4. *A Method for Sound Analysis in Hellenistic Greek*. I have subsequently pursued this idea in "Matthew: The Musical"; "Melody in Manuscript: The Birth Narrative in the Gospel of Matthew"; and "Sound and Structure in the Gospel of Matthew." Because literary works in the New Testament world were composed for oral delivery and were typically heard rather than read silently, they engage the unique dynamics of auditory reception, with its linear, time-bound character. This thesis outlines a method for analyzing New Testament texts as spoken sound, using Matthew's Sermon on the Mount (5–7).

5. Lee and Scott, *Sound Mapping*.

A Sound Approach

Sound mapping is an analytical technique with an empirical basis that draws from two tributaries of the same river: the characteristics of the Greek language and the precise configuration of sounds in a particular Greek composition. Put another way, a sound map plots distinctive features of both *langue* and *parole*. Aspects of the Greek language conducive to sound mapping include its flexible word order, rhyming inflections, and its aspectual system. Flexible word order creates a wide range of syntactic possibilities that allow an author to select where emphasis should fall and to specify precisely how syntactic elements are related. Rhyming inflections ensure that nominal elements can be perceived as clusters and not atomistically. The Greek aspectual system creates powerful verbal structures that open dimensions of meaning beyond a verb's temporal implications.

Such linguistic features generate a vast expressive repertoire that extends beyond the semantic domain. Authors can imply subtleties of meaning using tone and timbre, melody and rhythm, speech and silence. Without even knowing what the words mean, we can feel the urgency of Mark's gospel narrative with its repeated καί and its clipped cola. We sense the complexity of Paul's ruminations through his nested, elliptical cola linked by undeclined particles and prepositions. The fourth gospel's dramatic impact imposes imperatives on a listening audience through its distinctive exploitation of verbal aspect as an auditory cue, even before listeners come to terms with the meanings of its words. New Testament exegesis remains at best incomplete and at worst misguided when we neglect its soundscape.

A composition communicates its λόγος in the creative tension between its fixed, written form and its fluid, voiced quality. Like an opera's *libretto*, a manuscript remains incomplete until animated by the human voice.[6] Hellenistic Greek authors explicitly appreciate this range of expressive potential as they conceptualize literary compositions as woven fabric. They compare the written marks in a manuscript to the taut warp threads on a loom through which the varied and more colorful weft yarn that symbolizes the human voice is interlaced. In the Greek notion of literary composition as weaving or συμπλοκή, a composition consists of more than the manuscript that preserves it. Like empty warp threads hanging loose on a loom's frame, a written composition lacks integrity until a human voice articulates its written marks. For these ancient audiences, a composition's unity and meaning remained inaccessible until spoken; in fact, in the absence of speech, the

---

6. The metaphor of manuscript as *libretto* comes from Foley, *The Singer of Tales in Performance*, 61–66.

composition did not actually exist.[7] This ancient, governing image of composition as a woven fabric integrated by the human voice should guide our analytical approach to Greek literature.

Explorations of Sound Mapping by Other Researchers

Listeners experience spoken compositions as linear streams of sound that they must process in real time. As with musical motifs, auditory patterns in spoken literature can only be established by means of clear and redundant signals. Sound mapping should therefore produce results that can be replicated by other interpreters. Thus we now turn to major sound mapping studies by Jeffrey Brickle, Kayle de Waal, Thomas Boomershine, and Dan Nässelqvist.

Jeffrey E. Brickle

Jeffrey Brickle was the first to try his hand at sound mapping. In 2012, his *Aural Design and Coherence in the Prologue of First John* explored the possibility that "modern scholarship on the Prologue may have overlooked a critical element in the passage's underlying make-up: aural design."[8] He turns to sound mapping to discover the Prologue's aural design. Brickle attends systematically to euphony, repetition, and rhythm as they relate to the Prologue's structure. He concludes,

> The Prologue reflects an aural design that undergirds its framework, development, momentum and interplay of unified and contrasting elements. This design ingeniously projects chief features into the auditory foreground while subordinating other elements into the auditory backdrop. The correlation of these various elements results in a dynamic and interactive tapestry of sounds that cohere, generate progression and inform interpretation.[9]

Brickle's work affirms sound mapping's potential to reclaim aspects of ancient listening experiences. He writes, "By assuming the stance of a first-century audience attentive to the Prologue's aural dynamics, we elevate

---

7. See Lee and Scott, *Sound Mapping*, 72–77, and ancient sources cited there.
8. Brickle, *Aural Design*, 107.
9. Ibid., 110.

John's testimony from silent obscurity, encountering afresh what he saw and heard."[10]

Kayle B. de Waal

In 2015, three major studies emerged that employ sound mapping in somewhat different ways. Kayle de Waal uses sound mapping in his *Aural-Performance Analysis of Revelation 1 and 11* to inform his work as a contemporary preacher. Like Brickle, de Waal creates sound maps to shift "the focus away from authorial intent toward an audience's experience of the performance."[11] De Waal employs a scheme of audience constructs based on work by Christopher Stanley[12] and Sean Ryan[13] in which de Waal distinguishes among an informed audience, a minimal audience, and a competent audience.[14] De Waal finds in the text various "audience markers," including structural, social, ideological, and theological markers.[15] Most of these markers are conceptually delineated but structural markers emerge by virtue of their phonological characteristics, which plot a composition's "auditory topography," to borrow Brickle's term.[16] De Waal writes, "A structural marker will begin each period and introduces the content of the period or the predominant focus of a period. Structural markers inform the audience of what lay ahead in the period. The structural marker can be one word or even five or six words."[17]

De Waal also incorporates insights from cognitive psychology in his analysis, since "auditory processing focuses not so much on hearing as a function of the ear but rather on listening as a function of the brain."[18] For example, he cites the cognitive "bathtub effect" to interpret structural markers and to explain "the significance of the beginning and the ends [sic] of a word for human understanding."[19] By virtue of this phenomenon, a word's beginning and end remain more vivid in memory than the middle, just as a person's head and feet remain visible as the rest of the body disappears into

10. Ibid., 125.
11. De Waal, *An Aural-Performance Analysis of Revelation 1 and 11*, 125.
12. Stanley, *Arguing with Scripture*.
13. Ryan, *Hearing at the Boundaries of Vision*.
14. De Waal, *An Aural-Performance Analysis of Revelation 1 and 11*, 25–28.
15. Ibid., 28–29.
16. Brickle, *Aural Design*, 112.
17. Ibid., 28.
18. De Waal, *An Aural-Performance Analysis of Revelation 1 and 11*, 16.
19. Ibid., 80.

a bathtub. Documentation of this cognitive process supports the insight of sound analysis, which acknowledges the priority of beginning sounds to train the ear for what comes next and of ending sounds for signaling closure.

De Waal concludes his analysis of Revelation with a positive assessment of sound mapping for deriving Revelation's contemporary implications as performance. He writes,

> Re-hearing Revelation in the contemporary setting means the interpreters have to reposition themselves not as interpreters that read a text but rather as listeners that seek to hear afresh the message of Revelation.... Re-hearing Revelation also means that hearers are called to action in light of what they hear.[20]

Thomas E. Boomershine

Thomas Boomershine's *The Messiah of Peace* employs sound mapping in an effort to reverse the "Christian anti-Judaism" that modern interpreters perceive in Mark's gospel.[21] Boomershine claims that finding anti-Judaism in Mark's passion-resurrection narrative represents "a misreading and a mishearing" of Mark's message.[22] Based on Boomershine's experience as a performer and storyteller, he calls for a "detailed exegesis of biblical stories as *compositions of sound performed for audiences*" (emphasis in the original).[23] If a written composition represents a *libretto*, sound mapping furnishes a kind of musical score, organized into cola and periods, "the sound units in which the composers of Greek stories thought and spoke."[24] Boomershine's sound map informs his actual performance in Greek of Mark 14–16.[25] For Boomershine, performance comes first and performance data inform his exegesis.

Boomershine contends that recovering the sounded quality of New Testament compositions accomplishes more than simply retrieving various neglected dimensions of meaning. A performance engages both performer and audience as participants in a story and thereby alters fundamentally their relationships with a text. Like de Waal, Boomershine advocates performance criticism precisely because it establishes "a dialectical relationship

---

20. Ibid., 132–33.
21. Boomershine, *Messiah of Peace*, 1.
22. Ibid., 22.
23. Ibid., 1.
24. Ibid., 6.
25. Boomershine, "Commentary Videos—Messiah of Peace."

between engagement in the experience of the story and critical analysis."[26] Such engagement "will reveal dimensions of its meaning both in its original historical context and in its contemporary context."[27]

Dan Nässelqvist

Dan Nässelqvist's *Public Reading in Early Christianity* employs sound mapping in his analysis of John 1–4.[28] Nässelqvist's interest in finding unique characteristics of communication technology among Christian communities guides his exploration of the physical features of early Christian manuscripts and the circumstances under which the compositions they encode would be conveyed.[29] Nässelqvist elucidates the role of lectors in Christian communities as distinct from those who delivered "oral performances" in drama and oratory.[30] He concludes, "literary writings of most genres—including New Testament texts—were delivered through public reading directly from a manuscript and with fitting vocal expression."[31] Sound mapping furnishes a foundation for Nässelqvist's understanding of how lectors would have analyzed and prepared manuscripts for public reading. In his sound analysis of John 1–4, Nässelqvist advances the notion of "aural intensity" as a phenomenon enabling a lector to "identify which passages attracted most attention in public reading."[32] Among other benefits, the notion of aural intensity suggests "how climactic passages can be positively identified."[33] This result corroborates Brickle's observation of sound's role in backgrounding some sounds and foregrounding others. Nässelqvist's sound analysis informs structural problems in John 1–4, such as whether to include ὁ γέγονεν with 1:3 or 1:4. Nässelqvist derives interpretative insights from his sound map, on the basis of which he disputes certain interpretations of John's gospel. Nässelqvist also brings new attention to the importance of a lector's role in mediating understanding by means of the way a lector vocalizes a New Testament composition.[34]

---

26. Boomershine, *Messiah of Peace*, 13.
27. Ibid.
28. Nässelqvist, *Public Reading*.
29. Ibid., 17–60.
30. Ibid., 63–116.
31. Ibid., 323.
32. Ibid., 326.
33. Ibid., 328.
34. Ibid., 131.

Critiques of Sound Mapping

While finding sound mapping useful for their own projects, early practitioners have suggested ways to refine sound analysis in response to challenges they have encountered. The three most salient issues they have raised concern pronunciation, the delineation of cola and periods, and Greek prose style. We will examine each in turn.

Pronunciation

The first and most obvious challenge sound mapping presents pertains to pronunciation. No consensus yet prevails regarding the pronunciation scheme or schemes applied to New Testament literature. We know that pronunciation in the classical and Byzantine periods differed considerably but we lack conclusive evidence about intermediate stages. We also know that Erasmian pronunciation does not reflect any actual pronunciation scheme in antiquity.[35] How can we map and analyze a composition's sounds if we do not know how its syllables were pronounced?

In my dissertation I argued that sound mapping does not require final resolution of this issue,[36] although obviously that would be helpful. The phonetic character of the Greek language ensures that letters and diphthongs would be voiced consistently in any particular realization of a composition, regardless of the pronunciation scheme in use, enabling identification of repeated patterns. Scott and I maintained this position in *Sound Mapping the New Testament*[37] and Nässelqvist supported it in his study.[38] Still, we cannot be completely content with such a position while advocating close analysis of sound quality.

Boomershine treats the problem at some length in collaboration with Adam Gilbert Bartholomew.[39] They write, "in Mark's time Greek was pronounced more like modern Greek than the Erasmian pronunciation."[40] Nevertheless, Boomershine employs Erasmian pronunciation in his performances of Mark's passion-resurrection narrative to accommodate modern listeners who tend to be more familiar with Erasmian than modern Greek pronunciation. Boomershine writes, "While we cannot determine the exact

---

35. Campbell, *Advances in the Study of Greek*, 192–208.
36. Lee, *Method for Sound Analysis in Hellenistic Greek*, 4.
37. Lee and Scott, *Sound Mapping*, 6, 81.
38. Nässelqvist, *Public Reading*, 123–24.
39. Boomershine, *Messiah of Peace*, 383–86.
40. Ibid., 385.

sounds of Koine Greek in the first century, the differences in the different pronunciation systems are relatively minor and have minimal effect on the overall impact of the sound of Mark's Greek."[41] He admits that his solution is imperfect but finds it necessary to strike a compromise for pragmatic reasons.[42]

Brickle confronts the problem of pronunciation in *Aural Design* by testing various possibilities. He applies sound mapping's analytical strategies assuming two different pronunciation schemes for the same composition, Erasmian pronunciation and the Historical Greek Pronunciation (HGP) scheme advocated by Chrys Caragounis[43] and based on the writings of Dionysius of Halicarnassus.[44] Brickle's detailed analysis illustrates how Erasmian pronunciation distinguishes some sounds that would be indistinguishable in HGP. Therefore, auditory patterns detected using Erasmian pronunciation are intensified with HGP, he argues, since that scheme recognizes fewer discrete vowel sounds. He concludes, "The net effect [of HGP] does not result in the emergence of new sound patterns *per se* but brings existing patterns into clearer focus."[45]

Despite uncertainty about Greek pronunciation in the Roman period, Brickle, de Waal, Boomershine, and Nässelqvist have all succeeded in discerning meaningful audible patterns in their test cases while taking different approaches to Greek pronunciation and without finally resolving the problem. Until new information becomes available, perhaps it is best to make explicit whatever provisional position we take on pronunciation in sound analysis, as Boomershine has done, and where possible, to explore multiple pronunciation schemes, as Brickle has done. Still, we remain well advised not to miss the forest for the trees where pronunciation is concerned. The most salient aspect of ancient Greek pronunciation is that its phonetic alphabet, a unique innovation in the ancient world, was designed precisely to represent Greek literature as a linear stream of sound. As writing encodes Greek compositions it also preserves their sounded quality.

---

41. Ibid., 7.

42. Others, too, have defended the Erasmian pronunciation scheme on pragmatic grounds. See Campbell, *Advances in the Study of Greek*, 204–5.

43. Brickle, *Aural Design*, 339–96.

44. Ibid., 19–23.

45. Ibid., 110.

Delineation of Cola and Periods

The second challenge that early practitioners of sound mapping have identified concerns criteria for delineating cola and periods. Defining the unit of analysis constitutes a necessary first step for any analytical process, so this issue deserves close consideration.

I have argued consistently for the value of employing emic criteria for Greek sound units to more fully appreciate a listener's experience of Greek literature as speech and to exploit the insights of ancient commentators on Greek literature. Based on those ancient reflections on Greek prose, I have proposed a rule of thumb for identifying cola as syntactic units: a colon consists of a predicate, expressed or implied, and all nominal elements related to that predicate.[46] I advanced this guideline not as an absolute criterion but as a pragmatic starting point. Nässelqvist calls for greater precision. While he agrees that sound mapping correctly identifies the colon as the fundamental unit of sound analysis he argues that, since cola constitute breath units, they should include a minimum number of syllables and should not extend beyond a maximum number.[47] Regarding periods, he argues that a series of cola must exhibit certain characteristics to qualify as a period; in other words, not all cola are combined into periods.[48] Nässelqvist recognizes the kinds of periods that occur as prose figures but he does not acknowledge the period as a building block for all Greek prose.

The problem resides in our sources. Ancient writers describe both cola and periods as breath units, even though they also specify that periods consist of multiple cola. If cola comprise the length of a breath and periods consist of multiple cola, it is hard to understand how periods, too, span the length of a breath; yet this is how ancient authors describe them. I have failed to find a single Greek author who seems disturbed by this apparent inconsistency. Similarly, these same authors insist that cola are combined into periods and that cola and periods comprise the building blocks of Greek prose, yet they admit that not all prose is "periodic."[49] Again, ancient authors seem untroubled by the apparent contradiction inherent in these assertions.

Moreover, we find somewhat different approaches to the period in ancient Greek sources. Aristotle discerns a stylistic gradient between periodic

---

46. Lee, "A Method for Sound Analysis in Hellenistic Greek," 169–71; Lee, "Colon," 63.

47 Nässelqvist, *Public Reading*, 129–31.

48. Ibid., 134–38.

49. For cola and periods, see Lee and Scott, *Sound Mapping*, 108–11. For a discussion of periodic and unperiodic prose, see ibid., 111–14, and sources cited there.

and unperiodic prose. He advocates a middle path of mixed style, consistent with the general pursuit of the golden mean among the Peripatetics. By contrast, some later authors including Dionysius of Halicarnassus treat the period as a prose figure exhibiting rounding and balance. Yet even Dionysius identifies periods that do not exhibit these diagnostic features.[50]

Although Nässelqvist identifies as periods only those series of cola that function as prose figures, he notices where complete thoughts begin and end, based on syntax. Ancient commentators, too, implicitly observe syntactic boundaries for cola and periods. Since grammar serves as the τέχνη or science of vocalized sound in Greek, my rule of thumb based on syntax still provides a reliable starting point for delineating cola. Nevertheless, I admit that the rule of thumb can break down in practice: what about compound predicates, absolute constructions, long strings of participles, direct and indirect address and brief elliptical constructions with missing predicates? As for periods, we can discern syntactic units that extend beyond the colon but how should we account for "unperiodic" prose?

Our ancient sources fail to provide more specific criteria for period and colon delineation but neither do they designate a minimum or maximum number of syllables for a colon. We still need more specific criteria for delineating cola and methods for analyzing how cola are combined. Even if we adopt a strict definition of the period as a prose figure, we still need labels for the coherent clusters of cola formed by their sounded, voiced qualities. Such clusters, in turn, themselves cohere as larger structural units that organize a whole composition, based on audible characteristics. Although ancient Greek authors neither name nor describe intermediate prose units, such units invariably emerge from a sound map and comprise each composition's structural skeleton. We will return to this issue below.

Greek Prose Style

A third challenge that practitioners of sound mapping have encountered pertains to the analysis of Greek prose style. This issue relates to the problem of delineating cola and periods, since style (λέξις) primarily concerns the construction of cola and their combination into periods or other coherent segments to express a composition's λόγος. Ancient commentators observe that some cola fit together more smoothly than others; some cola are connected grammatically while others are simply juxtaposed. These ancient authors advocate a mixture of styles to achieve pleasing effects and a correspondence between an author's purpose and the manner in which cola

---

50. Dionysius of Halicarnassus, *Comp.* 22.

are combined.⁵¹ This point of unanimity among our ancient sources implies a pragmatic dimension to cola combination.

Ancient sources on style also analyze vowel quality and quantity, euphony, and hiatus. Unfortunately, these sources furnish little information about the aesthetic principles at work in their analysis. Authors disagree about which sounds they find pleasant and which seem cacophonous. They even criticize some literature as too polished, or mannered, in the use of figures. Apparently where beauty is concerned, more is not always better.

Ancient typologies of style also associate literary styles with particular genres, noting that continuous style is appropriate for histories while periodic style is suitable for philosophy. They further apply stylistic categories to units of prose within a genre according to an author's purpose, assigning the austere style to dignified speech and elegant style to speech that is designed to lull an audience into a kind of passivity.⁵² No single typology emerges as authoritative, making it difficult to apply these guidelines to the New Testament, especially since New Testament genres continue to be debated.⁵³

Nässelqvist has criticized my analysis of literary style for being incomplete and Boomershine calls for more clarity on this point. While accepting my method for identifying cola and periods, Boomershine observes a need for criteria to delineate prose units longer than the period.⁵⁴ I accept these critiques as fair, since I have advanced no criteria for Greek prose segmentation beyond the apprehension of a composition's auditory patterns. Nor have I applied standard labels to intermediate prose units that sound maps expose, sometimes calling them "parts," while at other times "sections" or "episodes," according to each composition's distinctive soundscape. Rather, I have worked inductively and pragmatically, attending to a composition's auditory features and systematically setting aside segmentation schemes based on conventional versification or abstract conceptions of themes or

---

51. See Lee and Scott, *Sound Mapping*, 119–21, and ancient sources cited there.
52. Ibid., 111–22, and ancient sources cited there.
53. Pearson and Porter, "The Genres of the New Testament."
54. Boomershine writes, "The sound map of the cola and periods is the major step in the recovery of the sound of Mark's story. But there is more to the sound than the rhythm of its cola and periods. There is also the organization of the cola and periods into larger storytelling units marked by changes in time and place, repetitions and verbal threads, particular grammatical constructions, changes in the principal characters, and the basic subject matter. These markers also call for various lengths of pause, changes of pace, or climactic expression as the means of marking the end of a storytelling move before going on to the next," *Messiah of Peace*, 7. Boomershine's observations relate specifically to narrative but the need to demarcate intermediate prose units applies equally to letters and other prose genres.

ideas. Because such schemes originate outside a composition they presume and import extrinsic, predetermined meanings.

Like the problem of delineating cola and periods, the issue of style presents challenges traceable to our ancient sources, which fail to enunciate consistent criteria for combining cola. Nevertheless, sound maps successfully identify intermediate prose units that cohere by virtue of their auditory characteristics.[55] Indeed, sound mapping's various practitioners have all advanced important interpretative insights that result from sound mapping's power to discern a composition's structural skeleton. Encouraged by this corroboration, we can now pursue systematic techniques for analyzing how repeated sounds form memorable patterns that organize a composition. Our search may need to reach beyond ancient sources, which cannot always satisfy a modern interpreter's desire for precision. Two logical places to look for additional methodological tools are philological studies of classical Greek, which circumscribe a larger context for Hellenistic prose literature, and discourse analysis in modern linguistics, which has long sought to define intermediate prose units based on the segmentation of contemporary speech.[56]

The Colon Hypothesis

Since the publication of *Sound Mapping the New Testament*, Frank Scheppers at Vrije Universiteit Brussel has advanced *The Colon Hypothesis* to establish criteria for word order, discourse segmentation and discourse coherence in ancient Greek prose.[57] Scheppers explores discourse segmentation in the context of modern linguistics while finding "common ground" in the tradition of classical philology. His book neither works with New Testament literature nor employs sound mapping yet he implicitly affirms sound mapping's most important tenets. Like sound mapping, Scheppers's hypothesis seeks an empirical foundation based on close reading, with "no pre-established theoretical and/or methodological framework."[58] As I have done for sound mapping, Scheppers advances his proposal as a "working

---

55. Previous attempts have been made to address the issue of delineating intermediate prose units in New Testament literature through colometry. See Kleist, "Colometry and the New Testament"; Kleist, "Colometry and the New Testament (Concluded)"; Nuwe-Testamentiese Werkgemeenskap van Suid-Afrika, "The Structure of Matthew 1–13"; *Structure and Meaning in Matthew 14–28*; Davis, *Oral Biblical Criticism*.

56. Moisés Silva, generally unsympathetic to discourse analysis, applauds this yet unmet goal. "Discourse Analysis and Philippians," 103.

57. Scheppers, *The Colon Hypothesis*.

58. Ibid., xi.

model," by which he means, "a problem-raising and hypothesis-raising analytical tool."[59] His thorough study can enlighten our questions about the delineation of cola and the segmentation of Greek prose into larger units.

Scheppers's Colon Hypothesis claims the following.

1. The colon is the elementary unit of analysis for ancient Greek prose.
2. The colon is virtually coterminous with the intonation unit (IU) in discourse analysis.
3. The colon is delimited pragmatically, encompassing phonological, cognitive, and grammatical dimensions of discourse.

Let us briefly examine these claims and then evaluate implications for sound mapping.

The Colon Is the Elementary Unit of Analysis

Scheppers begins in the mainstream of classical philology by examining Greek word order, beginning with the work of Jacob Wachernagel in 1892.[60] Scheppers observes that we must be able to identify correctly the unit of analysis to resolve questions of word order. He turns to Eduard Fraenkel's work from 1932–1966 that proposes the colon as this fundamental unit.[61] Scheppers concludes that "the colon is the elementary discourse unit, in other words: discourse *essentially* comes in cola" (emphasis in the original).[62] He finds that "the colon is the unit to which Greek word order rules . . . are applicable"[63] and he identifies morphosyntactic, prosodic, and pragmatic grounds for colon delineation.[64] Scheppers tests his insights on a corpus of Greek literature consisting of all the extant works of Lysias, excluding fragments, and four dialogues of Plato: *Cratylus*, *Sophista*, *Theaetetus*, and *Politicus*.[65] Notably, Scheppers's corpus selects literature that is framed as speech, just as sound mapping began with the Sermon on the Mount for the same reason. Scheppers's resulting segmentation criteria derive from "major

---

59. Ibid., 423, n.411.
60. Ibid., 4–7.
61. Ibid., 7–12.
62. Ibid., 17.
63. Ibid.
64. Ibid., 434–35.
65. Ibid., x.

grammatical and discourse boundaries," "formal word order phenomena," and "syntactic criteria."[66]

Cola Are Coterminous with IUs

Having examined the boundaries of cola as defined by rules of word order, Scheppers examines the IU in discourse analysis, based on work in American ethnolinguistics by Wallace Chafe from 1976–2001.[67] Like cola, IUs coincide with discourse units exhibiting phonological,[68] cognitive,[69] grammatical,[70] and pragmatic[71] integrity. In comparing the colon and the IU, Scheppers observes "that a colon is typically realized as a single IU, and that an IU typically conveys a single colon."[72] Scheppers concludes, "The overall resemblance between colon-typology . . . and IU typology . . . corroborates the idea that these notions are not really different and that Ancient Greek discourse (even in its written transmitted form) is apparently structured in a way that reminds us of contemporary spoken language."[73] This conclusion explicitly connects ancient Greek prose with contemporary speech and would seem to legitimate Boomershine's use of a sound map to inform his performances of Mark's passion-resurrection narrative in Greek for modern audiences.

Pragmatic Definition of Cola

In settling the issue of the elementary unit of analysis, Scheppers advances what he calls his "Pragmatics first" claim: "P(ragmatic)-structure, as a 'central' level of cognition (i.e. common to all kinds of sensible behavior), underlies the other, more specific, levels of linguistic structure."[74] Prioritizing this pragmatic dimension, Scheppers observes that colon linkages derive

---

66. Ibid., 223–25. Syntactic criteria include "verb-centered constituents" (finite clauses, participial clauses, and some types of infinitival constructions), "different members of coordinated, correlative and parallel structures," "parentheses, afterthoughts, and other syntactically non-integrated elements," and "fronted elements."
67. Ibid., 18–35.
68. Ibid., 21–24.
69. Ibid., 24–25.
70. Ibid., 26–32.
71. Ibid., 33–35.
72. Ibid., 42. Scheppers acknowledges some few exceptions.
73. Ibid., 440–41.
74. Ibid., 284.

from their syntactic structures.[75] Scheppers concludes, "Ancient Greek texts were written to be read in cola, i.e. the 'normal' or 'natural' way to read Ancient Greek texts essentially involves reading them as a sequence of cola, in exactly the same way that [contemporary] spoken discourse necessarily comes in IUs."[76]

Because Scheppers's approach builds on advances in modern linguistics and not on ancient reflections on Greek prose, his scheme does not designate the period as an intermediate discourse unit. Scheppers briefly considers the period in an excursus, in recognition of its use by ancient Greek commentators. He notes, as I have done in my dissertation[77] and in *Sound Mapping the New Testament*,[78] the somewhat different treatment of the period by Aristotle and subsequent authors, such as Demetrius and Dionysius of Halicarnassus. He concludes that more can and should be studied about the period but this aspect of colon analysis lies outside the scope of his project, which advances a typology of coherence relations in Greek prose.[79]

Scheppers's Colon Hypothesis confirms fundamental components of sound mapping: that ancient Greek prose can and should be analyzed as speech, that the colon constitutes the basic unit of analysis, and that cola are delineated pragmatically and not by syllable count or other criteria derived from any single linguistic feature. Scheppers's theory of Greek prose segmentation and coherence suggests more precise criteria for delineating intermediate prose units in sound mapping while affirming my rule of thumb for colon definition based on syntax. Scheppers's work also indicates how modern advances in linguistics may be applied to ancient Greek prose.[80] His Colon Hypothesis suggests a way forward toward greater precision in sound analysis, enabling others to expand and replicate our findings to date.[81]

---

75. Scheppers explains, "Syntactic structure would then be expected to reflect the pragmatic articulation of the P(ragmatic)-tree. Indeed, syntactic constituency and discourse articulation as a rule do show a certain degree of homology." Ibid.

76. Ibid., *Colon Hypothesis*, 177.

77. "A Method for Sound Analysis in Hellenistic Greek," 85–92.

78. Lee and Scott, *Sound Mapping*, 108–11.

79. Scheppers, *Colon Hypothesis*, 295–317.

80. Porter, "How Can Biblical Discourse Be Analyzed," 107, has noted the problem of using discourse analysis, which studies contemporary speech, with ancient literature. Scheppers overcomes this hurdle by finding an equivalence between the colon and the IU.

81. Although Goldstein in, "Review of *The Colon Hypothesis*," questions Scheppers's "idiosyncratic" theoretical framework and the extent of his claims for the colon, he admits, "This is the most thorough treatment of Greek *Kola* available, and offers a comprehensive inventory of words for segmentation criteria."

Implications for Further Study

The work of those who have found sound mapping helpful for their understanding of the New Testament affirms its value and urges us on. De Waal pushes interpreters beyond the simple apprehension of audible signals. He correctly observes that auditory processing relates to listening as a function of the brain. I see promise in engaging cognitive psychology to inform our understanding of pattern recognition, storage of patterns in individual memory, and mechanisms for recall.

De Waal and Boomershine have both found support in sound mapping for their constructions of a listening audience and Boomershine has begun to exploit sound mapping's potential for reconstructing public performances. Although Nässelqvist critiques the notion of oral performance in favor of public reading as the primary mode for communicating New Testament literature, he has shown that the way speakers vocalize a composition makes a difference for how it is apprehended and understood.[82]

Scheppers's analysis of coherence relations can be enlisted to refine our criteria for delineating cola and to develop a typology of intermediate prose units in the New Testament. But while his Colon Hypothesis brings new tools to bear from modern linguistics, it lacks the crucial dimension of sound. Sound mapping supplies this critical component, allowing us to hear New Testament compositions more like their first audiences heard them and thus to perceive anew their structure, meaning and beauty. Recent exegetical work based on sound mapping promises important payoffs in interpretative insight. We need systematic sound analyses of whole compositions to develop a more comprehensive picture of the New Testament's soundscape. We should not just create more sound maps but better ones, refining our methodology to make the results of sound analysis more accessible for exegesis.

Conclusions

Ancient Greek authors understood literary composition as συμπλοκή or weaving, which reminds us that the human voice must animate a composition before it can be understood and before it even actually exists. Sound mapping and analysis supplies this crucial, missing component by providing techniques for New Testament interpretation that demonstrate how meanings are mediated by and implemented through sound. Now interpretative proposals must pass the sound test, since a composition's λόγος can

---

82. Nässelqvist, *Public Reading*, 131.

only be conveyed through sound. Our assessment of sound mapping has demonstrated its permanent contribution to the range of analytical tools available for New Testament interpretation.

Bibliography

Boomershine, Thomas E. "Commentary Videos—Messiah of Peace." http://messiahofpeace.com/commentaryvideos/.

———. *Messiah of Peace: A Performance-Criticism Commentary on Mark's Passion-Resurrection Narrative / Thomas E. Boomershine*. Biblical Performance Criticism Series 12. Eugene, OR: Cascade Books, 2015.

Brickle, Jeffrey E. *Aural Design and Coherence in the Prologue of First John*. Library of New Testament Studies 465. New York: T. & T. Clark, 2012.

Campbell, Constantine R. *Advances in the Study of Greek: New Insights for Reading the New Testament*. Grand Rapids: Zondervan, 2015.

Davis, Casey Wayne. *Oral Biblical Criticism: The Influence of the Principles of Orality on the Literary Structure of Paul's Epistle to the Philippians*. Journal for the Study of the New Testament. Supplement Series 172. Sheffield: Sheffield Academic, 1999.

De Waal, Kayle B. *An Aural-Performance Analysis of Revelation 1 and 11*. New York: Lang, 2015.

Dean, Margaret E. "The Grammar of Sound in Greek Texts: Toward a Method of Mapping the Echoes of Speech in Writing." *Australian Biblical Review* 44 (1996) 53–70.

Dionysius of Halicarnassus. *De Compositione*.

Foley, John Miles. *The Singer of Tales in Performance*. Voices in Performance and Text. Bloomington: Indiana University Press, 1995.

Goldstein, D. M. Review of *Review of: The Colon Hypothesis: Word Order, Discourse Segmentation and Discourse Coherence in Ancient Greek*, by Frank Scheppers. *Bryn Mawr Classical Review*, May 2012. http://bmcr.brynmawr.edu/2012/2012-05-49.html.

Kleist, James A. "Colometry and the New Testament." *Classical Bulletin* 3 (1927) 18–19.

———. "Colometry and the New Testament (Concluded)." *Classical Bulletin* 4 (1928) 26–27.

Lee, Margaret Ellen. "Colon." In *Dictionary of the Bible and Ancient Media*, edited by Tom Thatcher, et al., 63. New York: Bloomsbury T. & T. Clark, 2017.

———. "Matthew: The Musical." *Currents in Theology and Mission* 37 (2010) 479–87.

———. "Melody in Manuscript: The Birth Narrative in the Gospel of Matthew." In *Testimony, Witness, Authority: The Politics and Poetics of Experience*, edited by Tom Clark, et al. Newcastle upon Tyne: Cambridge Scholars, 2013.

———. "A Method for Sound Analysis in Hellenistic Greek: The Sermon on the Mount as a Test Case." D.Theol., Melbourne College of Divinity, 2005.

———. "Sound and Structure in the Gospel of Matthew." In *From Text to Performance: Narrative and Performance Criticisms in Dialogue and Debate*, edited by Kelly R. Iverson, 97–130. Biblical Performance Criticism Series 10. Eugene, OR: Cascade Books, 2014.

———. "Sound Mapping." In *Dictionary of the Bible and Ancient Media*, edited by Tom Thatcher et al., 372–79. New York: Bloomsbury T. & T. Clark, 2017.

Lee, Margaret Ellen, and Bernard Brandon Scott. *Sound Mapping the New Testament*. Salem, OR: Polebridge, 2009.

Nässelqvist, Dan. *Public Reading in Early Christianity: Lectors, Manuscripts, and Sound in the Oral Delivery of John 1–4*. Novum Testamentus Supplements 163. Leiden: Brill, 2015.

Nuwe-Testamentiese Werkgemeenskap van Suid-Afrika. *Structure and Meaning in Matthew 14–28*. Neotestamentica 16. Stellenbosch: Department of Biblical Studies, University of Stellenbosch, 1983.

———."The Structure of Matthew 1–13: An Exploration into Discourse Analysis." In *Proceedings of the Thirteenth Meeting of "Die Nuwe-Testamentiese Werkgemeenskap van Suid-Afrika" Held at the University of Pretoria from the 5th to the 7th of July, 1977*. Stellenbosch: Department of Biblical Studies, University of Stellenbosch, 1980.

Pearson, Brook W. R., and Stanley E. Porter. "The Genres of the New Testament." In *Handbook to Exegesis of the New Testament*. New Testament Tools and Studies 25. Leiden: Brill, 1997.

Porter, Stanley E. "How Can Biblical Discourse Be Analyzed? A Response to Several Attempts." In *Discourse Analysis and Other Topics in Biblical Greek*, edited by Stanley E. Porter and D. A. Carson, 107–16. Library of New Testament Studies. Edinburgh: T. & T. Clark, 1995.

Ryan, Sean Michael. *Hearing at the Boundaries of Vision: Education Informing Cosmology in Revelation 9*. Library of New Testament Studies 448. New York: Bloomsbury T. & T. Clark, 2014.

Scheppers, Frank. *The Colon Hypothesis: Word Order, Discourse Segmentation and Discourse Coherence in Ancient Greek*. Brussels: VUBPress, 2011.

Scott, Bernard Brandon and Margaret E. Dean. "A Sound Map of the Sermon on the Mount." In *Society of Biblical Literature 1993 Seminar Papers*, 672–725. Atlanta: Scholars, 1993.

———. "A Sound Map of the Sermon on the Mount." In *Treasures Old and New: Recent Contributions to Matthean Studies*, edited by David Bauer and Mark Allan Powell, 313–80. Atlanta: Scholars, 1996.

Silva, Moisés. "Discourse Analysis and Philippians." In *Discourse Analysis and Other Topics in Biblical Greek*, 102–6. Journal for the Study of the New Testament. Supplements 113. Sheffield: Sheffield Academic, 1995.

Stanley, Christopher D. *Arguing with Scripture: The Rhetoric of Quotations in the Letters of Paul*. New York: Bloomsbury T. & T. Clark, 2004.

2

New Adventures in Sound Mapping
A First-Timer's Attempt at a New Methodology

ADAM G. WHITE

Introduction

I am the "new kid on the block" in this project. My interest in sound mapping came about only recently through reading Margaret E. Lee and Bernard B. Scott's *Sound Mapping the New Testament* as part of a larger, growing interest in the area of performance criticism. I had never come across anything like it before, so I read the book with great interest. This reading was followed up by a long breakfast with Margaret Lee at the 2016 Annual Meeting of the Society of Biblical Literature in San Antonio, who then very kindly invited me to take part in this project. Being so new to the method, and with other academic commitments in the way, I have not to this point had the chance to apply sound mapping to my work. So, what follows in this essay is a first attempt at sound mapping with a passage I am very familiar with and one very dear to me. I will conclude the analysis with a brief review of my experience.

This essay will look at 1 Cor 1:18–31. During my doctoral research, which focused on 1 Cor 1–4, I was examining verses 1:27–28 and was struck by the structure of the Greek. There was something very intentional about the way the passage was set out, a beautiful symmetry that was very clear even to my untrained eye. I noted this in the thesis, but at the time, had no method of understanding its significance. I never stopped thinking about that structure, however, and every time I have taught Corinthians since then, I have wanted to highlight it to my students but still had no way of explaining the reason for it. So, when Margaret approached me to contribute to this volume, it seemed like the perfect opportunity to apply sound mapping to not only vv. 27–28, but to the entire section of 1 Cor 1:18–31, and see what it reveals. For me at least, the results were eye-opening!

Let us begin with a brief background to the text. Some elite members of Paul's Corinthian community have come to understand the "wisdom of God" according to ethical categories taught (particularly) in philosophical schools and embodied in the (I argue) Stoic σοφός. In their assessment of themselves, they believe that they have made more progress along the path to wisdom in Christ than Paul has; in fact, by contrast with Apollos, they have deemed Paul inadequate. According to Paul, however, the "wisdom" they are boasting about is foolishness to God and incompatible with the message of the cross.[1] In this section (1:18–31), Paul defines the wisdom of God as the foolish message of the crucified Messiah and then describes who it is that rejects it and who it is that accepts it. He intends to juxtapose the two groups and make clear what type of person one finds in his community.

Sound Map of 1 Corinthians 1:18–31

1 Corinthians 1:18–25

Scholars typically divide 1 Corinthians 1:18–31 into two distinct but interrelated parts: 1:18–25 and 1:26–31.[2] In the first part, 1:18–25, Paul describes the wisdom of God as the foolish message of the cross and contrasts this with the "wisdom" of the world and those who embody this wisdom. Fee calls this section "one of the truly great moments in the apostle Paul—and in the whole of Christian scripture."[3] The passage functions to set up, not only the section of 1 Corinthians 1–4, but the entire letter.[4] Paul first de-

---

1. White, *Where Is the Wise Man?* 71–79.

2. Scholars also note that the overall section beginning at 1:18 ends at 2:5. The purpose of the passage is to respond to the suggestion that the gospel is some form of wisdom like the world's wisdom. It does this in three ways: 1:18–25, the message concerns a crucified Messiah; 1:26–31, the Corinthian recipients are far from wise; 2:1–5, foolishness is what characterizes Paul's preaching. See Thiselton, *The First Epistle to the Corinthians*, 148. But limitations of space prevent an analysis of 2:1–5.

3. Fee, *First Epistle to the Corinthians*, 70.

4. To that end, there are numerous suggestions as to the function of 1:18–25: that it serves as the *narratio*, the *probatio*, the *exordium*, or the *argumentatio*; others see it as a

New Adventures in Sound Mapping 29

scribes in gentle and more general terms what the message is and how it contrasts with the commonly held views of wisdom. He does not launch into a direct critique of the Corinthians; instead, he sets a more general platform upon which he will build the proceeding argument, outlining the content of the message and defining those who reject it.

Period 1:

1. Ὁ λόγος γὰρ ὁ τ<u>οῦ</u> σταυρ<u>οῦ</u>

   <u>τοῖς μὲν</u> ἀπολλυμέν<u>οις</u> μωρία ἐστίν,

2.   <u>τοῖς δὲ</u>   σῳζομέν<u>οις</u>   ἡμῖν

       δύνα<u>μις</u> θε<u>οῦ</u> ἐστιν.

The cola are marked by the presence of the subject and the predicate; they also form complete sense units. Colon 1a contains the subject (Ὁ λόγος ὁ τοῦ σταυροῦ) while 1b and 2b provide the predicate. Colon 2 is a subordinate clause that adds an additional predicate to the subject. The two cola are combined with the subordinate conjunction δέ, forming a period. The beginning and end of the period are marked by the repetition of the τοῦ σταυροῦ/θεοῦ sound, rounding out the period. Balance between the cola is also achieved through the parallel dative participle phrases that both end with the verb ἐστίν, as well as the similar length of the two cola. The repetition of ιν creates *homeoteleuton*. The addition of ἡμῖν emphasizes that salvation is found within the Corinthian community of which Paul is a representative, but breaks what would otherwise be a symmetrical parallel.[5] Instead, it seems to create a new structure that connects ἀπολλυμένοις, σῳζομένοις, and δύναμις with parallel sound and placement. The repetition of οις through the central section creates assonance and draws attention to the main characters in focus. The repetition of the τοῦ σταυροῦ/θεοῦ draws attention to the main theme of the period: God and the cross. The period exhibits clear periodic style.

The structure of the map reveals that τοῦ σταυροῦ in 1a and δύναμις θεοῦ of 2b, with their corresponding sound signatures, appear to form a parenthetical, cohesive thought: "the word of the cross is the power of God." Within this parenthetical structure, Paul describes the understanding of this message by two opposite groups: those who are being destroyed and those who are being saved. Through the use of comparison and contrast in

---

form of speech called a *schēma*. For discussion of the various views, see Lampe, "Theological Wisdom and the Word about the Cross," 117–31; Schnabel, *Der erste Brief an die Korinther*, 112–13; Ciampa and Rosner, *First Letter to the Corinthians*, 89–90.

5. Without the pronoun: τοῖς μὲν ἀπολλυμένοις μωρία ἐστίν, τοῖς δὲ σῳζομένοις δύναμις θεοῦ ἐστιν.

1b and 2a, these two groups are juxtaposed with parallel structure and the repeating sound signature οις. The repetition of the sound οις/ις (ἀπολλυμένοις, σῳζομένοις, δύναμις) identifies these terms as connected—that is, destruction and salvation are both achieved through God's power (δύναμις). Overall, the period establishes the central theme of the pericope: the word of the cross is foolishness to this world and does not conform to worldly wisdom. It also establishes a juxtaposition between those who reject the message, whom God will ultimately destroy, and those who receive it, whom God has saved. The Corinthians must decide to which group they belong. This juxtaposition is the foundation upon which Paul will now build.

Period 2:

1. γέγραπται γάρ·
2. Ἀπολῶ   τὴν σοφίαν τῶν σοφῶν,
3.   καὶ τὴν σύνεσιν τῶν συνετῶν   ἀθετήσω.

The cola are marked by the presence of the subject and the predicate; they also form complete sense units. Colon 1 functions as a comma and is a standard formula for Paul and recognizable in all his letters. Cola 2 and 3 share virtually identical structures and sound patterns, with the main verbs placed at the beginning and end to bracket the period. The cola are connected with the coordinating conjunction καί, forming a period. The beginning and end of the period are marked by the repetition of the ω sound in the main verbs, which rounds out the period. The quotation is taken verbatim from Isaiah 29:14 in the LXX, with only the final verb ἀθετέω changed from the original κρύπτω (to hide). Balance is achieved by almost identical and parallel cola and is made explicit by its chiastic structure. That Paul quotes this passage verbatim would suggest that it is made memorable by its poetic structure.[6] Harmony is achieved through repeated, identical patterns. The alliteration of the σ as well as the *homeoteleuton* created by ων highlights the characteristics of those being destroyed. Once again, the period displays clear periodical style.

In period 1, Paul draws attention to the ἀπολλύμενοι who see the message of the cross as foolishness. The repetition of ἀπόλλυμι in period 2 reveals in more concrete terms who are the ἀπολλύμενοι of the previous period. Those whom God is destroying are the ones who rely on human wisdom and understanding and, as period 1 makes clear, see the message of the cross as foolish. Period 2 introduces the σοφός/σοφία terminology, which is the logical antithesis to the μωρία of the previous period.

---

6. See Collins, *First Corinthians*, 103.

New Adventures in Sound Mapping   31

The sound map reveals the repetition of the σ, which, through alliteration, draws attention to the chief characters (σοφῶν/συνετῶν) and their wisdom (σοφίαν/σύνεσιν). This σοφός/σοφία language of period 2, and its antithesis μωρία in period 1, will characterize the rest of the pericope. The foolishness message of the cross is God destroying the wisdom upon which the "wise" are dependent and is nullifying their understanding.

The verbatim quotation from Isaiah 29:14 provides scriptural authority for the overall thesis. But by changing the final verb from Isaiah's "hide" (κρύπτω) to "nullify/reject" (ἀθετέω), Paul is pointing out an important fact: God is not hiding *God's* wisdom from the wise of the world, he is nullifying *theirs*.

Period 3:

1. ποῦ σοφός;
2. ποῦ γραμματεύς;
3. ποῦ συζητητὴς τοῦ αἰῶνος   τούτου;
4. οὐχὶ ἐμώρανεν ὁ θεὸς τὴν σοφίαν τοῦ κόσμου;

Each of the four cola poses a distinct and related question, and each forms a complete sense unit. Each colon (except colon 1) begins and ends with the ου sound, which also functions as a sound cluster to unify the period. Each colon lengthens as the period develops. The key actors in cola are marked with the ς/ος sound signature. The cola are linked through the repeated ου sound and the combination of related questions, forming a period. The period is bracketed with the thematic phoneme σοφ as well as the repetition of the ου sound in the first and last word, which rounds out the period. Balance is achieved through the repeated structure of questions; but the pattern established in the first two questions is gradually modified in the second two, with the final question introduced by a new word with a repeating sound. The modification of this final question introduces God as the chief actor in overturning the world order. Unlike the polished harmony found in the first two periods, this period is more austere, with harsh, jarring questions assaulting the hearer. Rounding and balance demonstrate a clear periodical style.

Period 3 picks up and draws together the σοφία and μωρία language of the previous periods. Paul says that God is making foolish the wisdom of the wise. The period, however, elaborates further the characters introduced previously. Period 1 introduced the ἀπολλύμενοι, while period 2 defined them with the generic τῶν σοφῶν/τῶν συνετῶν. Now, however, Paul gives further specification to who they are, describing them in more concrete terms.

Scholars define the three figures mentioned here (the σοφός, γραμματεύς, συζητητὴς τοῦ αἰῶνος) as the three forms of tertiary scholar in the Graeco-Roman world; that is, the rationalistic philosopher, the Jewish legal expert, and the rhetorician respectively.[7] These are the ones who embody the wisdom that God is nullifying.

The use of rhetorical questions in the period forces the Corinthian listeners to re-evaluate the social make-up of the community to which they belong. The anaphoric repetition of the initial ποῦ is pointed and quite jarring. In a performance setting, there would almost be a moment of shock on the part of the hearer, who is now forced to pause and physically look around for such members. The map also highlights the modification of colon 4, which breaks the pattern set in the previous three questions and introduces God as the chief actor in overturning the world order and echoes God's words in period 2. There, Paul says that God ἀπολῶ τὴν σοφίαν ("is destroying the wisdom"); now, Paul says, God ἐμώρανεν τὴν σοφίαν ("is making foolish the wisdom"). Paul's aim with this set of rhetorical questions is to show that "the truly wise person cannot be found, (because) God has annihilated the basis of learned culture, so that one can no longer claim to be what the name of σοφός suggests."[8] In other words, Paul wants the Corinthians to take a moment to look around and pay attention to the teachers in the Christian community. They will see that these teachers do not rank amongst the world's σοφοί. Quite the opposite, in fact. A closer inspection will reveal that such men are virtually nowhere to be seen, thus nullifying their false assessment of Paul as inferior.

Period 4:

1. ἐπειδὴ γὰρ ἐν   τῇ σοφίᾳ   τοῦ θεοῦ οὐκ ἔγνω ὁ κόσμος
                                  διὰ τῆς σοφίας τὸν θεόν,

2. εὐδόκησεν ὁ θεὸς   διὰ τῆς μωρίας   τοῦ   κηρύγματος
                                              σῶσαι τοὺς πιστεύοντας.

The cola are marked by the presence of the subject and the predicate; they also form complete sense units. Each colon repeats a parallel sound pattern: η/εν/α/ου/ος/ας. The period is marked by the clear balance provided by the parallel structures of the cola. The two cola pivot around the fulcrum of τὸν θεόν/ὁ θεός, who is here introduced as the active agent in salvation. Colon 1 rounds off the discussion of periods 1–3, where the world is

---

7. See Welborn, *Paul, the Fool of Christ*, 177–78; Lindemann, *Der Erste Korintherbrief*, 45. For discussion of the three figures, see Ciampa and Rosner, *The First Letter to the Corinthians*, 94–95; Winter, *Philo and Paul among the Sophists*, 188–89.

8. Welborn, *Paul, the Fool of Christ*, 177.

described as trying to find God through its wisdom. The repetition of the term σοφία connects it with the previous discussion. Colon 2 introduces the juxtaposition that salvation is only through God. The juxtaposition is made explicit with the opposite terms σοφία/μωρία and their corresponding final sounds. The introduction of the term μωρία shifts the emphasis of the proceeding periods and will become the focus of discussion. The two cola are set in parallel, and the key terms in each are placed in the same relative position in the colon; they are also emphasized through the corresponding phoneme: τῇ σοφίᾳ/ τῆς μωρίας, κόσμος/κηρύγματος, σοφίας/ πιστεύοντας. There is a return to the more polished style; euphony and harmony are achieved through the parallel structure and the relative absence of harsh consonants. There is a clear periodic style achieved through balance of the cola.

The period marks a transition point in the pericope. The focus moves away from the wise ones of the world who are perishing on account of their rejection of God and shifts towards those who believe and are being saved through God's foolish message. The juxtaposition of the terms σοφία/μωρία makes this clear. In this period, Paul contrasts the two ways by which a person might approach God.⁹ The sound map makes these two different ways explicit through the repeated sounds that draw out the keywords for attention: τῇ σοφίᾳ/τῆς μωρίας, κόσμος/κηρύγματος, σοφίας/πιστεύοντας. The world's way (which leads to destruction) is through the wisdom of the world. God's way is through believing in the foolish message. In the first scenario, it is the world trying through its resources to make a way to God. In the second, it is God actively drawing people in.¹⁰

Period 5:

1. ἐπειδὴ καὶ   Ἰουδαῖοι σημεῖα αἰτοῦσιν
                        καὶ Ἕλληνες σοφίαν ζητοῦσιν·
2. ἡμεῖς δὲ   κηρύσσομεν Χριστὸν   ἐσταυρωμένον,
                        Ἰουδαίοις μὲν σκάνδαλον   ἔθνεσιν δὲ μωρίαν,
3. αὐτοῖς δὲ   τοῖς κλητοῖς, Ἰουδαίοις τε καὶ Ἕλλησιν,
                        Χριστὸν θεοῦ δύναμιν καὶ θεοῦ   σοφίαν.

---

9. See Fee, *First Epistle to the Corinthians*, 75–77.

10. Thiselton (*First Epistle to the Corinthians*, 167) has noted the contrast between "through the wisdom of God" in colon 1 and "through the foolishness of what is proclaimed" in colon 2, both introduced by the διά. This rightly highlights the different ways by which God behaves towards two different groups; i.e., in God's wisdom, God prevents those finding God through human wisdom, but in the foolishness of God's message God saves. However, the map seems to reveal a starker contrast, as noted above.

Each colon as I have marked it here could, in fact, form two separate cola (that is, 1a and 1b could also be marked 1 and 2); I have kept them as one because the repetition of the conjunction δὲ appears to divide the period into three distinct cola. Each colon is introduced by a repeating sound pattern η/αι, ει/ε, οι/ε (following a modern Greek pronunciation). Colon 1a and b have the parallel sound pattern α/σιν. Colon 2a and b have the parallel sound pattern μεν and ον and pick up the σιν and αν of colon 1. Colon 3a repeats the sound pattern of colon 1a, while 3b repeats 2b. The period is connected by the subordinate clauses marked with the conjunction δέ. The cluster of repeated phonemes makes the connection of these cola quite apparent. All three cola are clustered around repeated phonemes; they are also connected by the repeated reference to Jews and Greeks/gentiles. The final colon repeats the δύναμις θεοῦ of period 1 that will now be further developed in subsequent periods. Harmony is achieved through repeated η/αι, ει/ε, οι/ε at the beginning of each colon, and the repetition of σιν and αν in the middle and at the end of each colon. This creates *homeoteleuton* throughout the period. The repetition in colon 3b of δύναμιν θεοῦ from period 1 creates an *inclusio* that rounds off the section.

The sound map reveals the individual cola of periods 4 and 5, and through this, we can see that period 5 mirrors and further elaborates period 4. Both periods set in contrast the wisdom of the world with the foolishness of the message of the cross. In period 4 colon 1, Paul states that the world (ὁ κόσμος) could not find God through its wisdom. In period 5 colon 1, the generic category of "the world" is specified to "Jews" and "Gentiles/Greeks" and the text explains that their failure to grasp God is due to their incorrectly seeking God through wisdom and signs.[11] The two cola are also connected through the repetition of the term σοφία. In period 4 colon 2, Paul says that God chose to save through the κήρυγμα of the implied Christ crucified. In period 5 colon 2, he says that they (he and his team) preach (κηρύσσω) Christ crucified. The two cola are also connected through the repetition of μωρία. Period 5 colon 3, which is now isolated on the map, in fact forms an *inclusio* with period 1. It also introduces a new term, τοῖς κλητοῖς, which seems to correspond to the τοῖς σῳζομένοις of period 1. The repetition of δύναμιν θεοῦ from period 1 makes the *inclusio* explicit.[12]

But the sound map also reveals an interesting development. The repetition of the term σοφία, which, until this point, has referred to the wisdom

---

11. Fee (*First Epistle to the Corinthians*, 77) also notes that the division of Jews and Greeks is specification; however, he argues that it describes the "perishing" of period 1. This is certainly the case, too, as the perishing ones there are also the generic category of "the world" in period 4.

12. See Collins, *First Corinthians*, 90.

of the world and the reason for which the world has not come to grasp God, is now redefined in colon 3 in the person of Christ. The incarnate Christ is the manifestation of both God's power and wisdom. In other words, the foolish message of the cross will now be defined as true wisdom, in contrast to the world's wisdom and it is only through this true wisdom that one may come to God. The sound map reveals that colon 3 is a new development in the pericope and, at the same time, begins a new *inclusio* that will be concluded in period 8.[13]

Period 6:

1. ὅτι τὸ μωρὸν   τοῦ θεοῦ σοφώτερον τῶν ἀνθρώπων   ἐστίν,
2. καὶ τὸ ἀσθενὲς τοῦ θεοῦ ἰσχυρότερον τῶν ἀνθρώπων.

Each colon is headed with the article τό, and each one forms a complete sense unit with a single controlling verb. The two cola share virtually identical structures and sound patterns. Each one juxtaposes a characteristic of God and a characteristic of humanity, setting them in opposition. This same pattern will be expanded in the proceeding period. The parallel cola form the period and make clear that this is a single unit of thought; the controlling verb ἐστίν is stated in colon 1 and then implied in colon 2. Balance is achieved through the parallel cola. Harmony is achieved through the repeated, identical patterns. Once again, the period displays clear periodic style through balance.

Period 6 summarises the section of period 1–5 (1 Cor 1:18–24) by explicating the extent of the δύναμις θεοῦ introduced in period 1. That is, the power of God is exceedingly more powerful than human wisdom and strength. Following the pattern seen so far, the period again juxtaposes two contrary ideas: wisdom and foolishness, strength and weakness. The map reveals that these opposing terms are set in parallel through the rhetorical technique of *synkrisis*.[14] The map also reveals that period 6 uses the same structure as period 2; this is appropriate, as both periods detail the active power of God in a manner that would be easily memorized by the listener.

Period 6 also serves to introduce the next section by establishing a pattern that will be repeated in what proceeds. The period does two things. It continues the preceding juxtaposition of God's wisdom against that of the world. But it also introduces categories by which Paul will now describe the people of God (τὸ μωρὸν/τὸ ἀσθενὲς).

---

13. Thiselton (*First Epistle to the Corinthians*, 174), citing Mitchell, alludes to this idea, but does not make explicit that an *inclusio* is formed.

14. See Collins, *First Corinthians*, 90.

1 Corinthians 1:26–31

In period 7–8 (1 Cor 1:26–31), Paul turns his attention to the audience. Having contrasted the two types of wisdom—the wisdom of the world and the foolish wisdom of God—and describing those who reject God's wisdom, he now asks the Corinthians to look at themselves and see where they stand in relation to all of these categories. In contrast to those of the previous section, who reject the message, Paul now describes those who accept it.

Period 7:

1. Βλέπετε γὰρ τὴν κλῆσιν ὑμῶν,   ἀδελφοί,
2.   ὅτι οὐ πολλοὶ σοφοὶ κατὰ σάρκα,
3.   οὐ πολλοὶ δυνατοί,
4.   οὐ πολλοὶ εὐγενεῖς·
5. ἀλλὰ τὰ μωρὰ   τοῦ κόσμου ἐξελέξατο ὁ θεός,   ἵνα καταισχύνῃ τοὺς σοφούς,
6. καὶ τὰ ἀσθενῆ   τοῦ κόσμου ἐξελέξατο ὁ θεός,   ἵνα καταισχύνῃ τὰ ἰσχυρά,
7. καὶ τὰ ἀγενῆ   τοῦ κόσμου
8. καὶ τὰ ἐξουθενημένα   ἐξελέξατο ὁ θεός,
   τὰ μὴ ὄντα,   ἵνα τὰ ὄντα καταργήσῃ,
9. ὅπως μὴ καυχήσηται πᾶσα σὰρξ ἐνώπιον τοῦ θεοῦ.

There are two sets of cola, each with a very different sound cluster. The first set of cola are is connected by the repetition of οι. The second set of cola is connected by the parallel structures that are virtually identical. Each colon in the second set begins with the conjunction, followed by τά. At the center of this set of cola is God, who aurally and visually stands between the two opposing types of person. Cola 5 and 6 repeat key terms that have already been introduced (μωρά, σοφούς, ἀσθενῆ, ἰσχυρά) and place these in otherwise identical structures. Colon 8 follows this same structure but modifies it through expansion. Here, we move from specific groups of people to universal terms (things that are and things that aren't) to make exceedingly clear that the calling of God is not in any way reliant on human ability. Paul also alters the verb καταισχύνῃ to καταργήσῃ, but still maintains the same phoneme. The period is bracketed by the verbs of cola 1 and 9, each with the same morpheme (βλέπετε/καυχήσηται), as well as the repetition of κατὰ σάρκα in colon 2 and πᾶσα σάρξ of colon 9. The adversative ἀλλά connects the two sets of cola. The impact of this conjunction is to make a stark difference between two contrasting but related realities. This period presents both an austere and more polished style. The first group of cola, as with period 3, is quite austere; once again, jarring statements awake the listener's attention to who they are and who is not in the room. The second set of cola is a more polished style that follows a similar pattern to period 6.

Period 7 picks up and repeats the terminology of period 6 (τὰ μωρὰ/τὰ ἀσθενῆ), language used to describe God's activity (period 6) and the character of those God calls (period 7). As with period 3, cola 1–4 force the listener to once again stop and re-evaluate the makeup of the community. Here, the relative absence of the worldly wise and powerful is explicit. These three terms (σοφός, δυνατός, εὐγενής) were all used to describe the members of the upper class, those who are distinguished by education, wealth, and birth.[15] But by looking around the room, the Corinthians will note they are all but absent. Instead, what they will see are the weak and foolish people of the world, whom God has called.

It is in the second part of the period (cola 5–9) that the sound map comes into its own. Its composition indicates the centrality of this passage and its importance in Paul's thinking.[16] The text contains three identical structures that create a juxtaposition of low- and high-status people, and in the very center of these opposite groups is God and God's purposes.[17] The rhetorical structure is unmistakable; there is an audible and visual separation of the two groups. The point in Paul's mind is to separate the wisdom of God, as represented in the weak and foolish things, from the wisdom of the world, as represented in the wise and powerful of this world. The period also serves to remind the Corinthians that, although some of them are educated and possess wisdom, these characteristics are not indicative of possession of God's wisdom. The wise of this world are those who reject God and stand on one side of his calling. If they want to stand on the opposite side, they must become foolish and weak (1 Cor 3:18).

The final colon provides an expansion of the pattern set in cola 6 and 7, thus portraying the stark reality of those whom God calls. It also echoes the sounds of colon 1 (βλέπετε/καυχήσηται; κατὰ σάρκα/πᾶσα σάρξ), thus bracketing the period.

---

15. Welborn, *Paul, the Fool of Christ*, 125. Similarly, see Schnabel, *Der erste Brief an die Korinther*, 140.

16. See Thiselton, *First Epistle to the Corinthians*, 183.

17. See Weiss, *Der erste Korintherbrief*, 36.

Period 8:

1. ἐξ αὐτ<u>οῦ</u> δὲ ὑμεῖς ἐστε <u>ἐν Χριστῷ</u> Ἰησ<u>οῦ</u>,
2. ὃς ἐγενήθη σοφία ἡμῖν ἀπὸ θε<u>οῦ</u>, δικαιοσύνη τε καὶ ἁγιασμὸς καὶ ἀπολύτρωσις,
3. ἵνα καθὼς γέγραπται·
4. Ὁ καυχώμενος <u>ἐν κυρίῳ</u> καυχάσθω.

The cola of this period differ from the previous ones in that they do not display the same polished patterns and structures; this creates a plainer style. However, the plainness of the period is perhaps intentional, as it is almost an anti-climax to the rhetorical heights of the previous cola and also reveals two repeated sounds, all associated with God. The repetition of the ου draws attention to the controlling agent: God/Christ Jesus. Their centrality is further highlighted in the second repetition of ἐν Χριστῷ/ἐν κυρίῳ, which serves to round out the period, as well as highlight the location within which salvation and wisdom are found. Finally, it was noted in period 5 that the incarnate Christ is the manifestation of both God's power and wisdom. The map revealed that this introduced a new *inclusio* that is concluded here in period 8, which rounds out the section begun there.

Review of the Method

By sound mapping this passage, we have been able to see in extensive detail what scholars have noted for a long time. In a twist of irony, the foolish message of the cross is described with powerful rhetorical devices.[18] In period 1, the sound patterns highlight and draw attention to the theologically significant point of the text; that is, God's δύναμις is both the destructive and saving force of humanity as well as the all-encompassing power at work. In period 2, the repetition of the σ drew attention to the main character being introduced, who will be a central feature in the rest of the pericope: σοφός/σοφία; specifically, the wisdom that God is and ultimately will destroy. In period 3, Paul sets out four rhetorical questions, whose jarring structure would force the Corinthians to stop and look around the room to see who could be categorized by such wisdom. The map revealed, however, that the final question, with its modified and extended structure, draws attention to the main character who is overturning this wisdom, namely, God. Having drawn attention to the fact that God is destroying the wisdom of the wise, which might assume God can be found through human striving, the structure of period 4 makes explicit through rhetorical contrast the only

---

18. See Collins, *First Corinthians*, 91.

way in which one may approach God. It is not through human wisdom, it is only through the foolish message. Period 5 then develops the argument of period 4 and its structure draws attention to the fact that it is Paul's preaching (by contrast to the other teachers that the Corinthians are enamored by) that they must depend on for the true message of wisdom. The final colon (revealed by the map) creates the *inclusio* with period 1 and explicates that true wisdom is Christ. Finally, periods 6 and 7 repeat all the previously used structures and sound patterns to create an extended juxtaposition that makes explicit the extent of God's power and the contrast between those God has called and those God is rejecting. Its structure in a performance setting would give the Corinthians cause to stop and actively look around to see who fits this description.

For those familiar with this passage, what I have drawn out here would come as no surprise. Paul's argument through this pericope is articulate and forceful, even without the sound map. However, what stood out to me in the analysis was the fact that the sound patterns and structures (revealed by sound mapping) further highlighted these established conclusions. Put another way, Paul's key argument through this passage is embedded in his audible structure. The map only made clear what we had already observed, but this fact ought to give us a moment of pause: what might sound mapping reveal in some of the more difficult passages we find in scripture?

What also stood out in the analysis was the way the map revealed the auditory effect this letter would have had on the Corinthians. A historical-critical approach will focus on the reading of the content—what are the key terms and arguments and how might they shape the thinking of the Corinthians—but sound mapping forced me to listen to the content. How were these key points heard during the original performance? What emotional effect would they have on the audience? For example, at points where God's power is described, euphony and harmony are employed in memorable statements (e.g., periods 1, 2, 6). But when Paul wants to waken the Corinthians to their standing to God, cacophony and dissonance are employed to force them to look around the room (e.g., periods 3 and 7).

Again, by setting out the passage in this way, numerous connections were revealed at a period-by-period level (e.g., the connection between period 4 and 5) as well as at an overall pericope level (e.g., the *inclusio* of period 1 and 5 and the *inclusio* of 5 and 9). By setting out the passage period-by-period, the map highlighted the centrality of the σοφία/σοφός μωρία/μορός language, present in every period. The analysis revealed the development of the understanding of true wisdom. Paul's argument begins in periods 1 and 2 by setting the world's wisdom in opposition to the foolishness of the message of the cross, and concludes that this very foolishness is in fact true wisdom.

Sound mapping for me was like having an extra pair of lenses to read the text. A typical analysis of a passage will begin with a close reading of the Greek text, which is the starting point of any research. It is from this process that new insights are found. Sound mapping adds another layer to this reading—like an extra tool in the toolbox. I began my analysis by mapping out the whole passage on a single document; that way I could see how each period was working by itself and in the broader context of the pericope. Already at this point, I was looking at the text in a way that I never had before. This then revealed the subtle techniques Paul used throughout and drew my attention to the points that seemed to be uppermost in his mind. In general, I found that sound mapping this passage made explicit the creativity and intentionality of Paul as he crafted this letter, and found myself one step closer to the first Corinthian listeners as they heard and experienced this letter being read to them.

I came to this project having never done sound mapping before. For me, this meant reading through Lee and Scott's *Sound Mapping the New Testament* several times in depth to learn the method and familiarize myself with the concepts and terminology. At first, I highlighted the main points in the book and then referred back and forth to it as I analyzed each verse of the text, which soon became frustrating. After a while, I decided to write my own glossary of key terms as a quick reference guide. This sped up the process substantially. By the end of the analysis, I had internalized some of the more common themes. A simple solution to this would be some type of handbook or reference chart that corresponds to *Sound Mapping the New Testament*. But such a handbook would only be necessary as the student learns the method and internalizes the concepts. The method itself is quite quick to learn. I found myself becoming familiar with the concepts and technique very quickly, so that, by the end of the analysis, the sound features of the passage were revealing themselves more easily.

Perhaps the most obvious deterrent to employing sound mapping as part of one's analytical process is the extra time it takes to map out the passage. Even if one is conversant with the method, it still requires the "gruntwork" of creating the map. There is no way around this. One's desire to use it is relative to the value that one sees in its findings. Even at a first attempt, I could see new features of the passage revealed by the map, and I could appreciate Paul's words from the point of view of a listener, rather than a reader. In the world of New Testament scholarship, where there is almost "nothing new under the sun," this was refreshing and exciting.

Bibliography

Ciampa, Roy E., and Brian S. Rosner. *The First Letter to the Corinthians.* Pillar New Testament Commentary. Grand Rapids: Eerdmans, 2010.

Collins, Raymond F. *First Corinthians.* Sacra Pagina. Collegeville, MN: Liturgical, 2006.

Fee, Gordon. *The First Epistle to the Corinthians.* Rev. ed. New International Commentary on the New Testament. Grand Rapids: Eerdmans, 2015.

Lampe, Peter. "Theological Wisdom and the Word about the Cross: The Rhetorical Scheme of 1 Cor 1–4." *Interpretation* 44 (1990) 117–31.

Lindemann, Andreas. *Der Erste Korintherbrief.* Handbuch zum Neuen Testament. Tübingen: Mohr/Siebeck, 2000.

Schnabel, Eckhard J. *Der erste Brief des Paulus an die Korinther.* Historisch Theologisch Auslegung. Brunnen: Brockhaus, 2006.

Thiselton, Anthony C. *The First Epistle to the Corinthians.* New International Greek Testament Commentary. Grand Rapids: Eerdmans, 2000.

Weiss, Johannes. *Der erste Korintherbrief.* Kritisch-exegetischer Kommentar über das Neue Testament. Göttingen: Vandenhoeck & Ruprecht, 1910.

Welborn, L. L. *Paul, the Fool of Christ: A Study of 1 Corinthians 1–4 in the Comic-Philosophic Tradition.* Journal for the Study of the New Testament Supplements 293. London: T. & T. Clark, 2005.

White, Adam. *Where Is the Wise Man? Graeco-Roman Education as a Background to the Division in 1 Corinthians 1–4.* Library of New Testament Studies 536. London: Bloomsbury T. & T. Clark, 2015.

Winter, Bruce W. *Philo and Paul among the Sophists: Alexandrian and Corinthian Responses to a Julio-Claudian Movement.* Grand Rapids: Eerdmans, 2001.

3

Luke's Strategy for Interpreting Parables

BERNARD BRANDON SCOTT

Introduction

Sound Mapping

Sound mapping in my view operates at the level of the syllable and colon.[1] For Greek, the primary unit for analysis is the colon.[2] Sound mapping supports other methodologies and belongs to "lower" criticism, much like text criticism, although at times a sound map can support or help explain text critical issues. A sound map will help a critic see how and what the composition has selected for interpretation by observing first of all repetitions,[3] anomalies, and artful arrangement. Close observation of detail will help the modern sound mapper observe what they heard, to observe how a composition is woven together to select the items for interpretation.

Yet sound mapping is not interpretation but is prior to, lays the foundation for interpretation and indicates what needs interpretation. Since

---

1. For a definition of colon, see Lee and Scott, *Sound Mapping*, 108–11. Scheppers, *Colon Hypothesis*, is an important study that both supports the contention of our book but goes beyond it by employing modern discourse analysis, as the subtitle indicates.

2. The Nestle–Aland Greek critical edition presents a reconstructed Greek text as though it were a modern European language. Consequently, the editors try to conform Greek cola to modern sentence structure. Sometimes it works; often it does not. For my purposes I will ignore the punctuation in Nestle–Aland 28.

3. Lee and Scott, *Sound Mapping*, 135–65.

"[w]riting and reading in the Greco-Roman world exhibited a shared dependence upon speech,"[4] a sound map attempts to present in graphic form what an ancient audience heard. It substitutes for our inability to be fluent hearers of a composition. A modern silent reading of a Greek composition impoverishes the original by turning it into a silent, interior experience, instead of a public (*publicatio*) experience, an experience between a speaker and an audience. Communication in the ancient world takes place in sound.

Parables

A truism of New Testament scholarship is that the gospel writers allegorized the parables of Jesus. Overall this assessment is true, especially in the case of Mark and Matthew. But this is less obviously true of Luke.[5] He is much more reserved in taking over Mark's form of allegory[6] and introduces no new allegories in the Marcan form, as does Matthew.[7] Rather, Luke often interprets parables by means of situating them in a narrative context. This approach has proven a much more effective means of interpreting the parables than Mark's point-by-point allegories. It appears more natural as part of the story than Mark's artificial effect. So effective has Luke's narrative incorporation of the parables been that commentators have found it difficult to separate them. For example, in dealing with the parable of the Prodigal Son, C. H. Dodd recognizes that Luke has constructed the context of the conflict with the Pharisees, but goes on to argue, "The application, however, is to the same situation in the ministry of Jesus. So Luke represents it, and we cannot doubt that he is right."[8] Luke's hold on the imagination has been powerful even when interpreters recognize it and even more so when masked.

This essay explores how Luke incorporated the uniquely Lucan parables into the narrative context of the gospel. The primary test case will be the Parable of the Samaritan (Luke 10:33–35), including the larger narrative section (10:1–42) and the immediate context of the dialogue with

---

4. Ibid., 91, with references.

5. I follow the convention of naming the author as "Luke," but have no idea who actually composed the gospel.

6. For example, compare Luke 8:11–15 with its source, Mark 4:13–20.

7. See the Parable of the Wheat and Tares (Matt 13:24–13) and its interpretation (Matt 13:36–43).

8. Dodd, *Parables of the Kingdom*, 93. Plummer, *Gospel according to St. Luke*, 371, remarks: "Even if it was delivered on some other occasion unknown to Luke, he could not have given it a more happy position than this." More recently, Hultgren, *The Parables of Jesus: A Commentary*, 85, struggles with the issue and finally comes down with, "There is no sufficient reason to discount the setting Luke has provided."

the lawyer (10:25-37). Finally, as further examples, the parables in Luke 15 (Lost Sheep, Lost Coin, Lost Kids) and Luke 16:1-16 (the Steward) will be probed to expand the understanding of Luke's narrative strategies and uncover related strategies for incorporating a parable into the narrative structure.[9]

Lawyer and Parable in Context

Section

Ancient readers were audiences, hearers. A composition was processed as a linear stream of sound[10] and composition took place in sound. Sound is the medium of ancient composition. This means that the structure of a composition must be held in memory. The ancients heard a composition's structure; they did not see it in a manuscript.[11] One of sound mapping's strengths is the delineation of a composition's segments. It maps out the segmentation as they would have heard it and kept it in memory. So, the analysis of Luke's compositional strategy begins with a delineation of the composition's segmentation.

The section[12] in Luke's gospel to which the parable unit belongs begins at Luke 10:1 with clear markers of a major shift from the previous narrative:[13]

Μετὰ δὲ ταῦτα ἀνέδειξεν ὁ κύριος ἑτέρους ἑβδομήκοντα

---

9. In preparation for this paper I sound mapped all the parables in Luke. To deal with all the parables would have made this paper too long. However, the three examples (five parables) selected for analysis in the paper are representative of Luke's various strategies.

10. Lee and Scott, *Sound Mapping*, 70-72.

11. The debate about whether the ancients could read silently has raged on interminably with no signs of abating. But it is irrelevant to the main point. Literary manuscripts were composed to be read aloud. For a summary of this debate see ibid., 25.

12. In my terminology, "section" is the larger grouping made up of "units." This usage is admittedly arbitrary but helpful in making appropriate distinctions.

13. This section belongs to what is commonly identified as the travel narrative (9:51—19:27), the trip to Jerusalem. At 19:28 Jesus arrives in Jerusalem. The four cola that inaugurate the travel narrative clearly set the direction for trip.

Ἐγένετο δὲ ἐν τῷ συμπληροῦσθαι τὰς ἡμέρας τῆς ἀναλήμψεως αὐτοῦ καὶ αὐτὸς τὸ πρόσωπον ἐστήρισεν τοῦ πορεύεσθαι εἰς Ἰερουσαλήμ
καὶ ἀπέστειλεν ἀγγέλους πρὸ προσώπου αὐτοῦ
καὶ πορευθέντες εἰσῆλθον εἰς κώμην Σαμαριτῶν ὡς ἑτοιμάσαι αὐτῷ
καὶ οὐκ ἐδέξαντο αὐτὸν ὅτι τὸ πρόσωπον αὐτοῦ ἦν πορευόμενον εἰς Ἰερουσαλήμ (Luke 9:51-3).

καὶ ἀπέστειλεν αὐτοὺς ἀνὰ πρὸ προσώπου αὐτοῦ εἰς πᾶσαν πόλιν
καὶ τόπον οὗ ἤμελλεν αὐτὸς ἔρχεσθαι[14]

These two cola formally inaugurate a new section and can be designated a section header. Μετὰ δὲ ταῦτα indicates completion of the previous unit. The strong repetition of α-sounds initially in the first four words draws attention to ἀνέδειξεν ὁ κύριος. Κύριος itself is a strong word whose less than frequent use to this point in the gospel[15] would draw the hearer's attention to the action of the κύριος. The second colon in the header has a string of π-sounds flowing from ἀπέστειλεν which draw out in sound the sending. The elongated second colon indicates the conclusion of section header. All these clues in combination indicate a new section.

The next strong marker denoting a new section is 11:1:

Καὶ ἐγένετο ἐν τῷ εἶναι αὐτὸν ἐν τόπῳ τινὶ προσευχόμενον

ὡς ἐπαύσατο, εἶπέν τις τῶν μαθητῶν αὐτοῦ πρὸς αὐτόν

κύριε, δίδαξον ἡμᾶς προσεύχεσθαι, καθὼς καὶ Ἰωάννης ἐδίδαξεν
τοὺς μαθητὰς αὐτοῦ

Καὶ ἐγένετο is frequently used in Luke to note a new section or unit.[16] The change of place and the reiteration of praying in this section header indicates a new section and the upcoming topic.

Units

The units in this section of Luke do not exhibit strong markers to denote the beginnings of narrative units. The initial markers are minimal and for the most part simple in contrast to the section beginning.

Sending Out (10:2–16)

ἔλεγεν δὲ πρὸς αὐτούς

---

14. When a colon extends beyond the length of a printed line, a hanging indent indicates its continuation on the line below.

15. Κύριος to this point in Luke has not been used frequently. It occurs six times in the birth narrative in reference to God. In this context 2:11 stands out as the only reference to Jesus in the angels' announcement of his birth to the shepherds: Σωτὴρ ὅς ἐστιν χριστὸς κύριος (2:11). After the birth narrative there are only two other uses of κύριος (6:5, referring to son of man, and 7:13, to Jesus) before this usage. Luke 10:1 begins a much more frequent use of the term (20 times) in reference to Jesus.

16. Ἐγένετο δέ begins the travel narrative in 9:51.

ὁ μὲν θερισμὸς πολύς, οἱ δὲ ἐργάται ὀλίγοι

δεήθητε οὖν τοῦ κυρίου τοῦ θερισμοῦ ὅπως ἐργάτας ἐκβάλῃ εἰς τὸν θερισμὸν αὐτοῦ

The sending out speech gets no special introduction: ἔλεγεν δέ (v. 2) does not so much introduce the speech as connect it to the section introduction. The threefold repetition of θερισμός indicates the speech's topic. The speech itself extends from verse 2 to 16, but commentators notice a break between verses 12 and 13 because the Woes do not seem to fit with the Sending Out speech.[17] A sound map does not posit any such break. Verse 12 connects to the Woes by means of keywords/sounds based on the names of the cities: Sodom, Chorazin, Bethsaida, etc.

The speech's conclusion (v. 16) is a strong but simply constructed series of cola:

Ὁ ἀκούων   ὑμῶν   ἐμοῦ ἀκούει

καὶ ὁ ἀθετῶν   ὑμᾶς   ἐμὲ ἀθετεῖ

ὁ δὲ ἐμὲ ἀθετῶν ἀθετεῖ τὸν ἀποστείλαντά με

The first two lines are balanced with a strong rhyming pattern, while the last line is elongated and the verb/object placement of the previous two lines is reversed, creating an AB/BA pattern between the first two lines and the final line.

Return (10:17-24)

The return of the seventy likewise gets no strong introduction (v. 17) and so a pattern is being established which will repeat throughout this section.

Ὑπέστρεψαν δὲ οἱ ἑβδομήκοντα μετὰ χαρᾶς λέγοντες

κύριε, καὶ τὰ δαιμόνια ὑποτάσσεται ἡμῖν ἐν τῷ ὀνόματί σου

Ἑβδομήκοντα and κύριος hark back to the section opening in 10:1. This unit continues to be strung together with weak connectors. Ἐν αὐτῇ τῇ ὥρᾳ (v. 21) introduces a thanksgiving whose audience is unclear. An audience is quickly introduced with the next transition: καὶ στραφεὶς πρὸς τοὺς μαθητὰς

---

17. Fitzmyer, *Gospel according to Luke*, 850, notes that 13–15 is "something of a problem." The Woes do not appear to fit with 2–12 (Sending), while verse 16 appears to form a logical conclusion to the speech of the sending out of the seventy. Nestle–Aland 28 starts a new paragraph at verse 13. Fitzmyer is allowing a form-critical observation to govern his understanding of Luke's redaction.

κατ' ἰδίαν εἶπεν (v. 23). Καὶ is a paratactic connector, not really separating this from what precedes it. Στραφείς (turning) plays upon ὑπέστρεψαν (they returned, v. 17) which introduced the return of the seventy. This keeps this unit tied to the previous action, while the "disciples" return to the stage. "Privately" attempts to introduce a context for the thanksgiving that makes sense.

The concluding beatitude (vv. 23-24) of three cola again is artfully constructed, this time by means of doublets and two final triplets built around seeing and hearing.

μακάριοι οἱ ὀφθαλμοὶ	οἱ <u>βλέποντες</u>	ἃ <u>βλέπετε</u>	
λέγω γὰρ ὑμῖν ὅτι	πολλοὶ <u>προφῆται</u>	καὶ <u>βασιλεῖς</u> ἠθέλησαν	
	ἰδεῖν	ἃ ὑμεῖς βλέπετε	καὶ <u>οὐκ εἶδαν</u>
	καὶ <u>ἀκοῦσαι</u>	ἃ <u>ἀκούετε</u>	καὶ <u>οὐκ ἤκουσαν</u>

The doublet οἱ βλέποντες ἃ βλέπετε balances with the doublet προφῆται καὶ βασιλεῖς. Prophets and kings is not a natural pairing,[18] but the β sound of βασιλεῖς blends it with the doublet οἱ βλέποντες ἃ βλέπετε. The final double triplet built around seeing and hearing expands the original seeing and elongates the final colon.

The analysis of this section to this point has displayed a series of unit introductions with weak markers of transition and conclusions that exhibit strong and artfully organized cola, training the hearer to listen for the conclusion.

The Lawyer (10:25-37)

Καὶ ἰδού (v. 25) draws attention to a shift in character to a lawyer, indicating a new unit.

Καὶ ἰδοὺ νομικός τις ἀνέστη ἐκπειράζων αὐτὸν λέγων
διδάσκαλε τί ποιήσας ζωὴν αἰώνιον κληρονομήσω

---

18. Verse 10:24 is the only place it occurs in the bible. Instead of βασιλεῖς Matthew has δίκαιοι (13:17). Much of the discussion concerns which is more original, with most interpreters assuming Luke is more original. The strangeness of the phrase draws little comment. Fitzmyer, *Gospel according to Luke*, 875, does not comment on the oddness of the combination. Marshal, *Gospel of Luke*, 439, notes, "The significance of 'kings' alongside prophets is less obvious." Robinson et al., *Critical Edition of Q*, 198-99, prefer the Lucan reading as Q. No one notices the sound map solution: the β sound of βασιλεῖς blends with the doublet οἱ βλέποντες ἃ βλέπετε.

Καὶ ἰδοὺ is a frequent attention marker in both Matthew and Luke,[19] but seldom is it used to mark a new narrative unit.[20] The narrative indicates no shift in time or location.[21] Verse 30 continues the pattern of weak signaling of unit beginnings and sets up a dialogue between the lawyer and Jesus. The dialogue is simply indicated by the repetition of ὁ δὲ εἶπεν or some variation for five times in a row.[22] The analysis of this unit will resume below (see "Lawyer's Dialogue") after consideration of the last narrative unit in this section.

Mary and Martha (10:38-42)

The next narrative unit, the story of Martha and Mary, is marked by a shift in place and characters (v. 38).

The story of Mary and Martha is the concluding narrative unit of a section that began at 10:1. It exhibits a weak beginning and a strong conclusion as did the other units in this section, giving the whole a cohesive sound. The weak marker of a new narrative unit (v. 38) denotes a transition in place:

Ἐν δὲ τῷ πορεύεσθαι αὐτοὺς αὐτὸς εἰσῆλθεν εἰς κώμην τινά

Immediately afterwards is the introduction of new character, Martha.

γυνὴ δέ τις ὀνόματι Μάρθα ὑπεδέξατο αὐτόν

These two cola serve to transition from the lawyer's dialogue with Jesus to Jesus's dialogue with Martha. While this dialogue is not as elegantly arranged as the lawyer's, it has the same dialogue structure.

The situation that provokes the dialogue is set up with the introduction of yet another character, Mary.

καὶ τῇδε ἦν ἀδελφὴ καλουμένη Μαριάμ

[ἣ] καὶ παρακαθεσθεῖσα πρὸς τοὺς πόδας τοῦ κυρίου ἤκουεν τὸν λόγον αὐτοῦ

---

19. Twenty-eight times in Matthew; twenty-six times in Luke. The phrase is absent in Mark and John. It is used much less frequently in Acts (eight times). This phrase is very frequent in the LXX and so might be considered part of Luke's imitation of the Septuagint's style. The phrase occurs three times in Lucan Q, but never to begin a colon. See Luke 11:31, 32; 13:30.

20. Four times in Luke it is clearly used to inaugurate a new narrative unit: 2:25, 23:50, 24:13. This happens only twice in Matthew (9:20, 19:16).

21. This is odd and narratively confusing, given that the previous unit was "private."

22. I am counting the variation at 10:30 and including the parable as part of this chain.

ἡ δὲ Μάρθα περιεσπᾶτο περὶ πολλὴν διακονίαν

ἐπιστᾶσα δὲ εἶπεν, κύριε, οὐ μέλει σοι ὅτι ἡ ἀδελφή μου μόνην με κατέλιπεν διακονεῖν

εἰπὲ οὖν αὐτῇ ἵνα μοι συναντιλάβηται

The dialogue ends with Jesus' making a carefully arranged pronouncement, as in all the previous units of this section.

ἀποκριθεὶς δὲ εἶπεν αὐτῇ ὁ κύριος

Μάρθα Μάρθα, μεριμνᾷς καὶ θορυβάζῃ περὶ πολλά

ἑνὸς δέ ἐστιν χρεία

Μαριὰμ γὰρ τὴν ἀγαθὴν μερίδα ἐξελέξατο ἥτις οὐκ ἀφαιρεθήσεται αὐτῆς

Conclusion 1

This section (Luke 10:1–42) contains four narrative units that are all organized in a similar fashion. They exhibit minimal unit beginning markers and artfully and strongly composed conclusions. Thus, Luke trains the listener's ear by the repetition of this pattern to pay attention to each narrative unit's conclusion.

Lawyer's Dialogue

The analysis of the Lawyer's dialogue with Jesus will now resume. This unit involves a confrontation between a lawyer and Jesus built around a series of questions and answers and illustrated by a parable with a concluding question.

Initial Colon (10:25)

The initial colon continues the pattern of weak initial markers at the beginning of narrative units throughout this section.

Καὶ ἰδοὺ νομικός τις ἀνέστη ἐκπειράζων αὐτὸν λέγων

Καὶ ἰδού singles out a lawyer and τις draws yet more attention to him.[23] The construction of the initial colon is arresting. Ἀνέστη ἐκπειράζων indi-

---

23. Τις, as is well known, is a common Lucan word. It occurs seventy-two times in

cates the dialogue will be a contest. Standing up is more confrontational than employing ἐλθών. The lawyer's standing up draws attention to him, making him stand out, although how a hearer is to view or imagine the audience for this dialogue is unclear. It would have been more neutral for the lawyer to have just addressed Jesus with εἶπεν as the disciple does in 11:1.

Contest (10:26–29)

Luke's editing of Mark 12:28b–32 involves shifting to a single character, a lawyer, instead of a scribe as part of a group of Sadducees, a quickly paced dialogue, and a much tighter focus than the Marcan version.

The topic for debate has been reworked from "Which commandment is the first of all" (Mark 12:38) to "What must I do to inherit eternal life?" (Luke 10:25). Rather than Jesus responding directly, as he does in Mark, in Luke's version the dialogue shifts back and forth, ending with the lawyer offering the decisive response. Four short phrases lead to the lawyer giving the answer, rather than Jesus.

ὁ δὲ εἶπεν πρὸς αὐτόν

ἐν τῷ νόμῳ τί γέγραπται

πῶς ἀναγινώσκεις

ὁ δὲ ἀποκριθεὶς εἶπεν

The shift from the question in Mark, "what is the greatest of commandments," to Luke's, "what must I do to inherit eternal life," allows for a condensing of two commandments into one. Mark's cola clearly set these off as two distinct commandments:

καὶ ἀγαπήσεις κύριον τὸν θεόν σου	ἐξ ὅλης τῆς καρδίας σου
καὶ	ἐξ ὅλης τῆς ψυχῆς σου
καὶ	ἐξ ὅλης τῆς διανοίας σου
καὶ	ἐξ ὅλης τῆς ἰσχύος σου

δευτέρα αὕτη ἀγαπήσεις τὸν πλησίον σου ὡς σεαυτόν (Mark 12:30–31)

In the Lucan redaction the two become one—the whole notion of commandment disappears.[24]

Luke, forty in Acts, twenty-four times each in both Matthew and Mark, and fifty times in John.

24. The Marcan text, while based on Deut 6:5, is similar but not identical. Luke's text, needless to say, is even further from Deuteronomy.

ἀγαπήσεις κύριον τὸν θεόν σου	ἐξ ὅλης [τῆς] καρδίας σου
καὶ	ἐν ὅλῃ τῇ ψυχῇ σου
καὶ	ἐν ὅλῃ τῇ ἰσχύϊ σου
καὶ	ἐν ὅλῃ τῇ διανοίᾳ σου
καὶ	τὸν πλησίον σου ὡς σεαυτόν

After the first iteration of ἐξ ὅλης [τῆς],[25] the colon continues with three ἐν ὅλῃ τῇ[26] phrases, which soften the expression. The third and fourth phrases in Mark (καὶ ἐξ ὅλης τῆς διανοίας σου καὶ ἐξ ὅλης τῆς ἰσχύος σου) are switched in Luke, increasing the number of syllables in line four, thus making lines four and five more matched. By switching ἰσχύϊ and διανοίᾳ, the harsher ἰσχύϊ balances with ψυχῇ, thus smoothing out the colon's end. The καὶ ἐν ὅ- sounds blend with the concluding καὶ τόν and the η sounds of ὅλῃ τῇ blend with πλησίον in the final phrase. The -ον ending sound of πλησίον picks up the initial τὸν and ties it to the final -τόν sound of σεαυτόν. The repetition of the sigma sounds further unifies this final phrase, contributing to the cohesion of the final phrase.

καὶ τὸν πλησίον σου ὡς σεαυτόν

The slight elongation of the final two phrases draws out the colon and makes the high degree of repetition more harmonious and euphonious. Instead of two cola as in Mark, Luke has constructed a single, unified, balanced and euphonious colon.

This section has trained a listener's ear to pay attention to euphonic and carefully constructed parallels. The effect of this careful construction is to draw the ear to the final phrase: καὶ τὸν πλησίον σου ὡς σεαυτόν. This sets up πλησίον, neighbor, as the topic.

The dialogue continues with the repetition of the continuing indicator of dialogue, εἶπεν δὲ αὐτῷ. Jesus' response to the lawyer's artfully composed colon is simple: ὀρθῶς ἀπεκρίθης τοῦτο ποίει καὶ ζήσῃ. The second part of Jesus' response, ζήσῃ, picks up on the lawyer's initial question: τί ποιήσας ζωὴν αἰώνιον κληρονομήσω. Ζήσῃ echoes ζωήν.

As the dialogue continues, the expected εἶπεν δὲ indicator of continuing dialogue is elaborated.

ὁ δὲ θέλων δικαιῶσαι ἑαυτὸν εἶπεν πρὸς τὸν Ἰησοῦν

---

25. The textual evidence for the inclusion of τῆς in Luke's first colon is very mixed. A number of manuscripts have ἐν with the dative instead of ἐξ, but this is surely a scribal effort to make the whole string agree.

26. In Mark, all the phrases have ἐξ.

καὶ τίς ἐστίν μου πλησίον

The lawyer is not named but described as ὁ δὲ θέλων δικαιῶσαι[27] ἑαυτὸν and the phrase is further elongated by πρὸς τὸν Ἰησοῦν, which is not really needed because to whom else would he be speaking? The lawyer, as part of his testing of Jesus, proposes the question, καὶ τίς ἐστίν μου πλησίον. The καὶ is connective but denotes "a previously expressed circumstance."[28] This conclusion repeats the conclusion of the lawyer's artful colon, but with a difference. Instead of πλησίον μου, as the colon has it in which the lawyer answered Jesus' question, in the lawyer's question now is μου πλησίον. The first colon as answer was constructed in a way to draw attention to τὸν πλησίον σου ὡς σεαυτόν. But the lawyer's question focuses the issue even tighter, focusing on μου πλησίον, ignoring everything else in the answer colon. By placing πλησίον in the final position in the question, it draws attention to that single word. The switching of μου from before the noun to after the noun does not change the meaning but it does change how sound structures the hearing and thus the meaning effect.

The Parable (10:30–35)

Ὑπολαβὼν ὁ Ἰησοῦς εἶπεν

The parable is clearly part of the dialogue, as indicated by ὁ Ἰησοῦς εἶπεν. The introductory participle ὑπολαβών indicates that Jesus is taking up the challenge proposed by the lawyer. The parable[29] is his answer.

While the structure of the dialogue was built around εἶπεν δὲ, the parable's connectors are more paratactic, setting it off in sound. There is a setup, two opponents, a hero and concluding action.

Setup (10:30)

The three cola of the Setup employ three verbs, κατέβαινεν, περιέπεσεν and ἀπῆλθον, to demark a pattern of descending motion, which portends the motion of the man and his downward fate.

---

27. Luke uses διακαιόω in both a positive (7:29, 35; 18:14) and negative sense (16:15).

28. Zerwick, *Biblical Greek*, #459, suggests it should be translated, "then who is my neighbor?"

29. It is, of course, not identified as a parable and is completely integrated into the dialogue.

Luke's Strategy for Interpreting Parables

ἄνθρωπός τις[30] κατέβαινεν ἀπὸ Ἰερουσαλὴμ εἰς Ἰεριχὼ

καὶ λῃσταῖς περιέπεσεν

οἳ καὶ ἐκδύσα<u>ντες</u> αὐτὸν καὶ πληγὰς ἐπιθέ<u>ντες</u> ἀπῆλθον ἀφέ<u>ντες</u> ἡμιθανῆ

The final colon is elongated, with one verb surrounded by three participles. The three cola are connected paratactically by καί, while the first two participles are also connected by καί, thus extending the parataxis. The participle endings -ε(α)ντες tie this final colon together. These first three cola of the parable indicate that the construction and resulting sound map of this Setup are different than the preceding dialogue.

Opponents (10:31–32)

The textual status of γενόμενος[31] in verse 32 is uncertain. Nestle–Aland[28] has it in brackets, indicating doubtful and uncertain status. As the analysis of the sound map of the Opponents goes forward, it will indicate, I think, that γενόμενος should be omitted.

I have divided the Opponents presentation into three cola, but it could just as easily be two.[32] The periodic structure is not strong because phrases are strung together in parataxis, so-called continuous style. There is an obvious parallelism between the presentation of the priest and the Levite as the following sound map indicates.

κατὰ συγκυρίαν δὲ ἱερεύς τις   κατέβαινεν ἐν τῇ ὁδῷ ἐκείνῃ

    καὶ ἰδὼν αὐτὸν ἀντιπαρῆλθεν

ὁμοίως δὲ   καὶ Λευίτης   κατὰ τὸν τόπον ἐλθὼν

    καὶ ἰδὼν   ἀντιπαρῆλθεν

The first colon dealing with the priest replays the structure of the introductory colon of the man, as this sound map indicates. It contains

---

30. This τις construction is a favorite of Luke's, as noted above (footnote 18). It was used of the lawyer in 10:25 and will be used again in this parable with the priest and Samaritan.

31. There is also a problem with ἐλθών. A number of manuscripts that have γενόμενος omit ἐλθών, although the evidence for ἐλθών is much stronger. Metzger, *Textual Commentary on the Greek New Testament*, 153, has a good discussion of the problem.

32. In my sound map the priest has two cola, while the Levite has one.

parallel subjects, man/priest, the same verb (κατέβαινεν), and a prepositional phrase. This parallelism makes κατὰ συγκυρίαν stand out.

	<u>ἄνθρωπός</u> <u>τις</u>	<u>κατέβαινεν</u>	<u>ἀπὸ Ἰερουσαλὴμ</u> <u>εἰς Ἰεριχὼ</u>
κατὰ συγκυρίαν δὲ	<u>ἱερεύς</u> <u>τις</u>	<u>κατέβαινεν</u>	<u>ἐν τῇ ὁδῷ ἐκείνῃ</u>

Τις is a favorite Lucan word, as indicated above (footnote 18). In this unit it is used four times in quick succession: of the lawyer (10:25), the man (10:30), the priest (10:31), and the Samaritan (10:33). Although I think sound mapping operates at a methodological level more elementary and primary than form criticism, it can make contributions to higher level criticism. Assuming that the parable is a piece of the oral tradition that Luke wove into his dialogue between the lawyer and Jesus, the repetition of τις in the cola of the man and the priest, almost certainly a Lucan editorial mark, indicates the author is following out the inherent parallelism already present in the parable.

The second colon, καὶ ἰδὼν αὐτὸν ἀντιπαρῆλθεν, describes the priest's action. As indicated above, this colon could just as easily be part of the first colon. The verb ἀντιπαρέρχομαι is very rare, making it stand out. It occurs in the New Testament only here. The double preposition ἀντί and παρά is a common prepositional compound in Greek indicating against (ἀντί) and beside (παρά). For example, ἀντιπαραβάλλω means to place side by side, to compare or contrast, while ἀντιπάρειμι mans to march on opposite sides of a river. Ἀντιπαρῆλθεν as describing the priests behavior indicates a gesture of pushing away (ἀντί) and passing by (παρά).

ὁμοίως δὲ καὶ Λευίτης κατὰ τὸν τόπον ἐλθὼν καὶ ἰδὼν ἀντιπαρῆλθεν

The third colon describes the second opponent in a parallel fashion, while reducing the colon, Κατὰ of κατὰ τὸν τόπον echoes κατέβαινεν, without repeating it. Only the participle/verb remain the same in both cola, thus drawing attention to the action of both the priest and Levite. The careful parallel construction of the opponents' cola draw attention to κατὰ συγκυρίαν and ἰδὼν ἀντιπαρῆλθεν.

Hero (10:33)

Following the rule of threes, an audience now expects a hero to appear. The first word of this colon announces the hero or, in this case, antihero. In contrast to the previous cola dealing with the priest and Levite, they were only identified after initial introductory words. In those cola, their identity was briefly postponed but here the identity of the Samaritan is boldly stated in initial position.

Σαμαρίτης δέ τις ὁδεύων ἦλθεν κατ' αὐτὸν καὶ ἰδὼν ἐσπλαγχνίσθη

This colon's construction echoes elements of the previous cola: ὁδεύων parallels ἐν τῇ ὁδῷ from the priest's colon; ἦλθεν is a variation on ἐλθὼν from the Levite's colon; κατ' αὐτὸν sounds like κατὰ τὸν τόπον, also from the Levite's colon, and κατέβαινεν from both the man's and priest's colon; and ἰδὼν occurs in the cola of all three characters, paired as the introduction to the final verb. In the case of both the priest and Levite the final verb is ἀντιπαρῆλθεν (pass on by), while it is ἐσπλαγχνίσθη (have compassion) in the case of the Samaritan. The construction of this colon causes its first (Σαμαρίτης) and last (ἐσπλαγχνίσθη) words to stand out. These are the words the sound map selects for interpretation. In the exegesis of the parable, these are the surprising and unexpected terms: the Samaritan as hero and compassion as his response.

Concluding Action (10:32–35)

The remaining cola elaborate the implications of ἐσπλαγχνίσθη. The connections remain paratactic and the construction remains simple, revolving around a main verb with participles.

> καὶ προσελθὼν κατέδησεν τὰ τραύματα αὐτοῦ ἐπιχέων ἔλαιον καὶ οἶνον
>
> ἐπιβιβάσας δὲ αὐτὸν ἐπὶ τὸ ἴδιον κτῆνος ἤγαγεν αὐτὸν εἰς πανδοχεῖον
>
> καὶ ἐπεμελήθη αὐτοῦ
>
> καὶ ἐπὶ τὴν αὔριον ἐκβαλὼν ἔδωκεν δύο δηνάρια τῷ πανδοχεῖ
>
> καὶ εἶπεν· ἐπιμελήθητι αὐτοῦ
>
> καὶ ὅ τι ἂν προσδαπανήσῃς ἐγὼ ἐν τῷ ἐπανέρχεσθαί με ἀποδώσω σοι

Unlike the previous cola, which exhibited a great deal of parallelism and echoing, these cola simply move the action forward. Parataxis is obvious, while repetition is minimal in contrast. The final description of the Samaritan's concern for the man is ἐπεμελήθη (care for) and that becomes his command to the innkeeper, ἐπιμελήθητι. Similarly, πανδοχεῖον and πανδοχεῖ occur at the ends of the second and fourth cola. At the beginning of several cola, καί is followed by π, επ, ειπ sounds. This is very minimal patterning when compared to the careful parallelism and echoing of the previous cola. Nothing in this part of the sound map is emphasized or singled out for attention. Exegesis, of course, would need to explain why that is so.[33]

Question (10:36–37)

The parable, while exhibiting its own structure in a sound map, has been part of Luke's overall dialogue structure. That structure now reasserts itself. The speaker, Jesus, shifting from third person narration, poses a question in the second person as part of the dialogue without any intervention by the narrator. This keeps the parable closely bound to the dialogue. The man in Jesus' question is described periphrastically as τοῦ ἐμπεσόντος εἰς τοὺς λῃστάς, echoing the description of his fate from the Setup. In the second colon the lawyer, without being named as such, responds, without naming the Samaritan, who is described by what he did. In these final cola, both the lawyer and the Samaritan remain as nameless as the man who fell among robbers.

> τίς τούτων τῶν τριῶν πλησίον δοκεῖ σοι γεγονέναι τοῦ ἐμπεσόντος εἰς τοὺς λῃστάς
>
> ὁ δὲ εἶπεν·ὁ ποιήσας τὸ ἔλεος μετ' αὐτοῦ
>
> εἶπεν δὲ αὐτῷ ὁ Ἰησοῦς· πορεύου καὶ σὺ ποίει ὁμοίως

Jesus' question and his response bracket the lawyer's answer. Jesus' question repeats the word πλησίον selected for attention in the lawyer's original dialogue with Jesus, "your neighbor as yourself." When Jesus originally responded to the lawyer's summary of what he should do to inherit eternal life, he said, τοῦτο ποίει καὶ ζήσῃ (10:28). Jesus' final response to the lawyer picks up this same sound with σὺ ποίει ὁμοίως, while omitting ζήσῃ. The clear implication is that doing this, being a neighbor, is life. Hence πλησίον and ποίει hark back to the first part of the dialogue, forming concluding inclusio.

Conclusion 2

This analysis has shown how the author of Luke's gospel carefully constructed a narrative context for a parable, a context that has circumscribed the

---

33. Normally in parables the twist occurs at the parable's conclusion. Here it occurs dramatically in the middle. I would suggest this elaborate description of his compassion serves to prepare an audience for accepting as hero someone they deem an anti-hero.

parable's interpretation by tying the parable closely to its narrative context. Mark's "what is the greatest of commandments" becomes in Luke the lawyer's answer to, "what he must do to inherit eternal life?" In the editing, Luke places the emphasis on the last element, the neighbor—the rest falls away from attention. In Luke, the question, "who is my neighbor?" becomes the hermeneutic lens for understanding the parable and through which the parable subsequently has been interpreted, following Luke's auditory clues. The care and skill by which the author has constructed the narrative framework that binds the parable to the narrative is what the ancients called σύνθεσις[34] (putting it together, composition). They conceived this process on the analogy of συνπλοκή[35] (weaving), so that the various parts selected by the author become interwoven and so disappear into a unified composition, like the warp and weft of a woven fabric. The individual threads disappear into the final product. The efforts of various commentators to undo Luke's narrative frame are a testimony to his skill at σύνθεσις. He has clearly interwoven (συνπλοκή) Mark's two commandments with the parable into a single composition in which the parts disappear. Who is my neighbor has dominated the parable's interpretation.

Adolf Jülicher demonstrated that the parable did not fit its narrative context; that "neighbor" in the parable took on a different sense than in the question. In the question, neighbor means, "who should I take care," an active sense; the parable illustrates, "who takes care," a passive sense.[36] But despite Jülicher's effort, interpreters too often adopt Luke's narrative frame as the hermeneutical frame.

The influence of Luke's implicit interpretation of the parable has had yet another unnoticed outcome. Because of the narrative context, interpreters have been convinced that this parable is an example story. Yet all the so-called example stories are Lucan. This should at least make one wonder whether example story as a form results from Luke's incorporation of the parable into a compelling narrative;[37] or, to put it another way, an example of Luke's creative (συνπλοκή) narrative genius.

34. Lee and Scott, *Sound Mapping*, 104–8.

35. Ibid., 72–77.

36. Jülicher, *Die Gleichnisreden Jesu*, 2:596. For a discussion of responses to Jülicher's suggestion, see Scott, *Hear Then the Parable*, 192. Not surprisingly, Hultgren, *The Parables of Jesus*, completely buys the Lucan fiction. He deals with the parable in a chapter entitled "Parables of Exemplary Behavior," clearly indicating his trajectory (chapter 3). He comments specifically on the parable, "it can be conceded that the parable must have been occasioned by a question or event concerning love for one's neighbor. The setting that Luke gives it, though by Luke himself, is fitting" (95). The logic is stunning, but it clearly demonstrates the power of Luke's artistry.

37. See my discussion of this issue in *Hear Then the Parable*, 28–30. Already in

Economy: Lost and Found

Chapter 15 appears to be a section consisting of the three units, all parables, all dealing with something lost. The connections between the units are minimal. The section beginning is clear with a new setting and characters. The section closing is much more problematic.

Narrative Frame (15:1–2)

The narrative setup in Luke 15:1–2 is very straightforward by comparison to that in Luke 10:1. It consists of only two cola.

Ἦσαν δὲ αὐτῷ ἐγγίζοντες πάντες οἱ τελῶναι καὶ οἱ ἁμαρτωλοὶ ἀκούειν αὐτοῦ
καὶ διεγόγγυζον οἵ τε Φαρισαῖοι καὶ οἱ γραμματεῖς λέγοντες ὅτι
οὗτος ἁμαρτωλοὺς προσδέχεται καὶ συνεσθίει αὐτοῖς (Luke 15:1–2).

Διεγόγγυζον in the second colon has deep resonance in the tradition. In Exodus and Numbers the verb is used of the people of Israel murmuring against Moses. Exodus 15:24 is a good example.

καὶ διεγόγγυζεν ὁ λαὸς ἐπὶ Μωυσῆν λέγοντες τί πιόμεθα

In this instance as well as the others in Exodus (16:2, 7, and 8) the murmuring has to do with food. Similarly in this passage, the Pharisees complain that Jesus is receiving and eating with sinners. Therefore, the very choice of διεγόγγυζον aligns the Pharisees with the place of the faithless people and Jesus with Moses. This subtle strategy implies that the Pharisees, like the faithless Israelites, are murmuring against what God wants. The Pharisees murmuring against Jesus' welcoming and eating with sinners becomes for Luke the narrative context for interpreting the three parables.

Lost Sheep (15:3–7)

Luke's introduction of the parables is simplicity itself—a single colon.

Εἶπεν δὲ πρὸς αὐτοὺς τὴν παραβολὴν ταύτην λέγων

This single colon, with a mention of parable in the singular, suffices for all three parables. In the first parable, when the shepherd finds the lost sheep

---

that book I argued that the example story was a creation of Luke. Sound mapping only makes that conclusion more likely.

he rejoices (χαίρων) and, upon returning home, calls his friends together, telling them to rejoice with him:

συγχάρητέ μοι ὅτι εὗρον τὸ πρόβατόν μου τὸ ἀπολωλός

Jesus then pronounces:

λέγω ὑμῖν ὅτι οὕτως χαρὰ ἐν τῷ οὐρανῷ ἔσται ἐπὶ ἑνὶ ἁμαρτωλῷ μετανοοῦντι
ἢ ἐπὶ ἐνενήκοντα ἐννέα δικαίοις
οἵτινες οὐ χρείαν ἔχουσιν μετανοίας

Λέγω ὑμῖν introduces a formal pronouncement. Χαρὰ picks up on χαίρων and συγχάρητέ from the parable. The very length of this colon as well as the long words in its second part draw attention to it. The "one" identifies the lost sheep with the "sinners" of the narrative frame and the ninety-nine sheep with the Pharisees. This is minimal narrative threading, but its hermeneutical effect is powerful.

Lost Coin (15:8–10)

In the next parable, which closely parallels the first, after the woman finds the one lost coin, the parable concludes:

καὶ εὑροῦσα συγκαλεῖ τὰς φίλας καὶ γείτονας λέγουσα
συγχάρητέ μοι ὅτι εὗρον τὴν δραχμὴν ἣν ἀπώλεσα

"Friends" is expanded to include neighbors and there is no mention of her joy upon finding the lost coin. The joy comes in her address to her friends and neighbors.

Once again Jesus makes a formal pronouncement.

οὕτως λέγω ὑμῖν γίνεται χαρὰ ἐνώπιον τῶν ἀγγέλων τοῦ θεοῦ ἐπὶ
ἑνὶ ἁμαρτωλῷ μετανοοῦντι

Οὕτως refers back to the previous pronouncement. "In heaven" (ἐν τῷ οὐρανῷ) becomes the "in the presence of the angels of God" (ἐνώπιον τῶν ἀγγέλων τοῦ θεοῦ) and there is mention of only ἑνὶ ἁμαρτωλῷ. The focus has narrowed down in comparison to the parable of the sheep, but the hermeneutical lens put in place in the first pronouncement persists in this pronouncement.

Lost Sons (15:11–32)

The third parable in this group, a story of a father and his two sons, is the longest parable in the Jesus tradition. Εἶπεν δέ (v. 11) inaugurates the parable.

At the conclusion of the episode dealing with the younger son (vv. 22–24), the father commands the slaves to begin the preparations to receive his son back. He tells them:

> καὶ φέρετε τὸν μόσχον τὸν σιτευτόν θύσατε
> καὶ φαγόντες εὐφρανθῶμεν
> ὅτι οὗτος ὁ υἱός μου νεκρὸς ἦν καὶ ἀνέζησεν
> ἦν ἀπολωλὼς καὶ εὑρέθη
> καὶ ἤρξαντο εὐφραίνεσθαι

The father's speech introduces eating, which recalls what the Pharisees were murmuring against: that Jesus had received and eaten with sinners. The note about the son having been dead and is now alive escalates this parable to a different level than either of the two previous parables. But "he was lost and found" parallels and repeats the phrases from the previous two parables.[38]

συγχάρητέ μοι ὅτι εὗρον τὸ πρόβατόν μου τὸ ἀπολωλός	Lost Sheep v. 5
συγχάρητέ μοι ὅτι εὗρον τὴν δραχμὴν ἣν ἀπώλεσα	Lost Coin v. 9
ἦν ἀπολωλὼς καὶ εὑρέθη	Lost Sons v. 24

The theme of rejoicing is repeated, but in different words—συγχάρητέ for the sheep and coin and εὐφρανθῶμεν for the younger son. The younger son is now clearly installed as the stand-in for the sinners, just as the one sheep and one coin were.

Elder Son (15:25–32)

Following the elder son's rejection of the father's invitation to come into the banquet, the father responds (v. 31):

> ὁ δὲ εἶπεν αὐτῷ

---

38. The strong parallel between these three phrases would suggest that they are a Lucan construction. Sound mapping cannot settle such a question, but it does provide relevant data for considering such a question.

τέκνον σὺ πάντοτε μετ' ἐμοῦ εἶ

καὶ πάντα τὰ ἐμὰ σά ἐστιν

The second line is emphatic in construction, following the narrator's simple, minimal, and bland introduction. Τέκνον is unexpected[39] and perhaps even demeaning or ironic, in light of the fact that the father is addressing ὁ πρεσβύτερος. The construction σὺ ... εἶ is emphatic since both are not needed. Furthermore, the construction brackets πάντοτε μετ' ἐμοῦ, verbally embracing the τέκνον like the father embraces the son. Ἐμοῦ is also emphatic. All of this makes the father's response dramatic and commanding. The final phrase of this colon, while not as emphatic, is still dramatic. Πάντα and ἐστιν bracket τὰ ἐμὰ σά as in the previous phrase, thus in sound joining the father and τέκνον.

The narrative frame has linked the elder son with the Pharisees. He, like the Pharisees, rejects the father's acceptance of the younger son/repentant sinners. But if this colon ends with the father giving everything to the elder son, where does that leave the younger son/repentant sinners? The narrative frame does not work. The father's address to the elder son is inconvenient for the narrative frame. But never fear, the narrative frame reasserts itself in the final colon (v. 32).

εὐφρανθῆναι δὲ καὶ χαρῆναι ἔδει

ὅτι ὁ ἀδελφός σου οὗτος νεκρὸς ἦν καὶ ἔζησεν

καὶ ἀπολωλὼς καὶ εὑρέθη

In the first colon, the double rejoicing picks up sounds that have been used by the narrative frame before in this section. Εὐφρανθῆναι refers back to verses 23, 24, and 29, while χαρῆναι echoes verses 5, 6, 7, and 9. Δὲ καὶ is an adversative conjunction,[40] emphasizing the necessity (ἔδει) of receiving back the younger son. These three elements—the double rejoicing, δὲ καὶ, and ἔδει, triple-down on the necessity of joy upon the return of the son/repentant sinner and draw attention away from the father's response to the elder brother and back to the younger son's story. The strategy of shifting attention from the implications of the father's address to the elder son to his acceptance of the younger son is completed by the last two lines of this colon, which reprise the conclusion of the younger son's episode. The re-

---

39. See Scott, *Hear Then the Parable*, 121. Bauer et al., *A Greek-English Lexicon of the New Testament*, 994, 1b, notes Luke 15:31 as "an affectionate address to a son," while in #2 it indicates that generally in the vocative it is "a form of familiar address, *my child, my son*," with evidence.

40. Blass, Debrunner, and Funk, *A Greek Grammar of the New Testament and Other Early Christian Literature*, 447(9).

prise draws attention back to the younger son's episode. Three elements, the father's receiving of the son like Jesus receiving sinners, the banquet, and the lost and found, successfully tie the narrative introduction of the Pharisees and the three parables together in a tight narrative frame, which supplies the section's hermeneutical key.

The narrative frame for the Samaritan parable was elaborate, while the one for the lost is a model of economy—murmuring, Pharisees, sinners, rejoicing, lost and found. But both of Luke's narrative frames have been very effective. Hearers and interpreters have understood these frames as the best context in which to interpret the parables. Even those who think Luke has created the narrative frame have either thought he got it right or have struggled to escape it.

Shell Game: The Steward

Conundrum (16:1–8)

It is unclear if Luke 16:1 marks a new section or is a continuation of the section begun at 15:1 with the Pharisees murmuring. The initial colon is minimal, indicating only a change of audience, the disciples, but no change of place. Δὲ καί supposes a continuation of the previous units of chapter 15. Unlike the other two examples we have examined, no narrative frame provides a context for this parable's interpretation.

> Ἔλεγεν δὲ καὶ πρὸς τοὺς μαθητάς
> ἄνθρωπός τις ἦν πλούσιος ὃς εἶχεν οἰκονόμον
> καὶ οὗτος διεβλήθη αὐτῷ ὡς διασκορπίζων τὰ ὑπάρχοντα αὐτοῦ

After the parable is introduced with a simple note of speaking to the disciples as audience, the parable begins. At the parable's conclusion (v. 8), the master states the parable's interpretive crux.

> καὶ ἐπῄνεσεν ὁ κύριος τὸν οἰκονόμον τῆς ἀδικίας ὅτι φρονίμως ἐποίησεν

What is one to make of the master commending the unjust steward for his wise action? The tension in the colon is heightened if one assumes that ὁ κύριος is not the master of the parable but Jesus as narrator of the parable. The colon is an interpretative oxymoron.

Strategy (16:9–16)

How to solve this conundrum? In the parable of the lost sons, Luke shifted attention from the father's giving of everything to the elder son by focusing the hearer's attention back on the welcoming the younger son. Similarly, in the case of the conundrum posed by the parable, he begins by changing the point of comparison:

ὅτι οἱ υἱοὶ τοῦ αἰῶνος τούτου φρονιμώτεροι

ὑπὲρ τοὺς υἱοὺς τοῦ φωτὸς εἰς τὴν γενεὰν τὴν ἑαυτῶν εἰσιν

This colon picks up a keyword/sound[41] φρονίμως, the positive pole of the conundrum, and shifts the comparison to one between the children of this age and those of the next. This strategy is like a shell game: hide the problem.

Καὶ ἐγὼ ὑμῖν λέγω ἑαυτοῖς ποιήσατε φίλους ἐκ τοῦ μαμωνᾶ τῆς ἀδικίας

ἵνα ὅταν ἐκλίπῃ δέξωνται ὑμᾶς εἰς τὰς αἰωνίους σκηνάς

The ἐγὼ ὑμῖν λέγω shifts from third person narration to first person pronouncement. If the keyword strategy worked once, try it again. Μαμωνᾶ τῆς ἀδικίας parallels οἰκονόμον τῆς ἀδικίας, although exactly what this means is unclear.[42] The continuing cola turn aphoristic.

Ὁ <u>πιστὸς ἐν ἐλαχίστῳ</u>	καὶ ἐν πολλῷ πιστός ἐστιν
καὶ ὁ <u>ἐν ἐλαχίστῳ ἄδικος</u>	καὶ ἐν πολλῷ ἄδικός ἐστιν

The initial word, πιστός, is yet another positive term but the keyword ἄδικος in the second line is set in chiastic parallel with πιστὸς. The two final elements are exactly parallel. The colon makes a decisive turn towards resolving the conundrum. The interpretation is now headed in a positive direction and the hearers are encouraged to be the faithful.

εἰ οὖν ἐν τῷ ἀδίκῳ μαμωνᾷ <u>πιστοὶ</u> <u>οὐκ</u> <u>ἐγένεσθε</u>

τὸ ἀληθινὸν τίς ὑμῖν πιστεύσει

καὶ εἰ ἐν τῷ ἀλλοτρίῳ <u>πιστοὶ</u> <u>οὐκ</u> <u>ἐγένεσθε</u>

---

41. I will not keep repeating keyword/sound, but the reader should remember that "keyword" is a not a lexeme but the sounds that express it.

42. Fitzmyer, *Gospel according to Luke*, 1109, among others, struggles mightily to make sense of the verse, eventually arguing that it means almsgiving. This is a frequent suggestion.

τὸ ὑμέτερον τίς ὑμῖν <u>δώσει</u>
Οὐ<u>δ</u>εὶς οἰκέτης <u>δύ</u>ναται <u>δ</u>υσὶ κυρίοις <u>δου</u>λεύ<u>ει</u>ν
ἢ γὰρ τὸν ἕνα μισ<u>ήσει</u> καὶ τὸν ἕτερον ἀγαπ<u>ήσει</u>
ἢ ἑνὸς ἀνθέξεται καὶ τοῦ ἑτέρου καταφρον<u>ήσει</u>
οὐ <u>δύ</u>νασθε θεῷ <u>δου</u>λεύειν καὶ μαμωνᾷ

Having made the decisive shift in verse 10 with the link between πιστός and ἄδικος, the association strategy continues by associating those two words with a previously heard sound μαμωνᾶς and two conditional cola connected paratactically. There is a strong repetition of similar sounds: δυν- and δουλ-. In the first two cola there is an ending rhyming pattern, and the final cola endings with ει. There is strong alliteration of the delta in the Οὐδεὶς οἰκέτης colon.

These cola are rounded off with an aphorism about serving two masters and concluding with not serving God and mammon. This aphorism leads a hearer far from the conundrum of the master commending an unjust steward for his wisdom.

Ἤκουον δὲ ταῦτα πάντα οἱ Φαρισαῖοι φιλάργυροι ὑπάρχοντες καὶ ἐξεμυκτήριζον αὐτόν
καὶ εἶπεν αὐτοῖς· ὑμεῖς ἐστε οἱ δικαιοῦντες ἑαυτοὺς ἐνώπιον τῶν ἀνθρώπων
ὁ δὲ θεὸς γινώσκει τὰς καρδίας ὑμῶν
ὅτι τὸ ἐν ἀνθρώποις ὑψηλὸν βδέλυγμα ἐνώπιον τοῦ θεοῦ
Ὁ νόμος καὶ οἱ προφῆται μέχρι Ἰωάννου
ἀπὸ τότε ἡ βασιλεία τοῦ θεοῦ εὐαγγελίζεται
καὶ πᾶς εἰς αὐτὴν βιάζεται

The parable and its transitioning aphorisms were addressed by Jesus to the disciples, indicating a modification of audience from the previous three parables which were addressed to the Pharisees (15:1–3). The narrator now reintroduces the Pharisees with a negative comment about their love of money, implying that they have been listening in and that they are disparaging Jesus. Thus 16:1–16 is part of the section begun in 15:1. Δὲ καί in the initial colon (16:1) of the parable's introduction had implied as much.

The Pharisees, first introduced at the section's beginning in 15:1–2 as mumbling against Jesus and reintroduced at 16:14 as lovers of money, by implication become the true lovers of μαμωνᾶς and so identified with the unjust steward. The strategy started out to resolve the conundrum of an unjust steward commended as wise has come full circle. Out of loosely constructed and connected cola (16:8a–16) an argument is built up that leads an audience to conclude that the Pharisees are at fault. The parable of the Steward then was told against them, just as were the three parables of lost sheep, lost coin, and lost sons of chapter 15! The final colon draws a line between the kingdom and the law and the prophets. Ἀπὸ τότε implies the line is temporal. The narrative context implies that the Pharisees are the violent men attacking the kingdom, because they have murmured against Jesus for welcoming and eating with sinners.

Conclusion 3

The Steward shows yet another Lucan strategy for interpreting a parable. This time a narrative frame is not employed. Instead, keywords/sounds shift attention away from the conundrum posed by the parable's conclusion. How is the unrighteous behavior of the steward a model for those righteous readers of Luke's Gospel? Gradually and subtly a series of cola shifts attention from the conundrum to pious moral aphorisms and finally it turns against the Pharisees. The problem fades away, hiding the problem. The logic may be hard to follow, but the effect is to reclaim the parable for Luke's gospel.

Luke's strategy of masking the conundrum posed by the parable's conclusion by keyword/sound association has been less successful than the examples of the Samaritan or the lost and found, examined above. Commentators see 16:8b-13 as applications of the parable,[43] but find them unconvincing as interpretations.

Sound mapping demonstrates sound/keyword connections and associations between the parable's conundrum and the cola of 16:8b-16. These connections and associations have largely gone unnoticed. Robert Tannehill, usually sensitive to literary connections, struggles to make sense of what is going in the passage. He sees the point as making friends with wealth, which he admits "may sound like crass manipulation of other for one's own benefit."[44] But the sound map shows that the unit and interpretation of the parable extends beyond v. 13 and includes the reintroduction of the Pharisees.[45] Thus Luke's strategy is to mask the conundrum with moral aphorisms and turn it against the Pharisees.

43. Dodd, *Parables of the Kingdom*, 30, famously observed, "We can almost see here notes for three separate sermons on the parable text," to which I would add the quip in a preacher's marginal notes, "Weak point. Pound hard on the pulpit."

44. *Narrative Unity of Luke-Acts*. 1:131. In his later commentary, he sees the unit as 16:1–13 and titles it, "Making Friends by Means of Wealth," *Luke*, 245–49.

45. The unit does not end until 16:31. Verse 17:1 begins a new unit with another of Luke's weak unit initial markers. Verse 17:1 closely parallels 16:1.

Εἶπεν δὲ πρὸς τοὺς μαθητὰς αὐτοῦ· ἀνένδεκτόν ἐστιν τοῦ τὰ σκάνδαλα μὴ ἐλθεῖν, πλὴν

Two problems remain beyond sound mapping's reach. Why did the author include the parable if it was so problematic? Why not omit it from the gospel narrative? Second, what did the parable originally mean?

Assessment

This paper has employed sound mapping to understand strategies the author of the gospel of Luke employed to interpret the parables unique to his gospel. The author did not interpret the parables by means of an explicit, point-by-point allegory, as did Mark. Rather, the author supplied a narrative framework that implicitly interprets the parables. Even in the case of the Steward, the interpretation, or rather, the distraction from the conundrum caused by the master's commendation of an unjust steward as wise was accomplished by stacking up aphoristic-like sayings based on sound/keyword associations until a more suitable interpretation emerged.

Could not this issue have been examined by more traditional methods? Yes, and it has been, although not with the precision that sound mapping brings. I had myself reached some of these conclusions using traditional methods in my *Hear Then the Parable*,[46] but they are not made as precisely nor clearly as they are with sound mapping. By examining the composition at the elementary level of syllable and colon, one can follow how elements of the composition were interlaced to create its effect. For example, by examining how Luke edited Mark's two commandments into a single, artful period that concludes and focuses the hearer's attention on πλησίον, "neighbor," it becomes evident how the Samaritan became "good" in the tradition. Traditional exegetical methods see that, of course, but they do not see it with the precision that sound mapping enables, nor do they explain how it was accomplished.

Murmuring Pharisees and repetition of rejoicing and lost and found, with these minimal elements the author wove together a powerful hermeneutical horizon for interpreting the three parables of chapter 15. Even more, by examining how that composition comes together at the level of syllable and colon, sound mapping raises important questions about how Luke might have edited the parables. For example, is the theme of lost and found, so important for the Lucan interpretative strategy, a Lucan redaction? Sound mapping cannot resolve this issue but surfaces data that raise the question.

οὐαὶ δι' οὗ ἔρχεται.

46. Although I completely failed to understand how the parable of Steward was woven into the larger section 15:1—16:31.

In the case of the Steward, a sound map illustrates how by keywords or sound connections and associations the author has built up a composition that eventually distracts from or masks the parable's conundrum. Luke's interpretation is massaged in a moral direction and a more acceptable trajectory until eventually it turns on the Pharisees, circling back to the opening at 15:1.

Close attention to a composition at the level of syllable and colon, below the level of semantics, compels an interpreter to pay attention to the composition's mechanics, how it was put together (σύνθεσις)[47] in minute detail. The Greek's analogy for composition was συμπλοκή (woven together),[48] the interlacing of various elements into a whole. That pays off with more precise data when one moves to the level of semantics, or what used to be called higher criticism. What sound mapping offers is a method for understanding with greater precision how a composition became συμπλοκή (woven together) or σύνθεσις (put-together) or, in Latin, *composito* (put-together).

Bibliography

Bauer, Walter, William F. Arndt, F. Wilbur Gingrich, and Frederick W. Danker. *A Greek-English Lexicon of the New Testament and Other Early Christian Literature*. 3rd ed. Chicago: University of Chicago Press, 2000.

Blass, F., A. Debrunner, and Robert Funk. *A Greek Grammar of the New Testament and Other Early Christian Literature*. Chicago: University of Chicago Press, 1961.

Dodd, C. H. *The Parables of the Kingdom*. New York: Scribner, 1935.

Fitzmyer, Joseph A. *The Gospel according to Luke X-XXIV*. Anchor Bible 28A. Garden City, N.Y.: Doubleday, 1985.

Hultgren, Arland J. *The Parables of Jesus: A Commentary*. Grand Rapids: Eerdmans, 2000.

Jülicher, Adolf. *Die Gleichnisreden Jesu*. 2 vols. 1899. Reprint, Darmstadt: Wissenschaftliche Buchgesellschaft, 1963.

Lee, Margaret Ellen, and Bernard Brandon Scott. *Sound Mapping the New Testament*. Salem, OR: Polebridge, 2009.

Marshall, Howard. *The Gospel of Luke: A Commentary on the Greek Text*. Grand Rapids: Eerdmans, 1978.

Metzger, Bruce M. *A Textual Commentary on the Greek New Testament*. New York: United Bible Societies, 1971.

Plummer, Alfred. *A Critical and Exegetical Commentary on the Gospel according to St. Luke*. International Critical Commentary on the Holy Scriptures of the Old and New Testaments 28. New York: Scribner, 1920.

47. "The elements of sound as analyzed in ἡ τέχνη γραμματική (the science of grammar) and the parts of speech analyzed as ἡ λέξις (speech, style) become interwoven in ἡ συνπλοκή (weaving) through the actual process of literary composition, which Greek authors conceived of as ἡ σύνθεσις," Lee and Scott, *Sound Mapping*, 104.

48. See ibid., 72–77.

Robinson, James M., Paul Hoffmann, and John S. Kloppenborg. *The Critical Edition of Q*. Hermeneia Supplements. Minneapolis: Fortress, 2000.

Scheppers, Frank. *The Colon Hypothesis: Word Order, Discourse Segmentation and Discourse Coherence in Ancient Greek*. Brussels: VUBPress, 2011.

Scott, Bernard Brandon. *Hear Then the Parable, A Commentary on the Parables of Jesus*. Minneapolis: Fortress, 1989.

Tannehill, Robert C. *Luke*. Abingdon New Testament Commentaries. Nashville: Abingdon, 1996.

———. *Narrative Unity of Luke-Acts: A Literary Interpretation*. Vol. 1, *The Gospel according to Luke*. Foundations and Facets. Philadelphia: Fortress, 1986.

Zerwick, Maximilian. *Biblical Greek Illustrated by Examples*. Rome: Pontifical Biblical, 1963.

4

Caves, Cattle, and *Koinonia*
Acoustic Shadows across Textual Walls

JEFFREY E. BRICKLE

Introduction

As a relatively new technique within biblical studies, the mapping of patterns of sound has generated innovative analyses and created alternative ways to approach texts.[1] Sound mapping—the interpretation of audible sounds generated by a vocalized text and converted into a visual display[2]—can affirm or challenge traditional methods of exegesis. This methodology invites biblical scholars to reconsider the rhetorical, structural, and aesthetic elements of ancient texts. When exploited as a wholistic approach that interfaces with other modes of ancient media culture, such as performance by a lector or use of the memory arts, the interpretive possibilities multiply and dare to alter the landscape of a modernistic hermeneutic.[3]

---

1. The pioneering work, Lee and Scott, *Sound Mapping*, has charted the course for subsequent research. See also the important contributions by Boomershine, *Messiah of Peace*; de Waal, *Aural-Performance Analysis*; and Nässelqvist, *Public Reading*.

2. Lee, "Sound Mapping," 372.

3. For a helpful survey treating the dynamic elements of ancient media, see Person and Keith, "Media Studies," 1–15. For explorations in conversation with multiple modes of media expression, see Chidester, *Word and Light*; Shiner, *Proclaiming the Gospel*; Botha, *Orality and Literacy*; and Kelber, *Imprints, Voiceprints, and Footprints*.

In this essay, I will first reflect on my own formative experiences in sound mapping as conveyed in my monograph, *Aural Design and Coherence in the Prologue of First John*.[4] Then, in an effort to "hear outside the box," we will branch out by briefly exploring ways to expand the reach of this technique into related domains. By tapping into the dynamics of ancient media culture and extending sound mapping's sensory range, we might be better enabled to see to hear and hear to see—in a word, to "translate the sayable into the seeable, while simultaneously reversing the process."[5]

Perceiving Patterns in the Prologue

The first major portion of my analysis of the Prologue of 1 John[6] sought to capture this passage's aural "logic" in the face of persistent claims that its complex syntax and grammar reflect confusion and disarray.[7] By acknowledging that this ancient Greek text was composed and functioned rhetorically in a largely oral climate—and was thus designed for aural consumption—I attempted to delineate its inherent soundscape. In short, I hoped to answer these essential questions: (1) How did an auditor hearing this text, written in *scriptio continua* and read aloud by a lector, comprehend its linear framework and semantics in real time? (2) What can one *see* in this text's inscribed form that might aid in vividly *hearing* it?

To answer these questions, I traced the text's interwoven threads of repetition and variation, resulting in the overall layout reflected in Figures 1 (reproduced here)[8] and 19.[9] (These figures are available in color online at https://media.bloomsbury.com/rep/files/brickle-colour-figures.pdf).

---

4. This work was originally produced as a dissertation, Brickle, "Aural Design," under the direction of Bruce G. Schuchard. It was later revised as *Aural Design*.

5. Squire, Iliad *in a Nutshell*, 11.

6. This section comprised chapter 3 (pp. 30–53) of Brickle, *Aural Design*.

7. Ibid., 1–2.

8. This author gratefully acknowledges the permission of T. & T. Clark, an imprint of Bloomsbury Publishing Plc., to reprint figure 1, which was originally published in Brickle, *Aural Design*, 53.

9. Ibid., 127.

FIGURE 1
Visually Evident Indications in 1 John 1:1–4 of an Overall Structure Featuring Aural Patterning

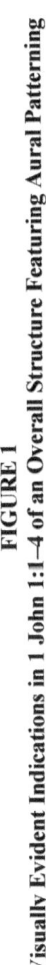

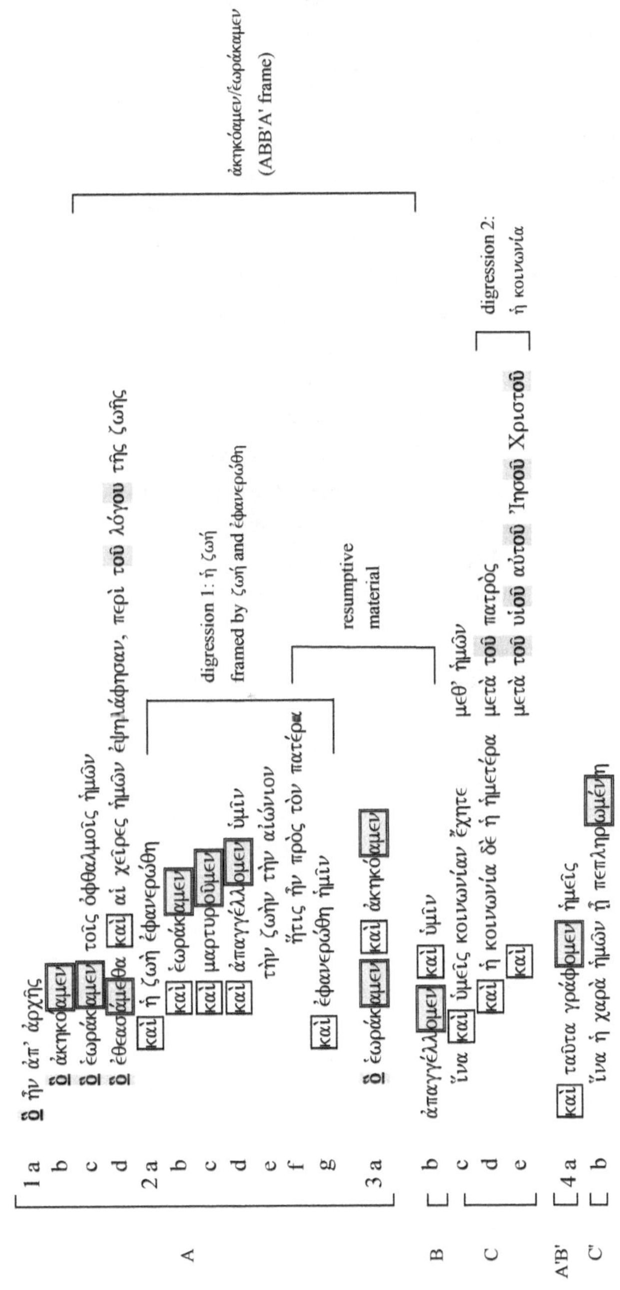

Left Margin Key: A/A' = direct object; B/B' = main verb; C/C' = purpose clause

The pattern is so striking that even those without any knowledge of Greek should clearly appreciate the arrangement. The prominent placement and recurrence of the oral elements ὅ (relative pronoun, "which"), vowel-μεν (first person plural verbal ending, "we ———"), and καί (conjunction, "and") constitute the central pillars of the text's auditory structure. These components function in concert with the unmistakable -ου nominal termination[10] that (re)sounds in vv. 1, 3 in string-like succession.[11]

In the course of this analysis I discovered in the Prologue what is, to my knowledge, the first identification of an overall ABCA'B'C' schema. The expansive ABC pattern reflected in vv. 1–3 is repeated in an extremely abridged form (A'B'C') in v. 4.[12] The Prologue's two digressions (vv. 2, 3) serve to bring to center stage the motifs of ζωή ("life"; three times in vv. 1–2) and κοινωνία ("fellowship"; twice in v. 3). When joined by the featured topic of χαρά ("joy"; once in v. 4), the three motifs appear in decreasing frequency from three to two to one, respectively (Figure 20).[13]

The upshot of this initial stage of the sound mapping experiment was that it accentuated critical aspects of the text's organization, emphases, and *topoi* that can be *seen*. It highlighted an existing aural landscape, complete with hills and valleys, parks and pathways. The result was that some aural elements appeared foregrounded, while others apparently functioned as a backdrop. I concluded this section by observing that

> the Prologue reflects a rhetorically powerful statement designed to arrest the audience's attention and incite cognitive, emotional and spiritual response. Through skilful aural and syntactical arrangement, including the incorporation of patterns of repetition, variation and echoing, these opening four verses of 1 John succeed in delivering a complex—yet coherent—statement capable of connecting with and winning over a first-century audience.[14]

The Contributions of Caragounis

In an effort to augment the previous results, the second stage of the analysis[15] applied the important research of Chrys Caragounis on Greek

---

10. The -ου termination marks genitive singular articles and nouns which serve as objects of περί ("concerning," v. 1) and μετά ("with," v. 3).
11. Brickle, *Aural Design*, 36–37.
12. Ibid., 39–40.
13. Ibid., 128.
14. Ibid., 52.
15. This section comprised chapter 4 (pp. 54–106) of Brickle, *Aural Design*.

pronunciation and aurality.¹⁶ This phase sought to hear what one cannot perceive through a mere visual examination of the text. These additional steps in the mapping process endeavored to enhance the auditory experience of the Prologue and further reconstruct what a first century audience may have heard.

Altering the Key through the HGP

The first step deployed Caragounis's proposed "Historical Greek Pronunciation" (HGP) as a test case to determine the potential effects on the passage's auditory terrain. In contrast to the more traditional Erasmian pronunciation scheme, HGP offers a compelling alternative to what *Koine* may have sounded like. It differs in a number of ways, particularly in the shared or similar sounds expressed by certain vowels, diphthongs, and consonants that *look* different.

By examining the distribution of particular Greek letters in the Prologue and comparing HGP to Erasmian, I discovered some interesting results. For example, while the vowel α and diphthong αυ sound distinct under Erasmian pronunciation, their shared *af* sound in the adjacent μετὰ τοῦ υἱοῦ α̲υ̲τοῦ Ἰησοῦ Χριστοῦ ("with his Son Jesus Christ," v. 3) and καὶ ταῦτα γράφομεν ἡμεῖς made for a striking pattern (a̲f̲tou . . . ta̲f̲ta . . . grafōmen) that was unnoticeable by a mere visual scan (compare Figures 13, 14).¹⁷ Factoring in additional labials like π and the double consonant ψ exposed further unseen audible correspondences (Figure 15).¹⁸

In short, plugging in this alternate pronunciation generated a significantly more unified and coherent soundscape than had been attainable by visually examining the text with an Erasmian "pair of eyes." This experiment illuminated formerly inconspicuous patterns and textures and thus served to supplement the former analyses. As I noted in *Aural Design*, "[p]reviously obscured sound correspondences are brought to light which demonstrate more frequent sound clusters and bolster the overall syntactical structure of the Prologue discussed in chapter 3 (ABCA'B'C')."¹⁹ It became clear from this research that pronunciation plays an integral role in sound mapping.

16. See especially, Caragounis, *Development of Greek*, 339–474.
17. Brickle, *Aural Design*, 101–2.
18. Ibid., 103.
19. Ibid., 58.

Subpoenaing the Auditor from Halicarnassus

The final step in this phase of *Aural Design* drew on Caragounis's investigation of a Greek treatise, titled *On Literary Composition* (Περὶ συνθέσεως ὀνομάτων), by the rhetorician and Atticist, Dionysius of Halicarnassus. In my estimation this sole-surviving work of its kind from antiquity is indispensible for understanding ancient perspectives on compositional methods targeting the ear. Caragounis's approach, developed through an examination of *On Literary Composition* and robust application to selected passages from the Pauline corpus, was attractive for sound mapping the Prologue of 1 John in that it promised a viable means to hear and evaluate the aural coherence of the text through a skilled ancient auditor.

For Dionysius, what a composition sounded like when read aloud was crucial to its ability to suitably impact and persuade its listeners. Fortunately, Greek's innately strong degree of grammatical inflection allowed a writer the flexibility to rearrange word order to achieve a more euphonious (or, if necessary, discordant) collation of sounds. To a degree unattainable in a more word-order dependent language like English, a Greek author could craft the soundscape of his prose composition to match the content, style, and tone he wished to express. For Dionysius this attention to the aural properties of a text extended to the choice of phonemes, syllables and word transitions.[20]

The final stage of my analysis thus sought to evaluate the Prologue in light of Dionysius's standards for achieving a range of qualities that enhanced a composition's auditory effectiveness, including, for example, euphony, melody, rhythm (note the scansion of the passage's cola and feet in Figure 17[21]), variety, and style. I determined that while the Prologue failed to achieve classical expectations, it did in fact display an impressive level of aural coherence, artistry, and rhetorical sophistication. Rather than exhibiting disarray, my studies suggested that this passage reflects an author who carefully crafted his opening statement and was attuned to its orally persuasive elements. By "listening" through the trained ears of an ancient expert in these matters, this analysis permitted a modern interpreter to hear what could not be seen from reading the text in silence.

Taken as a whole, the research carried out in *Aural Design* not only advanced an alternative appraisal of the Prologue's architectural design but espoused an approach for encountering and interpreting texts that is more consonant with an ancient paradigm. These attempts to map out patterns

---

20. Ibid., 24–29, 58–59.
21. Ibid., 105–6.

of sound assisted in better "seeing what we can hear" as well as "hearing what we cannot see."[22] As I observed in retrospect, the study's various investigations contributed to "the articulation of [the Prologue's] theological message. In other words, the Prologue's sound patterns—coupled with grammatical and syntactical shaping—serve as the conduit for semantic expression. The overall structure of the Prologue is supported and highlighted by the element of sound."[23]

Forging Ahead

The closing chapter of *Aural Design* summarized the project's analyses, offered a concise exegetical commentary on the Prologue, and pointed ahead to further areas of research.[24] These proposed studies encompassed wider ranging applications of sound mapping as well as branching out into related avenues of ancient media culture, such as performance and memory. Next I briefly prescribe some additional ideas for moving forward.

Tool Development

As noted in the introduction above, sound mapping involves the graphic display of perceived sounds. Margaret Lee and Bernard Scott provide helpful guidance in creating a basic sound map[25] as well as numerous examples of sound maps of selected New Testament texts.[26] Such maps serve as vital points of entry into the process.

At the panel session, "Sound Mapping: Potential and Implications," sponsored by the Bible in Ancient and Modern Media section at the 2016 Annual Meeting of the Society of Biblical Literature, I presented a paper in which I sought to ally euphony and spatial mnemonics by mapping soundspace.[27] I noted that the "Lee-Scott approach to sound mapping . . . is an especially invaluable model, not least because of its visual clarity, flexibility, and practicality for anyone seeking to depict acoustic patterns."[28] The paper utilized and depicted examples of sound maps stemming from the Lee

---

22. The respective titles of chapters 3 and 4 in Brickle, *Aural Design*.
23. Ibid., 111.
24. Chapter 5 (107–25).
25. Lee and Scott, *Sound Mapping*, 167–95.
26. Ibid., 199–384.
27. Brickle, "Dionysius of Halicarnassus."
28. Ibid., 7.

and Scott model but also featured two-dimensional images in which sound maps were incorporated onto representative shapes.

Additionally, this research highlighted the value of leveraging mapping techniques from other disciplines, such as the creative use of audio-visual cityscapes. These types of maps move beyond unisensory models by "superimpos[ing] representative sound images and/or audio files onto a visual backdrop, thus generating a multi-dimensional soundscape that interfaces with spatial cartography."[29] Promising also in this regard is the Macunx software currently being developed jointly by Linguisticator and the University of Westminster in which users can create customized memory palaces.[30] Software such as Macunx may be employed to overlay textual sound maps onto spatial displays through which users can navigate in virtual reality—and in the process transform their mind into a living library.[31]

Building on the seminal work of Lee and Scott, therefore, techniques and devices may be refined that move beyond static models to more sophisticated kinds which utilize three-dimensional, multi-sensory displays to depict and explore the fascinating interface between sound, space, and time evoked by texts.[32]

A Koine Community

Another factor that can enhance the skillset and toolkit of those pursuing sound mapping is the implementation of Communicative Language Teaching (CLT). Institutions such as the Biblical Language Center[33] and Conversational Koine Institute[34] offer training and resources to develop fluency in ancient Greek and ultimately foster communities of Greek speakers. The upshot of this approach to language learning is that, like many modern

---

29. Ibid., 8.
30. See https://linguisticator.com/macunx-vr/.
31. See Carruthers, "Mechanisms for the Transmission," 1–26.
32. For examples of sound maps from the standpoint of cognitive studies, see McAdams and Bigand, *Thinking in Sound*. For techniques in visually mapping spatial images, see, e.g., MacEachren and Taylor, *Visualization in Modern Cartography*; Dykes, et al., *Exploring Geovisualization*; Slocum et al., *Thematic Cartography*. For examples of time map figures, see those in Zerubavel, *Time Maps*.
33. See www.biblicallanguagecenter.com. This author has participated in a Biblical Language Center workshop and integrates CLT into his graduate-level Greek instruction.
34. See www.conversationalkoine.com. A publisher affiliated with the Conversational Koine Institute is GlossaHouse (www.glossahouse.com), which offers numerous resources specifically geared towards this pedagogy.

language pedagogies, it cultivates an internalization of the language—a decided advantage for those seeking to hear patterns of sound in Greek texts.

Engaging the Sound Level Meter

Before closing, we will now briefly discuss some possible implications of sound mapping on two texts from the Epistle to the Hebrews. Sound mapping proves even more fruitful when incorporating insights from narrative criticism and intertextuality.[35] An array of meticulously-constructed sound maps would seek to establish a probable, even measurable, connection of New Testament texts to other narratives or discourses. The short forays conducted here, however, merely raise questions about audible and conceptual linkages to texts that were widely known in the ancient Mediterranean world and inquire whether such potential intertextual echoes might be detectible in part through sound mapping.

Odyssean Echoes in the Proemium of Hebrews

We begin with another prologue. Hebrews opens with a carefully-crafted periodic statement. Among other sound plays, the sophisticated prose features striking alliteration and consonance of the letter π: πολυμερῶς καὶ πολυτρόπως πάλαι ὁ θεὸς λαλήσας τοῖς πατράσιν ἐν τοῖς προφήταις ("In many parts and in many ways long ago God spoke to the fathers by the prophets," Heb 1:1).[36] The author telescopes the entire Hebrew Bible revelation into two words (πολυμερῶς, "in many parts," and πολυτρόπως, "in many ways"), inviting readers to recall and imagine the rich spaces and imagery of Scripture's first Testament.[37]

While the Epistle clearly evokes the subtext of the Israelites's wilderness pilgrimage, warning its hearers not to repeat the tragic error of their forefathers when they rebelled against the voice of Yahweh (e.g., Heb 4:1–11), arguably its prologue also evokes another grand narrative with

---

35. For a piece that considers the intriguing interconnections between texts and the memory arts, see Brickle, "Sympathetic Resonance," 213–36. The brilliant study by Bewernick, *Storyteller's Memory Palace*, seeks to demonstrate that the memory arts may lie at the heart of narrative-making.

36. See "πολυμερῶς" and "πολυτρόπως," BDAG 847, 850. On alliteration of the consonant π, see Attridge, *Hebrews*, 37; Lane, *Hebrews 1–8*, 5–6; Ellingworth, *Epistle to the Hebrews*, 91; and Thompson, *Hebrews*, 32.

37. For the phenomenon of miniaturizing texts, see Squire, *Iliad in a Nutshell*.

which the text's Hellenistic recipients would have been familiar.³⁸ The adverb πολυτρόπως resonates with the adjective πολύτροπον ("many devices") in the prologue of the renowned archaic poem, the *Odyssey* of Homer, in an opening that also features alliteration and consonance of π: Ἄνδρα μοι ἔννεπε, Μοῦσα, πολύτροπον, ὃς μάλα πολλὰ πλάγχθη ("Tell me, Muse, of the man of many devices, driven far astray").³⁹

Πολύτροπον characterizes the ingenuity and resourcefulness of the epic's central hero, Odysseus, who, like Moses, led his people on an arduous journey in quest of their ancestral homeland. Like the doomed Israelites who stubbornly refused to heed the voice of their captain at Kadesh Barnea (Num 13:1—14:38; Deut 9:23), Odysseus's men recklessly forfeited their homecoming by foolishly disobeying his warning not to slay the cattle of Helios.⁴⁰ The Odyssey's narrator invoked the Muse to recount these adventures;⁴¹ the author of Hebrews notes the definitive way in which God's voice had spoken of a pioneer superior to Moses who would successfully lead the recipients to a place of rest (Heb 1:2; 3:1—4:16).

As we noted above, the fascinating correspondences that appear to be evident here could be further investigated through a series of sound maps.

Acoustic Shadows on Platonic Cave Walls

Our second example stems from Heb 8, in which the author summarizes his argument from the preceding chapters. He contrasts the fleeting nature of the personnel and sacrifices associated with the Old Covenant tabernacle with the priesthood of Christ, who, as the author points out elsewhere, is the true ὑπόστασις ("reality," "essence," "realization"; Heb 1:3; 11:1).⁴² He notes that the bygone Mosaic institutions were but "a sketch (ὑποδείγματι) and shadow (σκιᾷ) of the heavenly one; for Moses, when he was about (μέλλων) to erect the tent (σκηνήν), was warned, 'See (ὅρα) that you make everything according to the pattern (τύπον) that was shown you on the mountain'" (Heb 8:5, citing Exod 25:40; NRSV).

The affinities here to Platonism, especially Middle Platonism as articulated by adherents such as Philo, are well-known.⁴³ In Plato's celebrated

---

38. On the pervasive role of the Homeric literature in Hellenistic schools, see Hock, "Homer in Greco-Roman Education," 56–77.

39. Homer, *Od.* 1:1–2 (Murray).

40. *Od.* 1:5–10.

41. *Od.* 1:1.

42. BDAG, 1040.

43. As Thompson, "Middle Platonism," 31, asserts, "Platonic categories were the

dialogue from *The Republic*, known as the Allegory of the Cave, Socrates hopes to advance the education (παιδείας, *Resp.* 7.514; cf. Heb 12:5, 8, 11) of his interlocutors by having them imagine people chained up in a cave. These prisoners know nothing of the outside world, seeing only shadows on the wall in front of them projected by means of a fire behind them. If one of these prisoners were to be set free, he would initially be overwhelmed and confused by the glare, but would eventually be able to comprehend in part the true nature of reality outside the cave. Upon his return, the remaining prisoners would be unable to grasp what he had experienced and unwilling to leave the cave.

Despite plausible affinities between Hebrews and *The Republic*, Kenneth Schenck largely dismisses any substantive connection. While affirming that Heb 8:5 "is filled with classic Platonic vocabulary" and that the "Platonic feel of this language is undeniable," he concludes that "the similarities are more verbal than substantial."[44] I propose, on the other contrary, that by comparing the sound patterns of Heb 8:5 with, for instance, a selection from *The Republic*,[45] the correspondences appear more conspicuous and significant than first meets the eye. For example, a surface analysis exposes not only verbal links (e.g., forms of πᾶς ["all"], σκιά ["shadow"], ὁράω ["to see"]; δείκνυμι ["to show"]), but audible resonances as well (e.g., σκ- in σκόπει, σκιάς, σκιᾷ, σκηνήν; οι in οἵτινες, ποιήσεις/ποιῶν, σοι, οἷα, οἴει; vowel-ρ in ὅρα, ἐπουρανίων, ὄρει, ἑώρα, ἐγγυτέρω, ὀρθότερον; and μέλλων with μᾶλλον). Further support for or invalidation of such claims, of course, awaits detailed sound analyses.

---

common property not only of the elite but of all educated people . . . The refined language of the Epistle to the Hebrews leaves no doubt that the author belonged to the educated circles among whom the tenets of Platonism were commonplace." See also Mackie, *Eschatology and Exhortation*, 105–20; and Johnson, *Hebrews*, 15–21.

44. Schenck, *Brief Guide to Philo*, 84.

45. Σκόπει δή, ἦν δ' ἐγώ, αὐτῶν λύσιν τε καὶ ἴασιν τῶν τε δεσμῶν καὶ τῆς ἀφροσύνης, οἵα τις ἂν εἴη, εἰ φύσει τοιάδε συμβαίνοι αὐτοῖς· ὁπότε τις λυθείη καὶ ἀναγκάζοιτο ἐξαίφνης ἀνίστασθαί τε καὶ περιάγειν τὸν αὐχένα καὶ βαδίζειν καὶ πρὸς τὸ φῶς ἀναβλέπειν, πάντα δὲ ταῦτα ποιῶν ἀλγοῖ τε καὶ διὰ τὰς μαρμαρυγὰς ἀδυνατοῖ καθορᾶν ἐκεῖνα ὧν τότε τὰς σκιὰς ἑώρα, τί ἂν οἴει αὐτὸν εἰπεῖν, εἴ τις αὐτῷ λέγοι ὅτι τότε μὲν ἑώρα φλυαρίας, νῦν δὲ μᾶλλόν τι ἐγγυτέρω τοῦ ὄντος καὶ πρὸς μᾶλλον ὄντα τετραμμένος ὀρθότερον βλέποι, καὶ δὴ καὶ ἕκαστον τῶν παριόντων δεικνὺς αὐτῷ ἀναγκάζοι ἐρωτῶν ἀποκρίνεσθαι ὅτι ἐστίν; οὐκ οἴει αὐτὸν ἀπορεῖν τε ἂν καὶ ἡγεῖσθαι τὰ τότε ὁρώμενα ἀληθέστερα ἢ τὰ νῦν δεικνύμενα; (*Resp.* 7.515c-d).

Signature Sounds and Spatial Settings

Space here does not permit, but if one were to develop a series of thorough sound maps, therefore, additional resonances could be traced between these passages from Hebrews and their respective Homeric and Platonic counterparts. These two examples invite dialogue on whether sound mapping may (or may not) reinforce other criteria suggested by scholars for determining the probability of intertextual allusions and echoes.[46] When factors like pronunciation and euphony are introduced to the mix, prospective intertextual echoes become even more intriguing. Could it be that in some cases New Testament writers have embedded sound signatures to mark intertextual linkages, patterns largely imperceptible to modern readers yet clear to ancient hearers fluent in the language?

These examples also provoke questions about the inclination of sounds to recall narratives imagined by the audience. In what way, then, can sound patterns be shown to educe visualized plots, spatial settings, and vivid imagery previously mapped on listeners' memories?[47] As we have suggested, such stored impressions can range from stories related in the Septuagint to scenarios from epic poetry and philosophical dialogues.

Concluding Reverberations

While still in its infancy, the technique of mapping sound patterns of orally-read texts holds significant promise for biblical interpretation. Sound mapping permits readers to cross the threshold separating sight and sound. They can then continue on into the realm of ancient multimedia, where texts may be experienced in a way more closely resembling that of the original hearers.[48] Not only have I found this craft compelling and insightful—it is a game changer when used in conversation with other modes of ancient media culture. I anticipate exciting developments as scholarship continues to exploit this richly rewarding approach.

---

46. See, for instance, Hays, *Echoes of Scripture in the Letters of Paul*, 29–33; Beale, *Handbook on the New Testament*, 29–40.

47. For two essays that treat the interface of texts and memory, see Brickle, "Simonides," 367, and "Wax Tablet," 454. For insightful studies that consider the role of spatiality in texts, see Minchin, *Homer and the Resources of Memory*; Webb, *Ekphrasis*; Purves, *Space and Time*; Thatcher, "John's Memory Theatre," 73–91; Clay, *Homer's Trojan Theater*; Tsagalis, *From Listeners to Viewers*; Squire, *Sight and the Ancient Senses*; Selby, *Not with Wisdom*; and Robbins, Melion, and Jeal, *Art of Visual Exegesis*.

48. See Brickle, "Seeing, Hearing, Declaring, Writing," 11–28; Butler and Purves, *Synaesthesia*; and Butler, *Ancient Phonograph*.

Bibliography

Attridge, Harold W. *The Epistle to the Hebrews.* Hermeneia. Philadelphia: Fortress, 1989.
Beale, Gregory K. *Handbook on the New Testament Use of the Old Testament: Exegesis and Interpretation.* Grand Rapids: Baker Academic, 2012.
Bewernick, Hanne. *The Storyteller's Memory Palace.* Anglo-Saxon Language and Literature 458. Frankfurt: Lang, 2010.
Boomershine, Thomas E. *The Messiah of Peace: A Performance-Criticism Commentary on Mark's Passion-Resurrection Narrative.* Biblical Performance Criticism Series 12. Eugene, OR: Cascade Books, 2015.
Botha, Pieter J. J. *Orality and Literacy in Early Christianity.* Biblical Performance Criticism Series 5. Eugene, OR: Cascade Books, 2012.
Brickle, Jeffrey E. *Aural Design and Coherence in the Prologue of First John.* Library of New Testament Studies 465. London: T. & T. Clark, 2012.
———. "Aural Design and Coherence in the Prologue of First John." PhD. diss., Concordia Seminary, St. Louis, 2010.
———. "Dionysius of Halicarnassus Meets Pseudo-Cicero: Revisiting Johannine Orality at the Crossroads of Sight and Sound." Paper presented at the annual meeting of the Society of Biblical Literature, San Antonio, Texas, Nov. 19, 2016.
———. "Seeing, Hearing, Declaring, Writing: Media Dynamics in the Letters of John." In *The Fourth Gospel in First-Century Media Culture,* edited by Anthony Le Donne and Tom Thatcher, 11–28. Library of New Testament Studies 426. London: T. & T. Clark, 2011.
———. "Simonides." In *The Dictionary of the Bible and Ancient Media,* edited by Tom Thatcher et al., 367. London: Bloomsbury T. & T. Clark, 2017.
———. "Sympathetic Resonance: John as Intertextual Memory Artisan." In *Abiding Words: The Use of Scripture in the Gospel of John,* edited by Alicia D. Myers and Bruce G. Schuchard, 213–36. Resources for Biblical Studies 81. Atlanta: SBL, 2015.
———. "Wax Tablet." In *The Dictionary of the Bible and Ancient Media,* edited by Tom Thatcher et al., 454. London: Bloomsbury T. & T. Clark, 2017.
Butler, Shane. *The Ancient Phonograph.* New York: Zone Books, 2015.
Butler, Shane, and Alex Purves, eds. *Synaesthesia and the Ancient Senses.* The Senses in Antiquity. Durham: Acumen, 2013.
Caragounis, Chrys C. *The Development of Greek and the New Testament: Morphology, Syntax, Phonology, and Textual Transmission.* Grand Rapids: Baker Academic, 2006.
Carruthers, Mary. "Mechanisms for the Transmission of Cultures: The Role of 'Place' in the Arts of Memory." In *Translatio or the Transmission of Culture in the Middle Ages: Modes and Messages,* edited by Laura Hollengreen, 1–26. Arizona Studies in the Middle Ages and the Renaissance 13. Turnhout: Brepols, 2008.
Chidester, David. *Word and Light: Seeing, Hearing, and Religious Discourse.* Urbana: University of Illinois Press, 1992.
Clay, Jenny Strauss. *Homer's Trojan Theater: Space, Vision, and Memory in the Iliad.* Cambridge: Cambridge University Press, 2011.
Danker, Frederick W., ed. *A Greek-English Lexicon of the New Testament and Other Early Christian Literature.* 3rd ed. Chicago: University of Chicago Press, 2000.
De Waal, Kayle B. *An Aural-Performance Analysis of Revelation 1 and 11.* Studies in Biblical Literature 163. New York: Lang, 2015.

Dykes, Jason, Alan M. MacEachren, and Menno-Jan Kraak, eds. *Exploring Geovisualization*. Kidlington, UK: Elsevier, 2005.

Ellingworth, Paul. *The Epistle to the Hebrews*. New International Greek Testament Commentary. Grand Rapids: Eerdmans, 1993.

Hays, Richard B. *Echoes of Scripture in the Letters of Paul*. New Haven: Yale University Press, 1989.

Hock, Ronald F. "Homer in Greco-Roman Education." In *Mimesis and Intertextuality in Antiquity and Christianity*, edited by Dennis R. MacDonald, 56–77. Studies in Antiquity and Christianity. Harrisburg, PA: Trinity, 2001.

Johnson, Luke Timothy. *Hebrews: A Commentary*. New Testament Library. Louisville: Westminster John Knox, 2006.

Kelber, Werner H. *Imprints, Voiceprints, and Footprints of Memory: Collected Essays of Werner H. Kelber*. Resources for Biblical Study 74. Atlanta: SBL, 2013.

Lane, William L. *Hebrews 1–8*. Word Biblical Commentary 47A. Dallas: Word Books, 1991.

Lee, Margaret E. "Sound Mapping." In *The Dictionary of the Bible and Ancient Media*, edited by Tom Thatcher et al., 372–79. London: Bloomsbury T. & T. Clark, 2017.

Lee, Margaret Ellen, and Bernard Brandon Scott. *Sound Mapping the New Testament*. Salem, OR: Polebridge, 2009.

MacEachren, Alan M., and D. R. Fraser Taylor, eds. *Visualization in Modern Cartography*. Modern Cartography 2. Tarrytown, NY: Elsevier Science, 1994.

Mackie, Scott D. *Eschatology and Exhortation in the Epistle to the Hebrews*. Wissenschaftliche Untersuchungen zum Neuen Testament 2/223. Tübingen: Mohr/Siebeck, 2007.

McAdams, Stephen, and Emmanuel Bigand, eds. *Thinking in Sound: The Cognitive Psychology of Human Audition*. Oxford: Oxford University Press, 1993.

Minchin, Elizabeth. *Homer and the Resources of Memory: Some Applications of Cognitive Theory to the Iliad and the Odyssey*. Oxford: Oxford University Press, 2001.

Nässelqvist, Dan. *Public Reading in Early Christianity: Lectors, Manuscripts, and Sound in the Oral Delivery of John 1–4*. Novum Testamentum Supplements 163. Leiden: Brill, 2015.

Person, Raymond F., Jr., and Chris Keith. "Media Studies and Biblical Studies: An Introduction." In *The Dictionary of the Bible and Ancient Media*, edited by Tom Thatcher et al., 1–15. London: Bloomsbury T. & T. Clark, 2017.

Purves, Alex C. *Space and Time in Ancient Greek Narrative*. New York: Cambridge University Press, 2010.

Robbins, Vernon K., Walter S. Melion, and Roy R. Jeal, eds. *The Art of Visual Exegesis: Rhetoric, Texts, Images*. Emory Studies in Early Christianity 19. Atlanta: SBL, 2017.

Schenck, Kenneth. *A Brief Guide to Philo*. Louisville: Westminster John Knox, 2005.

Selby, Gary S. *Not with Wisdom of Words: Nonrational Persuasion in the New Testament*. Grand Rapids: Eerdmans, 2016.

Shiner, Whitney. *Proclaiming the Gospel: First-Century Performance of Mark*. Harrisburg, PA: Trinity, 2003.

Slocum, Terry A. et al. *Thematic Cartography and Geovisualization*. 3rd ed. Prentice Hall Series in Geographic Information Science. London: Pearson, 2008.

Squire, Michael. *The* Iliad *in a Nutshell: Visualizing Epic on the* Tabulae Iliacae. Oxford: Oxford University Press, 2011.

———, ed. *Sight and the Ancient Senses*. The Senses in Antiquity. London: Routledge, 2016.
Thatcher, Tom. "John's Memory Theatre: A Study of Composition in Performance." In *The Fourth Gospel in First-Century Media Culture*, edited by Anthony LeDonne and Tom Thatcher, 73–91. Library of New Testament Studies 426. London: T. & T. Clark, 2011.
Thompson, James W. *Hebrews*. Paideia Commentaries on the New Testament. Grand Rapids: Baker Academic, 2008.
Thompson, James W. "What Does Middle Platonism Have to Do with Hebrews?" In *Reading the Epistle to the Hebrews: A Resource for Students*, edited by Eric F. Mason and Kevin B. McCruden, 31–52. Resources for Biblical Study 66. Atlanta: SBL, 2011.
Tsagalis, Christos. *From Listeners to Viewers: Space in the Iliad*. Hellenic Studies 53. Washington, DC: Center for Hellenic Studies, 2012.
Webb, Ruth. *Ekphrasis, Imagination, and Persuasion in Ancient Rhetorical Theory and Practice*. Surrey, UK: Ashgate, 2009.
Zerubavel, Eviatar. *Time Maps: Collective Memory and the Social Shape of the Past*. Chicago: University of Chicago Press, 2003.

5

Investigations into the Sound's Message of Philippians 1:27—2:18

BERNHARD OESTREICH

Introduction

The aim of this study is to use the sound of the spoken language of a section of Paul's letter to the Philippians as a tool in order to come to conclusions concerning the overall impact of the passage and the meaning of specific parts and expressions. It is not the written text that is interpreted directly, a practice that is common in our culture where information encoded in written texts is often processed immediately from the signs on paper or screen. In this study—following the pioneering work of Margaret E. Lee and Bernard B. Scott[1]—the attempt is made to return first to the spoken language and only then to proceed to interpretation. What is the advantage? Is not the written text all we have? Of course, the spoken word carries more information than the written text because oral language has many additional ways to communicate, for example tone, rhythm, emphasis, pace, inflection and the countless nuances of facial expression and gesture. However, all that has been lost for a long time.

This study is based on the assumption that traces of the additional wealth of oral language have found their way into the written encoding of language. This is possible because the above mentioned different channels

---

1. Lee and Scott, *Sound Mapping*.

of communication available for speakers overlap to a certain extent. Of course, they can work completely independent of each other. It is well possible that the semantic content of an utterance has nothing to do with what the speaker's eyes signal, or that a friendly formulation can be accompanied by a voice that signals anger or ridicule. But very often some of the channels are used in tandem with each other in order to amplify the effect. The additional message of the speaker's eyes can result in a verbal image that slips into the formulation or it can lead to an ambiguous expression that makes room for the message that is expressed nonverbally. The voice of ridicule could be accompanied by a phrase of exaggeration or the voice of anger or abasement by expletives (σκύβαλα in Phil 3:8). To transform the written text into the oral expression cannot fully retrieve the multi-layered communication, especially not those parts of the message that the speaker expressed by voice or gesture and that work independently of the semantic content. Our method can only reveal what is encoded in writing. However, the effort to reconstruct the oral language can sharpen our senses in order not to overlook what is there, what is perhaps only hinted at or very subtly expressed. Processing the reconstructed spoken language, i.e., paying attention to the sound as we normally do when we listen to a spoken message, does not provide new data about the biblical texts. It rather puts the only available data in a different light that might reveal structures and meanings and overtones that could otherwise easily be overlooked. This study is undertaken with the conviction that this different light will prove effective in revealing aspects in the text that always have been there but escaped notice of its students.

The Phonology of Koine Greek in Paul's Time

The phonological system of any spoken language is in constant change. However, most speakers do not notice the changes because the differences are small and do not disturb communication.[2] While pronunciation of words changes slowly and constantly, the spelling of their written representations remains the same[3] until it is eventually adapted to the new pronunciation. Because the adaptation of writing can happen even centuries after the oral changes, the written text of Paul's letter does not reveal how its readers and performers pronounced it. Researchers of the development of the Greek language use clues from frequent misspellings, onomatopoetic words, the

---

2. Nikiforidou, "Language Change," 124.
3. Petrounias, "Pronunciation of Ancient Greek," 547.

representation of Greek words or names in other languages, and the spelling of foreign words in Greek to reconstruct pronunciation schemes.[4]

Since pronunciation is crucial in producing all forms of acoustical repetitions, the device that gives structure to oral language,[5] it is not of small significance how the vowels and consonants are phonetically realized. For example, we would miss rhyme if we did not take into account that the letter <ι> as well as the digraph <ει> were both pronounced as [i] in Koine Greek.[6] Likewise, we would not notice alliteration if we would take the letter <κ> as representing the voiceless stop [k] while the letter <χ> the velar fricative [x]. In classical Greek and far down in Hellenistic times <χ> was an aspirated velar stop [kʰ] that could form alliteration with [k]. It is also of importance for studying the oral impact of a Pauline text, whether the classical metrical rhythm of Greek was still known and sometimes applied in his time or whether it had already been completely ousted by a stress accent. Therefore, the attempt to interpret a letter of Paul starting from its audible representation requires a decision on the stage of language development that is taken as a basis for this study.

On the way from classical Greek *via* Koine Greek to Modern Greek there are some general developments in pronunciation.[7] The most important ones include fricativization of the aspirated and the voiced stop consonants (e.g., <δ> from [d] to [ð]), movement of the vowel system from back open vowels to more front closed vowels (e.g., <η> from [ɛ:] to [e:] to [i]), the change of diphthongs to monophthongs, the loss of the distinction between long and short vowels accompanied by the change of the speech rhythm from an alternation of light and heavy syllables (the heavy syllables extending approximately twice the length of light syllables) to an alternation between stressed and unstressed syllables. While the general development of Greek phonology has been reconstructed quite well, it is often not at all clear at what time the different changes actually happened.[8] Additionally,

4. Nikiforidou, "Language Change," 125; Petrounias, "Pronunciation of Ancient Greek," 545–55.

5. Lee and Scott, *Sound Mapping*, 141–45.

6. To symbolize language sounds, I am using the alphabet of the International Phonetic Association (IPA) as listed in Christidis, ed., *History of Ancient Greek*, 1560. For reference to sounds, the symbol is in brackets: [i]; for reference to the written letters, the symbol is in angle brackets <ι>; for reference to *phonems* (sounds of a language that are relevant for meaning but can be acoustically realized somewhat variably), the reference is in slashes /i/.

7. Horrocks, *Greek*, 160–88; Malikouti-Drachman, "Phonology," 526–44.

8. Nikiforidou, "Language Change," 125: "To reconstruct the pronunciation of earlier periods is perhaps one of the most difficult chapters in the historical reconstruction of a language."

the speed of accepting changes of pronunciation differs according to geographical area, the social stratum of the speaker, and the linguistic register. Colloquial speech and the language of less educated people would likely show more of the various respective trends of development. There were alternative pronunciations competing with each for a long time until one variant prevailed.[9]

In this study, the results of experts on the Greek language are adopted that are collected in the voluminous edition of Christidis and are supplemented by previous studies.[10] The letters of Paul must have been read by people who had received enough literary education to perform letters significantly more complex than the short letter papyri found in Egypt.[11] Since more educated speakers tend to abide by a more traditional pronunciation, I assume that the reading of Paul's letters would not display the most advanced state of Greek language development in his time.[12] The local differences of pronunciation cannot be considered here.

In Hellenistic and Roman times, the voiced stop consonants <β, δ, γ>, spoken in classical times as [b, d, g], changed to fricatives [β or v, ð, ɣ].[13] However, they did not all become fricatives at the same time. In some contexts, <γ> changed very early. Before [i] it changed to the fricative [j] forming a palatal glide [ji]. <γ> before velar consonants <γ, κ, χ>, and before [m] was spoken as a nasal [ŋ].[14] Also, <β> changed in the second century BCE to a bilabial [β], then to a labiodental [v]. The fricativization of <δ> and <γ> followed in the second century CE.[15] However, <β, δ, γ> remained

9. Joseph, "Early Movement," 693–94.

10. Christidis, ed., *History of Ancient Greek*; Allen, *Vox Graeca*, 12–103; Devine and Stephens, *Prosody*; Horrocks, *Greek*. Cf. also Caragounis, *Development of Greek*, 350–96; however, he tends to assume that the changes from classical pronunciation to Koine and finally to Modern Greek happened very early, even in classical time or early Hellenistic time.

11. See Stirewalt, *Paul*, 25–55, who compares the Pauline letters with official letters of kings and officials.

12. Horrocks, "Syntax," 620, emphasizes that Koine was not "a single variety. Rather we should see the relatively uniform 'high' written and spoken forms used by the upper classes, which interacted naturally with literary Attic . . . , as forming the apex of a pyramid, beneath which were subsumed the many different spoken (and sometimes written) varieties that inevitably developed in the lower levels of society among Greeks and speakers of local dialects and languages other than Greek in the vast territories of the Roman empire." See the tables of the pronunciation of different social strata in Horrocks, *Greek*, 164–66. See also Kyrtatas, "Greek World," 352, referring to the upper classes that abandoned Koine for Atticism.

13. Nikiforidou, "Language Change," 127; Allen, *Vox Graeca*, 31–32.

14. Allen, *Vox Graeca*, 34.

15. Horrocks, *Greek*, 170.

stops if they followed a nasal consonant [m, n].[16] The aspirated stops <φ, θ, χ>, originally [pʰ, tʰ, kʰ], also gradually changed to voiceless fricatives [f, θ, x or χ].[17] These changes began in the second century BCE.[18] The fricative pronunciation of <φ> is surely demonstrable in the first century CE, while <θ> and <χ> are still not uniform fricatives in the second century CE.[19]

The consonant [h] was not written any more since the end of the fifth century BCE but was marked later by *spiritus asper* above the vowel. It was still spoken in the Hellenistic period until the first century CE, although it was vanishing and was completely lost by the following century.[20]

The letter <ζ>, originally [zd], perhaps sometimes [dz], had become [z] already in classical times; <σ> was normally voiceless, voiced only before voiced stops and [m]. The letter <ν> at the end of a word was assimilated to the first consonant of the following word.[21] Other consonants remained relatively stable until Modern Greek.

The pronunciation of the letters <α, ε, ι, and ο> did not change much. In everyday language the long vowels <η and ω> lost more and more of their long value in the Hellenistic period. The vowel <η>, originally open [ɛː], became more closed [eː] or [e]. In the first century CE in Attica and Asia Minor, it was not yet closed to [i] as in Modern Greek.[22] The vowel <υ> was not yet [i] but [y].[23] The digraph <ει> had been spoken [iː] since the end of the classical period.[24] Also the long open <ω>, in classical time spoken [ɔː], became more closed, approximating the vowel <o>. Already in classical time the diphthongs began to change to monophthong pronunciation. After the classical period <αι> became long [æː], then later in Hellenistic time [ɛː] or [ɛ], and only after the second century CE [e].[25] The diphthongs with <υ>,

16. Petrounias, "Pronunciation of Classical Greek," 562.

17. Allen, *Vox Graeca*, 23–24, finds first evidence in the first century CE, however in certain areas it may have begun earlier.

18. Nikiforidou, "Language Change," 127–28.

19. Joseph, "Early Movement towards Modern Greek," 695; Allen, *Vox Graeca*, 18–26; Horrocks, *Greek*, 170.

20. Petrounias, "Pronunciation during Hellenistic Period," 607; Allen, *Vox Graeca*, 52–55.

21. Allen, *Vox Graeca*, 33–34.

22. Bubenik, "Eastern Koines," 634–35; Allen, *Vox Graeca*, 74; Horrocks, *Greek*, 168.

23. Petrounias, "Pronunciation of Ancient Greek," 550; Joseph, "Early Movement Towards Modern Greek," 697; Allen, *Vox Graeca*, 68; Horrocks, *Greek*, 160–62, 169.

24. Petrounias, "Pronunciation during the Hellenistic Period," 602; Drettas, "Septuagint," 891; Allen, *Vox Graeca*, 70. Before vowels, however, it was spoken [e] with palatal glide [ej] until the second century CE. See Allen, *Vox Graeca*, 72–73, esp. n.28.

25. Allen, *Vox Graeca*, 79.

i.e., <αυ> and <ευ>, were pronounced with a fricative glide (first bilabial [aβ/eβ], then labiodental [av/af] and [ev/ef]), beginning in Hellenistic time but not yet finalized in the second century CE.[26] The diphthongs <οι and υι> changed value to the vowel [y:] or [y] early in Hellenistic time and remained in this state until the tenth century CE.[27] The long diphthongs <αι, ηι, ωι>, later written <ᾳ, ῃ, ῳ>, were already spoken as long [a:, ε:, ɔ:] since the second century BCE,[28] the original diphthong <ου> had been pronounced [u:] since classical time.

These developments of Greek pronunciation lead to the following assumptions for the Koine Greek of the Pauline churches that are adopted for this study:

<β>	perhaps still labial [β] or already labiodental [v/f], but [b] after nasals
<δ>	perhaps still [d] or already [ð], but [d] after nasals
<γ>	perhaps still [g] or already [ɣ], but [g] after nasals, before [i] fricative [j], before velars [ŋ]
<φ>	[f]
<θ>	probably still [t], sometimes already [θ]
<χ>	probably still [k], sometimes already [x]
<ζ>	[z]
final <ν>	assimilated to the consonant of the following word (e.g., <ν β> → [mb], <ν κ> → [ŋk], <ν σ> → [ss], <εν στ> → [e st], <ν ρ> → [rr])
spir. asper	spoken as [h] only in an upper register of language
<α, ᾳ>	[a]
<ε, η, ῃ>	[e]
<αι>	[ɛ]
<ι, ει>	[i], <ι> before vowel with glide [j]
<ο, ω, ῳ>	[o]
<ου>	[u]
<υ, οι, υι>	[y]
<αυ>	[aβ, av/af], the fricative voiced before vowel or voiced consonant
<ευ>	[eβ, ev/ef], the fricative voiced before vowel or voiced consonant

26. Ibid., 80; Joseph, "Early Movement towards Modern Greek," 696; Horrocks, Greek, 163.

27. Allen, Vox Graeca, 80–81; Joseph, "Early Movement towards Modern Greek," 697.

28. Allen, Vox Graeca, 84.

Beginning perhaps already in the fourth century BCE with less educated or foreign speakers, the Greek language lost its differentiation of long and short vowels and heavy and light syllables.[29] This resulted later in a complete change of Greek prosody from tonal accent to stress accent.[30] This development is visible in writing around 100 CE, but was not finished before the third or fourth century CE.[31] We assume that in the Pauline churches the ordinary speech did not differentiate between long and short syllables. However, in an upper register of speech people were still able to appreciate the rhythmic value of classical metric language.[32]

Delimitation of the Passage and Methodical Considerations

After the letter opening (1:1–2), Paul describes his relationship with the Philippians by expressing thankfulness and prayer wishes (1:3–11). It follows a section in which Paul speaks about his imprisonment, how his situation influences the proclamation of Christ and how he himself relates to his uncertain future (1:12–20). At the end of this section, Paul goes through the possible results of his trial, either death or release from prison, and assesses them in view of himself and of his churches (21–26).

Verse 26 finishes Paul's reflection on his fate. The word μόνον, the first word in verse 27, serves as a boundary marker introducing a new train of thought. It signals that Paul leaves behind the wavering between the two future ways, namely, death or further work for the benefit of his converts, and turns to another subject that is less ambivalent than his fate but has only (μόνον) one clear concern.[33] Of course, Paul's undecided future continues

---

29. Devine and Stephens, *Prosody*, 215.

30. Malikouti-Drachman, "Phonology," 541–44.

31. Allen, *Vox Graeca*, 93–94, 130–31.

32. On Greek meter, see Kazasis, "Ancient Greek Meter," 1033–144. He states (p. 1034): "In the case of Ancient Greek, which displayed 'prosody'—i.e., rhythm of a quantitative nature—from its origins up until the fourth century AD, these relations involved an interplay of long and short syllables . . . There is no evidence whatsoever for a 'dynamic' (or stress-) accent (roughly corresponding to Latin *ictus*) exercising a structural influence on the Greek prosodic verse before the imperial period. With the radical change in the language occurring from the fourth century AD onwards, the distinction between long and short gradually recedes, and accentuation, denuded of its musical quality, turned into a dynamic, i.e., simple acoustic, emphasis."

33. For Lohmeyer, *Philipper*, 73, the μόνον seems not to be related to the context ("beziehungslos"). But then he concludes that the μόνον emphasizes the only thing that counts. Also according to Müller, *Philipper*, 72, the μόνον refers to that what is solely important: Christian conduct. Both do not refer to the ambivalence in Phil 1:21–26 as

to bother him. The new subject does not fully erase all thoughts that Paul employed before. Whether he will see the Philippians or not is still an open alternative in his mind, as 1:27 and, later, 2:12 indicate. And his possible death is again in view in 2:17. However, in none these instances does Paul resume the deliberation of his future.

It is a feature of good rhetoric to avoid jumping from one subject to the next in hard and sudden changes and instead to glide smoothly into the next section of a speech. This is realized by referring to the pride of the Philippians in Christ in verse 26 (καύχημα) that indirectly refers forward to their conduct worthy of the gospel of Christ (v. 27: ἀξίως). Inversely, by mentioning the two possible future ways in verse 27 Paul refers back to the previous section.

The end of the passage is clearly marked by the fourfold repetition of joy (χαίρω/συγχαίρω) in 2:17-18. Already the previous section was closed by reference to joy in faith and pride in Christ (1:25-26).[34] Paul places the two verbs χαίρω and συγχαίρω, the latter with its dative object, in a parallelism, thereby forming a closing formula.

In 2:19, Paul changes from exhortations to recommendations for two of his co-workers, Timothy and Epaphroditus, whom he plans to send to the Philippians. This change in genre indicates the beginning of a new section of the letter. Again, the move to this section is not without connections to the previous part. Especially the recommendation of Timothy as a worker who seeks not after his own interests but Christ's (2:20-21) refers back to 2:4-5. But also Epaphroditus is recommended because of his willingness to risk his own life for the work of Christ and the service to Paul (v. 30). Thus Timothy and Epaphroditus become models for the attitude that Paul pushes in 2:1-11.[35]

---

cause for the μόνον.

34. Joy continues to function as signal of turning from one subject to the next, often marking the beginning of a new section (3:1; 4:1; 4:4; 4:10).

35. On a discussion of this delimitation of the section 1:27—2:18, see Wojtkowiak, *Christologie*, 124-27. He sees 1:27-30 as general and abstract admonition, 2:1-4 as the corresponding concrete guidelines. He takes the thematic parallels between 1:27-30 and 2:12-18 as evidence that they belong to one exhortative section. Walter, *Philipper*, 51, however, realizes the break between 1:30 and 2:1, because in the previous section the apostle is concerned with outside influence, "jetzt geht der Blick nach innen." However, both authors do not consider sound and language but argue almost solely with aspects of content. Holloway, *Philippians*, 38-40, 102-3, takes the section 1:27—2:16 as a "hortatory digression" that is inserted in the consolatory argument 1:22 to 2:18. "It was typical of ancient consolation to include exhortation" (p. 82). For him, 2:17-18 resume the consolation from 1:26. Holloway takes 2:16b with the *geminatio* of εἰς κενὸν as a "modest clausula" (pp. 130, 135) that ends the thought that began at 2:12. But is the break between 2:16 and 2:17 strong enough to signal the end of the whole section

Structure is created by repetition.[36] We study now the auditory features of the passage in order to understand if its sound will reveal its inner structure, the emphasized thoughts, and Paul's overall concern.

Sound will be investigated under several aspects. First, at the level of the colon, we will look for salient features of the sound of the syllables. These are vowel repetitions (*assonance*) and vowel patterns, as well as consonant repetitions (*alliteration*) and their patterns. Also, inflectional endings or repeated words can result in repetition of sounds. Additionally, the speaker can select words or opt for a certain word sequence that can create or amplify a sound pattern.[37] Not only the sound but also the rhythm of the colon is of interest. Is there a *caesura* in the line? Is there a noticeable succession of stressed and unstressed syllables? Is there perhaps a reminiscence of Greek language meter that creates rhythm?[38]

We then transcend the level of a single colon and compare the sounds of adjacent cola. Are there repetitions at the onsets of cola or at their ends (rhyme)? Are there repeated endings, words, phrases, sound patterns or rhythms? This will reveal all forms of parallelism.

If we enlarge the scope further and include groups of cola we can determine chains, frames, and chiasms. Comparing cola length reveals deviations that can indicate introductions, terminating lines (e.g., short or extended final sentences), inserted cola, or emphasis. Are there cola deviating in rhythm or style that could indicate climax or period ending? This way, periods can be delimitated.

This study does not provide an exegesis of the passage. However, the results of the investigation into sound will be confronted with the semantical content of the passage. The question is, whether the sound pattern

---

that starts from 1:27? The fact that 2:17–18 could easily follow after 1:26 (p. 39) is no proof that what stands in between is a digression or insertion but could also signal that both sections have the same aim and lead to the same conclusion. Paul speaks of the Philippians' χαρά and καύχημα in 1:25–26 and of his own χαρά and καύχημα in 2:16–17 and the χαρά of the Philippians in v. 18. This holds 2:16–18 closer together than the "modest clausula" could separate them. It parallels the endings of two sections instead of framing a digression.

36. See Lee and Scott, *Sound Mapping*, 141–45.

37. On some aspects of meaning carried by sound, see Seal, "Sensitivity," 41–44.

38. Normal speech in the first century CE would probably not—like classical Greek—distinguish between long and short vowels or heavy and light syllables. Among the educated, however, a return to the classical Greek language style and literature was part of a repristination of the cultural heritage in the first and second century CE (Second Sophistic). See Kazazis, "Atticism," 1200–212. Using the meter of Classical Greek would lend a grand sound to the speech and add to its solemnity. However, the effort payed only under the condition, that there had been not too few in the audience who at least were able to recognize metrical verses.

supports the meaning, changes it, or contradicts it. Especially the delimitation of periods, the structure of cola and periods, and their emphases have the potential to clarify semantically ambiguous expressions. It would also be possible that the sound level of the language reveals a substructure of the utterance that can have an additional emotional meaning or even deny the surface meaning.

Unit 1

Unit 1
Period 1
1:27 1.1.1 Μόνον ἀξίως τοῦ εὐαγγελίου τοῦ Χριστοῦ πολιτεύεσθε
  1.1.2 ἵνα εἴτε ἐλθὼν καὶ ἰδὼν ὑμᾶς
  1.1.3 εἴτε ἀπὼν ἀκούω τὰ περὶ ὑμῶν
  1.1.4 ὅτι στήκετε ἐν ἑνὶ πνεύματι
  1.1.5 μιᾷ ψυχῇ συναθλοῦντες τῇ πίστει τοῦ εὐαγγελίου
Period 2
28 1.2.1 καὶ μὴ πτυρόμενοι ἐν μηδενὶ ὑπὸ τῶν ἀντικειμένων
  1.2.2 ἥτις ἐστὶν αὐτοῖς ἔνδειξις ἀπωλείας
  1.2.3 ὑμῶν δὲ σωτηρίας
  1.2.4 καὶ τοῦτο ἀπὸ θεοῦ
Period 3
29 1.3.1 ὅτι ὑμῖν ἐχαρίσθη τὸ ὑπὲρ Χριστοῦ
  1.3.2 οὐ μόνον τὸ εἰς αὐτὸν πιστεύειν
  1.3.3 ἀλλὰ καὶ τὸ ὑπὲρ αὐτοῦ πάσχειν
30 1.3.4 τὸν αὐτὸν ἀγῶνα ἔχοντες
  1.3.5 οἷον εἴδετε ἐν ἐμοὶ
  1.3.6 καὶ νῦν ἀκούετε ἐν ἐμοί

Period 1.1

The first colon starts with the repeated sound [o] (μόνον) and ends with the repetition of [e] (-εύεσθε [-e-ves-te]). In the center, we find a pattern that is repeated four times—even though the fourth has only half of it: The front vowel [i] is followed by two back vowels [o] or [u] connected with [t]. The syllable λι constitutes the beginning of the second and fourth instance:

  1.1.1 (1)-ξίως τοῦ ... (2)-λίου τοῦ (3)Χριστοῦ πο(4)λιτ-

Moreover, that the verb is placed at the end is a deviation from the normal word order of Koine Greek.[39] This results in an elevated and euphonious colon with four evenly distributed stressed words. If it is spoken

---

39. Horrocks, "Syntax," 621–22. See Blass, Debrunner, Rehkopf (=BDR), §§472–78.

according to classical prosody it comes close to a *katalectic anapaestic tetrameter*.⁴⁰

1.1.1   Μόνον ἀξίως τοῦ εὐαγγελίου τοῦ Χριστοῦ πολιτεύεσθε
         ᴗ ᴗ ‒ ‒   ‒ , ‒ ‒   ᴗ ᴗ ‒,   ‒   ‒   ‒   ᴗ ᴗ, ‒ ‒   ᴗ

This beautifully shaped colon is a grand opening for a greater section of speech.⁴¹ It functions as a summary of what will follow, i.e., like a rhetorical *propositio*.⁴²

The two following cola are parallel by the repeated word εἴτε, the participles ἐλθών and ἀπών, the verbs of perception (ὁράω, ἀκούω), and the pronoun second person plural. The vowels [i] (ἵνα, εἴτε, ἰδών, περί) and [o] dominate, the vowel [a] can be found in the first line at the beginning and end, in the second line three times in the middle. At the end of both cola the penultimate syllable has the additional sound [y]. The first colon is introduced by ἵνα, the second line is prolonged by τὰ περί.

1.1.2   ἵνα εἴτε ἐλθὼν καὶ ἰδὼν ὑμᾶς
1.1.3   εἴτε ἀπὼν ἀκούω τὰ περὶ ὑμῶν

This results in a rhythm of four stressed syllables following one or two unstressed ones.⁴³ Each line has hiatuses that make the utterance of the cola somewhat halted,⁴⁴ thereby giving time for deliberation:

1.1.2   ἵνα **εἴ**τε ἐλ**θὼν** καὶ ἰ**δὼν** ὑ**μᾶς**
        [i-na*i-te*el-tʰon-kɛ*iðo-ny-**mas**]

1.1.3   **εἴ**τε ἀ**πὼν** ἀ**κού**ω τὰ πε**ρὶ** ὑ**μῶν**
        [i-te*a-**po**-na-**ku***o-ta-pe-ri*y-**mon**]

---

40. The sign – denotes a heavy syllable, ᴗ a light syllable, x denotes a syllable that can be heavy or light, ᴗ ᴗ indicates two light syllables that replace a heavy one, comma marks the end of the meter, and * indicates hiatus. In the *anapaestic* foot (ᴗ ᴗ –), the heavy syllable can be replaced by two light ones and vice versa. The [i] in ἀξίως could be reduced to a glide [j] in order to avoid hiatus (Devine and Stephens, *Prosody*, 255), the first two short syllables of πολιτεύεσθε are taken here together and replace the second long syllable of the third *anapaest*, which is somewhat unusual. The last meter is *katalectic*, i.e., incomplete. On Greek prosody, see also BDR §487.

41. Lohmeyer, *Philipper*, 74, speaks of a "gewisse Getragenheit des Tons."

42. See Friedrich, *Philipper*, 146: "Überschrift"; Holloway, *Philippians*, 103: "thematic exhortation"; O'Brien, *Philippians*, 143. Brucker, *Christushymnen*, 294, takes the whole unit 1:27–30 as the *propositio* of the whole letter.

43. Syllables in bold face indicate stress.

44. Lee and Scott, *Sound Mapping*, 234: hiatus "draws attention to what comes next." See also Drettas, "Septuagint," 893.

Sound's Message of Philippians 1:27—2:18

If the two cola are spoken according to classical meter they both have 2½ *iambic* meter (x – ∪ –), the second one shortened at the beginning.[45]

1.1.2 ἵνα εἴτε ἐλθὼν καὶ ἰδὼν ὑμᾶς
       (∪∪)– ∪ –, x – ∪ –, ∪ –

1.1.3 εἴτε ἀπὼν ἀκούω τὰ περὶ ὑμῶν
       –(∪∪) –, ∪ (– –) ∪ ∪ ∪, ∪ –

The two cola are marked by the four occurrences of the ending -ων. However, in colon 3 the ending only once indicates a participle present. Colon 3 has the only finite verbal form of the parallel cola: ἀκούω. In a compound sentence with several participles, the finite verb denotes the most important action of the whole construction. This indicates that Paul, while dictating these words, has in mind his absence, not his coming to the Philippians. We detect here that sound structure and grammatical form of these two cola contradict the semantic message of the immediately preceding period.[46] There Paul displays great confidence that he will soon come and see the Philippians (πεποιθὼς οἶδα ὅτι μενῶ καὶ παραμενῶ πᾶσιν ὑμῖν ... διὰ τῆς ἐμῆς παρουσίας πάλιν πρὸς ὑμᾶς). Why does Paul presuppose his absence only one sentence later? Was it a short-lived enthusiasm that led Paul to formulate 1:25–26? Was it a concession to the needs of the Philippians that he revokes in verse 27 because the "far better" option (1:23) gained the upper hand again? Or did Paul think in this moment that it would overcharge the Philippians if he frankly spoke of his death? Did he postpone the discussion of this possible fate until 2:17–18?[47] In any case, the language reveals a tension in the speaker.

The next two cola have a different sound pattern.

1.1.4 ὅτι στήκετε ἐν ἑνὶ πνεύματι
1.1.5 μιᾷ ψυχῇ συναθλοῦντες τῇ πίστει τοῦ εὐαγγελίου

The dominant [o] sound has disappeared and [e] and [i] prevail. The beginning is specially marked. It has four stop consonants and a hiatus (ὅτι στήκετε* ἐν). The verb ending of the imperative plural (στήκετε) picks up the ending of the verb at the end of the first colon (πολιτεύεσθε). Thus the

---

45. The light syllable of the *iambus* (∪ –) can be replaced with two light syllables at certain places. The heavy syllable can be replaced by two light ones (∪ ∪). The long vowels of ἀκούω are perhaps drawn together to one syllable.

46. See Betz, *Apostel*, 30, who senses the tension, but does not give an explanation.

47. Thus Holloway, *Philippians*, 39: "This would be a distressing thought for the Philippians at this point in time, so Paul warms to the topic slowly." However, that the meter gets irregular at the moment when it contradicts what Paul uttered a few seconds earlier is easier to explain as an inner tension than as a deliberately chosen pedagogical means. O'Brien, *Philippians*, 148–49, resorts to the explanation that Paul has in mind his future travel to other churches that will prevent him from seeing the Philippians.

beginning of colon 4 forms a bridge to colon 1 and manifests that the parallel cola 2 and 3 are an insertion.

Colon 5 is in part semantically parallel to the previous one (ἐν ἑνὶ πνεύματι ‖ μιᾷ ψυχῇ). It is also acoustical parallel by the voiceless labial stop [p] in the onset of the parallel words (π̲νεύματι ‖ ψ̲υχῇ). This parallelism is underlined by the repeated sound sequence [i] [e] in both cola:

    1.1.4 ὅτι στήκετε ἐν ἑνὶ πνεύματι
    1.1.5 μιᾷ ψυχῇ συναθλοῦντες τῇ πίστει τοῦ εὐαγγελίου.

However, the second colon of this parallelism has the additional sounds of the vowels [y] and [u]. In addition, it is prolonged exactly with the six syllables of the expression τοῦ* εὐαγγελίου. This expression is set off against the context by hiatus. This way the end of colon 5 takes up another part of the first colon, forming a frame that encompasses the five cola and at the same time reinforces the bridge over cola 2 and 3 in a chiastic manner:

    1.1.1 Μόνον ἀξίως τοῦ εὐαγγελίου τοῦ Χριστοῦ
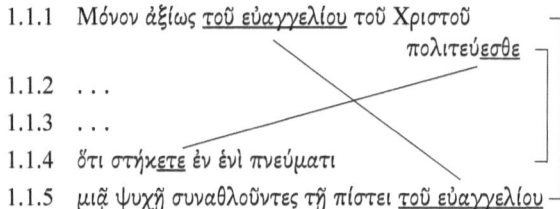
                                          πολιτεύεσθε
    1.1.2 ...
    1.1.3 ...
    1.1.4 ὅτι στήκετε ἐν ἑνὶ πνεύματι
    1.1.5 μιᾷ ψυχῇ συναθλοῦντες τῇ πίστει τοῦ εὐαγγελίου

What is the effect of the insertion of cola 2 and 3? It relates Paul's exhortation to himself as a person, no matter if he is present or absent. The first colon has related the behavior of the Philippians to the *gospel* (ἀξίως τοῦ εὐαγγελίου). The final colon does the same, but in the middle, Paul refers to *himself*, reminds of his unsafe status, and indirectly claims authority to determine the conduct of the Philippians.[48] We will return to this feature below.

Colon 5 has a finalizing value. This is marked by the frame[49] and by the elongation of the last colon.[50] We can consider verse 27 as the first period of our passage.

    48. For Holloway, *Philippians*, 104–5, the wish to hear from the other party is a sign of the consolatory letter genre. The authors regularly include the wish to receive information about the absent friends in order to find consolation themselves. Thus a good report from Philippi will give consolation to Paul. But the fact that Paul speaks repeatedly about the dependence of his joy (2:4.12.17) and even his success in God's judgment (2:16) on the Philippians' obedience seems to require an explanation that is not based on the genre of the letter but on Paul's role as apostle.

    49. Lee and Scott, *Sound Mapping*, 110, call it rounding.

    50. Lengthening or shortening of a colon are means to mark the end of a period. See Holloway, *Philippians*, 40–42, on "Paul's paragraphing."

Period 1.2

No major break is established between the last colon of the first period and the first colon of the next period. The colon is connected to the previous one with the conjunction καὶ and continues with a second participle μὴ πτυρόμενοι that is dependent on the imperative στήκετε.

Also the sound pattern of the next two cola continues with the succession of [e]/[ε] (mid open vowels) and [i] supplemented by [y] (closed front vowels, one not rounded, the other rounded). This indicates that the second period is still part of the first main unit.

    1.2.1   καὶ μὴ πτυρόμενοι ἐν μηδενὶ ὑπὸ τῶν ἀντικειμένων
           [kɛ-me-pty-ro-me-ny*en-me-de-ni]   [an-ti-ki-me-non]

    1.2.2   ἥτις ἐστὶν αὐτοῖς ἔνδειξις ἀπωλείας
           [e-ti-ses-ti-nav-ty-sen-dik-sis]

The length of the first colon (note that the sound pattern [e] [y/i] occurs four times in this colon, in the next only two times), the strong word πτύρομαι ("be terrified") and the doubling of the negation μὴ together with the negative prefix ἀντι all indicate emotional involvement. Paul's exhortation is markedly colored by his own experience of opposition, not only from non-Christian authorities that took him captive but also from fellow Christians that agitated against him (Phil 1:15-17). Paul himself decided not to give room to negative feelings but to rejoice that the gospel is being advanced. He even cements his decision to be filled with joy for the future (1:18), probably knowing that future experiences of antagonists will endanger his victory over bad feelings. Here, Paul's own emotional struggle is revealed by sound and by his choice of words. It gives his message vividness and authenticity.

The second colon, still displaying the same vowel pattern, features a new consonantal sound. While colon 1 has no *phonem* /s/, colon 2 has six /s/, often alternating with dental stops [t] and [d].[51] The consonant <σ> was considered to be the symbol of the most unpleasant sound by Dionysios of Halicarnassos.[52] The negative content of this colon is underlined by the hissing sound that is additionally enforced by the many front vowels [i] and [y].

    1.2.2   ἥτις ἐστὶν αὐτοῖς ἔνδειξις ἀπωλείας

---

    51. Voiced stop after nasal was not fricative in the Koine: <νδ> is spoken [nd].

    52. *On literary composition*, 14. However, the <σ> could also have been rejected because the letter's form <Σ> reminded of a snake. Gurd, *Dissonance*, 105-7: "It is not the sound of the sigma but its symbolic associations that make the sigma 'bad'" (p. 106).

The third colon is parallel to the previous one through the personal pronouns (αὐτοῖς and ὑμῶν) and the words describing the final outcome (ἀπωλείας and σωτηρίας). These last words have natural emphasis in the sentence. Both are additionally parallel by rhyme (liquid and [ijas]). But at the same time they display a sharp contrast, not only semantically but also pertaining to sound. The [e] [i] vowel pattern is broken off by [o] sounds and the colon is drastically shorter.

1.2.3 ὑμῶν δὲ σωτηρίας

The speaker will slow down the pace of utterance to give the third colon with 7 syllables approximately the same time as the second one with 13 syllables. This makes this colon especially impressive. Paul strengthens the Philippians' certainty of their salvation even in times of hardship and hostility.

It follows an additional short colon, again with 7 syllables, that has no front vowels, but two [u] sounds at the beginning and the end. It has only stop consonants and hiatus.

1.2.4 καὶ τοῦτο* ἀπὸ θεοῦ

This lets the speaker set words emphatically side by side.[53] Although the Philippians are exhorted to conduct their life according to the gospel and stand firmly together on the battle field, their victory is the work of God. The short colon has a closing quality and marks the end of the second period. Its sound quality and its semantic content qualify it to trigger a response of the audience, perhaps an "Amen."

Period 1.3

The next period starts with an introductory colon that sets out to substantiate Paul's advice about how to live in the face of hostility. The colon has a *caesura* that is established by a repetition of sound. The first word, ὅτι, corresponds to the article τό with the same sounds [t] and [o]. It is followed by the vowel <υ>. The following words have several consonants and vowels in common—the correlation is even stronger if <θ> was still pronounced as a stop. The rhythm of the colon is *anapaestic*: first a *pherecrateus* (x x - ⏑ ⏑ - x), then an *anapaest*. The language becomes rhythmic, similar to the first colon of the first period (1:27).

1.3.1 ὅτ' ὑμῖν ἐχαρίσθη | τὸ ὑπὲρ Χριστοῦ
       ⏑ ⏑ - ⏑ ⏑ - -, ⏑ ⏑ -   - -

---

53. Lee and Scott, *Sound Mapping*, 234.

Both parts of the colon have positive connotations. Besides the rhythm, the reference to Christ also refers back to the beginning of the first period. The verb ἐχαρίσθη is divine passive[54] and takes up the last colon of the second period: τοῦτο ἀπὸ θεοῦ. Repeating previous features is typical for final parts of speech. The audience becomes prepared for a closing of a unit of speech.

Two parallel cola follow. Cola 2 and 3 are parallel in the article to the infinitive; the hiatus after the article that sets the verbal phrase off from the opening of the colon, creating expectation; the third person singular pronoun after a preposition; the *alliteration* <π> in the onset of the verb; and the infinitive verbal ending forming rhyme (*homoioteleuton*).[55]

The poetic language continues and underlines the parallel. Both cola start with a *trochaic* meter and have then, after a hiatus, a *spondaic trimeter* (with the second colon *catalectic*).

1.3.2 οὐ μόνον τὸ* εἰς αὐτὸν πιστεύειν
       − ∪ − ∪, − −, − −, − −

1.3.3 ἀλλὰ καὶ τὸ* ὑπὲρ αὐτοῦ πάσχειν
       − ∪ − ∪, ∪ ∪ −, − −, −

The parallelism is comparative. The enhancing phrase, οὐ μόνον . . . ἀλλὰ καί, and the shortening of the second colon both place special emphasis on the last infinitive, πάσχειν. Together with the meaning of the main verb χαρίζομαι in the first colon that carries very positive connotations, the parallelism results in a paradox: suffering becomes something positive.[56] The special beauty of the language of these cola underlines the positive value. The hiatus before ὑπὲρ might even arrest the utterance for a moment and enhance the force of the paradox in the perception of the listeners.

The fourth colon comments on the paradox of "positive suffering." Again we have a beautiful metrical structure, a *dactylic trimeter*.

1.3.4 τὸν αὐτὸν ἀγῶνα* ἔχοντες
       (∪) − ∪ ∪, − ∪ ∪, − ∪

The sound structure links this colon to the previous cola of this period: the word αὐτόν of the two previous cola is repeated. The vowels alternate very regularly between stressed [o] and unstressed [a]: τὸν αὐτὸν ἀγῶνα. Both vowels have been prominent in the parallel cola standing before, the [o] especially in μόνον, the [a] in ἀλλὰ.

---

54. Holloway, *Philippians*, 108 n.35.
55. See BDR §§488–94 for several figures of expression.
56. Wick, "Ahmt Christus nach," 318: The gracious gift of suffering has the promise of reward in the same way as the suffering of Christ was rewarded by God through exaltation in 2:9–11.

The verb ἔχοντες refers back to the verb ἐχαρίσθη in the first colon because of the sound [ekʰ] (or already fricative [ex]) forming a frame around the parallel cola 2 and 3. So far we have found in the middle of each period a pair of parallel lines (1.1.2 || 1.1.3; 1.2.2 || 1.2.3; 1.3.2 || 1.3.3). The short colon 4 could well be the final colon of this period.

However, two more parallel cola are added. The parallelism is obvious from the exact agreement of the endings with as many as five equal syllables (*homoioteleuton*). Both cola have the vowel [y] (<υ> and <οι>) at the beginning and the end, echoing the two [y] in the first colon (ὑμῖν and ὑπὲρ). The two cola have *dactylic dimeters*, the first incomplete. After a hiatus, both dimeters are followed by an *anapaest*.

1.3.5 οἷον   εἴδετε*   ἐν ἐμοὶ
      ‒ ◡,   ‒ ◡ ◡,   ◡ ◡ ‒

1.3.6 καὶ νῦν ἀκούετε* ἐν ἐμοί
      ‒ ◡   ◡, ‒ ◡ ◡, ◡ ◡ ‒

This additional parallelism closes the whole speech unit consisting of three periods. The third period repeats many features of the first, forming a frame for the whole unit.[57] The second person plural ending -ετε in 3.5 and 3.6 refers back to the verbal endings that we have in cola 1.1 and 1.4 in the first period. Christ is mentioned as the foundation of the conduct of the believers in 1.1 and 3.1. The Philippians should live worthy of the gospel of Christ (1.1) they have heard and adopted and should realize that their sufferings are for Christ's sake (3.1). But both periods refer also to Paul. In the first period (1.2 and 1.3), Paul used a parallelism with the verbs ὁράω and ἀκούω to refer to his own fate. At the end (3.5 and 3.6) he returns to these verbs in the same order and speaks about his own experience of hardships. The Philippians should act worthy of the gospel for his sake (1.1–1.3) and should rejoice in suffering following his example (3.4–3.6).

That Paul repeatedly places Christ and himself—in this order—side by side in his explanatory statements given to the receivers of his letter reveals an important aspect of how he sees himself and his role as an apostle. The information about the gospel of Christ needs to be accompanied by a witness that embodies the faith that the gospel creates. To know about Christ is not enough. One needs someone to follow and to emulate. That does not mean that the witness must be without fault. Paul does not hesitate to speak of his weaknesses. This makes him a witness of Christ's forgiveness and of Christ's strength in a weak vessel.[58]

---

57. See Brucker, *Christushymnen*, 295.

58. Wick, "Ahmt Christus nach," 318–19: Paul presents himself as someone who—together with many others—imitates the selflessness of Christ described in the Christ hymn and invites the Philippians to become part of this network of imitators of Christ (3:17).

Unit 2

Unit 2
Period 1
2:1	2.1.1	Εἴ τις οὖν παράκλησις ἐν Χριστῷ
	2.1.2	εἴ τι παραμύθιον ἀγάπης
	2.1.3	εἴ τις κοινωνία πνεύματος
	2.1.4	εἴ τις σπλάγχνα καὶ οἰκτιρμοί

Period 2
2	2.2.1	πληρώσατέ μου τὴν χαρὰν
	2.2.2	ἵνα τὸ αὐτὸ φρονῆτε
	2.2.3	τὴν αὐτὴν ἀγάπην ἔχοντες
	2.2.4	σύμψυχοι, τὸ ἓν φρονοῦντες

Period 3
3	2.3.1	μηδὲν κατ' ἐριθείαν
	2.3.2	μηδὲ κατὰ κενοδοξίαν
	2.3.3	ἀλλὰ τῇ ταπεινοφροσύνῃ ἀλλήλους ἡγούμενοι ὑπερέχοντας ἑαυτῶν
4	2.3.4	μὴ τὰ ἑαυτῶν ἕκαστος σκοποῦντες
	2.3.5	ἀλλὰ τὰ ἑτέρων ἕκαστοι

Period 2.1

The next period comes with a solemn language,[59] a new style,[60] but the οὖν refers back to the previous unit.[61] Four cola start with the same words εἴ τι(ς) (*anapher*) and form a beautiful parallelism. They share the same sounds: /p/ occurs at the onset of one of the main words in each colon and the [i] vowel (<ι> and <ει>) is prominent, not only at the beginning of each colon [itis], but throughout. It is complemented with the vowels [a] and [y] (<υ> and <οι>). Note the middle position of [y] in the second and third cola, but the end position in the fourth colon. All four cola are approximately of the same length, but they shorten at the end (10, 10, 9, 8 syllables). At the same time, the last colon, although it is the shortest, has a doubling of terms, while the others have only one term with an attribute. This indicates final position in this parallelism. The meter is irregular. However, each colon has two nouns bearing stress. The first and the last cola have the last syllable stressed, while the second and third end with unstressed syllables. This cre-

---

59. Brucker, *Christushymnen*, 307, speaks of a "gehobenen Stil."
60. O'Brien, *Philippians*, 164, speaks of a "rhythmical or lyrical style."
61. See Lohmeyer, *Philipper*, 81. However, he divides the unit in five periods of three cola each and sees in the first three cola a Trinitarian formula: Christ, Love (of God), and Pneuma (82).

ates a framing effect, tying together the four cola to one period.⁶² The language is solemn.

2.1.1 εἴ τις οὖν παράκλησις ἐν Χριστῷ
2.1.2 εἴ τι παραμύθιον ἀγάπης
2.1.3 εἴ τις κοινωνία πνεύματος
2.1.4 εἴ τις σπλάγχνα καὶ οἰκτιρμοί

Period 2.2

The whole second unit consists of only one sentence. The second period starts with a colon that has the main verb of the clause: πληρώσατε. This imperative connects the colon back to the imperatives of the first period of the first unit (1.1.1 and 1.1.4). The colon is beautifully regular. If it is pronounced with a stress accent it has stressed and unstressed syllables alternating regularly. However, if it was presented by a native Greek speaker in a more elevated register, it would have been spoken according to Greek prosody. The meter has two *ionic maior* feet:

2.2.1 πληρώσατέ μου τὴν χαρὰν
      ‒ ‒ ⏑ ⏑,   ‒ ‒ ⏑ ⏑

The next three cola are closely connected with the first one by repeated sounds. The first and second cola both have [o] and the second person plural verbal ending (-ατε and -ητε). The second and third cola both have the pronoun αὐτός/αὐτή; the second and fourth cola both have the verb φρονεῖν. The vowels [a] and [e] are the dominant sounds in colon 3, but are also important in the second half of colon 1. Cola 3 and 4 rhyme ([-ontes]/[-untes]). The four interconnected cola form a period. The final colon is especially marked by the sound [y], repeated three times in the word σύμψυχοι. Additionally, the last colon closes with a *trochaeic meter*.⁶³

2.2.4 σύμψυχοι, τὸ ἓν φρονοῦντες
      (‒ ‒ ‒) ⏑,‒   ⏑ ‒ ⏑

Thus the regular meter that we find in colon 2.2.1 and the meter at the end of 2.2.4 form a frame for the whole period, while the cola are interconnected by sound, rhyme, and words.

---

62. Wojtkowiak, *Christology*, 127, takes 2:1–4 as the concrete application of the general admonitions 1:27–30 and 2:12–18.

63. On the connection of the word σύμψυχοι with this colon see Gnilka, *Philipperbrief*, 102; Wojtkowiak *Christologie*, 134 n.65; differently Brucker, *Christushymnen*, 306.

2.2.1 πληρώσατέ μου τὴν χαρὰν	[-osate]	[a] [e]	meter
2.2.2 ἵνα τὸ <u>αὐτὸ</u> <u>φρονῆτε</u>	[-onete] αὐτό		φρονεῖν
2.2.3 τὴν <u>αὐτὴν</u> ἀγάπην <u>ἔχοντες</u>	αὐτή [-ontes] [a] [e]		
2.2.4 σύμψυχοι τὸ ἓν <u>φρονοῦντες</u>	[-untes]		φρονεῖν meter

It is remarkable that this period displays no parallelism. In the first unit, each period had at least one parallelism, often antithetical, reflecting that Paul is concerned with alternatives: his coming or not coming to the Philippians, salvation or destruction, believing and suffering. In the second unit, we found a fourfold synonymous parallelism in the first period, describing what the Philippians have in Christ. The cola of this second period, however, are related to each other through interconnectedness. The language performs what Paul wants the Philippians to be: despite their diversity being connected to each other in harmony and love.

Period 2.3

The third period has five cola and continues the description of what it means to be of the same mind. The participles connect this period with the previous one by rhythm and by their endings: ἡγούμεν<u>οι</u> refers back to σύμψυχ<u>οι</u>, σκοπ<u>οῦντες</u> to φρον<u>οῦντες</u>. Additionally, the participle ἔχοντες from cola 1.3.4 and 2.2.3 is taken up and superelevated to ὑπερέχοντας in colon 2.3.3.

Cola 1 to 3 form one opposition, cola 4 and 5 another (μὴ ... ἀλλὰ). This period has a symmetrical form with a very long colon in the middle. The first two cola form a synonym parallelism. They display the same sounds at the beginning [me-de(n)-kat-] and rhyme at the end [-ijan]. The two last cola form an antithetical parallelism. They both have similar sound at the beginning ([ta-(h)e-av-ton] || [ta-(h)e-te-ron]) followed by the word ἕκαστος. The last colon elides the verb and signals the end of the period by shortening.

The prosody of the period is not perfectly metrical. However, *trochaic* feet dominate and connect this period to the last colon of the previous period. The last colon is a perfect *trochaic dimeter*.[64]

2.3.5 ἀλλὰ τὰ ἑτέρων ἕκαστοι
− ∪ ∪∪ ∪,− ∪ − x

---

64. There is a good text tradition that has καὶ in this colon: ἀλλὰ καὶ τὰ ἑτέρων ἕκαστοι. It is missing only in some manuscripts and some Latin translations. It seems to be an early alleviation. Thus Holloway, *Philippians*, 113; differently O'Brien, *Philippians*, 164, 185.

What does the structure of this unit reveal? The first period refers to what the Philippians—more or less—have in Christ. The Greek conditional sentence introduced by the particle εἰ does not consider or even doubt whether the condition is true or not true (this would be expressed with ἐάν), it rather places the emphasis on the outcome: when a certain condition is fulfilled, you can be sure that the result that is expressed in the main clause will happen.[65] Paul's wording (οὖν) connects this period to the gospel of Christ (1.1.1) and the wealth of gifts that the Philippians have received from God (1.3.1).

Paul exhorts the Philippians to live in unity (2.2.2), but before he does so, he suggests that the conditions of the Philippians are such that their following along is almost a matter of course.[66] Paul's words do not simply describe the condition of the audience but move it into the realm of the gospel, where the expected conduct becomes possible.

Moreover, before Paul finally comes to his subject matter, he utters an exhortation that concerns himself. The Philippians are asked to make his joy perfect: πληρώσατέ μου τὴν χαράν. This imperative is the main verb in the whole period. The remarkable position of the possessive pronoun elevates the clause in a higher register. What the Philippians actually should do is hereafter expressed only in the subordinate final clause (ἵνα τὸ αὐτὸ φρονῆτε) and is unfolded with participles.

What is the result of this formulation? The desired conduct is living for the benefit of *others* (2.3.4–2.3.5). If Paul argued with the advantages of the right behavior for the audience, as many exhortations do—your life becomes peaceful, you win God's favor and prepare yourselves for his kingdom—then he would have contradicted his goal. How can the Philippians truly live for others if they are motivated by their own interests? Why should they strive to win something, if they have already so much by God's grace (period 1)? Therefore the apostle draws the audience away from their own advantages and offers himself as the first one of whose joy they should be mindful. Again, the language performs what is says: The Philippians practice or rehearse the unselfish behavior using their apostle as a first object.[67]

---

65. See BDR §371.

66. See Brucker, *Christushymnen*, 305; O'Brien, *Philippians*, 176.

67. O'Brien, *Philippians*, 176–77, is not aware of this performative language. He comments that Paul's wish in 2.2.1 is a "tactful expression" that "gives the Philippians a further motif for living in harmony."

Unit 3

Unit 3
Period 1
2:5	3.1.1	Τοῦτο φρονεῖτε ἐν ὑμῖν ὃ καὶ ἐν Χριστῷ Ἰησοῦ
6	3.1.2	ὃς ἐν μορφῇ θεοῦ ὑπάρχων
	3.1.3	οὐχ ἁρπαγμὸν ἡγήσατο τὸ εἶναι ἴσα θεῷ
7	3.1.4	ἀλλ' ἑαυτὸν ἐκένωσεν
	3.1.5	μορφὴν δούλου λαβών
	3.1.6	ἐν ὁμοιώματι ἀνθρώπων γενόμενος
	3.1.7	καὶ σχήματι εὑρεθεὶς ὡς ἄνθρωπος
8	3.1.8	ἐταπείνωσεν ἑαυτὸν
	3.1.9	γενόμενος ὑπήκοος μέχρι θανάτου
	3.1.10	θανάτου δὲ σταυροῦ

Period 2
9	3.2.1	διὸ καὶ ὁ θεὸς αὐτὸν ὑπερύψωσεν
	3.2.2	καὶ ἐχαρίσατο αὐτῷ τὸ ὄνομα τὸ ὑπὲρ πᾶν ὄνομα
10	3.2.3	ἵνα ἐν τῷ ὀνόματι Ἰησοῦ πᾶν γόνυ κάμψῃ
	3.2.4	ἐπουρανίων καὶ ἐπιγείων καὶ καταχθονίων
11	3.2.5	καὶ πᾶσα γλῶσσα ἐξομολογήσηται
	3.2.6	ὅτι κύριος Ἰησοῦς Χριστὸς
	3.2.7	εἰς δόξαν θεοῦ πατρός

This unit contains, after an introductory colon, the passage that, since Lohmeyer, has often been considered to be a traditional hymn that Paul quotes in his exhortation.[68] I take the term "hymn" in a very broad sense, not restricted to a literary piece that has exact poetic meter and strophes of the same length.[69] I do not attempt to reconstruct an "original" version of the "hymn." I adopt here the disposition of Hofius who—following Jeremias—has convincingly demonstrated that the "hymn" is structured by

---

68. Lohmeyer, *Kyrios Jesus*, 90–99.

69. Fee, "Exalted Pauline Prose," 30–34, misses these features of a hymn in Phil 2:6–11 and takes the passage as "exalted prose." This present study is not concerned with the distinction of "hymn" or "exalted prose," which also Fee himself never really explains.

Semitic parallelism and divided in two stanzas, each concluded with a short final colon.[70] The last two cola of each period rhyme (*homoioteleuton*).[71]

The introduction connects this unit to the previous one with the repetition of the verb φρονεῖν (2.2.2 and 2.2.4). The cola are interconnected by repetitions of words: μορφὴ (3.1.2 and 3.1.5), ἑαυτὸν (3.1.4 and 3.1.8), ἄνθρωπος (3.1.6 and 3.1.7), γενόμενος (3.1.6 and 3.1.9), θανάτου (3.1.9 and 3.1.10, *anadiplosis*), αὐτὸν and αὐτῷ (3.2.1 and 3.2.2), ὑπὲρ (3.2.1 and 3.2.2), ὄνομα (2x 3.2.2 and 3.2.3), Ἰησοῦ(ς) (3.2.3 and 3.2.6), πᾶν (3.2.2, 3.2.3, 3.2.5). The word θεὸς marks the beginning, center and end of the unit (3.1.2/3.1.3, 3.2.1, 3.2.7). We have also the threefold ending [-ijon] (3.2.4) and the repetition of the sound [sa] (3.2.2, 2x 3.2.5, and 3.2.7).[72]

It is remarkable that—besides repetition of words—the parallelisms are mainly semantically expressed. Repetition of phrases and sounds plays a secondary role. There is also no convincing prosodic meter in this unit.[73] Compared with the previous units with their wealth of parallelisms, sophisticated sound repetitions, and construction of frames, and with their often appearing Greek meter, this third unit is strikingly poor in its application of sound arrangement. Sometimes it has been suggested that Paul himself

---

70. Jeremias, "Gedankenführung," 274–76; Hofius, *Christushymnus*; followed by O'Brien, *Philippians*, 230. See also the detailed structure of Brucker, *Christushymnen*, 308–10. Fee, "Exalted Pauline Prose," 39–43, structures the passage according to syntax, not to sound (see also his outline on p. 46). He suggests a chiastic structure with 3.2.4 as the center and turning point. Colon 3.2.4 would thus be applicable to both of the adjoining cola. This structure, however, sets in parallel the first and last colon of this period, which are quite different in form and function. Brucker himself notes that the repetition of the name Jesus in 3.2.3 and 3.2.6 does not fit in this chiastic order.

71. On final cola in Paul's letters, i.e., *clausulae* like maxims, summaries, exclamations, wordplay, and all forms of rhetorical embellishment, see Holloway, *Philippians*, 40–42.

72. See the study of repetitions of words and sounds in Kennel, *Frühchristliche Hymnen*, 202–7.

73. See Brucker, *Christushymnen*, 311; Kennel, *Frühchristliche Hymnen*, 207–9. The attempt to establish a metrical order of the passage by Eckman, "Metrical Analysis," 258–66, is not convincing. She selects five repeated patterns of heavy and light syllables wherever they appear—or roughly appear—in the text and reconstructs from these patterns—after some emendations—an "original" hymn that is built from these five prosodic patterns. However, the five patters appear in an irregular order, the emerging very short cola often disrupt the thought. Caragounis, *Development of Greek*, 428–29, has attempted to find rhythmic pattern in Phil 2:5–7b. However, he partitions each colon in *different* feet as he finds a group of syllables matching any Greek feet. ("In the first colon the first foot is a bacchius, the second is a dactyl, while the third foot is a spondee," etc.) He does not distinguish between feet and meter. The result is not a metrical pattern of the cola, but a chaotic succession of Greek feet in each colon.

could have crafted this "hymn."[74] If he had done so, it would be difficult to explain why he did not use his rich repertoire of language forms and his creative ability of shaping aesthetically appealing cola and periods as he does in the preceding and—as we will see—following units. As a consequence, I suggest that it is not the formal quality of the Greek language of this unit but rather the lack of features of Greek lyric that indicates that Paul uses a traditional piece.[75]

Paul selects the form of a psalm for his speaking of Christ's way from heavenly harmony to death on a cross and then his exaltation to becoming the *kyrios* of all. This indicates that this unit is more than a mere description. It seems as if Paul thought it would not be apt to speak about Christ in normal descriptive language. Descriptive language presupposes a certain distance of the speaker to his or her subject. But if one speaks of Christ, impartial language is not adequate. The speaker confesses to being affected and involved by relating not only what happened but also what this means for him or her. The language of the third unit of the passage under investigation here displays many features of the speaker's personal involvement. These include, first, speaking in parallelism. It is not enough to express a fact; the fact must be illuminated from different angles (e.g., 3.1.6 and 3.1.7). Second, the speaker selects all-encompassing, drastic, or even exaggerated words (κενόω, δοῦλος, ὑπερυψόω, πᾶσα/πᾶν) or phrases (μέχρι θανάτου, θανάτου δὲ σταυρου; ἐπουρανίων καὶ ἐπιγείων καὶ καταχθονίων) indicating excitement. Third, the final short colon praises God and invites the listeners to respond with praise or an "Amen!" The language impels the presenter to speak in a way that expresses marveling and praise.

---

74. Betz, *Apostel*, 34; Fee, "Exalted Pauline Prose," 34–37; Fee, *Philippians*, 41–46; Brucker, *Christushymnen*, 311–15.

75. Mostly the argument is that this unit displays formal qualities of language that qualify it as a hymn. This is true if one assumes a Semitic background, not a Greek one. See Jeremias, "Gedankenführung"; Hofius, *Christushymnus*. Against the qualification as a hymn see Brucker, *Christushymnen*, 318–19.

Unit 4

Unit 4
Period 1
2:12   4.1.1   Ὥστε, ἀγαπητοί μου
        4.1.2   καθὼς πάντοτε ὑπηκούσατε
        4.1.3   μὴ ὡς ἐν τῇ παρουσίᾳ μου μόνον
        4.1.4   ἀλλὰ νῦν πολλῷ μᾶλλον ἐν τῇ ἀπουσίᾳ μου
        4.1.5   μετὰ φόβου καὶ τρόμου τὴν ἑαυτῶν σωτηρίαν
                                                   κατεργάζεσθε
13   4.1.6   θεὸς γάρ ἐστιν ὁ ἐνεργῶν ἐν ὑμῖν καὶ τὸ θέλειν καὶ τὸ
                                                   ἐνεργεῖν
        4.1.7   ὑπὲρ τῆς εὐδοκίας
Period 2
14   4.2.1   Πάντα ποιεῖτε χωρὶς γογγυσμῶν καὶ διαλογισμῶν
15   4.2.2   ἵνα γένησθε ἄμεμπτοι καὶ ἀκέραιοι
        4.2.3   τέκνα θεοῦ ἄμωμα μέσον γενεᾶς σκολιᾶς καὶ
                                                   διεστραμμένης
        4.2.4   ἐν οἷς φαίνεσθε ὡς φωστῆρες ἐν κόσμῳ λόγον ζωῆς
                                                   ἐπέχοντες
16b   4.2.5   εἰς καύχημα ἐμοὶ εἰς ἡμέραν Χριστοῦ
        4.2.6   ὅτι οὐκ εἰς κενὸν ἔδραμον
        4.2.7   οὐδὲ εἰς κενὸν ἐκοπίασα
Period 3
17   4.3.1   Ἀλλ' εἰ καὶ σπένδομαι ἐπὶ τῇ θυσίᾳ καὶ λειτουργίᾳ τῆς
                                                   πίστεως ὑμῶν
        4.3.2   χαίρω καὶ συγχαίρω πᾶσιν ὑμῖν
18   4.3.3   τὸ δὲ αὐτὸ καὶ ὑμεῖς χαίρετε καὶ συγχαίρετέ μοι

Period 4.1

The first colon indicates the beginning of a new unit by two features: introducing a result (ὥστε) and addressing the audience. Already in the first cola of units 1 and 2 we have found words that signal a conclusion drawn from what was said before (μόνον and οὖν).

In the third unit, mainly Christ was in view. Now the relationship of apostle and audience is evoked again. It is a relationship of love (ἀγαπητοί μου), but also of obedience (ὑπηκούσατε). A parallelism, comparable to the first unit (1.1.2 and 1.1.3), reflects Paul's absence. The parallel cola 3 and 4 of this period have a chiastic structure: in colon 3 the phrase ἐν τῇ παρουσίᾳ μου is followed by the word μόνον. In colon 4 the corresponding word μᾶλλον comes before the phrase ἐν τῇ ἀπουσίᾳ μου. Additionally, the *morphem* /m/ is prominent in the beginning and end of colon 3.[76] Colon 4 has a threefold repetition of the geminated *morphem* /l/ in connection with the vowels [a] and [o]: ἀλλὰ νῦν πολλῷ μᾶλλον. In this series of words, the word νῦν with the vowel [y], corresponding to the first colon (ἀγαπητοί), functions like a signal that demands attention. The four cola of this period, additionally held together by the prominence of the alternating vowels [a] and [o], have an ever growing number of syllables. The parallel cola 3 and 4, like a retarding factor, serve to heighten the expectation of what follows. All this creates an increasing tension.

4.1.1	Ὥστε ἀγαπητοί μου	[y]	7 syllables
4.1.2	καθὼς πάντοτε ὑπηκούσατε		10 syllables
4.1.3	μὴ ὡς ἐν τῇ παρουσίᾳ μου μόνον	[-usijamu]	11 syllables
4.1.4	ἀλλὰ νῦν πολλῷ μᾶλλον ἐν τῇ ἀπουσίᾳ μου	[y] [-usijamu]	14 syllables

The next two cola (4.1.5 and 4.1.6) lead to the climax. The number of syllables continues to increase (20 and 21). Both rhyme within the colon: φόβου καὶ τρόμου and ἐν ὑμῖν καὶ τὸ θέλειν καὶ τὸ ἐνεργεῖν [e-ny-<u>min</u> kɛ-to-θe-<u>lin</u> kɛ-to-e-ner-<u>jin</u>]—note also the increasing number of syllables in the members of this threefold rhyme.

The Greek prosody of these two cola is also revealing. The first has two regular *cretics* (– ⏑ –) at the onset, underlining the words μετὰ φόβου καὶ τρόμου. Afterwards the meter is irregular. The following colon (4.1.6) has regular meter throughout. It starts with a *jambic* meter. After a *caesura*, four *ionic* meter follow. The regular meter as well as the length of this colon indicate that it is the climax and bears the main message of this period. Hiatus before the verbs produces emphasis on ἐνεργεῖν. Only a very short colon follows (4.1.7 with 7 syllables), with two *ionic* metric feet, the second *katalectic*.[77] As often, the short colon indicates the closing of the period.

4.1.5 μετὰ φόβου καὶ τρόμου | τὴν ἑαυτῶν σωτηρίαν κατεργάζεσθε
⏑⏑ ⏑ –, – ⏑ –,

4.1.6 θεὸς γάρ ἐστιν | ὁ* ἐνεργῶν ἐν ὑμῖν καὶ τὸ θέλειν καὶ τὸ* ἐνεργεῖν
(⏑)– ⏑ – ⏑, ⏑ ⏑ – –, ⏑ ⏑ – –, ⏑ ⏑ – –, ⏑ ⏑ – –

4.1.7 ὑπὲρ τῆς εὐδοκίας.
⏑ – – –, ⏑ ⏑ –

In order to understand these cola (4.1.5 and 4.1.6) we must pay attention to what Paul emphasizes. In colon 4.1.5, Paul does not begin the

---

76. The negation μὴ is used because Paul has already the imperative in mind. The negation of a constative sentence would be οὐ. The parallel cola 4.1.3 and 4.1.4 are part of the imperative 4.1.5, they do not refer back to the obedience of the Philippians.

77. The meter is inexact. At the place of the second syllable of ὑπὲρ should be a light syllable.

sentence with the verb, which is the increasingly common word order in Koine Greek, but places μετὰ φόβου καὶ τρόμου first. Paul's concern is not that the Philippians do not end in destruction but reach salvation. His admonition is not: κατεργάζεσθε τὴν ἑαυτῶν σωτηρίαν.[78] This would contradict his confidence in 1:28 (cola 1.2.2–1.2.4). He is rather concerned with the *manner* in which they live while approaching the final goal: μετὰ φόβου καὶ τρόμου. This is in accordance with ἀξίως τοῦ εὐαγγελίου τοῦ Χριστοῦ πολιτεύεσθε in 1.1.1. Note that also in the very first colon of our passage the word ἀξίως is placed at the beginning of the sentence, emphasizing the manner in which the Philippians live their Christian life. It is to this imperative that Paul returns in 4.1.5. This indicates that we have reached the final unit. However, it is not simply a repetition. In the meantime, there has been the beautiful description of the self-humbling way and the exaltation of Christ in unit 3.

In the next colon, again the emphasis falls on the words that have the prominent place at the beginning: θεὸς γάρ ἐστιν. But there is another parallel. In both cola, the emphasized words are rhythmically separated from the rest of the colon by a *caesura*. At the *caesura*, the speaker pauses for a short moment before continuing to utter the colon. This feature results in a parallelism of the first words: fear and trembling are related to God's presence (θεὸς γάρ ἐστιν . . .). The relationship of fear and God's presence has a long tradition. Humans tremble when God comes close.[79] This is the climax, probably spoken with great solemnity: θεὸς γάρ ἐστιν ὁ ἐνεργῶν ἐν ὑμῖν. The Philippians are not only exhorted to live their Christian life in the presence of God, but the language creates an event that helps them to realize that God is with them. That does not mean that they are under God's critical observation but that they are subjects of God's activity, because the Philippians' aims and accomplishments (καὶ τὸ θέλειν καὶ τὸ ἐνεργεῖν) are all effects of God's work.

78. Brucker, *Christushymnen*, 320, understands κατεργάζεσθε and μετὰ φόβου καὶ τρόμου as referring to mission work. In his paraphrasing he gives the imperative the main stress. But Paul's concern in this colon is the salvation of the Philippians (ἑαυτῶν), not of the unbelievers. He emphasizes the closeness of God.

79. See Gnilka, *Philipperbrief*, 149, who speaks of the "Erschrockenheit von Menschen, die in die Nähe Gottes geraten sind." Wojtkowiak, *Christologie*, 161, following Pedersen, "Furcht und Zittern," 1–31 rejects this notion of God's self-revelation in this verse. Pedersen investigates the phrase "with fear and trembling" in Paul's letters and finds it applied in the context of Paul's mission as a description of his self-humiliation (1Cor 2:3) or the self-humiliation of the Corinthians (2Cor 7:15). However, these passages do not exclude the notion of an encounter with God; they rather presuppose it, as O'Brien, *Philippians*, 282–84, demonstrates. He explains φόβος καὶ τρόμος as "awe and reverence," the human reaction to God's mighty acts, however without reflecting in what way and at what time the Philippians experience the acts of God.

This is God's satisfaction and delight (4.1.7).⁸⁰ The final short line releases the tension. What a positive ending! While God is active in the Philippians, should it be a problem to obey? The last line is suitable for triggering reactions from the audience: perhaps an "Amen," a nod, or a smile.

The question arises how the awesome presence of God becomes a reality. Does Paul speak only in an abstract manner about fear and trembling? Does he imagine a relaxed and unexcited audience sitting at their places or does his letter effect reactions like trembling or thrilling?

We need to pay attention to the wording: with whom is the audience associated? The first four cola of the period reflect the relationship between the addressees and the apostle (Paul's loving address, their obedience, the absence of the apostle). The last three cola speak about the relationship between the addressees and God. In colon 5 God is indirectly in view through the effects of his presence on the addressees (φόβος καὶ τρόμος). In colon 6, however, God is explicitly mentioned at prominent place, the first word. Thus, during the period Paul recedes and God emerges. The language does to the audience what it semantically expresses.

Moreover, the exhortation of this period ties up to the previous unit (ὥστε) that proclaims Christ in a beautiful way. It is the excitement that the presenter—hopefully—has triggered in the audience with his most committed speech that is assumed to be an experience of God's presence. In other words, the proclamation of the gospel moves the audience in God's presence. Paul's admonitions are built on this foundation. God is at work in the Philippians and in the preaching of the Gospel everywhere (see Phil 1:6, 14–18).

How can Paul be sure that his letter will be presented in such an exciting way that the audience would feel the presence of God? He cannot be sure. He has no influence on the selection of the presenter.[81] The reference to Paul's absence in cola 4.1.3 and 4.1.4 serves to distance the audience from the actual performance of his letter. They are reminded that Paul is absent. They are aware of the fact that they do not listen to Paul himself but to someone who lends his voice and body to the apostle. If he is less than successful, even if he presents the letter without commitment, the audience is invited to imagine how Paul would utter the words himself.[82]

---

80. This colon speaks of God's εὐδοκία; see O'Brien, *Philippians*, 288–89; Wojtkowiak, *Christologie*, 161.

81. It is not likely that Paul's envoy who delivered the letter, in the case of Philippians most probably Epaphroditus (2:25), was also the reader. See Oestreich, *Performance Criticism*, 73–75, where the assumption is substantiated that the envoy was not the reader.

82. See Oestreich, *Performance Criticism*, 136–51.

Period 4.2

The colon starts with *alliteration* (πάντα ποιεῖτε) and ends with two words connected with καί (*hendiadys*) that form a rhyme (γογγυσμῶν καὶ διαλογισμῶν). *Alliteration* and *hendiadys* are repeated in cola 2 to 4. (*Hendiadys*: ἄμεμπτοι καὶ ἀκέραιοι, σκολιᾶς καὶ διεστραμμένης; *alliteration*: ἄμεμπτοι, ἄμωμα (διεστραμμένης); φαίνεσθε ὡς φωστῆρες.) The first words of cola 1 and 3 rhyme (πάντα, τέκνα). Additionally, some endings are repeated: γένησθε, φαίνεσθε; διεστραμμένης, φωστῆρες, ἐπέχοντες. All these sound repetitions keep the four cola together.

4.2.1	Πάντα ποιεῖτε χωρὶς γογγυσμῶν καὶ διαλογισμῶν	hend.	rhy. μων	allit. π
4.2.2	ἵνα γένησθε ἄμεμπτοι καὶ ἀκέραιοι	hend.	rhy. οι	allit. -σθε αμ
4.2.3	τέκνα θεοῦ ἄμωμα μέσον γενεᾶς σκολιᾶς καὶ διεστραμμένης	hend.		allit. αμ -νης
4.2.4	ἐν οἷς φαίνεσθε ὡς φωστῆρες ἐν κόσμῳ λόγον ζωῆς ἐπέχοντες			allit. φ -σθε -ρες -τες

The period's form is similar to what we have found in the second period of the second unit. Moreover, these two periods have the same structure: an imperative is followed by a final clause (ἵνα) and participles. This provides the reason why the phrase λόγον ζωῆς ἐπέχοντες is part of the last colon of this period, not the beginning of the next period.[83] Additionally, the cola's repetitions and balance of length require this allocation. The participle ἐπέχοντες substantiates what the final clause (4.2.4) expects. The Philippians will be like stars in a dark world because they hold to the word of life. What is meant with λόγος ζωῆς? It is the gospel[84] that is the foundation for Christian conduct, as Paul pronounced in his *propositio* (1.1.1). It is the message of Christ's descent and ascent to which Paul has given full expression in unit 3. While the first period of the fourth unit refers back to unit 3 in an emotional and existential way (God's self-revelation that causes fear and trembling), the second period refers to it as a message or gospel (λόγος).

There is another aspect that refers back to the first unit. Paul speaks of the Philippians living among warped people in a dark world. At the beginning he referred to the opposing world (1.2.1) approaching destruction (1.2.2). It is the world that crucifies the innocent (3.1.10). Paul sets off the audience against this world by attributing blamelessness to them, but at

---

83. See O'Brien, *Philippians*, 297.
84. Ibid., 298.

the same time he implies that they might suffer like Christ and for Christ's sake (see the gift of suffering in 1.3.3) because they are not mixed with evil (ἀκέραιοι). This is what Paul has in mind while speaking of obedience (3.1.9 and 4.1.2).

It is important to realize the manifold references to the middle and the beginning of the whole passage in this last unit. These are signals that the speech comes to a close.[85] There might be also a linguistic feature that points in the same direction: the frequent use of *hendiadys* in this period. There have been other instances before (σπλάγχνα καὶ οἰκτιρμοί at the end of 2.1.4, μετὰ φόβου καὶ τρόμου in 4.1.5, that is in the colon before the climax), but the frequency in this period is striking. *Hendiadys* is a way to express something comprehensive that the speaker feels unable to embrace with one term alone. Naturally, this feeling increases if the speech has already developed a comprehensive subject and it is time for a final summary.

The period closes with a reference to the apostle. There is a revealing sound pattern in colon 5. It has two halves. The vowel [i] marks the beginning of each half (εἰς), and is repeated before the end of the colon. The last vowel of each half stands out: [y] and [u]. The remaining vowels alternate between [a] and [e]. The two-part structure is enforced by rhythm, an *iambic* meter.

4.2.5 εἰς καύχημα ἐμοὶ | εἰς ἡμέραν Χριστοῦ
       –, x –(⌣⌣)–, x – ⌣ –, x –

In this colon, sound and structure reveal that Paul and Christ, each at the end of one of the halves, are related to each other. This relationship is of eschatological importance. The next two parallel cola provide the explanation.

4.2.6 ὅτι* οὐκ εἰς κενὸν ἔδραμον
       – ⌣ ⌣ ⌣ ⌣, x

4.2.7 οὐδε* εἰς κενὸν ἐκοπίασα
       – ⌣ – ⌣, ⌣ ⌣ ⌣ ⌣⌣ ⌣

The rhythm is *trochaic*;[86] not perfect in the first colon, but beautifully aligning prosody and stress in the second. Both cola have a hiatus after the first word that heightens expectation of what follows. The parallelism is synonym.

Paul relates his position on the day of the Lord to his success with the Philippians. If they are obedient he will receive honor. Paul motivates the audience to follow his admonitions by an appeal to care for their apostle. If

---

85. See Brucker, *Christushymnen*, 296.

86. *Muta cum liquida* δρ, does not make the preceding syllable heavy. The syllable -μον at the end of the line is lengthened.

they have any compassion (see period 2.1) they will see to it that he is not put to shame at the end. We have found this strategy throughout the passage at several places, mostly expressed in parallelism. The Philippians should obey the *apostle*, especially as he is absent (1.1.2 || 1.1.2; 4.1.3 || 4.1.4). They should perfect *his* joy (2.2.1) by adopting Christ's selfless attitude. We have seen above that Paul's strategy is not to motivate the audience by pointing to their own advantages but by directing them to the advantages of others. By stirring empathy with the imprisoned apostle and by pointing to the way the Philippians can contribute to the fulfillment of his hope, he gives the Philippians the chance to practice what he requires: selflessness. The apostle offers himself as the object of selfless action that is worthy of the gospel.

Period 4.3

A final short period follows. It has the same structure as the last three cola of the preceding period: first a long colon, then two parallel cola. The first colon again has *hendiadys* and rhyme.[87] The vowel [i] is prominent. This connects this period directly to the previous one.[88]

4.3.1 Ἀλλ' ε̲ἰ̲ καὶ σπένδομαι ἐπ̲ὶ̲ τῇ θυσ̲ίᾳ̲ καὶ λε̲ιτουργίᾳ̲ τῆς
                                                           π̲ί̲στεως ὑμῶν

In the following two parallel cola the verb is doubled (χαίρω καὶ συγχαίρω), resulting in a fourfold repetition of the verbal root -χαιρ (*paronomasia*). The velar consonant <χ>, probably not yet spoken fricative, and the velar stop <κ> (καὶ) form an impressive *alliteration* /ke/. This emphasis on joy is a closing signal.

The last colon has an additional introductory phrase. If we consider the meter we see that the parallel cola have a regular *anapaestic* rhythm (ᴗ ᴗ -). However, the introductory phrase in the last colon breaks the meter and is irregular. Additionally, it has two hiatuses. The presenter would speak emphatically. The sound of the last colon creates a solemn closure.

---

87. Walter, *Philipper*, 67, assigns the phrase ἐπὶ τῇ θυσίᾳ καὶ λειτουργίᾳ τῆς πίστεως ὑμῶν not to the verb σπένδομαι as Nestle/Aland do but to the verb χαίρω. This would shorten the first colon and prolong the second exuberantly. The harmonious dimensions of the whole period would be destroyed.

88. O'Brien, *Philippians*, 301–3, argues convincingly that the connections between periods 4.2 and 4.3 indicate that the unit does not end with 2:16. Lohmeyer *Philipper*, 71, however, takes 2:17–18 as the beginning of the next section, but calls it a transition ("Überleitung," 112). He is followed by Holloway, *Philippians*, 38–39, 136, who takes the section 1:27—2:16 as a digression and 2:17 as the return to the thoughts of 1:26.

Sound's Message of Philippians 1:27—2:18

4.3.2 χαίρω καὶ συγχαίρω πᾶσιν ὑμῖν
  -, - - - -, - ⌣ ⌣ -

4.3.3 τὸ δὲ* αὐτὸ καὶ* ὑμεῖς χαίρετε καὶ συγχαίρετέ μοι
  (⌣ ⌣ - ⌣ - ⌣) - - ⌣ ⌣ -, - - ⌣ ⌣ -

The last period starts with a conditional sentence with the conjunction εἰ. The truth of the condition is not in focus. The emphasis is rather on the result expressed in the two final cola, i.e., Paul's and the Philippian's joy. What is the condition? The words θυσία καὶ λειτουργία refer to a situation of worship.[89] Paul's letter was certainly read to the Philippians in a worship setting. At the end of the passage the current performance situation is addressed and the apostle reflects his role in this assembly. He makes the reader look around, getting in eye contact with the audience. While the last cola are uttered, Paul's message is: you all, assembled at this place at this very moment, you are the true reason for joy. Paul reflects his own fate (σπένδομαι) as an addition to the worship of the Philippians. Part of the worship of pagan and Jewish cults was the pouring out of some liquid (wine) on the main offering (ἐπὶ τῇ θυσίᾳ) or on the ground beside it. In using this image for his work and even his possible death, Paul diminishes his own contribution to a minor part in the worship service of the Philippians.[90] The apostle has delivered an emphatic admonition. He has shaped his speech in such a way that Christ was clearly portrayed before their eyes as crucified (see Gal 3:1: οἷς κατ' ὀφθαλμοὺς Ἰησοῦς Χριστὸς προεγράφη ἐσταυρωμένος). At the end of the passage, the apostle recedes in the background. Even in the case of his death, the Philippians have every reason to conduct their life worthily of the gospel and joyfully in selfless caring for each other.

Summary

We can now summarize the results of the investigation of the sound quality of the selected passage. Six aspects are worth mentioning.

1. Sound is an important aspect of structuring the passage and determining the beginnings and endings of units. All periods and units of this passage have been demarcated according to sound, sometimes with results that differ from widely held assumptions, as in colon 2.2.4 where in contrast to Nestle/Aland, the word σύμψυχοι is drawn to the

---

89. See Varenhorst, *Kultische Sprache*, 235–38.
90. See Wick, "Ahmt Christus nach," 315.

phrase τὸ ἓν φρονοῦντες. It has also been made clear that 2:17–18 are part of the unit 2:12–18.

2. Sound structures indicate the relationship of the speaker to the audience. We have seen that Paul again and again relates the conduct of the Philippians to his own presence or absence (period 1.1, 1.3, 4.1), to his own joy (colon 2.2.1, period 4.3), and even to his success on the day of the Lord (period 4.2). Paul asks the Philippians that they, *for his sake*, live up to the conditions that have become possible through Christ. While they are doing it for him they practice the attitude that Paul wants them to adopt: not to strive after their own advantage but after the joy for others. The delivery of the letter becomes an occasion to practice the attitude that Paul wants to instill into the audience.

3. Sound is a key to the emotional aspects of the passage. Paul's experience of opposition shapes the sound of his language in period 1.2 (verse 28). Unit 3 is marked by emotional language, especially at the end of the periods. The intensifying emotional tension in period 4.1 (2:12) is indicated by increasing length of cola and by prosodic rhythm. When the climax is reached, hiatuses mark off the most important words (cola 4.1.5 and 4.1.6).

4. Beauty (e.g., the beauty of period 1.3 that displays the positive "gift of suffering") or aggressiveness of sound (e.g., the /s/ in colon 1.2.2) underlines the semantic message.

5. Sound reveals a subtext that can even contradict the semantic content of the utterance. We have seen in period 1.1 (v. 27) that syntax and rhythm reveal a tension in Paul concerning his promise to visit the Philippians.

6. Paying attention to the sound reveals the overall beauty and solemnity of the language. We have seen that the whole passage is marked by an elevated style and language and not just unit 3, which is widely considered an early Christian hymn.

Our investigation has shown that paying attention to the oral aspects of a text that we have only in written form is a rewarding tool for the interpretation of New Testament texts. It cannot replace any other exegetical method, but can provide additional insights especially concerning text structure, the emotional impact of speech, and interpersonal relationships between an author and aural recipients. It is especially useful to appreciate the acoustical beauty of the texts. A well-ordered and euphonious text indicates that the author highly treasures the message he or she want to transmit

and lovingly appreciates his or her audiences. This is certainly true for Paul
and his letter to the Philippians.

Bibliography

Allen, W. Sidney. *Vox Graeca: The Pronunciation of Classical Greek*. Cambridge: University Press, 1987 [reprinted 3rd ed.; first published 1968].
Betz, Hans-Dieter. *Der Apostel Paulus in Rom*. Julius-Wellhausen-Vorlesung 4. Berlin: de Gruyter, 2013.
Blass, Friedrich, Albert Debrunner, Friedrich Rehkopf. *Grammatik des neutestamentlichen Griechisch*. 15th ed. Göttingen: Vandenhoeck & Ruprecht, 1979.
Brucker, Ralph. *'Christushymnen' oder 'epideiktische Passagen'? Studien zum Stilwechsel im Neuen Testament und seiner Umwelt*. Forschungen zur Religion und Literatur des Alten und Neuen Testaments 176. Göttingen: Vandenhoeck & Ruprecht, 1996.
Bubenik, V. "Eastern Koines." In *History of Ancient Greek: From the Beginnings to Late Antiquity*, edited by A. F. Christidis, 632–37. Cambridge: University Press, 2007.
Caragounis, Chrys C. *The Development of Greek and the New Testament: Morphology, Syntax, Phonology, and Textual Transmission*. Wissenschaftliche Untersuchungen zum Neuen Testament 167. Tübingen: Mohr/Siebeck, 2004.
Christidis, A. F., ed. *A History of Ancient Greek: From the Beginnings to Late Antiquity*. Cambridge: University Press, 2007.
Devine, A. M., and L. D. Stephens. *The Prosody of Greek Speech*. Oxford: Oxford University Press, 1994.
Drettas, G. "The Translation (Targum) of the Septuagint." In *History of Ancient Greek: From the Beginnings to Late Antiquity*, edited by A. F. Christidis, 886–96. Cambridge: University Press, 2007.
Eckman, Barbara. "A Quantitative Metrical Analysis of the Philippians Hymn." *New Testament Studies* 26 (1980) 258–66.
Fee, Gordon D. *Paul's Letter to the Philippians*. The New International Commentary on the New Testament. Grand Rapids: Eerdmans, 1995.
———. "Philippians 2:5–11: Hymn or Exalted Pauline Prose?" *Bulletin of Biblical Research* 2 (1992) 29–46.
Friedrich, Gerhard. *Die Briefe an die Galater, Epheser, Philipper, Kolosser, Thessalonicher und Philemon*. Neues Testament Deutsch 8. Göttingen: Vandenhoeck & Ruprecht, 1990.
Gnilka, Joachim. *Der Philipperbrief*. Herders Theologischer Kommentar 10.3. Leipzig: St. Benno, 1968.
Gurd, Sean A. *Dissonance: Auditory Aesthetics in Ancient Greece*. New York: Fordham University Press, 2016.
Hofius, Otfried. *Der Christushymnus Philipper 2,6–11: Untersuchungen zu Gestalt und Aussage eines urchristlichen Psalms*. 2nd ed. Wissenschaftliche Untersuchungen zum Neuen Testament 17. Tübingen: Mohr/Siebeck, 1991.
Holloway, Paul A. *Philippians*. Hermeneia. Minneapolis: Fortress, 2017.
Horrocks, Geoffrey. *Greek: A History of the Language and Its Speakers*. 2nd ed. Malden, MA: Wiley-Blackwell, 2010.

———. "Syntax: From Classical Greek to the Koine." In *History of Ancient Greek: From the Beginnings to Late Antiquity*, edited by A. F. Christidis, 618–31. Cambridge: University Press, 2007.

Jeremias, Joachim. "Zur Gedankenführung in den paulinischen Briefen." In *Abba: Studien zur neutestamentlichen Theologie und Zeitgeschichte*, 269–76. Göttingen: Vandenhoeck & Ruprecht, 1966.

Joseph, B. D. "Early Movement Towards Modern Greek." In *History of Ancient Greek: From the Beginnings to Late Antiquity*, edited by A. F. Christidis, 693–98. Cambridge: University Press, 2007.

Kazazis, J. N. "Ancient Greek Meter." In *History of Ancient Greek: From the Beginnings to Late Antiquity*, edited by A. F. Christidis, 1033–44. Cambridge: Cambridge University Press, 2007.

———. "Atticism." In *History of Ancient Greek: From the Beginnings to Late Antiquity*, edited by A. F. Christidis, 1200–212. Cambridge: Cambridge University Press, 2007.

Kennel, Gunter. *Frühchristliche Hymnen? Gattungskritische Studien zur Frage nach den Liedern der frühen Christenheit*. Wissenschaftliche Monographien zum Alten und Neuen Testament 71. Neukirchen-Vluyn: Neukirchener, 1995.

Kyrtatas, D. J. "The Greek World During the Roman Empire." In *History of Ancient Greek: From the Beginnings to Late Antiquity*, edited by A. F. Christidis, 346–55. Cambridge: Cambridge University Press, 2007.

Lee, Margaret E., and Bernard B. Scott: *Sound Mapping the New Testament*. Salem, OR: Polebridge, 2009.

Lohmeyer, Ernst. *Die Briefe an die Philipper, Kolosser und an Philemon*. Kritisch-exegetischer Kommentar über das Neue Testament 9. Göttingen: Vandenhoeck & Ruprecht, 1956.

———. *Kyrios Jesus: Eine Untersuchung zu Phil. 2,5–11*. Sitzungsberichte der Heidelberger Akademie der Wissenschaften, Philosophisch-Historische Klasse, 1927/28, 4. Heidelberg: Winter, 1928.

Malikouti-Drachman, A. "The Phonology of Classical Greek." In *History of Ancient Greek: From the Beginnings to Late Antiquity*, edited by A. F. Christidis, 524–44. Cambridge: Cambridge University Press, 2007.

Müller, Ulrich B. *Der Brief des Paulus an die Philipper*. Theologischer Handkommentar zum Neuen Testament 11.1. Leipzig: Evangelische, 1993.

Nikiforidou, K. "Language Change." In *History of Ancient Greek: From the Beginnings to Late Antiquity*, edited by A. F. Christidis, 124–31. Cambridge: Cambridge University Press, 2007.

O'Brien, Peter T. *The Epistle to the Philippians: A Commentary on the Greek Text*. New International Greek Testament Commentary. Grand Rapids: Eerdmans, 1991.

Oestreich, Bernhard. *Performance Criticism of the Pauline Letters*. Translated by Lindsay Elias and Brent Blum. Biblical Performance Criticism Series 14. Eugene, OR: Cascade Books, 2016.

Pedersen, Sigfred. "'Mit Furcht und Zittern' (Phil 2,12–13)." *Studia Theologica* 32 (1978) 1–31.

Petrounias, E. B. "Development in Pronunciation during the Hellenistic Period." In *History of Ancient Greek: From the Beginnings to Late Antiquity*, edited by A. F. Christidis, 599–608. Cambridge: Cambridge University Press, 2007.

———. "The Pronunciation of Ancient Greek: Evidence and Hypotheses." In *History of Ancient Greek: From the Beginnings to Late Antiquity*, edited by A. F. Christidis, 545–55. Cambridge: Cambridge University Press, 2007.

———. "The Pronunciation of Classical Greek." In *History of Ancient Greek: From the Beginnings to Late Antiquity*, edited by A. F. Christidis, 556–70. Cambridge: Cambridge University Press, 2007.

Seal, David. "Sensitivity to Aural Effects of a Text: Some Acoustical Elements in Revelation." *Journal of Biblical and Pneumatological Research* 3 (2011) 38–51.

Stirewalt, M. Luther. *Paul, the Letter Writer*. Grand Rapids: Eerdmans, 2003.

Vahrenhorst, Martin. *Kultische Sprache in den Paulusbriefen*. Wissenschaftliche Untersuchungen zum Neuen Testament 230. Tübingen: Mohr/Siebeck, 2008.

Walter, Nikolaus, et al. *Die Briefe an die Philipper, Thessalonicher und an Philemon*. Das Neue Testament Deutsch 8/2. Göttingen: Vandenhoeck & Ruprecht, 1998.

Wick, Peter. "'Ahmt Jesus Christus mit mir zusammen (Phil 3,17) nach!' Imitatio Pauli und imitatio Christi im Philipperbrief." In *Der Philipperbrief des Paulus in der hellenistisch-römischen Welt*, edited by Jörg Frey and Benjamin Schliesser, 309–26. Wissenschaftliche Untersuchungen zum Neuen Testament 353. Tübingen: Mohr/Siebeck 2015.

Wojtkowiak, Heiko. *Christologie und Ethik im Philipperbrief: Studien zur Handlungsorientierung einer frühchristlichen Gemeinde in paganer Umwelt*. Forschungen zur Religion und Literatur des Alten und Neuen Testaments 243. Göttingen: Vandenhoeck & Ruprecht, 2012.

6

Underexplored Benefits of Sound Mapping in New Testament Exegesis

Dan Nässelqvist

Introduction

One may easily assume that the primary, or even the solitary, function of sound mapping is confined to the study of the oral delivery of Biblical texts (regardless of whether that it is envisioned as dramatic performance of a memorized text, reading aloud from a manuscript, or something in between).[1] I first engaged in sound mapping as a means to understand how compositional features of the Fourth Gospel impacted its oral delivery.[2] I found that the composition and oral delivery of ancient literary writings corresponded in several ways, which means that we can gain information about how a New Testament text was delivered in public reading from compositional features found within it. Sound mapping also presented an unexpected bonus for exegetes in that a detailed analysis of the aural properties of a text provides numerous interpretative clues. These clues are in no way restricted to the impact on oral delivery. On the contrary, they provide

---

1. For a critical analysis of different views on which type of oral delivery predominated in early Christianity, see Nässelqvist, "Dual Conventions." See also the recent debate in New Testament Studies between Larry Hurtado ("Oral Fixation," "Correcting") and Kelly Iverson ("Oral Fixation").

2. The resulting interpretation of John 1–4 can be found in Nässelqvist, *Public Reading*, 180–320.

information on matters such as how the text is punctuated, which passages are emphasized, and how one should understand its leading questions.

In the rest of this chapter, I will illustrate the potential of sound mapping for New Testament exegesis by describing how it produces such interpretative clues and in what manner they can be used to better understand the texts. I will examine each step in the process of sound mapping (as presented by Lee and Scott),[3] discuss how it may be improved and made even more concrete,[4] as well as illustrate how it provides the type of interpretative clues mentioned above.

Delimit Cola

Lee and Scott rightly stress the importance of first identifying the boundaries of a text's cola, since these are the basic speech units of ancient Greek and thus comprise the most fundamental interpretative unit in sound mapping.[5] I have argued elsewhere that the varying descriptions of cola in ancient theory can only be implemented if we work with a wide and yet quite exact definition. A colon is then understood to be a sense unit (it involves a complete thought, or a complete part of a thought) with a limited extent (not too brief and not longer than it can be uttered in a single breath; the acceptable length is *circa* 7–30 syllables), which can be combined into a period.[6]

It may easily be thought that the delimitation of cola cannot provide anything fruitful beyond being the point of departure for sound analysis. I have found, however, that an understanding of the colometric nature of ancient literary writings aids in elucidating complex passages. One example where sound mapping guides the interpretation of convoluted passages involves the question of how to punctuate John 1:3–4, a problem that has confounded both ancient and modern readers and is exacerbated by the scarcity of punctuation in ancient manuscripts.[7] At least four different punctuations of John 1:3–4 have been suggested, although only two of them have received wide support. A colometric analysis of the passage according to the definition of colon presented above does, however, indicate that three of the possible readings result in unbalanced cola and at least one example

---

3. These steps are outlined in Lee and Scott, *Sound Mapping*, 168–89.

4. For a full-length reassessment of each step in light of further studies of ancient literary critics, grammarians, and rhetoricians, see Nässelqvist, *Public Reading*, 126–64.

5. Lee and Scott, *Sound Mapping*, 169.

6. Nässelqvist, *Public Reading*, 127.

7. The following example is based upon a longer argument found in Nässelqvist, "Punctuation."

of a colon which is too short.[8] Compare how John 1:3–4 is punctuated in the following readings, both of which have received strong scholarly support. Note especially the length and balance of the cola (the number in the left-hand margin indicates the number of syllables in each colon).

Reading A[9]

8	πάντα δι' αὐτοῦ ἐγένετο,	All things came into being through him,
12	καὶ χωρὶς αὐτοῦ ἐγένετο οὐδὲ ἕν.	And without him not one thing came into being
10	ὃ γέγονεν ἐν αὐτῷ ζωὴ ἦν,	What has come into being in him was life,
11	καὶ ἡ ζωὴ ἦν τὸ φῶς τῶν ἀνθρώπων·	and the life was the light of all people.

Reading B[10]

8	πάντα δι' αὐτοῦ ἐγένετο,	Through him all things were made;
16	καὶ χωρὶς αὐτοῦ ἐγένετο οὐδὲ ἓν ὃ γέγονεν.	without him nothing was made that has been made.
6	ἐν αὐτῷ ζωὴ ἦν,	In him was life,
11	καὶ ἡ ζωὴ ἦν τὸ φῶς τῶν ἀνθρώπων·	and that life was the light of all mankind.

The two readings differ in whether the full stop comes before or after ὃ γέγονεν and the results are noticeably dissimilar, not only in how balanced the cola are, but also in which meaning they produce. In instances such as these, ancient descriptions and examples of cola length can guide our reading. Reading A produces balanced cola of acceptable length (8–12 syllables), which support the rhetorical figures present in this part of the Prologue (such as the *gradatio*, or 'staircase parallelism,' which begins with ὃ γέγονεν

---

8. The designations "balanced" and "unbalanced" in reference to cola refer to whether or not they are of similar length and thus produce a balanced (almost rhythmic) impression when read aloud. When cola are clearly balanced, they produce the rhetorical figure of *isocolon*. See Lausberg, *Handbook*, §719; Nässelqvist, *Public Reading*, 168–69.

9. The English translation is that of NRSV, which adopts this reading (full stop before ὃ γέγονεν).

10. The English translation is that of NIV, which adopts this reading (full stop after ὃ γέγονεν).

and continues in 1:4–5).¹¹ Reading B results in unbalanced cola, hampers the beginning of the staircase parallelism in 1:4–5, and comprises a line of only six syllables, which is too brief to function as an independent colon.

Features of ancient compositional practices and the "grammar of sound,"¹² which are summarized in the sound mapping method, are thus able to guide the interpretation of complicated passages, such as John 1:3–4. Other approaches have produced four possible readings of the passage,¹³ but the colometric analysis with which sound mapping begins argues strongly for reading A (i.e. that the full stop comes before ὃ γέγονεν).

Identify Periods

The manner in which periods—artistically arranged cola with a circuital structure—are identified and understood constitutes the area where I found that the sound mapping method could profit most from a reconsideration in light of ancient rhetorical handbooks and literary critics.¹⁴ These include a number of descriptions and examples, which affect our considerations about what constitutes a period and according to which criteria we can identify them.

The fundamental requirement of a period is that the passage in question "bends back" at the end, in the sense that the final colon connects the end of the period with its beginning and thus produces the requisite circuital structure (a sort of micro-scale *inclusio*).¹⁵ The Greek term for a period, περίοδος, indeed denotes a circle or a circuitous journey. Additionally, authors regularly signal the existence of a period through the use of at least one other periodic feature, such as symmetry (repetition of sounds or words in parallel position), *hyperbaton* (inversion of regular word order), elongation (an extended final clause or colon), or a *clausula* (a rhythmic ending).¹⁶

The identification of periods comprises the second step of the sound mapping method, coming immediately after the cola have been delimited,

---

11. For the rhetorical figures found in John 1:1–5, see Nässelqvist, *Public Reading*, 185–90.

12. See Lee and Scott, *Sound Mapping*, 96–100.

13. Nässelqvist, "Punctuation."

14. Their treatment of periods can be found in Lee and Scott, *Sound Mapping*, 171–73.

15. Demetrius, *Eloc.* 10, defines a period as "a combination of cola or *commata* which has brought the underlying thought to a conclusion with a well-turned ending."

16. For a fuller treatment of requisite and optional features of periods, see Nässelqvist, *Public Reading*, 134–38.

yet the identification of a passage as a period does not profoundly impact the following steps. Sound patterns, compositional units, and instances of noticeable sound quality (steps three to five) can be identified regardless of whether or not the text comprises any periods. It is only in the sixth and final step of sound mapping, in which literary style is considered, that the periods make a real impact upon the analysis. Since periods are artistic arrangements of cola, they are more suited to the middle (or florid) style, which is characterized by smoothness and a fluid combination of rhetorical figures, than to the plain (see further below). The frequency of periods often follows the shift between different stylistic levels in the composition in question.[17]

The identification of periods in a text thus aids us in understanding the stylistic level and fashioning of a literary text, but the fact that a passage comprises a period also provides interpretational clues about its nature and use. How we understand these clues depends upon from which perspective we approach periods. They provided information to ancient lectors (those who read texts aloud in early Christian communities) about which sentences to lift out for special delivery, after which they regularly inserted a brief pause for emphasis, reflection and possibly also some interaction from the listeners.[18] To ancient listeners (or those reading a text for themselves) periods indicated which parts were particularly emphasized and important. Readers and listeners thus focused their attention upon these sentences, may well have memorized some of them, and used them to interpret the rest of the text.

When we identify a period, we should therefore not be satisfied with the mere act of attaching this label, but rather raise further questions about the nature and use of the period in question. Why is this passage emphasized? Which role does it play in the composition at large? How does it affect the interpretation of the surrounding text? How would it have functioned in oral delivery?

Identify Sound Patterns and Compositional Units

I have combined the third and fourth steps of sound mapping (as described by Lee and Scott), as they largely overlap. These steps involve an analysis of how sounds are repeated in a text and of how these repetitions produce emphasis and create sound patterns on micro (within a sentence or a brief

---

17. For a description of ancient literary style categories which also takes sound mapping into account, see Nässelqvist, "Style."

18. See Quintilian, *Inst.* 9.4.61; Cicero, *Or. Brut.* 168.

passage) as well as macro (spanning whole sections or even the entirety of the composition) levels.[19]

Nowhere does sound mapping come closer to more traditional exegetical methods than in the identification of repetition and analysis of how repetition creates structure. Rhetorical criticism also focuses upon repetition and how it is used in rhetorical figures to stress and amplify arguments. Although they overlap in their attention to repetition, the two methods have different focuses. Whereas rhetorical criticism primarily relates the use of repetition (predominantly in the form of rhetorical figures) to persuasion and thus to the argumentative layer of a text, sound mapping has deeper and wider roots. It identifies how repetition produces structure not only in individual rhetorical figures at a specific point, but throughout the text. It depicts and describes how these structures create large-scale patterns through the use of repetition, variation, modification, and transformation of sound.[20]

When the sound mapping method is used on a large portion of text, or on a literary writing in its entirety, it is possible to analyze the large-scale effects of how repetition (and other aural effects) creates emphasis and structure. I have used the term "aural intensity" for this depiction of the shifting soundscape of a literary writing in oral delivery. It supports sound mapping by aiding the delimitation of larger compositional units and by setting emphasized passages in the context of a varying soundscape. Aural intensity is represented in a chart that depicts the degree to which each passage attracts emphasis in oral delivery.[21]

The aural intensity of a passage (which may comprise one or several cola) is defined as low, medium, or high, depending upon the frequency and combination within it of distinctive aural features, compositional features that produce much emphasis. These include noticeable prose rhythm, well-formed periods, significant tempo shifts, especially euphonious or dissonant sounds, and the most attention-attracting rhetorical figures.[22] An example chart of aural intensity (this one with an analysis of John 1:47–51) can be seen below:[23]

---

19. Lee and Scott, *Sound Mapping*, 141–51, 174–76.
20. See ibid., 151–55.
21. Nässelqvist, *Public Reading*, 164–66.
22. For a full list with descriptions, see Nässelqvist, *Public Reading*, 167–76.
23. An analysis of the soundscape and aural intensity of John 1:47–51, see Nässelqvist, *Public Reading*, 215–18, 225–28.

Aural intensity			Verse	Cola	Summary of content
High	Med	Low			
		X	1:47a–c	3	Jesus saw Nathanael and calls him "a true Israelite"
		X	1:48a–b	2	Nathanael: "From where do you know me?"
	X		1:48c–d	2	Jesus: I saw you before, under the fig tree
X			1:49a–c	3	Nathanael: "Rabbi, you are the Son of God"
	X		1:50a	3	Jesus: Do you believe because of what I said?
		X	1:50d	1	You shall see greater things than these
		X	1:51a–c	3	You shall see God's angels upon the Son of Man

As becomes clear from the depiction above, it is possible to depict the aural intensity of large sections of a text on a single page. The analysis of aural intensity thus begins with several full-scale sound maps and within these identifies brief passages with similar use of distinctive aural features. It is then possible to depict the shifting soundscape—passage by passage—by indicating its intensity level, location in the text, span (in number of cola), and a short note about the content. The pattern of varying intensity resembles an electrocardiogram, as it depicts how the text shifts from sections without emphasis or effect, followed by passages of great intensity on a saying or an action.[24]

Describe Sound Quality

One of the greatest contributions of sound mapping, in my opinion at least, is the way that it provides a methodology for understanding the impact of sound quality in ancient literary writings. Ancient rhetoricians and literary critics mention the importance, as well as the strong effect, of how a text sounds as it is read aloud or declaimed. Lee and Scott have done a great service to Biblical studies through their interpretation and employment of these recurring references to sound in literary writings.[25]

Sound quality refers to the aural effects of a text as it is orally delivered. It involves features such as euphonious and dissonant sounds, which affect

---

24. For a full-scale chart of the aural intensity of the first four chapters of John's gospel, see Nässelqvist, *Public Reading*, 347–53.

25. See especially Lee and Scott, *Sound Mapping*, 176–79.

the smoothness of a passage, and clashes of letters between words, which alter the rhythm. In some instances, the sound quality of a passage interacts with its content and influences the interpretation of the text. This is especially true for particularly euphonious or dissonant passages. One area where this occurs, unexplored by Lee and Scott, is in the context of leading questions.

Leading question are questions that are posed in such a manner that they indicate which answer is expected. In Greek, this is readily accomplished with the help of a negative particle at the beginning of the question (some form with οὐ to indicate that a positive answer is expected and some form with μή for a negative answer).

Most leading questions in the New Testament do not have a distinctive or particularly noticeable sound quality.[26] When they do, however, the type of sound quality (euphonious or dissonant) almost always fits the expected answer; euphonious sounds for an expected positive answer and dissonant sounds for a negative. These cases not only confirm that sound quality guides the interpretation of questions, but also that it amplifies the impression of them.

A good example can be found in the question posed by the Samaritan woman to her neighbors in Sychar about the identity of Jesus, in John 4:29.

4:28b	καὶ ἀπῆλθεν εἰς τὴν πόλιν	She returned to the city
4:28c	καὶ λέγει τοῖς ἀνθρώποις·	and said to the people:
4:29a	δεῦτε ἴδετε ἄνθρωπον	"Come and see a man
4:29b	ὃς εἶπέ μοι πάντα ὅσα ἐποίησα·	who told me everything I have ever done.
4:29c	μήτι οὗτός ἐστιν ὁ χριστός;	Surely, he is not the Messiah?"

The question in 4:29c (the final line) is a leading question with an expected negative answer: "He cannot be the Messiah, can he?" or "Surely, he is not the Messiah?" Despite the clear indication given by the initial negative particle μήτι, some commentators state that the leading question should be understood as a semi-confession, or even as the positive expression of a "mentally and socially transformed" individual.[27] The sound quality of the question in this case acts as an interpretative key, which cautions against such readings.

---

26. This is because it is usually a semantic and pragmatic feature of question-asking, and rarely syntactic.

27. For the first interpretation, see Brandt, *John*, 87. For the second, see Matthews, "Conversation and Identity," 224–25.

The question in 4:29 is accompanied by dissonant sounds, mainly due to frequent hissing consonants that begin already in 4:29b and continue until the end of the question. The dissonant sounds reinforce and confirm the expected negative answer. Rather than point to a semi-confession on the part of the Samaritan woman, they imply a skeptical attitude towards Jesus and towards the notion that he should be the Messiah.[28] Sound quality thus affirms and strengthens the guidance given by the pragmatic factor of a leading question.

Analyze the Connection between Style and Content

It is notoriously difficult to comprehend how literary style functions in ancient Greek writings and which factors are the most important in establishing and communicating style. Indeed, ancient literary critics and rhetoricians do not provide a clear definition of style, even though the topic occurs regularly in their discussions. It may safely be stated, however, that style involves how a message is embodied and expressed in a text. By extension, style also entails the choices made by the author (to embody and express the message) and the interpretative work performed by readers and listeners, who decode the stylistic features according to conventions of the time.[29]

The conventions of literary style in the ancient Mediterranean world focused upon ideal patterns, which authors tried to approximate. The predominant system in the first century CE involved three such patterns, most often referred to as "levels of style." These patterns used the same stylistic features, albeit to varying degrees and occasionally in contrasting ways, to produce literary styles that could fit various types of texts. The three levels of style represented an increasing stylistic intensity, from "plain" to "middle" (or "florid") to "grand."[30]

---

28. This impression is strengthened by the sound quality of a question that she poses directly to Jesus (4:9): "How can you, a Jew, ask me, a Samaritan woman, for a drink?" This question, which is not leading, produces a strongly dissonant sound quality (the question and its introductory formula include several dissonant vowel clashes, due to long vowels at the end and beginning of adjoining words, and two dissonant consonant clashes when hissing consonants collide between words). The already skeptical question is thus rendered even less friendly by the dissonant sounds. Ancient listeners may well have perceived it as an intentional insult.

29. For an introduction to the history of literary style in antiquity, see Russell, *Criticism*, 129–47.

30. Nässelqvist, "Stylistic Levels," 34–35.

The most succinct explanations of the levels of style can be found in Cicero: "For these three functions, there are three styles: plain style for proof, middle style for pleasure, vigorous [i.e., grand] style for persuasion."[31] Plain style is used to present information and proofs, as well as to explain and teach. It is clear, concise and restrained, and thus includes few embellishments. Middle/florid style is used to charm and please the listeners and thus to win their favor. It produces a smooth, polished and ornamented text, which is characterized by a combination of rhetorical figures. Grand style is used to forcefully win over the listeners through vigor, boldness and appeal to the emotions. Although it employs many rhetorical figures, it differs from middle style by combining them to produce emotional force rather than a smooth and charming piece. Authors regularly varied the stylistic level in different parts of a literary text, in order to create a pleasant variation and, more importantly, to fit the stylistic fashioning of a passage to its content.[32]

There are many pitfalls in combining sound mapping with an analysis of literary style, as Lee and Scott endeavor to do in the sixth and final step of the sound mapping method.[33] In part, this has to do with the fact that this step does not involve any expansion of the sound map. In order to analyze the literary style in the context of sound mapping, we thus have to identify aural features already depicted in the sound map (produced in the earlier steps) and examine whether they fit a particular level of style.

Two of the most promising aural features for stylistic analysis are periods and exceptional sound quality. As mentioned above, periods—particularly well-formed periods—are most suited to middle or grand style compositions. The austere prose of plain style writing does not allow much room for such elaborate arrangements. It is thus no coincidence that the unadorned second chapter of John's Gospel includes only a single period, in 2:19 (λύσατε τὸν ναὸν τοῦτον καὶ ἐν τρισὶν ἡμέραις ἐγερῶ αὐτόν, "destroy this temple and in three days I will build it up"). In contrast to this, the surrounding chapters, which are characterized by middle and grand style as well as numerous aural features, contain at least twelve periods.[34] The existence of periods (as determined in the second step of sound mapping) can thus guide our analysis of the literary styles found in a composition.

31. Cicero, Or. Brut. 69.

32. For a more thorough description of each stylistic level, see Nässelqvist, "Style," 25–29; and Nässelqvist, "Stylistic Levels," 34–37.

33. Lee and Scott, Sound Mapping, 179–89. For a cautionary note as to this enterprise, see Nässelqvist, Public Reading, 163–64.

34. The periods can be found in John 1:7, 1:11, 1:13, 1:18, 1:26b–27, 1:45b–c, 1:48c–d, 1:50b–c, 2:19b–c, 3:17, 3:21, 3:26d–e, and 3:36. See Nässelqvist, Public Reading, 191–264.

The existence of distinctive sound quality provides even more information about the stylistic level of a passage than the presence of periods. This is especially true of particularly dissonant or euphonious passages. Since strong dissonance destroys the requisite smoothness of middle-style writing, such passages are more suited to plain or grand style. If the dissonance is combined with vehemence, it produces the forcefulness and emotional appeal usually found in grand-style compositions. An example of such a combination of vehemence and dissonance can be found in a passage from Euripides' *Medea*, which is often commented upon in ancient discussions of dissonance:[35]

ἐγώ τε γὰρ λέξασα κουφισθήσομαι	I shall ease the burden of my soul
ψυχὴν κακῶς σε καὶ σὺ λυπήσῃ κλύων.	by reviling you, and you will be sorry for it.
ἐκ τῶν δὲ πρώτων πρῶτον ἄρξομαι λέγειν.	I will begin from the very beginning:
ἔσωσά σ', ὡς ἴσασιν Ἑλλήνων ὅσοι	I saved you; this knows every son of Greece
ταὐτὸν συνεισέβησαν Ἀργῷον σκάφος	that went aboard with you on Argo's hull

The reproachful words of Medea are strong enough in terms of their content. When we take account of their sound quality as well, however, we find that Euripides has dressed the opening of Medea's verbal attack on her unfaithful husband in the most dissonant way possible. At the very moment when she begins her story, her words are full of hissing consonants (indicated with underlining in the depiction above), a strongly dissonant feature. There are no less than twelve *sigmas* in twenty-four syllables at this point (i.e., in the last two lines shown above). It can readily be heard, even by those who understand no Greek: *esōsa sōs ísasin hellēnōn hósoi tauton syneisébēsan argōon scaphos.*

Noticeable sound quality often impacts the understanding of the passage in which it is found. In the case of *Medea*, it sharpens the reproachful and antagonistic air of her response to Jason. This combination of dissonance in sound, vehemence in content, and emotional appeal correspond with ancient descriptions of the grand style. Similar use of exceptional sound quality to fit the style (and content) of a passage can also be found in New Testament writings, such as in Jesus' dissonant reaction to Nathanael's hasty confession in John 1:50.[36]

---

35. Euripides, *Med.* 473–477. The translation, which is mine, does not aspire to recreate the meter.

36. See Nässelqvist, *Public Reading*, 216–18.

Conclusions

The reconsideration of the different steps of the sound mapping method, presented above, serves two purposes. First, it provides the opportunity to indicate areas in which the method may be strengthened, made more concrete, and even further adapted to the evidence found in the works of ancient literary critics and rhetoricians. Second, the retracement of the method reveals how each step also produces interpretative clues that are not primarily related to sound mapping or the study of oral delivery in antiquity, but can shed light on other aspects of the text being analyzed.

Each step of the sound mapping method thus generates more information than what is contained in the sound maps themselves. This information can be used to guide the interpretation of the text being analyzed. I have given examples related to each step of how these—often underexplored—interpretative clues may be utilized by the exegete. In the first step of delimiting the cola, the information gathered can guide the understanding of complex passages, such as the punctuation of John 1:3–4. The second step, which involves the identification of periods, provides further information about the stylistic level and fashioning of the text, as well as about how the passage with the period functioned for different types of text users in antiquity (such as lectors, listeners, and private readers). The third and fourth steps, which involve the identification of sound patterns and larger compositional units, supply the information needed to analyze the large-scale effects of repetition and aural effects. When combined into a chart of the text's shifting aural intensity, we get a depiction of how it shifts in intensity and at which points it especially attracted the attention of ancient readers and listeners. The fifth step, in which the sound quality is analyzed, provides data that also can be used in the interpretation of leading questions (as long as the passage has a distinctive sound quality), such as John 4:29. The sixth and final step, which involves the connection between style and content, does not produce any addition to the sound map. The exegete rather uses already depicted aural features, periods and sound quality in particular (such as the dissonant features of John 1:50 or *Medea* 476–77), to understand how they impact the stylistic fashioning and level of a passage.

The method for sound mapping introduced by Lee and Scott can and should be constantly revised and developed. I have tried to indicate how this can be achieved through a more detailed adaptation of its steps to the guidelines and information presented by ancient rhetoricians and literary critics. Such an enterprise also produces interpretational clues, which can be used beyond the confines of sound mapping to understand features such as punctuation, emphasis, leading questions, and style.

Bibliography

Brandt, Jo-Ann. *John*. Paideia. Grand Rapids: Baker Academic, 2011.

Hurtado, Larry W. "Correcting Iverson's 'Correction.'" *New Testament Studies* 62 (2016) 201–6.

———. "Oral Fixation and New Testament Studies? 'Orality', 'Performance' and Reading Texts in Early Christianity." *New Testament Studies* 60 (2014) 321–40.

Iverson, Kelly R. "Oral Fixation or Oral Corrective? A Response to Larry Hurtado." *New Testament Studies* 62 (2016) 183–200.

Lausberg, Heinrich. *Handbook of Literary Rhetoric: A Foundation for Literary Study*. Translated by Matthew T. Bliss et al. Edited by David E. Orton and R. Dean Anderson. Leiden: Brill, 1998.

Lee, Margaret Ellen, and Bernard Brandon Scott. *Sound Mapping the New Testament*. Salem, OR: Polebridge, 2009.

Matthews, Victor H. "Conversation and Identity: Jesus and the Samaritan Woman." *Biblical Theology Bulletin* 40 (2010) 215–26.

Nässelqvist, Dan. "Dual Conventions: The Oral Delivery of New Testament Writings in Light of First-Century Delivery Practices." In *Social Memory and Social Identity in the Study of Early Judaism and Early Christianity*, edited by Samuel Byrskog et al., 111–24. Novum Testamentum et Orbis Antiquus 116. Göttingen: Vandenhoeck & Ruprecht, 2016.

———. *Public Reading in Early Christianity: Lectors, Manuscripts, and Sound in the Oral Delivery of John 1–4*. Novum Testamentum Supplements 163. Leiden: Brill, 2015.

———. "The Question of Punctuation in John 1:3–4: Arguments from Ancient Colometry." *Journal of Biblical Literature* 137 (2018) 173–89.

———. "Style." In *How John Works: Storytelling in the Fourth Gospel*, edited by Douglas Estes and Ruth Sheridan, 23–39. Resources for Biblical Study 86. Atlanta: Society of Biblical Literature, 2016.

———. "Stylistic Levels in Hebrews 1.1–4 and John 1.1–18." *Journal for the Study of the New Testament* 35 (2012) 31–53.

Russell, D. A. *Criticism in Antiquity*. London: Duckworth, 1981.

7

Discourse Segmentation, Discourse Structure, and Sound Mapping

(Including an Analysis of Mark 15)

FRANK SCHEPPERS

The emerging literature on sound mapping includes an impressively diverse set of approaches and methods and covers a vast array of interesting topics: the interpretation of ancient scholarship and literary criticism (including ancient conceptions of euphony), orality and the functions of writing, genre-related issues, ancient and modern views on discourse segmentation, pause and other prosodic phenomena, etc. A number of these topics were also at hand in the research on classical Greek word order, discourse segmentation and discourse structure that I engaged in between 1991 and 2004 and again in 2010–2011, which most notably gave rise to my book *The Colon Hypothesis: Word Order, Discourse Segmentation and Discourse Coherence in Ancient Greek*, published in 2011 (henceforward *TCH*). The overall perspective I adopted in my work was based on discourse analysis in the vein of the so-called Santa Barbara school (most notably Wallace Chafe),[1] previously applied to ancient Greek by such authors as Egbert Bakker and Siem Slings.[2]

---

1. Chafe, "The Deployment of Consciousness"; Chafe, *Discourse, Consciousness, and Time*; Chafe, "The Analysis of Discourse Flow"; and many other titles.

2. See for instance: Bakker, *Homeric Discourse and Enjambement*; Bakker, "Boundaries, Topics, and the Structure of Discourse"; Bakker, "Discourse and Performance";

For the purposes of the present contribution to a volume dedicated to the sound mapping project, I focus on those aspects that are directly related to the reconstruction of the "sound" of discourse (which however has not been the main focus of my own work). As I have no particular experience with the sound mapping methodology as such, nor with the New Testament (henceforward NT) corpus, my contribution will mainly consist of (1) a few remarks on those methodological aspects on which there is an overlap between my own work and sound mapping (sections 1 to 3), and (2) an application of my own approach to an excerpt taken from the NT corpus (section 4), focusing on those aspects that should be most relevant for the purposes of the sound mapping project, either by confirming or by contradicting views that are part of this emerging research tradition. In this already lengthy contribution, there will be not enough space for a thorough exposition of the theoretical background of what I propose, let alone a serious discussion of the literature. I apologize for often confining myself to admittedly inelegant references to the relevant paragraphs of *TCH*. Throughout my contribution, Lee and Scott's 2009 *Sound Mapping the New Testament* (henceforward *SMNT*) will be my main interlocutor.

1. General Remarks

Let me start by briefly addressing a few very general issues that play a role within sound mapping as well as in my own work.

1.1 Orality and Literacy

The issues surrounding the notion of "orality" as applied to NT texts, gave rise to sometimes heated debates,[3] which are very interesting in their own right and allow for genuine progress in our understanding of the original circumstances of both production and consumption of the written texts that have been transmitted to us. However, the idea that one has to choose between an orality-based and a writing-based position as mutually exclusive options is—in my opinion—not fruitful for the purposes at hand. Thus, if the concept of "orality" is taken to specifically refer to the epic tradition, then "orality" will obviously not be straightforwardly applicable to NT texts. But this rejection of the model of the oral epic as appropriate for the de-

---

Slings, "Written and Spoken Language"; Slings, "Figures of speech and their lookalikes."

3. See for instance: Hurtado, "'Orality', 'Performance' and Reading Texts"; Nässelqvist, *Public Reading in Early Christianity*, 2–13.

scription of NT texts should not have as a result that all and any research that uses "orality" as one of its key concepts gets summarily dismissed as well. It would be a pity not to avail oneself of sources of interesting insights,[4] because of an allergic reaction to the word "oral." Even if both the production and the consumption of NT texts turned out to involve a lot more writing than some proponents of "orality" would like to admit (e.g., if NT texts were essentially written by a silent author and their consumption in a liturgical context involved reading the written text), it would still be the case that writing was less differentiated from speech ("more oral") in the ancient Mediterranean context than is the case now. This fact is of course essential for the very relevance of sound mapping, but it also entails that a number of other supposed aspects of "orality" (in the wider sense) will automatically be relevant to sound mapping as well. In any case, one should focus on what is fruitful and relevant for the project at hand,[5] while ensuring that any of the claims one wishes to make remains compatible with what is known about the linguistic and the more general context of the text.

1.2 Cultural Background, Genre, and Structural Patterns in Discourse

Sound mapping (as represented by *SMNT*) has paid a lot of attention to the intertextual relations between the NT and Greek literary traditions, including ancient rhetoric and its typical sensitivity to euphony and phonetic expressive devices in general (see especially *SMNT* chapter 3), and appears to have based its core methodology—at least partly—on these ancient Greek approaches. However, the relation between the NT and the classical Hellenic tradition is a rather complicated one, in that the NT texts obviously also have a Jewish intertext (in various languages) and originated in a culturally and linguistically hybrid Judaeo-Aramaeo-Helleno-Roman context.[6] It should therefore be taken into account that the NT texts also participate in

---

4. For instance, Tannen, *Spoken and Written Language*; and Tannen, "Oral and Literate Strategies." For a recent contribution concerning classical Greek in which "orality" is used in the wider sense meant here, see Vatri, *Orality and Performance*.

5. Whereas the "epic" implementation of the notion of "orality" is too narrow for our purposes, some takes on the orality issue may be too wide to be relevant: if "orality" is taken to refer to the very general idea that spontaneous conversation is the "original"/"natural" context for human language use, which may be interesting and inspiring (and even correct) as such, this insight need not necessarily contribute anything specific to the technical issues of the project at hand.

6. Janse, "Bilingualism, Diglossia and Literacy"; Ong, *Multilingual Jesus*; Porter, "The Role of Greek Language Criteria."

a definitely non-Hellenic context and intertext, which may manifest itself in a number of very concrete ways (including idiosyncrasies in the phonology, grammar and vocabulary of the Greek,[7] and—obviously—various content-related aspects).

Perhaps the most immediately relevant aspect of the cultural background of the texts can be captured in terms of the issue of the genre to which they belong, in that genre mediates between the pragmatic context within which the text functions and a number of formal/linguistic aspects. The question of the genre-theoretical status of the gospels as a whole has been debated at length and Greek biography ("βίοι"), historiography and novel have been mentioned among the candidates.[8]

Among many other aspects, genre is important for the study of discourse structure in that it predetermines a number of genre-specific patterns, both at the global level of the overall structure of the text, and at the more local levels (*TCH* §13.3.5).

In the case of the gospels, the internal structure of the discourse is determined by mostly narrative patterns and—like ancient novels and biographies—also includes various types of public speeches and dialogues. Some aspects of narrative plots are probably universal: a broadly chronological sequence of connected actions by a limited number of interacting main agents. Thus, many of the patterns in Mark's narrative seem very similar to the narrative patterns I found in Lysias (*TCH* chapters 15–17): e.g., the pattern "agent 1+ δέ, followed by actions performed by agent 1; agent 2 + δέ, followed by actions performed by agent 2" in Mark 15:11–24 looks very classical (although καί appears to not always behave in the same way as in classical prose; see section 3.2 below). But a number of other aspects looked very different to me. For one thing, the typically Greek binary contrasts of the type "X μέν—Y δέ" (*TCH* §21.3(2c) and cross-references) are much less frequent in NT Greek than in contemporary (or earlier and later) Greek high literature.[9]

Similarly, a brief preliminary analysis of the Sermon on the Mount (Matt 5–7), for which there is unfortunately no room in this contribution,

---

7. For the fact that NT Greek is a form of Semitized koinè, see Janse, "The Greek of the New Testament"; Rico, "New Testament Greek." I am not necessarily convinced by Rico's (summary) account of word order, though it does give a perhaps useful first impression of the difficulty of translating from the Greek into modern languages. Also, the degree of Semitization is debated (Porter, "The Role of Greek Language Criteria.")

8. Vines, *The Problem of Markan Genre*; Burridge, *What are the Gospels?*; Walton, "What are the Gospels?"; Köstenberger, "The Genre of the Fourth Gospel"; Maier, "Luke as a Hellenistic Historian."

9. Except for the eliminative contrasts of the type "οὐ X, ἀλλὰ Y," of course, which are an altogether different phenomenon.

immediately shows a number of structural patterns that look unfamiliar from the point of view of classical Greek speech writing, and conversely, some of the patterns that are most typical for classical Greek public speeches—most notably a wide array of binary contrasts, as well as argumentative patterns (for examples, see *TCH* chapter 18)—appear to be absent from the Sermon. Apart from the structural patterns *stricto sensu*, the Sermon also implies a quite different relation between audience and speaker than is the case in—say—the forensic or political speeches of Lysias and similar classical authors. It would perhaps be more fruitful to look for points of comparison within didactic and/or prophetic genres in the Jewish tradition than to Lysias or Demosthenes.[10]

1.3 Sound Mapping, Ancient Rhetorical Theories, the "Poetics" of Speech, and Contemporary Linguistics

SMNT presents a both extensive and detailed account of the potential impact of ancient rhetorical concepts for the purpose of sound mapping and its analytical practice shows remarkable continuity with ancient practices. In the 1990s, I started out with a similar interest in ancient accounts,[11] but came to the conclusion that many of these were rather *ad hoc* and sometimes internally incoherent, almost invariably were not up to the standards of present-day linguistic approaches, and at any rate would not give rise to a systematic account of the aspects I was interested in.

Thus, I came to the conclusion that for the purposes of analyzing continuous stretches of text, one should get rid of the shaky notion of "period" altogether,[12] and instead get used to a whole range of patterns with a variable number of hierarchical levels, such as the one I propose in chapter 13 of *TCH* (see also the literature quoted there).

---

10. Within the Hellenic tradition, the closest one gets to the authoritarian tone displayed in the Sermon may be the didactic poetry of such religiously inspired pre-Socratic gurus as Empedocles. But even then, no direct links with the NT need to be surmised.

11. Scheppers, "Kola"; see also *TCH* §10.4.4 for a few notes on Aristotle. For a similarly critical approach to the traditional rhetorical notion of "figure of speech," see Slings, "Figures of Speech and their Lookalikes."

12. Aristotle introduced the notion of period to describe particular binary effects and not as a unit of analysis that is applicable throughout a text. Similarly, the notion of colon as it is used in ancient rhetorical sources was at first (i.e., in Aristotle and authors closely following him) defined in terms of the period, and only later also acquired the almost modern sense of an elementary discourse unit, defined by pauses at its edges, whether it is part of a period or not.

In the same vein, what is said about hiatus sometimes makes very little sense. For instance, on p. 205 of *SMNT*, the very common combination of the particle καί + forms of the article ὁ is marked as a case of hiatus (to be fair, Lee and Scott downplay the importance of the occurrence in this case). However, it is *a priori* hard to conceive that such a common combination was indeed a problem for the contemporary ear: either the hiatus was not a problem at all, or the language would have solved it by routinely applying one of the many sandhi mechanisms available (in this case probably crasis).[13]

Similarly, from a present-day perspective, informed by the success of methodologically more rigorous approaches, one may have reservations about the ancients' penchant for esthetic judgments and content-related interpretations of phonetic patterns (or even individual phonemes), such as the ones that sound mapping has been interested in so far. For instance, Lee and Scott offer the following remark on the succession of two aspirated onsets in ὅτι οὕτως ἐξέπνευσεν in Mark 15:39 (*SMNT*, 212): "The ὅτι clause reiterates ὁ sounds, requiring exhalation and imitating the action narrated in the next word ἐξέπνευσεν, which dramatizes Jesus' expiration."[14] In view of the enormous frequency of pronouns, subordinators, articles and adverbs starting in [ho] in ancient Greek, it is—in my opinion—hard to attribute any intrinsic expressive or mimetic value to this collocation *per se* (i.e., only an extremely small portion of the occurrences of this collocation would coincide with contents that involve the notion of expiration). Still, it is not inconceivable that a performer would choose to make *SMNT*'s interpretation audible by somehow exaggerating the aspiration at the onset of these otherwise perfectly neutral words. However, this hypothetical type of "special effect" is not straightforwardly plausible either, in that it presupposes a lot about what would be acceptable—let alone customary—performance practices: would it necessarily be a desirable effect, if a performer were to

---

13. For the fact that prepositives are treated differently with respect to hiatus, even by authors that otherwise appear to avoid it, see Allen, *Vox Graeca*, 97, and chapter 5 of the same book for an overview of the issues related to "vowel-junction" in general. For cases of crasis involving the article, see ibid., 99 and Devine and Stephens, *The Prosody of Greek Speech*, 266–69.

14. Note that it is an obvious fact that not only [ho]-sounds require exhalation, but all (Greek or English) phonemes, so exhalation as such is not the relevant feature. Also note that the supposed effect occurs within an anaphoric complement clause ("what the centurion saw") referring back to the event of Jesus' last breath, and not to the actual description of the event when it was first mentioned in Mark 15:37, which does not improve the plausibility of Lee and Scott's hypothesis: why would a performer choose to emphasize/"act out" the notion of expiration at that point (after the mentioning of the tearing of the curtain)?

emphasize it? Would it not be considered vulgar? Or more in general: what textual patterns triggered what kind of performance effects?

I believe it would be beneficial if future developments within the sound mapping project would adopt a more critical stance towards these ancient interpretative practices, and not take them for granted.[15] In any case, any characteristics one may want to attribute to NT Greek should be compatible with what is known about human languages and language use in general, and it would be useful to start elucidating questions such as the following in the light of a more methodologically rigorous and more empirically-minded approach: is the function of the sound patterns ("signatures," etc.) something that is typical of ancient Greek in general? Of certain genres in ancient Greek? Of biblical Greek only? Or is it perhaps supposed to be universal? How exactly are these patterns supposed to have an effect on the listener? What are the cognitive mechanisms involved? Is this something that has to be specifically acquired through training/education, or is it a side effect of more general mechanisms? Can these effects be observed in present-day spoken discourse? If not, why not? Can these patterns exist across strong boundaries? If so, how does that work in cognitive terms? Is there any functional difference between (1) very common patterns that are, e.g., the result of rhymes between high-frequency inflectional endings and (2) more rare and therefore more salient/marked patterns?[16] A good starting point for further development may be the work on the "poetics" of spontaneous speech in the tradition of conversation analysis.[17]

---

15. We may have a poor understanding of what any particular ancient author meant to achieve by his contribution within the context in which he wrote, which may have been very different from our own. The fact that ὀνόματα and ῥήματα in Plato (SMNT, 99) impossibly can have meant "nouns and verbs" (see Hoekstra and Scheppers, "'Ὄνομα, ῥῆμα, et λόγος") may be a good case in point. It should perhaps also be pointed out that ancient rhetorical criticism was not necessarily always of a high intellectual level, and many contributions mostly survived because of their use in a "middle school" context. In any case, a very critical approach to all those contents is in order.

16. For instance, in the case of the interpretation of [ho]-sound mentioned above, it would be easy to constitute a corpus containing any number of occurrences of similar sound patterns, in which the same pattern may or may not be interpretable as significant, so as to fuel a reflection on what exactly makes a pattern significant or not, what it would require from a performer to make its significance audible to an audience, etc.

17. Jefferson, "On the Poetics of Ordinary Talk"; Sacks, *Lectures*, vol. 2, 318–25, and elsewhere within the same volume. See also Tannen, *Talking Voices*.

2. Discourse Segmentation: Colon and Intonation Unit (IU)

One of the most obvious ways in which my work may contribute to sound mapping is that it offers a systematic linguistic account of discourse segmentation, as well as a practical way of segmenting Greek texts into elementary discourse units, which I called "cola." However, my use of this term is not so much grounded in any of its ancient uses in either rhetoric or literary criticism or metrics (although there is an obvious historical connection), but rather in modern approaches in which it was observed that certain word order rules appeared to apply to smaller-scale units than the clause or sentence. Building on observations by such authors as Eduard Fraenkel, Kenneth Dover and M.H.B. Marshall,[18] I tried to systematically develop the idea that these units coincided with the units called "Intonation Units" ("IUs") in contemporary linguistics. Following most importantly the works of Wallace Chafe (as mentioned above), I then defined the IU/colon as the elementary discourse unit, which means that discourse *essentially* comes in cola. The elementary nature of this unit has consequences on many levels:

(i) the colon is primarily a cognitive unit, corresponding to a "chunk" of information that is processed at once; this aspect has for a consequence that it will typically coincide with a prosodic and grammatical unit;

(ii) *qua* elementary discourse unit, the colon is also a pragmatically elementary unit, i.e., a single "verbal action," coinciding with a single pragmatic function ("point");

(iii) the above explains why the colon is the unit to which certain Greek word order rules apply (see section 2.1 here below).

2.1 Word Order within the Colon

Word order played a relatively important part in my own work on classical Greek, in that it offered me clear, formal and objective evidence that "grounded" the research empirically.[19] Thus, a number of word order rules

---

18. Fraenkel, "Kolon und Satz I" and "Kolon und Satz II"; Dover, *Greek Word Order*; Marshall, *Verbs, Nouns, and Postpositives*.

19. Still, the focus of the work was clearly on discourse segmentation and coherence, and not on word order as such (*pace* Nässelqvist, *Public Reading in Early Christianity*, 131): my claim was that the observed word order phenomena are a direct consequence of the fact that discourse is produced one colon at a time, not that the

predict that certain types of words will have to take this or that position within the colon in classical Greek:

- a number of postpositive particles take second position (P2) after the first word (whatever this word may be), and unemphatic personal or indefinite pronouns, as well as ἄν, take P2 after the first full word of the colon, excluding such words as the article, prepositions and certain introductive particles (*TCH* §4);
- a number of "introductive" particles takes first position (P1) within the colon (*TCH* §2.1) and a number of "preferential" words have a clear statistical tendency towards P1 (*TCH* §5.1).

Once these rules have been established, they can be used to reconstruct colon-boundaries in an ancient Greek written text.

However, the P2-rules ("Wackernagel's Law"), which yield numerous and reliable criteria for segmentation in classical and archaic Greek, appear to be a lot less useful for the purpose of analyzing NT Greek. Firstly, particles (including P2-particles) are less frequent in NT Greek than in the classical literature. Next, the P2-rule for non-emphatic pronouns does not seem to hold in biblical Greek in the same way it holds in classical Greek: apparently, the rules for enclitics changed so that the domain to which they cling was now the one to which they belong syntactically, rather than the first word of the colon.[20]

This does not mean that it would not still be worthwhile to study this aspect of word order for the purposes at hand. However, this is a rather technical matter that would require a more thorough and extensive corpus study than I can afford within the context of this contribution. Let me just refer to the position of αὐτ- in Mark 15:17–19:

17a	καὶ ἐνδιδύσκουσιν <u>αὐτὸν</u> πορφύραν
17b–d	καὶ περιτιθέασιν <u>αὐτῷ</u> πλέξαντες ἀκάνθινον στέφανον·
18a	καὶ ἤρξαντο ἀσπάζεσθαι <u>αὐτόν</u>
18b	Χαῖρε βασιλεῦ τῶν Ἰουδαίων
19a	καὶ ἔτυπτον <u>αὐτοῦ</u> τὴν κεφαλὴν καλάμῳ
19b	καὶ ἐνέπτυον <u>αὐτῷ</u>,

---

colon was somehow *defined* by word order (*TCH* §0.1.5).

20. For this diachronic aspect, see Taylor, *Clitics and Configurationality*; Janse, "Convergence and Divergence." The tendency was already noticeable in classical Greek (*TCH* §0.1.1(3) and §6.3; Marshall, *Verbs, Nouns, and Postpositives*).

It is noteworthy that all these occurrences of αὐτ- cling to the word to which they syntactically belong with, except for αὐτοῦ in 19a (but then again, body parts often produce grammatically "special" constructions: "*I hit his head" vs. "I hit him on the head"). At the same time, all occurrences (including 19a) obey the P2-rule, except perhaps 18a (but even in this case, one may argue that "to begin" may function as a kind of auxiliary verb, forming a unit with the infinitive; see *TCH* §6.1(3b)). Similarly, one may invoke unit formation for the collocation "cast lots," and thus still read ἐπ' <u>αὐτά</u> in P2 of the colon βάλλοντες κλῆρον ἐπ' <u>αὐτά</u> (Mark 15:24). However, this explanation would not work for καὶ διαμερίζονται τὰ ἱμάτια <u>αὐτοῦ</u> in the same verse, which is a clear example of the tendency for enclitics to cling to their syntactic host.

However, phonological prominence (including clisis) may also be important for the reconstruction of the sound of Greek discourse as such. Whether a particular word or syllable is prominent or not may make a difference for determining the kind of phonetic patterns that are studied in sound mapping. Most importantly, all postpositives (and most introductives, depending on their function) are—by definition—prosodically weak.[21] For instance, I wonder whether the phonetic weakness of καί or αὐτ- (e.g., in Mark 15:16–24) does or does not disqualify these words as a major factor in establishing a sound pattern (cf. *SMNT*, 199–201). More in general, I would surmise that the fact that certain words carry focus may make them stand out more within a sound pattern than those that do not carry focus.[22]

Let me mention one more aspect of colon-internal word order, as it turns out that it occurs a number of times in the excerpt analyzed below. There is a general, apparently cross-linguistic, tendency for cognitively "new" items to occur as late as possible in a unit.[23] One of the manifestations of this tendency in Greek are so-called "presentative constructions" in which a verb (typically a rather low-content or otherwise predictable "staging verb") occurs at the beginning of the unit and a new topic (e.g., a new main agent in a narrative) comes last. A prototypical example occurs in Mark 15:8 καὶ ἀναβὰς ὁ ὄχλος, in which the verb ἀναβὰς is a staging verb

---

21. The claims about the function of δέ on p. 188 of *SMNT* do not make sense from the point of view developed in this paper: it is simply not correct that the fact that δέ is postpositive makes it a weak connector that does not create an obvious paratactic link: it has been shown that δέ (and *a fortiori* other postpositives such as τοίνυν in classical Greek) does indicate parataxis and *can* indicate (and in classical Greek typically *does* indicate) stronger shifts than καί (see, e.g., *TCH* §21,3(2)). It may be useful, in order to avoid misunderstandings, to add that καί is weak in most of its uses, as well.

22. For the notion of focus, see *TCH* §0.3.4(1), §7.2, and §21.4.

23. Chafe, *Discourse, Consciousness, and Time*, 82–92.

in a very literal sense:[24] the crowd walks up onto the stage; after this entry, it remains present on the stage as a main interlocutor to Pilate for the whole of Mark 15:8–15; also note the aoristus participle, which appears to be standard in these constructions.[25]

2.2 Segmentation Criteria Based on the Grammatical and Pragmatic Functions of the Segment

One of the main empirical arguments for the "colon hypothesis" is the observation that the grammatical typology of units yielded by the segmentation procedures based on word order in classical and pre-classical Greek (*TCH* §0.1.3) coincides more or less completely with the grammatical typology of IUs in spontaneous speech (*TCH* §0.2.4). Thus, it can be shown that the following types of grammatical constituents as a rule constitute separate discourse segments (comprising one or more cola/IUs), or—in other words—that the boundaries of these constituents typically coincide with colon boundaries (*TCH* §10.2 and §10.5(3)):

(i)	Verb-centered constituents / clauses: • finite clauses (main clauses or subordinate clauses); • participial clauses (genitivus absolutus, participium coniunctum); • some types of infinitival constructions.
(ii)	The different members of coordinated, correlative and parallel structures.
(iii)	Parentheses, tags, afterthoughts, and other syntactically non-integrated elements.
(iv)	Fronted elements: • fronted argument NPs (very often subjects) as topics; • fronted PPs as settings or as markers; • fronted markers; • highly salient words may also be subject to "emphatic fronting."

Ad (i): Verb-centered constituents are colon-autonomous if they coincide with a separate pragmatic point, for instance if they present a separate action in a plot. In other cases, they can be realized within the same IU as other material, for instance infinitives in combination with an almost auxiliary verb ("begin to V," "want to V," "should V," etc.), identifying/restrictive relative clauses in combination with their antecedents, or perhaps certain

---

24. Unless one chooses to follow the alternative reading ἀναβοήσας, defended by, e.g., Cranfield, *The Gospel According to St Mark*, 450.

25. For parallels in classical Greek, see *TCH* §5.2.2(3) and §21.2(f).

participial constructions involving *verba percipiendi* (*TCH* §0.2.4(2) and §10.2.1).

Ad (ii): This category covers traditional rhetorical patterns such as chiasmus or antithesis. Note that Aristotle's original usage of περίοδος and κῶλον was limited to this kind of binary pattern.[26]

Ad (iii): The status of non-integrated items makes sense from a cognitive point of view, in that they are often the result of a voluntary or involuntary interruption of the cognitive flow, which explains at the same time both their syntactic and their prosodic autonomy. Short and formulaic parentheses or tags may be integrated within an IU; in the case of ancient Greek, some of these (vocatives, ἔφη, etc.) can function like a P2-clitic (*TCH* §10.2.3).

Ad (iv): Often, the scope of these fronted elements is a criterion for considering them as a separate colon or not (*TCH* §2.0(2c), §2.1(3), and many examples throughout Part II and Part III).

It may be useful to mention that the occurrence of parenthetical units, as well as some types of fronting, may result in "rest-cola," i.e., units that are the result of the interruption of what otherwise would have been a "natural" colon, but that now do not fit the above typology (*TCH* §10.2.5).[27]

It is impossible to adequately argue for this set of segmentation criteria here and —again— I can only refer to *TCH* for very extensive argumentation and exemplification. Suffice it here to remind the reader of the fact that my main argument derives from a comparison between (i) word order phenomena in classical Greek, and—importantly—also (ii) a typology of IUs in spontaneous speech. The practical usefulness of this typology for the analysis of ancient Greek will be amply demonstrated in my analyses in section 4 below.

2.3 Prosodic Aspects: Intonation, Pause and "Breath"

Ever since ancient rhetoric,[28] there exists a persistent idea that the colon is somehow a "breath unit" and/or that pauses necessarily are spaces for breathing. Of course, breath is physiologically important (sooner or later

---

26. *TCH* §10.4.4; and Scheppers, "Kola."

27. Furthermore, it is also true that—depending on performance style, degree of preparation and rhetorical engineering, etc.—some types of "natural" cola can in actual performance undergo various degrees of merger with adjacent IUs; for the notions of "intonational sandhi" and "syntactic sandhi," see, i.a., *TCH* §0.2.2(3) and §13.1.4(3).

28. For the ambiguous status of πνεῦμα in some ancient rhetorical treatises, see Scheppers, "Kola."

any speaker will have to breathe in) and a competent performer should have enough breath control to not be forced to pause when he or she would not choose to. However, there is no one-to-one relation between pause and breath: while any pause can be used to breathe, not all pauses are actually used for breathing.[29] More importantly, there is no one-to-one relation between pause and discourse boundary either: some discourse boundaries are not marked by particularly long pauses (at the level of the individual IU, some boundaries may not be marked by pauses at all), and, conversely, it is perfectly possible and actually quite common to pause in the middle of an IU (whether as so-called "hesitation pauses" or for dramatic effect—there is no real difference in effect between both). Any sufficiently detailed transcription of recorded speech—or even simple self-observation and experimentation—should suffice to establish these facts.[30] The delimitation of IUs is not exclusively and not even mainly a matter of pauses, but crucially involves a convergence of various parameters (such as a decrease in baseline pitch level and/or acceleration-deceleration and/or a recognizable intonation contour and/or "creaky" voice quality at the end, etc.).[31]

3. Discourse Structure

Section 2 (here above) dealt with the issue of how to determine the boundaries of elementary discourse units (cola/IUs) in an ancient Greek text, as well as with certain aspects of the nature of these units, and how my work on these matters may contribute to sound mapping. In the present section 3, I would like to discuss the relevance of larger—or, rather, higher-level—discourse units.

---

29. For instance, the phenomenon of "filled pauses" ("uhm," etc.) shows that pauses need not consist of an inhalation at all; *TCH* §0.1.2(2), §0.2.2(2), §10.2.5(2b), §13.3.4(3).

30. It follows that the claim that cola should include a minimum number of syllables and should not exceed a maximum number of syllables (e.g., Nässelqvist, *Public Reading in Early Christianity*, 129–31) is not self-evidently correct, at least if one uses the colon in the "modern" sense adopted here (which Nässelqvist, to be fair, does not). Although Tom Boomershine's performances (e.g., "The Messiah of Peace") perhaps cannot be used as direct and conclusive evidence as to the correctness of any of my (or anyone else's) reconstructions, it is interesting to note that this professional performer opts for segmentations into IUs that are very close in size to what I propose on more theoretical grounds.

31. See, e.g., Chafe, *Discourse, Consciousness, and Time*, 57–60.

3.1 The Phonetics of Discourse Structure

In speech (as studied in discourse analysis and related fields), the major and uncontroversial phonetic reflections of discourse segmentation/articulation are not so much the phonematic "sound signatures" that sound mapping focuses on, but rather the prosodic phenomena directly related to discourse structure:[32]

- intonation contours at the level of the individual IU (and more complex patterns beyond the single IU);
- pauses of various lengths (including filled pauses);
- (sudden) changes in baseline pitch;
- changes in speed;
- changes in volume;
- changes in voice quality.

Importantly, there is also the phenomenon of the "phonological sentence" characterized by a drop of the baseline pitch (sentence final falling pitch).

As the sound mapping project is focusing on the "sound" aspect of discourse structure, it may be worthwhile to engage in educated speculation on the various prosodic ways in which discourse segmentation and articulation is enacted: reconstructing prosody has to be a crucial part of reconstructing a performance of the corpus, which would also help giving phonematic patterns such as "sound signatures" their proper place in the overall picture. More in particular, I believe it would be worthwhile to consider how prosodic boundaries affect the perception of the phonetic patterns that sound mapping is focusing on (see my remarks in section 1.3 above).

3.2 Discourse Markers and Discourse Structure

It is a well-known fact that the repertoire of discourse particles in the NT texts is somewhat limited as compared to classical Greek,[33] which means that we are presented with fewer overt clues to establish discourse structure

---

32. For an overview and references, see, e.g., Couper-Kuhlen, "Intonation and Discourse," and Sicoli, "Voice Registers." As was already mentioned above, pause is often quoted as *the* boundary marker, but in actual fact pauses are remarkably unpredictable (both ways: they sometimes don't occur where expected, and often they occur in the middle of IUs).

33. Thrall, *Greek Particles*, 39.

Discourse Segmentation 147

in NT Greek than in classical and pre-classical Greek. Still, whenever they occur, these markers should be taken into account for the reconstruction of the overall sound of the NT corpus, and not merely as repeating phonetic entities. The following examples illustrate this point (*TCH* §21.3):

- οὖν indicates that whatever is introduced by it has a more substantial function than whatever preceded, which—sound-wise—would probably imply some kind of more emphatic elocution (perhaps slower, perhaps louder or less loud than what preceded, etc.);
- one of the typical uses of γάρ is to introduce an explanation, often parenthetical or afterhought-like,[34] which would perhaps imply faster, lower pitched, and/or less loud speech.

One of the key aspects for establishing the structure of the excerpt of Mark's gospel analyzed below is the occurrence of two particles: καί (as also noted in *SMNT*) and δέ.[35] Most of the uses of these particles in classical Greek derive from their "primary" functions:

- δέ indicates a switch;
- καί indicates continuity.

In classical Greek narratives, this typically yields patterns where δέ indicates more or less major boundaries (often coinciding with a switch from one main agent to the next, or from one setting to the next), and καί linking events *within* a segment introduced by δέ.[36] In the excerpt of Mark analyzed

---

34. A lot has been made of allegedly illogical or awkward cases of Mark's use of γάρ (see, e.g., Evans, "How Mark Writes," 136–38; Thrall, *Greek Particles*, 41–50). I would like to argue that this evaluation of Mark's usage is based on the erroneous presumption that the particle marks a causal relation: to me all of the cases cited seem to fall well within the domain of classical usage. For instance, Evans, "How Mark writes," 137: "Mark's explanation, 'for the stone was very large,' is a classic. The evangelist's misplacement of the qualifying *gar* clause in this passage is so illogical as to be humorous. The relevant part of the passage reads: "And they were saying to one another, 'Who will roll away the stone for us from the door of the tomb?' And looking up, they saw that the stone was rolled back—for it was very large" (16.3–4). If this is taken literally, Mark seems to be saying that the stone was rolled back because it was very large (as though smaller stones were less likely to roll back!)." However, the "literal meaning" (?) of γάρ does not coincide with "because" or "for," and the clause ἦν γὰρ μέγας σφόδρα is not problematic at all as a background explanation of why the stone was an issue to start with. I agree with Voelz that the tag "you know" would often be a more adequate translation of γάρ (in ancient Greek at large, not only Mark) than "for" or "because" (Voelz, "The Characteristics of the Greek of St. Mark's Gospel," 142–43).

35. For a critique of some of the more bizarre speculations on the functions of δέ in Mark, see Thrall, *Greek Particles*, 50–67.

36. For a simple example, see my analysis of Lysias 1,23, *TCH* §15.

below, δέ still often indicates an agent-switch (or other switches), but καί appears to have taken a much wider usage, including at major boundaries. This sometimes yields patterns in which a certain instance of καί has scope over several segments introduced by δέ.[37] Note that this does not mean that καί cannot also mark very minor boundaries, because it obviously very often does, even within the same excerpt. In view of these observations, I would like to propose the hypothesis that, in Mark's idiolect, καί is the unmarked/default clause-connector, which implies that—as such—it is useless for determining the hierarchical level of the boundary it marks.[38]

Apart from the presence of particles, major boundaries are often marked explicitly by i.a. temporal markers, overt agent-switches and location-switches (often involving the particle δέ), or meta-linguistic discourse markers (e.g., "that is all I know about X," "let us now address the next point," etc.). Such major boundaries are also marked prosodically, not only by pauses of various lengths, but also by a number of other phenomena (see section 3.1 above). A reconstruction of this aspect should perhaps be included in a sound map.

3.3 Discourse Structure and Discourse-Space

Discourse—as it actually occurs in real life contexts—does not just consist of sound and not even just of specifically linguistic phenomena, in that it crucially involves "a world" that unfolds according to the underlying pragmatic structure of the discourse:[39] subsequent events, agents, objects, and

---

37. Chapter 2 of Runge's *Discourse Grammar of the Greek New Testament* deals with the functions of καί and δέ in NT Greek. Similarly, see also Black, *Sentence Conjunctions in the Gospel of Matthew*.

38. Rodney Decker calculated that 80/88 sections and 64% of all sentences in Mark's gospel start with καί; interestingly, Decker connects this usage with the influence of a Hebrew particle *nan* (Decker, "Markan Idiolect," 47–49). I am not able to verify these claims, but they do seem to confirm my first impressions. Cf. Voelz, "The Characteristics of the Greek of St. Mark's Gospel," 139: "The heavy use of καί as the basic conjunction throughout the gospel is easily recognized as Marcan. It may be a Semitism or simply characteristic of an oral milieu. See 3:1–27, 5:35–41, 8:1–13, 14:32–41 (also 12:1–5, 14:53–72, 16:1–8)." See also Porter, "Pericope Markers and the Paragraph," 184–87. As stated above, I disagree with the conclusion that καί is a marker of major boundaries at all: the fact that καί occurs at major boundaries does not *ipso facto* turn it into a marker of these boundaries *qua* major boundaries, especially if it occurs very frequently at very low-level boundaries as well.

39. I personally find this aspect (*TCH* §13.1.3 and elsewhere in Part III) the most interesting part of my work and it is one that I will pursue in future research. However, I do not believe it is particularly relevant to the sound mapping project, beyond the practical aspects I mention here. For the idea that this aspect is particularly relevant for

other items successively occur at the foreground or in the background of the "stage," the action shifts from one setting to the next, our focus shifts from one main agent to the next, etc. From this point of view, it is to be expected that major discourse boundaries essentially coincide with major shifts in the world/stage/space that constitutes the contents of the discourse.

Depending on one's methodological choices, one might consider these aspects as lying outside the objectives of the sound mapping project *per se*, but I believe it would be self-defeating to not take this aspect into account while trying to establish structural boundaries or prosody more in general. My analyses here below will demonstrate how this aspect can be operationalized and how this sometimes yields results that are at odds with the results published in *SMNT*.

4. Analysis: Mark's Crucifixion Story (Mark 15)

In this section I offer an analysis of Mark's crucifixion story (Mark 15).[40] For the sake of ease of presentation, I have divided the text into 10 units (A to J), which I tried to make coincide with "natural" episodes, as much as possible (for an analysis of the overall structure, see my conclusion to this section). I also present a tentative segmentation of the text into cola/potential IUs, which I will number for ease of reference, using the traditional numbering of the verses followed by letters referring to my segmentation (the first colon of Mark 15:1 will be referred to as 1a, and the fourth colon of Mark 15:40 as 40d).

As always in this paper, my main interlocutor will be Lee and Scott's *SMNT*, in this case chapter 6, dealing with the excerpt analyzed here. I will occasionally also refer to Tom Boomershine's performance of this excerpt as made available at the Youtube channel of the GoTellStory organization.[41]

---

the analysis of oral discourse, see, e.g., Bakker, "Discourse and Performance: Involvement, Visualization and 'Presence' in Homeric Poetry."

40. For the sake of practicality, I used the Greek text of Westcott and Hort, *The New Testament*, as published by the Perseus Digital Library. I also consulted Holmes, *The Greek New Testament*, and Nestle et al., *Novum Testamentum Graece* [27th edition], mostly for their critical apparatus and their choices in punctuation and lay-out. My draft translation (very ad hoc) has made use of the 'World English Bible' version (http://ebible.org/web/).

41. Boomershine, "The Messiah of Peace."

A. The Head-priests Turn in Jesus (Mark 15:1)

This episode starts with a fronted temporal marker καὶ εὐθὺς πρωΐ (1a), which parallels other temporal markers at 25a (ἦν δὲ ὥρα τρίτη), 33a (καὶ γενομένης ὥρας ἕκτης), 34a (καὶ τῇ ἐνάτῃ ὥρᾳ), and 42a (καὶ ἤδη ὀψίας γενομένης). The use of καί (1a) at a major discourse boundary is very un-classical but obviously quite frequent in Mark (see similar use in 15:42, 16:1, and at the beginning of each of the separate episodes that make up Mark 8). It appears that—at least in Mark—καί can serve to connect segments of any level to each other, provided they are of the same level: from single words in a list, over various actions by a single agent (see below), to—apparently—whole episodes.

One should also ask the question as to the scope of both καί and the temporal marker (and the answers can but need not be the same in both cases). Depending on how one chooses to analyze the overall structure of the gospel, i.e., whether Mark 15 is considered a separate segment on its own or whether one reads it as forming an integrated whole with the preceding chapter, one could argue that καί in 1a has scope over chapter 15 as a whole, or—together with the temporal marker—over Mark 15:1-24 (until the next temporal marker), or even until 2a only. Nothing much may hinge on it for the interpretation of this passage as such, but the issue may shape the way in which one views the functions of discourse particles and temporal markers in general and thus still has some interest.

In any case, the first episode under the scope of 1a is made up by 4 successive actions by the same agent (the head-priests, introduced in 1b): hold a consultation (1b-d), bind Jesus (1e), carry away Jesus (1f), turn Jesus in to Pilate (1g), each of them expressed by an aorist verb, which corresponds to classical usage. Also note that this episode coincides with one single syntactic sentence.

1a   Καὶ εὐθὺς πρωΐ
     And immediately in the morning
1b   συμβούλιον ποιήσαντες οἱ ἀρχιερεῖς
     a consultation was held by the head-priests
1c   μετὰ τῶν πρεσβυτέρων καὶ γραμματέων
     with the elders and scribes,
1d   καὶ ὅλον τὸ συνέδριον
     and the whole council
1e   δήσαντες τὸν Ἰησοῦν
     and they bound Jesus

1f	ἀπήνεγκαν
	and carried him away,
1g	καὶ παρέδωκαν Πειλάτῳ.
	and they turned him in to Pilate

As far as the details of my segmentation go, I can briefly mention the following elements (referring to the typology introduced in section 2.2 above):

1a	Fronted temporal marker with a potentially very wide scope (see above).
1b	Participial clause presenting a self-contained action within a sequence of actions (// 1e, 1f, 1g). Note the presentative construction (see section 2.1 above), with the verb in P1, allowing the introduction of a new main agent on the scene, at the end of an introductory colon; the head-priests function as the main agent until that role shifts to Pilate in 2a.
1c	Parallel member within a complex NP (// 1d).
1d	Parallel member within a complex NP (// 1c).
1e	Participial clause presenting a self-contained action within a sequence of actions (// 1b, 1f, 1g).
1f	Main finite clause, minus fronted subject (1b), presenting a self-contained action within a sequence of actions (// 1b, 1e, 1g).
1g	Main finite clause, minus fronted subject (1b), presenting a self-contained action within a sequence of actions (// 1b, 1e, 1f).

B. Pilate Interrogates Jesus (Mark 15:2–5)

Beginning with this episode, a pattern establishes itself that will last until Mark 11:28 (interrupted by the excursus in Mark 15:6–7):

- καί introduces an episode;
- fronted subject + δέ marks agent-switches within an episode.

2a	καὶ ἐπηρώτησεν αὐτὸν ὁ Πειλᾶτος
	and Pilatus asked him
2b	Σὺ εἶ ὁ βασιλεὺς τῶν Ἰουδαίων;
	"Are you the king of the Jews?"
2c	ὁ δὲ
	and he

2d	ἀποκριθεὶς αὐτῷ	
	he replies to him	
2e	λέγει	
	and says	
2f		Σὺ λέγεις.
		"If you say so."
3	καὶ κατηγόρουν αὐτοῦ οἱ ἀρχιερεῖς πολλά.	
	And the head-priests accused him of many things.	
4a	ὁ δὲ Πειλᾶτος	
	And Pilate	
4b	πάλιν ἐπηρώτα αὐτὸν [λέγων]	
	again, he asked him	
4c		Οὐκ ἀποκρίνῃ οὐδέν;
		"You don't reply anything?
4d		ἴδε πόσα σου κατηγοροῦσιν.
		Look how many accusations they make!"
5a	ὁ δὲ Ἰησοῦς	
	and Jesus	
5b	οὐκέτι οὐδὲν ἀπεκρίθη,	
	he still didn't reply anything	
5c	ὥστε θαυμάζειν τὸν Πειλᾶτον.	
	to the astonishment of Pilate.	

First, the details of the segmentation proposed:

2a	Full finite main clause, minus the complement clause (2b). Note again the presentative construction, introducing a new main agent; the verb "asking" is perhaps not low-content *per se*, but asking is predictable within the context of the trial and is *de facto* redundant when the actual question asked is made explicit.
2b	Full finite clause.
2c	Fronted subject, presenting a switch to another agent (// 4a, 5a and more examples after the excursus Mark 15:6–7).
2d	Participial clause. One might want to argue that the "answering" represents actually the same action as the "he said" in 2e, and that therefore 2d should not be considered a separate colon, despite the formal resemblance to *participia aoristi* that definitely do constitute separate cola (for typical examples, see Mark 15:36 analyzed below).
2e	Main clause, minus the fronted subject (2c) and minus complement clause (2f).

2f	Full finite clause.
3	Full finite main clause. Presentative construction (subject follows verb); apparently, πολλά bears the main focus and appears even later than the "new" subject.
4a	Fronted subject (// 2c and 5a).
4b	Main clause, minus the fronted subject (4a) and minus complement clause (4c–d).
4c	Full finite clause.
4d	Full finite clause.
5a	Fronted subject (// 2c and 4a).
5b	Main clause, minus the fronted subject (5a).
5c	Afterthought-like infinitival clause, presenting a separate action from the one in the main clause (5b).

The internal structure of this episode is determined by agent-switches back and forth between Pilate, Jesus and the head-priests, and at the formal level by alternations between καί and δέ.[42] There is no ambiguity about the fact that what is introduced by δέ here falls under the scope of καί: it would be very unlikely to postulate a major boundary between the two members of question-answer adjacency pair. The exact function of καί in (3) is somewhat more difficult to determine. In view of the very wide range of uses of καί in Mark, one could want to read this colon as (1) the continuation of Jesus' silence in the previous segment, with the next switch back to Pilate as the stronger boundary, or (2) the beginning of a new sub-unit, and the switch back to Pilate as a reaction to what the head-priests said. Colon 4d ἴδε πόσα σου κατηγοροῦσιν seems to suggest (2), in that Pilate's question in 4 corresponds to the accusations mentioned in 3. In that case 3–4 parallels 2.

C. Excursus: Pilate's Yearly Amnesty; Barabbas (Mark 15:6–7)

For lack of space, I will not analyze this excursus in detail, but it may be useful to still print the text for ease of reference: [6a] Κατὰ δὲ ἑορτὴν [6b] ἀπέλυεν αὐτοῖς ἕνα δέσμιον [6c] ὃν παρῃτοῦντο. [7a] ἦν δὲ ὁ λεγόμενος Βαραββᾶς [7b] μετὰ τῶν στασιαστῶν δεδεμένος [7c] οἵτινες ἐν τῇ στάσει φόνον πεποιήκεισαν.[43]

---

42. In many classical authors, such action-reaction patterns would probably be presented by means of the μέν—δέ combination (*TCH* §21.3(2c)).

43. [6a] And at the festival [6b] he used to release to them one prisoner, [6c] whom they asked of him. [7a] And there was one called Barabbas, [7b] in prison with those

That there is a boundary here is indicated by the fact that the sequence of events that makes up the plot is interrupted for some background info. This corresponds to the following formal aspects:

- the pattern "fronted agent + δέ, followed by one or more actions by that agent" is interrupted: δέ in (6a) still signals a switch, but no longer a switch between main agents;
- the verbs are no longer presenting successive actions making up the plot (no more aorists).

It is clear that this information is backgrounded with respect to the main plot (the sequence of agent-switches resumes at Mark 15:8), but the relation with what precedes or follows is not immediately evident from any of the formal features, though it is clear that this info is needed at this spot in order to make the following interaction between Pilate and crowd intelligible.

Qua backgrounded, parenthetical contents, it can be expected that this excursus is performed faster and/or in a lower-pitched voice and/or at a lower volume than the main line of the narrative. Boomershine's rendition of this excursus[44] does indeed employ a less emphatic diction than the surrounding main line of the plot (shorter pauses between IUs, less spectacular variation in pitch and volume).

D. Pilate and the Crowd (Mark 15:8–15)

The pattern established from the beginning of our excerpt continues here. The episode starts with καί and the internal structure is determined by a strongly homogeneous pattern: after the introduction of the crowd in 8a καὶ ἀναβὰς ὁ ὄχλος, the text is structured by a series of agent-switches, each time marked by the fronting of the agent + δέ:

8a	(ὁ ὄχλος)
9a	ὁ δὲ Πειλᾶτος
11a	οἱ δὲ ἀρχιερεῖς
12a	ὁ δὲ Πειλᾶτος
13a	οἱ δὲ
14a	ὁ δὲ Πειλᾶτος

---

who had rebelled, [7c] men who in the rebellion had committed murder.

44. "The Messiah of Peace," 22:26–22:49.

14d οἱ δὲ
15a ὁ δὲ Πειλᾶτος

I will have to confine myself here to a brief analysis of the end of this episode.

15a	ὁ δὲ Πειλᾶτος and Pilate	
15b	βουλόμενος τῷ ὄχλῳ τὸ ἱκανὸν ποιῆσαι who wanted to please the crowd	
15c	ἀπέλυσεν αὐτοῖς τὸν Βαραββᾶν, he released Barabbas to them,	
15d	καὶ παρέδωκεν τὸν Ἰησοῦν and he handed over Jesus,	
15e	φραγελλώσας — he flogged him —,	
15f		ἵνα σταυρωθῇ. to be crucified.

The following elements should help motivate my segmentation:

15a	Fronted subject. Parallel to a number of similarly fronted subjects (see above).
15b	Full participial clause, presenting a separate content from the action in the main clauses 15c–d. Note that this participle, in the present tense (as opposed to the aoristi in, e.g., Mark 15:36 analyzed below and—for that matter—φραγελλώσας in 15e), does not present a separate step in the sequence of actions, but the background to one of these actions (the reason why Pilate sets Barrabas free and has Jesus executed). This conforms with classical usage (*TCH* §21.1(3)).
15c	Main clause, minus the fronted subject 15a (// 15d).
15d	Main clause, minus the fronted subject 15a (// 15c).

15e	Participial clause. Participium aoristi, typically presenting a separate step in the plot sequence. However, the participle does not occur before the finite verb as would be the case in more prototypical usage. One wonders whether the flogging occurs before the handing over (which would be necessarily the case if it was intended that Pilate did the flogging himself), or if the order of the verbs perhaps still follows the chronological order of the successive actions, but the choice between finite and participial verb forms is somewhat off. Note that the problem only exists because of the author's strategic choice to not operate a subject-switch from Pilate to the soldiers at this point. Nestle et al., *Novum Testamentum Graece* (27th edition) mentions variant readings that do away with the problem by putting the participle before the finite verb (lectio facilior). Holmes, *The Greek New Testament*, 111 does not mention any such variation. Interestingly, the bland, classical word order in Matt 27:26 (τὸν δὲ Ἰησοῦν φραγελλώσας παρέδωκεν ἵνα σταυρωθῇ) also avoids the anomaly.
15f	Subordinate finite clause.

Lee and Scott's analysis of this passage (*SMNT*, 200) has a new "unit" start with καὶ παρέδωκεν τὸν Ἰησοῦν (15d). This looks very unlikely to me, in the light of the following elements:

- the pattern "fronted agent + δέ + a series of actions in which he/she is the main agent," is both classical and well-established in Mark's text;
- καὶ παρέδωκεν τὸν Ἰησοῦν is obviously under the scope of ὁ δὲ Πειλᾶτος and Mark 15:16–24 is obviously under the scope of οἱ δὲ στρατιῶται;
- there is an obvious contrast between ἀπέλυσεν αὐτοῖς τὸν Βαραββᾶν and καὶ παρέδωκεν τὸν Ἰησοῦν, both under the scope of ὁ δὲ Πειλᾶτος, which suggests an immediate relation between both contrasted members;
- Mark 15:16 coincides with an explicit change of scenery (from the court to some other place at the praetorium).

All these elements taken together suggest that there cannot be a major boundary between (15c) and (15d). This is a case in point of an issue with—what I called—the "holistic" character of discourse (section 3.3 above): if the syntactic and pragmatic, and therefore presumably also the prosodic, levels of discourse structure suggest the (in this case) absence of a major boundary, it is hard to see how a change in sound pattern (however defined) could fruitfully go against that. What underlying mechanism (cognitive or otherwise) would generate a relevant boundary at the level of a sound pattern and another one just after it on all other levels? What would its function be?

E. The Soldiers and Jesus (Mark 15:16–24)

Let us start by briefly looking at the very beginning of this episode:[45]

16a	Οἱ δὲ στρατιῶται
	and the soldiers
16b	ἀπήγαγον αὐτὸν ἔσω τῆς αὐλῆς,
	they led him away within the court,
16c	(ὅ ἐστιν πραιτώριον),
	which is the praetorium
17a	καὶ συνκαλοῦσιν ὅλην τὴν σπεῖραν.
	and they call together the whole cohort.
17b	καὶ ἐνδιδύσκουσιν αὐτὸν πορφύραν
	and dress him in purple

This episode (unlike most previous ones) is not introduced by καί and instead continues the pattern of agent-switches marked by δέ. However, καί is not exclusively a marker of major boundaries (i.e., the absence of καί does not at all imply the absence of a major boundary) and several other elements indicate that there is major boundary here:

- the switch to a *brand new* main agent (the soldiers, who were not previously on the scene) and the disappearance of all other agents (except Jesus) from the scene;
- an explicit change of location;
- a very consistent internal structure of all the segments within the unit: all the successive actions are introduced by καί immediately followed by the main finite verb; in most cases Jesus is then referred to by means of the unemphatic anaphoric pronoun αὐτ-, which stereotypically clings to the verb.[46]

Of course, there is a lot of internal structure to this episode, including several changes in location, but the way the events are presented, including the fact that the soldiers remain the central agents throughout (and Jesus the—bizarrely but effectively—backgrounded passive object of their

---

45. The segmentation is straightforward: a fronted brand new main agent with a very wide scope, followed by successive actions by this agent (16c is an obvious parenthetical explanation, coinciding with a full finite relative clause).

46. Though this point is similar to the argument made by *SMNT*, I do not fully agree with their description "καί + predicate + αὐτ- + additional details": what *SMNT* call "additional details" are often the most indispensable "focused" items in the colon.

actions) ensures the internal cohesion of the episode. The internal structure of the episode—at first sight—contains three major sub-units:

- The whole block 17b–20 belongs together, as it consists as a whole of the mockery of the "king." This is marked explicitly by the resumptive ὅτε ἐνέπαιξαν αὐτῷ at the beginning of [20], as well as the fact that the disguise was taken off of Jesus.
- The stretch from the second part of 20 (καὶ ἐξάγουσιν αὐτὸν) until 22 (included) presents the trajectory between the praetorium and Golgotha; note that the finite verbs are all in the present tense, whereas the actions in what immediately preceded were presented in past tenses.
- The last verses 23–24 of the episode present what happens upon the soldiers' arrival at Golgotha (they try to give Jesus wine; they crucify him; they divide his cloths). Note the switch to past tense ἐδίδουν at verse 23, but back to present tense καὶ σταυροῦσιν αὐτὸν in 24.[47]

I cannot go into the details of the whole episode, but would like to quote the very ending:

23a	καὶ ἐδίδουν αὐτῷ ἐσμυρνισμένον οἶνον,
	and they gave him wine mixed with myrrh
23b	ὃς δὲ οὐκ ἔλαβεν.
	but he didn't take it.
24a	καὶ σταυροῦσιν αὐτὸν
	and they crucify him
24b	καὶ διαμερίζονται τὰ ἱμάτια αὐτοῦ
	and they divide his clothes among them
24c	βάλλοντες κλῆρον ἐπ' αὐτὰ
	casting lots on them
24d	τίς τί ἄρῃ.
	who gets what.

The segmentation is straightforward: each colon coincides with a separate finite clause, except for 24c, which is a participial clause, also representing a separate action. Not all of the clauses represent separate steps in

---

47. There is a lot more to be said about the switches between the historical present and past tenses in Mark's narrative, but at least in this case it looks plausible that the switches are a direct reflection of the occurrence of boundaries between sub-episodes. I haven't found anything insightful to say about the tenses in 16–17 above. For an account that suggests a significantly different use of the "historical present" in Mark (and perhaps John) as compared to classical usage, see Decker, "Markan Idiolect," 57–58.

the plot, though: 24c describes the way they divide the clothes (explanation/elaboration of 24b) and 24d in its turn explains 24c. Note that δέ in 23b obviously falls under the scope of καί in 23a, in a way that reminds us of the action-reaction patterns in 2a–2c and 3–4a above.

Something needs to be said about the fact that the actual crucifixion, which presumably is the narrative (and emotional?) climax of the whole episode, is dealt with in a very understated way: Mark deals with the event in only one full word (σταυροῦσιν).[48] Furthermore, after mentioning the crucifixion, the author does not stop, but goes on offering the detail about the cloths, as if this was even more important than the crucifixion *per se* (and perhaps, for the author the fulfillment of a prophecy *was* more important). This understated way of presenting potentially climactic material should be kept in mind, as it recurs below.

F. The Third Hour (Mark 15:25–32)

This episode starts as follows:

25a	ἦν δὲ ὥρα τρίτη	
	and it was the third hour	
25b		καὶ ἐσταύρωσαν αὐτόν.
		and they crucified him
25c		καὶ ἦν ἡ ἐπιγραφὴ τῆς αἰτίας αὐτοῦ ἐπιγεγραμμένη
		and the inscription of his accusation was inscribed: [. . .]

A wide array of elements indicates that the most important discourse boundary since Mark 15:1 occurs at verse 25. First of all, there is the overt temporal marker ἦν δὲ ὥρα τρίτη (without parallel since Mark 15:1). Next, there is also the resumptive repetition of 24a (καὶ σταυροῦσιν αὐτόν) in 25b: καὶ ἐσταύρωσαν αὐτόν (only the tense is different), which is indicative of the cognitive workload associated with a major shift. At the boundary 25a, there is also a switch from a rapid succession of successive punctual actions (verbs in aorist or historic present) without much descriptive material, to a much more diversified mix of static situations, continuous activities and punctual actions:

- 26–27: descriptive elements concerning the crucifixion itself (the superscript + the presence of two other convicts);

48. Of course, the event is resumptively referred to again in 25b (here below), but as laconically as in 24a.

- 29–32: Jesus is insulted by passers-by, head-priests and co-convicts.

G. The Sixth Hour (Mark 15:33)

The full text of this very short episode goes as follows:

33a	Καὶ γενομένης ὥρας ἕκτης
	And when the sixth hour had come,
33b	σκότος ἐγένετο ἐφ' ὅλην τὴν γῆν
	there came darkness over the whole land
33c	ἕως ὥρας ἐνάτης.
	until the ninth hour.

First, a few details concerning the segmentation into cola:

33a	Fronted participial clause, functioning as a temporal marker.
33b	Main finite clause.
33c	Extraposed prepositional phrase. Its potential autonomy as a colon is the result of its functional autonomy: the notion that the darkness lasts until the 9th hour is "new" with respect to the idea that the darkness came at the 6th hour.

This episode is extremely short, as compared to the other episodes, and perhaps one could read it as part of the next episode,[49] although the formal parallelism between the marking of the third hour (25a), the sixth hour (here), and the ninth hour (34a) is hard to ignore. Perhaps such extreme asymmetry is not problematic in Mark's style. It may be the case that Mark presents the supernatural darkness (and its three-hour duration) as having the same structural weight as the lengthy episodes containing many human actions. It may be worthwhile to speculate on how one could make this interpretation audible in actual performance, perhaps by a very long pause between 33 and 34, or by an extreme change in pitch, volume or speed at that point.

---

49. Thus, Boomershine's performance ("The Messiah of Peace," 29:30) does not show any conspicuous prosodic indications of a major boundary.

H. The Ninth Hour: Jesus' Death and the Centurion's Statement (Mark 15:34–39)

The beginning of this episode is marked by the temporal marker καὶ τῇ ἐνάτῃ ὥρᾳ (34a), parallel to 25a and 33a. It has a very wide scope, over six syntactic sentences, coinciding with the traditional division into verses 34–39.[50] Again, the alternation between various main agents at the level of the discursive space and between the particles καί and δέ at the purely formal level can serve as starting points for our reading of the overall structure of this episode:

- Jesus (34b–34i);
- καί the bystanders (35a–35f);
- (presentative construction + δέ) an unnamed individual bystander (36a–i);
- Jesus + δέ (37a–b);
- καί the curtain is torn (38a–b);
- (presentative construction + δέ) the centurion (39a–f).

As usual, the variety of the functions of καί in Mark (sometimes occurring at major boundaries with scope over an occurrence of δέ, sometimes occurring at minor boundaries within the scope of an occurrence of δέ) prevents us from reaching a conclusion on the basis of this criterion alone. However, the episode seems to be structured around two actions by Jesus and the reactions they provoke in the bystanders. Let us therefore start by tentatively distinguishing two units within this episode:

- H1: Jesus' cry (34) + the reaction of the bystanders, who think he's calling Elijah (35–36);
- H2: Jesus' death + the reaction of the centurion (37–39).

---

50. The scope of καὶ τῇ ἐνάτῃ ὥρᾳ (34a) may extend even further, if we include verses 40–41, about the women. For the sake of ease of presentation, I will not come back to this option until the conclusions to section 4 below.

H1. Jesus' Cry + the Reaction of the Bystanders (Mark 15:34–36)

The first unit under the scope of καὶ τῇ ἐνάτῃ ὥρᾳ consists of (1) Jesus cry (34b–i), and (2) the reaction of the bystanders (35–36); (2) consists in its turn of two sentences.

34a	καὶ τῇ ἐνάτῃ ὥρᾳ
	and at the ninth hour
34b	ἐβόησεν ὁ Ἰησοῦς φωνῇ μεγάλῃ
	Jesus cried with a loud voice
34c	ἐλωί
	"Eloi,
34d	ἐλωί
	Eloi,
34e	λαμὰ σαβαχθανεί;
	lama sabachthani?"
34f	ὅ ἐστιν μεθερμηνευόμενον
	which in translation means
34g	ὁ θεός μου
	"My God,
34h	[ὁ θεός μου],
	my God,
34i	εἰς τί ἐγκατέλιπές με;
	why have you let me down?"

The details of the segmentation into cola/IUs are as follows:

34a	Fronted temporal marker, with very wide scope (see above).
34b	Full finite main clause, minus complement clause 34c–34d.
34c	Vocatives, like all other syntactically non-integrated contents, typically make up separate IUs. Parallel to 34d (parallel members typically make up separate IUs, as well). Note that this would imply that the relevance of hiatus (*SMNT*, 209) between the two occurrences becomes—at the very least—questionable.
34d	Vocative (// 34c).
34e	Finite main clause.
34f	Finite relative clause, minus complement clause 34g–i. Afterthought-like explanation of 34c–e.
34g	Vocative (see 34c).

34h	Vocative (// 34g).
34i	Finite main clause (see 34e).

The reaction of the bystanders to Jesus' cry is introduced by καί and the two sentences that make up this unit are linked by δέ, the second sentence singling out one person from the crowd. The text can be segmented as follows:

35a	καί and then	
35b	τινες τῶν παρεστηκότων some of those who stood by	
35c	ἀκούσαντες they heard this	
35d	ἔλεγον and they said	
35e		Ἴδε "Look,
35f		Ἡλείαν φωνεῖ. he's calling Elijah!"
36a	δραμὼν δέ τις and one person came running	
36b	γεμίσας σπόγγον ὄξους filled a sponge with vinegar,	
36c	περιθεὶς καλάμῳ put it on a reed	
36d	ἐπότιζεν αὐτόν, and made him drink,	
36e	λέγων saying:	
36f		Ἄφετε "Come on,
36g		ἴδωμεν let's see
36h		εἰ ἔρχεται Ἡλείας if Elijah is coming

36i	καθελεῖν αὐτόν. to take him down.

As usual, we first discuss a few details concerning my segmentation into cola:

35a	I analyzed καί as having wide scope over the whole stretch until 36i, or even 39f (depending on how close one chooses to read 37 seqq. to 36). One may also choose to read καί as having scope over only 35, in which case there is no reason to posit a boundary between 35a and 35b. Not much hinges on this.
35b	Fronted subject/agent, with scope over 35c-f. The conventional enclitic spelling of the indeterminate pronoun τινες may very well be mistaken in this case (see *TCH* §23.4(4a) and cross-references).
35c	Participial clause (participium aoristi), presenting a separate action within the plot sequence.
35d	Finite main clause, minus fronted subject (35b) and complement clause 35e-f.
35e	Fronted interactional marker.
35f	Finite main clause.
36a	Participial clause, presenting a separate action within the plot sequence. This can easily be read as a presentative construction, introducing a new agent on the scene (scope over 36b–36h). The conventional enclitic spelling of the indeterminate pronoun τις may be mistaken (see 35b).
36b	Participial clause (participium aoristi), presenting a separate action within the plot sequence. Note the existence of an alternative reading in which γεμίσας is preceded by καί; this reading is followed by many editions, though not by the Westcott and Hort edition used here. For the fact that matters of word order (including clitic-related issues) may be prone to a lot of variation in manuscript traditions as well as editorial processing, see Saerens, "Papyrus d'Hérodote et tradition manuscrite."
36c	Participial clause (// 36b).
36d	Finite main clause, minus subject.
36e	Participial clause, minus complement clause 36f-h. The present tense and the fact that it follows the main verb are indicative of its different function as compared to the aoristi above (not a separate step in the plot, but coinciding with the action expressed by the main verb).
36f	Fronted interactional marker.
36g-i	36h is a finite subordinate clause, minus the infinitival clause in 36i. In actual realization, one might realize 36g-i as a single IU. Not much hinges on it.

Discourse Segmentation 165

The use in 35–36 of aorist participles to present successive actions in a plot sequence, the last of which is expressed by a finite verb, conforms to classical usage (more so than the flat succession of main finite clauses linked by καί that we observed in, e.g., Mark 15:16–24 above). Note that the unity of this unit is confirmed by the fact that Elijah remains present throughout H1, and then disappears from the scene in H2.

H2. Jesus' Death and the Reaction of the Centurion (Mark 15:37–39)

The second unit under the scope of καὶ τῇ ἐνάτῃ ὥρᾳ (34a) consists of three syntactic sentences, coinciding with the traditional verses.

37a	ὁ δὲ Ἰησοῦς	
	and Jesus	
37b	ἀφεὶς φωνὴν μεγάλην	
	he let out a loud sound	
37c	ἐξέπνευσεν.	
	and he breathed out his last breath.	
38a	καὶ τὸ καταπέτασμα τοῦ ναοῦ	
	and the curtain of the temple	
38b	ἐσχίσθη εἰς δύο ἀπ' ἄνωθεν ἕως κάτω.	
	was torn in two from the top to the bottom.	
39a	ἰδὼν δὲ ὁ κεντυρίων ὁ παρεστηκὼς ἐξ ἐναντίας αὐτοῦ	
	and the centurion who stood facing him	
39b		ὅτι οὕτως ἐξέπνευσεν
		saw that he breathed out his last breath that way
39c	εἶπεν	
	and he said:	
39d		Ἀληθῶς
		"Truly,
39e		οὗτος ὁ ἄνθρωπος
		this man
39f		υἱὸς θεοῦ ἦν.
		was a son of a god."

The segmentation into cola is based on the following considerations:

37a	Fronted subject NP, scope over 37b-c.
37b	Participial clause (participium aoristi), presenting a separate action within the plot sequence.
37c	Finite main clause, minus fronted subject (37a).
38a	Fronted subject NP, scope over 38b.
38b	Finite main clause, minus fronted subject (38a). In a very slow and emphatic performance the parallel PPs may be read as separate IUs. Nothing hinges on it for the present purposes.
39a	Participial clause presenting a separate step in the plot, minus finite complement clause 39b. Also note the presentative function of the colon: a new agent (the centurion) is introduced (scope over 9b-f); the verb typically takes P1. The attributive participle "standing opposite" identifies the centurion and is therefore likely to be realized within the same IU (cf. restrictive relative clauses in English).
39b	Finite complement clause. May be realized within the previous colon. Nothing hinges on this for the present purposes. For interesting variations in the transmitted text, see Comfort, *New Testament Text and Translation Commentary*, 155. The addition of the notion of "shouting" after οὕτως (probably taken over from Matt 27:50), solves certain problems, but perhaps also distorts the original meaning. For a comment on the potential sound effect in this colon, as surmised by *SMNT*, see section 2.3 above.
39c	Main finite clause, minus fronted subject (39a) and minus finite complement clause (39d-f).
39d	Fronted epistemic marker. The fact that the epistemic marker ἀληθῶς is fronted (as well as the subject οὗτος ὁ ἄνθρωπος) may require further interpretation. Again, looking into parallel passages in other gospels and their textual variants may prove to be rewarding. For instance, a quick look at Read-Heimerdinger and Rius-Camps, *A Gospel Synopsis*, 193 shows that Mark's version of this sentence is the only one in which the subject is fronted. In any case, this marked word order makes a performance in three IUs (39d-e) very likely, which must be relevant for sound mapping purposes.
39e	Fronted subject NP. Note the presence of a demonstrative pronoun, which has a strong P1-tendency (*TCH* §5.1).
39f	Main finite clause, minus fronted subject (39e). *Pace SMNT*, 212, I don't think ἦν is "grammatically unnecessary" and its P2 within the colon (υἱὸς θεοῦ is a plausible unit) looks inconspicuous to me. For the P2-tendency of the copula in classical Greek, see *TCH* §5.2.1.

The unit under scrutiny presents 3 events (or series of events), coinciding with the traditional division into verses, formally linked by two occurrences of δέ and one occurrence of καί:

- 37: Jesus (δέ) cries out and dies;
- 38: (καί) the curtain tears;

- 39: the centurion (presentative + δέ) sees how Jesus dies and says, "It is true: this man was a son of a god."[51]

The question as to the exact relations between these sentences and the functions of the particles is in this case particularly interesting in that it may have consequences for the exegesis of this crucial passage.[52]

As we have seen before, Mark's use of καί does not help us decide between a narrow and a wide scope for this particle, which leaves open the possibility of two types of readings:

- *reading (1):* καί (38a) may mark a major boundary and have rather wide scope, perhaps over 38–39;[53]

---

51. The standard translation, "the Son of God," as well as the capitalization of Son and God, which loses the ambiguity of the Greek as to how many gods there are and how many sons (compare ὁ θεός μου in Mark 15:34, where no such ambiguity was intended, for obvious reasons), simply cannot be correct, not even within the presumably monotheistic framework of the author and his original intended audience. The fact that the phrase *can* be used to refer to a situation in which there is only one (relevant) god and only one (relevant) son is beside the point. For the fact that the notion "son of a god" applied to many different situations in the context from which the gospels emerged, as well as some potential consequences, see, e.g., Fredriksen, *Christians in the Roman Empire*, 589–93. For early Christians, the idea of multiple gods, and many sons of gods, must have been quite familiar. *A fortiori*, the phrase was put into the centurion's mouth, who could not be expected to have adopted a monotheistic outlook (see Cranfield, *The Gospel according to St Mark*, 460: "What exactly *the centurion* meant by υἱὸς θεοῦ we cannot be sure. Quite possibly he used the term in a Gentile sense— "demi-god," "hero"), which actually may be functional within Mark's conception of the so-called "messianic secret." It may also be interesting to refer to the critical apparatus of—for instance—Mark 1 and point out the variant readings υἱοῦ θεοῦ and υἱοῦ τοῦ θεοῦ, which shows that there have been problems with this issue at a relatively early (?) date in the transmission (the reading referred to in *SMNT*, 217, appears to be not the only one).

52. For a more or less representative summary of the issues and their importance, see Culpepper, *Mark*, 563: "The centurion's confession, 'truly this man was the Son of God,' is the last interpretive element in Mark that defines the significance of Jesus' death. Verse 39 connects with v. 37, and v. 38 disrupts the flow of the narrative. The reader also knows of the rending of the veil in the temple, whether or not Mark assumes that the centurion could see that the veil was torn. It was the manner of Jesus' death, and specifically his last cry that prompted the centurion's confession. Mark is precise about the position of the centurion relative to the cross (lit., "he stands by over against Jesus"). The reader is well aware that this is the climax of Mark's revelation of Jesus' identity."

53. This reading appears to be supported by the layout in Nestle et al., *Novum Testamentum Graece* (27th edition), by the capital letter of καί in Westcott and Hort, *The New Testament*, 111 and the layout of the same edition on the Perseus website, and by *SMNT*, 211. Boomershine's rendition ("The Messiah of Peace," 30:52) shows a very long pause occurring at this juncture, which—at least—shows that a skilled performer *can* pause at this point. Of course, pauses need not indicate major boundaries and a pause

- *reading (2)*: καί (38a) may have narrow scope over only 38 and hence mark a closer link between 37 and 38 and a less important boundary at 38a.

Let us first consider the pros and cons of *reading (1)*. This reading implies that Jesus' last breath should be read in closer conjunction with the reactions of the crowd (including the Elijah joke) and that the tearing of the curtain is presented as not only a separate event, but also the beginning of a new series of events. The obvious advantage of this reading would be that Jesus' death would occupy the expected climactic position at the end of a sequence of events. However, this reading would make it hard to interpret the relation between the centurion's reaction in verse 39 and the tearing of the curtain immediately preceding it. Firstly, it would be hard to understand what kind of switch would be indicated by δέ in 39a: how is the reaction of the centurion a reaction to the tearing of the curtain, rather than to Jesus' death? Secondly, there is also a problem with the reference of οὕτως in 39b: does it refer back to verse 37, skipping verse 38 and the major boundary occurring before verse 37?

Alternatively, we may want to adopt *reading (2)*, according to which καί has a narrow scope over only verse 38 and hence marks a closer link between 37 and 38 and a less important boundary at 38a. This would have important consequences:

- The tearing of the curtain is presented as the immediate continuation (consequence?) of Jesus' death (this use of καί conforms with classical usage, and with Mark's use of the particle in 16–24 and many other places).
- The switch marked by δέ in 39a is of a familiar type: (1) Jesus dies (in such a way that the curtain tears) and (2) the centurion sees it and speaks up. The issue as to the reference of οὕτως ceases to exist: οὕτως straightforwardly refers to Jesus' death, *including* the tearing of the curtain.[54]

---

after the dramatic climax (?) may be in place here, anyway. Still, the extreme length of this pause, as well as the marked sentence-final intonation contour occurring before it, suggest that Boomershine did intend a major break at this point.

54. The centurion cannot literally have seen the tearing of the curtain, but this need not be a problem, after all: the fact may simply escape notice in the context of the natural narrative flow, "seeing" may have to be understood in a non-literal/non-physical way, it can be yet another preternatural aspect of the events depicted, etc. In any case, the same problem would be equally (if not more) pressing in the alternative reading.

Note that this reading suggests that there is a direct narrative link, perhaps a causal one, between Jesus' death and the tearing of the curtain.[55] The actual relation marked by καί may then be read in two ways:

- *reading (2a):* the tearing of the curtain is an afterthought to the main point of Jesus' dying;
- *reading (2b):* the tearing of the curtain is itself the main point, even more so than Jesus' dying.

Reading (2a) would perhaps be more appealing from a certain (emotional?) point of view: many a (modern?) reader would like to think of the actual death of Jesus as the climax of the story, more so than the supernatural event of the tearing of the curtain. However, *reading (2b)* may actually be correct. Ending the climactic event of the whole chapter (so far) with an afterthought would be a very strange narrative strategy, indeed. Furthermore, it may simply be the case that the supernatural aspect, or the fact that an event was predicted in the Old Testament, in Mark takes precedence over the human and emotional aspect: for instance, we have already noted the very understated way in which Mark describes (or, rather, does not describe) the horrors of the beating and the crucifixion; we have also noted the fact that he seems to give the same structural weight to one verse mentioning the supernatural and predicted darkness as to the many events surrounding the crucifixion and the many events surrounding Jesus' death.[56]

I. Excursus: And There Were also Women (Mark 15:40–41)

40a	Ἦσαν δὲ καὶ γυναῖκες
	And there were also women
40b	ἀπὸ μακρόθεν θεωροῦσαι,
	watching from afar
40c	ἐν αἷς
	amongst them: [list follows]

---

55. For ancient readings that see a causal relation between the death (or the cry) and the tearing of the curtain, see Lamb, *The Catena in Marcum*, 448–50.

56. For the remarkable lack of detail on the "human" aspect and the relative heaviness of prophetic material, see also Cranfield, *The Gospel according to St Mark*, 453–454: "If all the features containing O.T. echoes are removed, there are very few details left; and it is scarcely credible that the early Church should have preserved the memory of so few details of happenings so central to its life and so dramatic and which had been witnessed by so many people. But it was natural that the O.T. passages should influence the language in which the details were related."

The beginning of vs. 40 looks like a major boundary: there is no more action, only the description (mostly a list) of the people watching from afar. Note that these women must have been there all along: that they are mentioned here and not earlier is clearly a matter of narrative strategy, not of subject matter. It is hard to pinpoint the function of this segment in standard narrative terms:[57] it does not look like a typical coda providing some meta-comment on the action and appears to not be part of the narrative at all. In other words, the function of this segment with respect to the overall narrative is to offer information that will be needed further on (in the next episodes), but it is not immediately clear why this information is attached here rather than somewhere else.

J. The Evening (Mark 15:42–47)

This episode starts with a fronted temporal marker ("and it became evening" / καὶ ἤδη ὀψίας γενομένης) that makes up a direct parallel with the one at the very beginning of our excerpt ("and early in the morning" / καὶ εὐθὺς πρωὶ), thus overtly marking the switch from what happened at Golgotha, to Joseph of Arimathaea's efforts to get Jesus' body buried.

Conclusion: The Overall Structure of Mark 15

Explicit temporal markers are the most obvious way in which the author organizes his discourse within this excerpt, as well as in the immediate context. Thus, the end of our excerpt is straightforwardly delineated by καὶ διαγενομένου τοῦ σαββάτου at Mark 16:1. Similarly, the day it is was already mentioned in ἦν δὲ τὸ πάσχα καὶ τὰ ἄζυμα μετὰ δύο ἡμέρας at Mark 14:1, and καὶ τῇ πρώτῃ ἡμέρᾳ τῶν ἀζύμων, ὅτε τὸ πάσχα ἔθυον at Mark 14:12. Note that the transition to the day narrated in our excerpt is more fluid than the very clear-cut switch to the next day, perhaps also because the action continued all night and the trial and conviction in the morning are the direct consequence of the arrest and the preliminary hearing (?) of the evening before. Also note that at least part of the main agents (most notably the head-priests and Jesus) continue to be on the scene across the boundary that coincides with the traditional boundary between Mark 14 and Mark 15. Perhaps we should read 14 and 15 as one continuous discourse unit.

---

57. For an account of what elements constitute a basic narrative structure, see Chafe, *Discourse, Consciousness, and Time*, 127–36; TCH §13.3.5.

Within our excerpt, the criterion of the overt temporal markers yields three major units:

(I) in the morning (1–24);

(II) from 3 to 9 (25–41);[58]

(III) in the evening (42–48).

As elsewhere, the boundaries between major units are not merely a matter of linguistic form (various markers, subject-switches and syntactic units, verbal tenses, perhaps the phonetic patterns studied by sound mapping), but also a matter of which items are presented on the scene (agents, objects, location, actions). The following table gives an overview of a few of the latter aspects:[59]

	Location	Main Agents	Main Actions
I	the way to the praetorium; the praetorium; the way from the praetorium to Golgotha; Golgotha.	A–D: head-priests, Jesus, Pilate, crowd. E: soldiers, (Jesus in a passive role), Simon (only in 21).	A–D: judicial procedure: trial (accusations, questions, answers), conviction, execution. E: mocking (incl. dressing and mock-salutation of the "king"); torture (beating and spitting); undressing; leading away; crucifixion; dividing clothes.
II	Golgotha.	Jesus + bystanders (incl. head-priests + centurion) + co-convicts + the women.	F: insults and mockery (bystanders, head-priests, co-convicts). G: none. H: cry out, die (Jesus); comment (bystanders). I: none.

---

58. I agree with Lee and Scott (*SMNT*, 215–16) that the very fact that within this segment the time is marked in hours, and in a parallel way, confirms that it is a "natural" discourse unit indeed. For further confirmation, see below.

59. When working on the structure of texts or transcripts of spoken discourse or non-verbal behavior, I like to use very large tables, with a separate row for each segment (e.g., the episodes A to J above), and columns for (1) segment identifier, (2) main agents, (3) actions, (4) space, (5) boundary markers, (6) internal structure, (7) verbal tenses, (8) other features, (9) number of lines/words/sentences/pages/minutes (with variations, depending on the material under scrutiny). These tables are very helpful and I do recommend them as a tool, but they tend to get unwieldy and publishing houses do not like them. The remainder of this section consists mainly of some of the data in such a large table transposed into prose (and one very small table).

| III | Pilate's office (?); the market (?) where linen is sold; Golgotha; the tomb. | 42–45: Joseph, Pilate, centurion. 46–47: Joseph, (Mary 1 & Mary 2). | preparation to burial; burial. |

Let us now briefly look into the internal structures of the three major units, their unity and the way their external and internal boundaries are marked.

Unit I: in the Morning; towards, at, and away from the Praetorium; the Trial and the Execution

Besides the temporal setting, the unity of this unit is relatively clear at the level of the location (in and around the praetorium) and the strong connectivity between the successive steps in the plot, mostly determined by the judicial procedure that is being executed. After the transitional episode A (the handover by the head-priests), there is great continuity throughout B to D, which coincides with the trial itself, including the interactions between Pilate, Jesus, the crowd, and the head-priests (structured by recognizable patterns in the use of particles to mark switches). Episode C merely interrupts these patterns, as a kind of excursus.

A major break within the unit occurs at vs. 16, which coincides with the agent-switch towards the soldiers. After this, all other agents disappear from the scene, Jesus gets cast in an entirely passive role, no more interaction is being presented (δέ no longer appears), and agency gets limited to the soldiers (except perhaps for the brief cameo by Simon). The internal unity of E is also further enhanced by the syntax (E coincides with a single grammatical sentence).

Despite the relatively strong internal unity of E and the relatively pervasive switch at its *initium*, I would like to argue that A–D and E do make up an encompassing unit, not only because of the absence of an overt temporal marker, but also because the switch to the soldiers as the new main agent is only the last of a number of such switches (marked by δέ like all the others), and because both the main line of action and the location are continuous with what preceded, but not so much with what follows.

Unit II: from 3 to 9, Golgotha, Jesus' Agony and Various Reactions of the Bystanders

The unity of this unit is guaranteed by the three parallel temporal markers (indicating the third, sixth, and ninth hours), the absence of location-switches (the action remains at Golgotha), and a relative continuity in the action (Jesus is dying and various bystanders react). Still, the boundaries marked by the three temporal markers do coincide with more or less important switches as to which of the bystanders come to the foreground (see my analyses of episodes F through I here above).

The exact function of Mark 15:40–41 (episode I, on the presence of the women) remains hard to pinpoint: the contents do not really add to the plot of Jesus' agony and death as such, and appear to be only mentioned because the women will play an important role later on. Still, this excursus seems to be attached to what precedes rather than to what follows: the location and general timeframe remain the same and no explicit marker separates it from the rest of Unit II (whereas the beginning of Unit III is marked explicitly).

Unit III: in the Evening, Joseph Obtains the Body from Pilate and Buries Jesus

Again, we notice that the temporal marker coincides with a drastic shift in location (away from Golgotha to wherever Pilate is at this time of day), main agents (Joseph becomes the main agent throughout, interacting with various deuteragonists), and types of action (shift away from the agony (+ reactions) to the mundane business of organizing a burial).

5. Final Remarks

My analysis in section 4 will remain inherently tentative in that I cannot claim sufficient familiarity with this type of text and its cultural context, nor even with the variety of Greek in which the text is written. My purpose was therefore more to show the potential of the approach advocated, than to pretend to offer definite and immediately useful results (although I hope there will be at least a few of those as well). Even if I were wrong on all the details (I hope I am not), I believe my comments would still have shown how the type of considerations I tried to demonstrate are relevant to the overall purposes of the sound mapping project.

My focus in this contribution was not in the first place on the study of the phonetic patterns that make up the core interest of sound mapping, but

I believe the following methodological considerations may help the project move forward (see my remarks in section 1 above):

- A more critical stance towards ancient "theorizing" (if that is the right word)[60] would be beneficial, even if that would mean giving up some long-standing practices. More specifically, I believe that, at this point in the development of sound mapping as a long-term project, an approach characterized by a certain level of bottom-up empiricism (starting from the formal features of the text) would be useful.[61]
- At the same time, sound mapping should continue to try and embed its methods and conceptual apparatus in as large and as solid a methodological and theoretical context as possible: what is proposed should fit in with what is known about human language and cognition in general, the various social and cultural contexts of the texts under scrutiny, etc.

In this contribution, I also argued for the following more specific claims:

- that the sound-related aspect that has the most direct impact on listeners is prosody (intonation/pitch, volume, speed, voice quality), that a number of relevant aspects of prosody (as well as of syntax, for that matter) are direct reflections of the underlying discourse structure, and that these aspects are immediately relevant to sound mapping;
- that discourse is a holistic phenomenon and that—in all more or less "normal" circumstances—the *sound* of the discourse cannot be separated from the *world* that is presented in it, which entails that the structure of discourse, including its contents, cannot be ignored when reconstructing the sound of a written text.

Of course, the proof of the pudding is in the eating, and I hope that the practical demonstration of the above methodological considerations in section 4 of this contribution will be useful to the readership of this volume.

Sound mapping went already a long way in the direction I am pointing towards in this contribution and I hope my remarks can help stimulate

---

60. Of course, these ancient approaches make up a fascinating object of study in their own right, not in the least because of the very foreignness and idiosyncrasy that make them hard to apply according to present-day standards. Sound mapping should eventually be able to help and shed light on the realities behind these ancient accounts.

61. I am not a fan of statistics as an explanatory device, but—as a starting point—a judiciously formulated quantitative approach may help to establish the basic facts as to the existence or non-existence of marked phonetic patterns, in a way that ad hoc, qualitative approaches never can.

further efforts. Given the energy displayed by those who participate in the sound mapping enterprise and their willingness to take on board methodological achievements from outside sources, I am looking forward to the results that this emerging field will produce in the future.

Bibliography

Allen, W. Sidney. *Vox Graeca: A Guide to the Pronunciation of Classical Greek*. 3rd ed. Cambridge: Cambridge University Press, 1987.
Bakker, Egbert J. "Boundaries, Topics, and the Structure of Discourse. An Investigation of the Ancient Greek Particle dé." *Studies in Language* 17 (1993) 275–311.
———. "Discourse and Performance: Involvement, Visualization and 'Presence' in Homeric Poetry." *Classical Antiquity* 12 (1993) 1–29.
———."Homeric Discourse and Enjambement: A Cognitive Approach." *Transactions of the American Philological Association* 120 (1990) 1–21.
Black, Stephanie. *Sentence Conjunctions in the Gospel of Matthew: Kai, De, Tote, Gar, Oun and Asyndeton in Narrative Discourse*. Journal for the Study of the New Testament Supplements 216. London: Bloomsbury T. & T. Clark, 2002.
Boomershine, Tom. "The Messiah of Peace: Mark 14–16 Told in Greek by Dr. Tom Boomershine." https://www.youtube.com/watch?v=3dw03z9T7HY.
Burridge, Richard A. *What Are the Gospels? A Comparison with Graeco-Roman Biography*. Society for New Testament Studies Monograph Series 70. Cambridge: Cambridge University Press, 1992.
Chafe, Wallace. "The Analysis of Discourse Flow." In *The Handbook of Discourse Analysis*, edited by Deborah Schiffrin, Deborah Tannen, and Heidi E. Hamilton, 673–87. Oxford: Blackwell, 2001.
———."The Deployment of Consciousness in the Production of a Narrative." In *The Pear Stories: Cognitive, Cultural, and Linguistic Aspects of Narrative Production*, edited by Wallace Chafe, 9–50. Norwood, NJ: Ablex, 1980.
———. *Discourse, Consciousness, and Time: The Flow and Displacement of Conscious Experience in Speaking and Writing*. Chicago: University of Chicago Press, 1994.
Comfort, Philip. *New Testament Text and Translation Commentary*. Carol Stream, IL: Tyndale, 2008.
Couper-Kuhlen, Elizabeth. "Intonation and Discourse." In *The Handbook of Discourse Analysis*, edited by Deborah Tannen, Heidi E. Hamilton, and Deborah Schiffrin, 2nd ed., 82–104. Malden, MA: Wiley–Blackwell, 2015.
Cranfield, C. E. B., ed. *The Gospel according to St Mark: An Introduction and Commentary [Reprinted with Revised Additional Supplementary Notes 1977]*. London: Cambridge University Press, 1959.
Decker, Rodney J. "Markan Idiolect in the Study of the Greek of the New Testament." In *The Language of the New Testament: Context, History, and Development*, edited by Stanley E. Porter and Andrew W. Pitts, 43–66. Linguistic Biblical Studies 6. Leiden: Brill, 2013.
Devine, A. M., and Laurence D. Stephens. *The Prosody of Greek Speech*. Oxford: Oxford University Press, 1994.
Dover, K. J. *Greek Word Order*. Cambridge: Cambridge University Press, 1960.

Evans, Craig A. "How Mark Writes." In *The Written Gospel*, edited by Markus Bockmuehl and Donald A. Hagner, 135–48. Cambridge: Cambridge University Press, 2005.

Fraenkel, Eduard. "Kolon und Satz: Beobachtungen zur Gliederung des antiken Satzes I [1932]." In *Kleine Beiträge zur klassischen Philologie. Erster Band. Zur Sprache. Zur griechischen Literatur*, 73–92. Rome: Storia e Letteratura, 1964.

———. "Kolon und Satz: Beobachtungen zur Gliederung des antiken Satzes II [1933]." In *Kleine Beiträge zur klassischen Philologie. Erster Band. Zur Sprache. Zur griechischen Literatur*, 93–130. Roma: Storia e Letteratura, 1964.

Fredriksen, Paula. "Christians in the Roman Empire in the First Three Centuries CE." In *A Companion to the Roman Empire*, edited by David S. Potter, 587–606. Blackwell Companions to the Ancient World: Ancient History. Malden, MA: Wiley-Blackwell, 2006.

Hoekstra, Marieke, and Frank Scheppers. "Ὄνομα, ῥῆμα, et λόγος dans le *Cratyle* et le *Sophiste* de Platon: Analyse du lexique et analyse du discours." *Antiquité Classique* 72 (2003) 55–73.

Holmes, Michael W., ed. *The Greek New Testament: SBL Edition*. Atlanta: Society of Biblical Literature / Logos Bible Software, 2010.

Hurtado, Larry W. "'Orality', 'Performance' and Reading Texts in Early Christianity." *New Testament Studies* 60 (2014) 321–40.

Janse, Mark. "Bilingualism, Diglossia and Literacy in First-Century Jewish Palestine." In *Encyclopedia of Ancient Greek Language and Linguistics*, 238–41. Leiden: Brill, 2014.

———. "Convergence and Divergence in the Development of the Greek and Latin Pronouns." In *Stability, Variation and Change of Word-Order Patterns over Time*, edited by Rosanna Sornicola et al., 231–58. Philadelphia: Benjamins, 2000.

———. "The Greek of the New Testament." In *A History of Ancient Greek: From the Beginnings to Late Antiquity*, edited by A. F. Christidis, 646–53. Cambridge: Cambridge University Press, 2007.

Jefferson, Gail. "On the Poetics of Ordinary Talk." *Text and Performance Quarterly* 16 (1996) 1–61.

Köstenberger, Andreas J. "The Genre of the Fourth Gospel and Greco-Roman Literary Conventions." In *Christian Origins and Greco-Roman Culture: Social and Literary Contexts for the New Testament*, edited by Stanley E. Porter and Andrew W. Pitts, 435–62. Texts and Editions for New Testament Study 9. Leiden: Brill, 2013.

Lamb, William R.S., ed. *The Catena in Marcum: A Byzantine Anthology of Early Commentary on Mark*. Texts and Editions for New Testament Study 6. Leiden: Brill, 2012.

Lee, Margaret Ellen, and Bernard Brandon Scott. *Sound Mapping the New Testament*. Salem, OR: Polebridge, 2009.

Maier, Paul L. "Luke as a Hellenistic Historian." In *Christian Origins and Greco-Roman Culture: Social and Literary Contexts for the New Testament*, edited by Stanley E. Porter and Andrew W. Pitts, 413–34. Texts and Editions for New Testament Study 9. Leiden: Brill, 2013.

Marshall, M. H. B. *Verbs, Nouns, and Postpositives in Attic Prose*. Edinburgh: Scottish Academic Press, 1987.

Nässelqvist, Dan. *Public Reading in Early Christianity: Lectors, Manuscripts, and Sound in the Oral Delivery of John 1–4*. Novum Testamentum Supplements 163. Leiden: Brill, 2016.

Nestle, Eberhard, Erwin Nestle, Barbara Aland, Kurt Aland, Johannes Karavidopoulos, Carlo M. Martini, and Bruce M. Metzger, eds. *Novum Testamentum Graece.* 27th edition, 9th print. Stuttgart: Deutsche Bibelgesellschaft, 2006.

Ong, Hughson T. *The Multilingual Jesus and the Sociolinguistic World of the New Testament.* Linguistic Biblical Studies 12. Leiden: Brill, 2015.

Porter, Stanley E. "Pericope Markers and the Paragraph. Textual and Linguistic Implications." In *The Impact of Unit Delimitation on Exegesis,* edited by Raymond de Hoop et al., 175–95. Pericope 7. Leiden: Brill, 2009.

———. "The Role of Greek Language Criteria in Historical Jesus Research." In *Handbook for the Study of the Historical Jesus,* edited by Tom Holmén and Stanley E. Porter, 361–404. Leiden: Brill, 2011.

Read-Heimerdinger, Jenny, and Josep Rius-Camps, eds. *A Gospel Synopsis of the Greek Text of Matthew, Mark and Luke: A Comparison of Codex Bezae and Codex Vaticanus.* Leiden: Brill, 2014.

Rico, Christophe. "New Testament Greek." In *The Blackwell Companion to The New Testament.* edited by David E. Aune, 61–76. Blackwell Companions to Religion. Malden, MA: Wiley-Blackwell, 2010.

Runge, Steven E. *Discourse Grammar of the Greek New Testament: A Practical Introduction for Teaching and Exegesis.* Peabody, MA: Hendrickson, 2010.

Sacks, Harvey. *Lectures on Conversation (Volumes I & II).* Edited by Gail Jefferson and Emanuel A. Schegloff. Oxford: Wiley-Blackwell, 1995.

Saerens, Cecilia. "Papyrus d'Hérodote et tradition manuscrite." In *Studia varia Bruxellensia ad orbem Graeco-Latinum pertinentia. II, Twintig jaar Klassieke Filologie aan de Vrije Universiteit Brussel,* edited by Cecilia Saerens et al., 177–92. Leuven: Peeters, 1990.

Scheppers, Frank. *The Colon Hypothesis: Word Order, Discourse Segmentation and Discourse Coherence in Ancient Greek.* Brussels: VUBPress, 2011.

———. "Kola. Antieke en moderne visies op taalkundige geleding." *Handelingen der Koninklijke Zuidnederlandse Maatschappij voor Taal- en Letter-kunde en Geschiedenis* 47 (1993) 293–314.

Sicoli, Mark A. "Voice Registers." In *The Handbook of Discourse Analysis,* edited by Deborah Tannen et al., 105–26. 2nd ed. Malden, MA: Wiley-Blackwell, 2015.

Slings, Siem R. "Figures of Speech and Their Lookalikes. Two Further Exercises in the Pragmatics of the Greek Sentence." In *Grammar as Interpretation: Greek Literature in Its Linguistic Contexts,* edited by Egbert J. Bakker, 169–214. Mnemosyne Supplements 171. Leiden: Brill, 1997.

———. "Written and Spoken Language: An Exercise in the Pragmatics of the Greek Sentence." *Classical Philology* 87 (1992) 95–109.

Tannen, Deborah. "Oral and Literate Strategies in Spoken and Written Narratives." *Language* 58 (1982) 1–21.

———, ed. *Spoken and Written Language: Exploring Orality and Literacy.* Norwood, NJ: Praeger, 1982.

———. *Talking Voices: Repetition, Dialogue, and Imagery in Conversational Discourse.* 2nd ed. Studies in Interactional Sociolinguistics 6. Cambridge: Cambridge University Press, 2007.

Taylor, Ann. *Clitics and Configurationality in Ancient Greek.* Ph.D. diss., University of Pennsylvania, 1990.

Thrall, Margaret E. *Greek Particles in the New Testament. Linguistic and Exegetical Studies*. New Testament Tools and Studies 3. Leiden: Brill, 1962.

Vatri, Alessandro. *Orality and Performance in Classical Attic Prose: A Linguistic Approach*. Oxford: Oxford University Press, 2017.

Vines, Michael E. *The Problem of Markan Genre: The Gospel of Mark and the Jewish Novel*. Academia Biblica 3. Leiden: Brill, 2002.

Voelz, James W. "The Characteristics of the Greek of St. Mark's Gospel." In *Texts and Traditions: Essays in Honour of J. Keith Elliot*, edited by Peter Doble and Jeffrey Kloha. New Testament Tools, Studies and Documents 47. Leiden: Brill, 2014.

Walton, Steve. "What Are the Gospels? Richard Burridge's Impact on Scholarly Understanding of the Genre of the Gospels." *Currents in Biblical Research* 14 (2015) 81–93.

Westcott, Brooke Foss, and Fenton John Anthony Hort, eds. *The New Testament in the Original Greek*. New York: Harper, 1882. http://data.perseus.org/citations/urn:cts:greekLit:tlg0031.tlg002.perseus-grc1:1.1.

8

A Sound Map of Revelation 8:7–12 and the Implications for Ancient Hearers

KAYLE B. DE WAAL

The Book of Revelation was written for a listening community of faith living in Asia Minor in the late first-century CE.[1] The members of the seven churches were largely illiterate and so their communication would have been oral and aural.[2] Harry Gamble states, "we must assume . . . that the large majority of Christians in the early centuries of the church were illiterate, not because they were unique but because they were in this respect typical."[3] These facts, while acknowledged by recent commentators, have not had a significant impact on the interpretation of the book of Revelation.[4]

---

1. For a full discussion of the two dominant views on the date of Revelation, see Mounce, *Book of Revelation*, 31–36. For a discussion on the *Abfassungszeit* of Revelation that further endorses a Domitianic date late in his reign see Müller, *Offenbarung des Johannes*, 41–42; and also Skaggs and Benham, *Revelation*, 8–9.

2. Harris, *Ancient Literacy* 272, 284, 328–30, in his celebrated study of ancient literacy, concluded that no more than 10–20 percent of the populace would have been able to read or write at any level during the classical, Hellenistic, and Roman imperial periods.

3. Gamble, *Books and Readers in the Early Church*, 7. See also Millard, *Reading and Writing in the Time of Jesus*.

4. Collins, *Crisis and Catharsis*, 144, is correct when she states, "it is better to speak of the first 'hearers' of Revelation, rather than the 'readers.'" Others who reach similar conclusions include: Charles, *Revelation*, 6; Barr, "Apocalypse as Oral Enactment," 243–56; Aune, *Revelation 1–5*, 20–21; and Pattermore, *People of God in the Apocalypse*, 53.

This can be seen in the various publications that continue discussion of the contextual or non-contextual use of the Old Testament in Revelation, thematic approaches to the book and the deployment of traditional schools of thought in interpretation.[5]

According to John D. Harvey, "most biblical scholars continue to examine the NT documents using presuppositions that apply more to nineteenth and twentieth-century literary/print culture than to the culture in which those documents were originally produced."[6] Generally speaking the aural features of this enigmatic book and the role of the lector have been neglected in scholarship even though John pronounces a blessing on both those that read and hear his book (Rev 1:3).[7]

More specifically, the passages about the seven trumpets (Rev 8:1—11:19) have been deemed by some to be the most difficult to interpret in Revelation. R. H. Charles says chapter 8 and 9 present "insuperable difficulties."[8] According to Herman Hoeksema, "the interpretation of the trumpets in the book of Revelation is very difficult."[9] Roy Naden confirms that "Revelation 8 and 9 contain the most graphic example of apocalyptic writing in the Bible. The complexity of the imagery has led to more speculative nonsense than can be found written about any other chapter of John's final work."[10]

Methodology

This chapter will develop a sound map of Rev 8:7–12 in an attempt to uncover fresh meaning-making potential from this passage.[11] Revelation 8:7–12 is acknowledged as a unit of text that symbolically depicts the blowing of the first four trumpets.[12] It is hoped that the sound map will assist in

---

5. See Sweet, *Revelation*, Swete, *Commentary on Revelation*; Talbert, *Apocalypse*; Morton, *One upon the Throne and the Lamb*.

6. Harvey, "Orality and Its implications for Biblical Studies," 99; Achtemeier, "*Omne Verbum Sonat*."

7. One possible exception is the work of David Aune. While he does contend "that ancient authors not only chose words to convey the meanings they intended but also chose words whose *sounds* effectively communicated those meanings" he does not provide an analysis of sound in his otherwise exhaustive commentary. See Aune, *Revelation 1–5*, 21 [his emphasis]. For the importance of the lector in Early Christianity see Shiell, *Reading Acts: The Lector and the Early Christian Audience*.

8. Charles, *Revelation*, 218.

9. Hoeksema, *Behold He Cometh*, 300.

10. Naden, *Lamb among the Beasts*, 137.

11. See Lee and Scott, *Sound Mapping*.

12. Smalley, *The Revelation to John*, 218; Osborne, *Revelation*, 349.

identifying the organic structure of this unit of text in the wider trumpet series and perhaps minimize some of the complexity of understanding the imagery identified by the previous scholars. Margaret Lee and Bernard Scott suggest,

> Sound mapping is an analytical tool, not an interpretative method or exegetical approach. Sound mapping should precede exegesis and sound analysis should indicate the features that demand attention. Every tool serves a specific purpose and implies practical consideration.[13]

Sound quality refers "to the way sounds are combined, and to the relation between sound and meaning."[14] Furthermore, sound mapping identifies the natural boundaries of a composition's structure and represents its acoustic patterns.[15] A sound map delineates cola and periodic structures, and attends to the matter of sound quality (euphony and harmony; cacophony and dissonance).

A sound map examines the aural features of Scripture by paying attention to sound quality, sound style and sound patterns. After an aural analysis of the text aural critics attempt to reconstruct how ancient hearers would have appropriated the text. The aural critic engages in this reconstruction by looking for thematic and structural markers and mnemonic hooks which aid in the process of communication.[16]

Lee and Scott contend that Greek grammar progressively builds from the level of the syllable, to the colon and then to the period.[17] These basic speech units build on each other: syllables form cola, cola form periods, periods build compositions. They point out that each speech unit controls an aspect of the discourse and that taken "together the syllable, colon and period comprise a composition's building blocks and account for organizational structure."[18] From a historical standpoint it is impossible to reproduce the aural experience of the early Christian hearers. The ironic questions that therefore guide this chapter are "what sounds can we see?" or "what can we hear based on what is visible?"[19]

---

13. Lee and Scott, *Sound Mapping*, 385.
14. Ibid., 176.
15. Ibid., 158.
16. Davis, *Oral Biblical Criticism*, 60.
17. Lee and Scott, *Sound Mapping*, 136.
18. Ibid.
19. Brickle, *Aural Design*, 18.

The Listening Audience

The listening audience of Revelation is multifaceted and complex. Steven Friesen states,

> Revelation had several social settings, not one; that these settings were characterized by distinct problems having mostly to do with relations to outsiders; that the assemblies agreed with John about abstention from imperial cults; and that John used their agreement about imperial cults as a rhetorical tool in order to link their settings together within the framework of the rejection of mainstream Roman imperial society.[20]

Friesen suggests that John brings together various issues and links them into a broader critique of religion, economy and imperialism. Since emperor worship dominated the lives of the people in Asia Minor, John creatively links emperor worship with local issues to provide a broader assessment of imperial society.

Ancient hearers' cultural register, a term coined by Werner Kelber, would allow some of them to recall the Old Testament stories, texts and passages that had shaped their life experience as Jews or their conversion to Christianity as Gentiles.[21] Other hearers would recall the immediate or perhaps wider Greco-Roman context of a symbol or phrase. Different symbols would also have varying levels of influence for ancient listeners depending on which city they lived in. Their cultural register would consist of associated traditions, memories, experiences and images. Meaning-making for this essay will therefore take place in the context of the ancient hearer's cultural register.

From a practical standpoint it is doubtful whether the hearers would understand the book on the first hearing. It is reasonable to postulate that the lector would re-read and study the text and teach it to less literate members of the community over time. That teaching would take place in the worship service.[22] It could have happened in about an hour and a half, according to John Sweet, but more likely it could have happened over numerous worship services.[23]

---

20. Friesen, "Satan's Throne," 353.

21. Kelber, *Oral and Written Gospel*.

22. Siew, *War between the Two Beasts and the Two Witnesses*, 9.

23. Sweet, *Revelation*, 13. Aune, "Prophet Circle of John of Patmos," contends that the book is first communicated to John's fellow prophets and then read and interpreted by the prophets to the seven churches.

A Sound Map of Revelation 8:7–12   183

The sound map of Rev 8:7–12 will now be generated followed by an analysis of its features. Repeated words that begin and end periods are italicized, repeated sounds are underlined and repeated words are also "spaced" correctly so that the sounds can be easily seen.

The Sound Map of Revelation 8:7–12

Period 1

1 *Καὶ ὁ πρῶτος*   ἐσάλπισεν·
2 καὶ ἐγένετο χάλαζα
3 καὶ πῦρ μεμιγμένα ἐν αἵματι
4 καὶ ἐβλήθη εἰς τὴν γῆν
5 καὶ τὸ τρίτον τῆς γῆς   κατεκάη
6 καὶ τὸ τρίτον τῶν δένδρων   κατεκάη
7 καὶ πᾶς χόρτος χλωρὸς   κατεκάη.

Period 2

1 *Καὶ ὁ δεύτερος ἄγγελος*   ἐσάλπισεν·
2 καὶ ὡς ὄρος μέγα πυρὶ   τὴν θάλασσαν,
  καιόμενον ἐβλήθη εἰς
3 καὶ ἐγένετο τὸ τρίτον   τῆς θαλάσσης αἷμα

Period 3

1 καὶ ἀπέθανεν   τὸ τρίτον τῶν   τῇ θαλάσσῃ τὰ
                               κτισμάτων τῶν ἐν ἔχοντα ψυχὰς
2 καὶ   τὸ τρίτον
                               τῶν πλοίων
                               διεφθάρησαν.

Period 4

1 Καὶ   ὁ τρίτος ἄγγελος
                               ἐσάλπισεν·
2 καὶ ἔπεσεν ἐκ τοῦ
  οὐρανοῦ ἀστὴρ μέγας
  καιόμενος ὡς λαμπὰς
3 καὶ ἔπεσεν   ἐπὶ τὸ τρίτον τῶν
                               ποταμῶν
4 καὶ   ἐπὶ τὰς πηγὰς τῶν
                               ὑδάτων,

Period 5

1 καὶ τὸ ὄνομα τοῦ ἀστέρος   ὁ Ἄψινθος,
  λέγεται
2 καὶ ἐγένετο τὸ τρίτον   τῶν ὑδάτων   εἰς ἄψινθον
3 καὶ πολλοὶ <u>τῶν</u> ἀνθρώπων
  ἀπέθανον ἐκ <u>τῶν</u> <u>ὑδάτων</u>
  ὅτι ἐπικράνθησαν.

Period 6

1 Καὶ ὁ τέταρτος ἄγγελος   ἐσάλπισεν·
2 καὶ ἐπλήγη τὸ τρίτον τοῦ
  ἡλίου
3 καὶ τὸ τρίτον τῆς σελήνης
4 καὶ τὸ τρίτ<u>ον</u> <u>τῶν</u>
  ἀστέρ<u>ων</u>,
5 ἵνα σκοτισθῇ τὸ τρίτ<u>ον</u>
  αὐτ<u>ῶν</u>
6 καὶ ἡ ἡμέρα μὴ φάνῃ τὸ
  τρίτον αὐτῆς
7 καὶ ἡ νὺξ ὁμοίως.

Aural Analysis

Significant Word and Phrase Usage	
Word/Phrase	Occurrence
καὶ	25
τρίτον	13
ἐβλήθη	2
ἄγγελος	4
ὡς	2
θάλασσαν	3
Ἄψινθος	2

Period one has seven uses of the word καὶ. It has the ε sound in cola one through four. The phrase καὶ τὸ τρίτον is used on two occasions in cola five and six. The word κατεκάη ends cola five through seven and serves as a transition between colon five, six and seven. These endings are important as they define the colon and orient an audience to structure and organization.[24] The ον sound is important in colon six and the ος sound is important

---

24. Lee and Scott, *Sound Mapping*, 152.

in colon seven. Colon seven also has the two guttural sounds of χ. Period two has three uses of the word καί. It has the ος sound in colon one and two and the ἐ sound in colon one, two and three. The use of the σ sound on two occasions would have been offensive to the hearers.[25] The symbol of σάλπισεν connects both period one and two.

Period three has two uses of the word καί. The θαλάσσης connects both periods as it is found in colon one and two of period two. The phrase τὸ τρίτον τῶν is found in both colon one and two. The ῶν sound dominates colon one and two. Period four has four uses of the word καί. The ῶν sound dominates colon three and four. Καὶ ἔπεσεν begins both colon three and four. The word τρίτον is found in colon one and three. Period five has three uses of the word καί. The word Ἄψινθος connects both the end of colon one and two. The phrase τῶν ὑδάτων is found in both colon two and three. The ῶν sound is important in colon three as it connects different words. Aune contends that ὅτι ἐπικράνθησαν is a casual clause.[26]

The phrase τὸ τρίτον dominates period six as it is found in cola two through six. The word καί is used six times in this period. Colon five is an exception to all the previous cola as it does not begin with the word καί. This sudden change and distinctive sound that diverges from the previously set pattern would surprise hearers.[27] The ancient hearers would be alert to this difference as a pattern variation.[28] Furthermore, the use of σ in σκοτισθῇ on two occasions would be offensive for ancient hearers.[29]

Aural Commentary

The commentary is not meant to be exhaustive but a guide as to how a hearing audience may have appropriated the text. The first feature to notice in Rev 8:7–12 is the importance of the word καί which is used in Revelation comparatively more than any other work in the New Testament.[30] Kermit Titrud maintains commentaries and monographs have not seriously engaged

---

25. Dionysius, *Comp.* 14.
26. Aune, *Revelation 1–5*, cxcviii.
27. Lee and Scott, *Sound Mapping*, 155.
28. Ibid., 157.
29. Dionysius, *Comp.* 14.
30. Aune, *Revelation 1–5*, cxci. Following the Nestle-Aland text, Aune claims that of the 337 sentences in Revelation 245 of these begin with καί. Aune also provides nine uses of καί, (see pp. cxcii–cxcv). Lupieri, *A Commentary on Revelation*, 100, maintains that καί occurs "on average twelve times every hundred words." I follow David Rhoads who refers to the First and Second Testament; see Rhoads, "Performance Criticism."

with the use of καί.³¹ He asserts that καί, in its adverbial function serves as a spotlight or an intensifier. Its function is emotive. In similar fashion, Resseguie states that John uses the word to thicken sentences and lengthen the list of qualities he seeks to highlight. "This paratactic style has the advantage of isolating each member of a list, allowing it to stand out and to be noticed," he asserts.³² Every line of the various periods begins with καί, except period six colon five. The reason for this will be explored later in this chapter.

The combination of hail, fire, and blood heard at cola two, three and four is widely used in the Old Testament, Jewish apocalyptic and the Greco-Roman literature.³³ While the hearing audience would not know a range of texts that combined hail, fire and blood, the general idea conveyed by all of them is judgment against the forces that oppose God and God's people. It is hence likely that the hearing audience would have understood the Roman Empire as the target of the first trumpet plague.

A feature of period one colon three is the use of πῦρ. The effect of the fire burns a third of the earth, the trees, and all the green grass. Fire is part of the apocalyptic arsenal John utilizes to convey the extent of the devastating judgment that falls in this trumpet. Since this symbol is used widely ancient hearers would have known that it pointed to judgement.³⁴

Most scholars assume the Exodus story as the background to this first trumpet passage.³⁵ Adela Collins suggests, "the story of the exodus is being used as a model for understanding the situation in which John's first readers found themselves. An analogy is seen between their ill treatment by the Romans and the slavery experienced by the children of Israel in Egypt."³⁶ Her statement demonstrates the thematic link between the Exodus and Revelation text. While ancient hearers with a Jewish heritage would have perceived the Exodus story when hearing these periods, it is debatable whether recently converted pagans would have made the same associations.

---

31. Titrud, "Function of *kai* in the Greek New Testament," 243.

32. Resseguie, *Revelation*, 50.

33. Fire was a weapon of Yahweh to deliver his true people and demolish his enemies (Ps 11:6; 18:13; Isa 29:1–6; Ezek 39:1–6; Amos 1:4; 7:4). For hail see Isa 30:30; Ezek 13:11–13; and for fire see Ps 80:14–16; Jer 21:12–14. Jewish texts include *Sib. Or.* 5:377–378; and Wis 16:16–24.

34. Paulien, *Decoding Revelation's Trumpets*, 248, states that in the OT it has the meaning of Yahweh's judgment, whether against Israel and Judah (Ps 80:8–11; Jer 11:16–17; Ezek 5:1–4; 15:6–7; Joel 1:19–20) or against her adversaries (Isa 10:16–20; 30:30; Jer 51:41–42). Fire was a weapon of Yahweh to deliver his true people and demolish his enemies (Ps 11:6; 18:13; Isa 29:1–6; Ezek 39:1–6; Amos 1:4; 7:4).

35. Resseguie, *Revelation*, 67; and Smalley, *Revelation to John*, 36, 317.

36. Collins, *Apocalypse*, 58.

In period one colon four the hail and fire mingled with blood "were thrown" (ἐβλήθη) to the earth, with the judgment coming from heaven. Commentators usually engage with a list of Old Testament texts. For example, according to Paulien,

> Trees and grass can symbolize both the enemies of Yahweh's people such as Lebanon and Assyria (Zech. 11.1, 6; Isa. 2.13) and also Israel (Ezek. 15.6–7; 20.47–48; Joel 1.19–20). When grass and trees are green and flourishing they symbolize Yahweh's faithful people, but when they are dry and withered they symbolize the fate of evil-doers (Isa. 44.3–4; Ps. 1.3; 52.8; 92.12–13)."[37]

While the texts provide the interpreter with clues to meaning, it is doubtful whether ancient hearers would have remembered all these verses from the Old Testament. Ancient hearers would have perceived the action of God with the use of ἐβλήθη.

Period two colon two refers to a huge mountain (ὄρος μέγα). Ancient hearers perceive two points of reference. Some may hear in this symbol the "tragic eruption of Vesuvius on 24 August A.D. 79."[38] Most scholars contend that John is alluding to Jer 51:25, which states, "'I am against you, O destroying mountain, you who destroy the whole earth,' declares the LORD. 'I will stretch out my hand against you, roll you off the cliffs, and make you a burned-out mountain (ὄρος).'"[39] Babylon is prophetically denounced and portrayed as a burning mountain. This line of reasoning is reinforced, since Babylon is destroyed by means of the Euphrates river, and the sea in period two endangers Rome. This endangerment comes about through the "pollution of the sea waters, the consequent death of sea life."[40]

However, even with this additional line of reasoning it is doubtful whether Jewish hearers would have remembered or recalled this text. An aural critical engagement with Scripture does not minimize the intertextual dynamics of the text but rather situates meaning-making in the context of the original hearers. It is more likely that ancient hearers would have appropriated the eruption of Vesuvius as a possible fulfilment of this text.

---

37. Paulien, *Decoding Revelation's Trumpets*, 251.

38. Aune, *Revelation 6–16*, 519–20.

39. Boxall, *Revelation*, 138; Sweet, *Revelation*, 163; Caird, *Revelation*, 114; Beale, *Revelation*, 476; Osborne, *Revelation*, 352–53. Contra Thompson, *Revelation*, 116, who does not mention the Jeremiah text. Why Beasley-Murray, *Revelation*, 157, says it is unlikely that Jer 51:25 is in view here is not expounded on.

40. Smalley, *Revelation to John*, 221.

The sea (θάλασσα) in the Old Testament was viewed as the abode of the enemies of God and with whom God was engaged in a cosmic battle and is another symbol with a rich literary and cultural dynamic to it.[41] Moreover, the use of the divine passive (ἐβλήθη) in period two coupled with the use of "third" on three occasions amplifies the interplay between cosmic forces in this trumpet judgment.[42]

The symbol of ships (πλοίων) heard at period three colon two would have been understood only within the audience's immediate Greco-Roman context. According to Danker, the word used at period three colon two refers to a rather large sea-faring merchant ship.[43] John's audience knew firsthand that ships portray the ability of Rome to procure wealth through commerce and trade and demonstrate her international power.[44] In the first-century world, ships carried large quantities of luxury items, especially grain.[45] Ordinary citizens were provided with grain by the empire and so would have valued these shipping merchants in maintaining their day-to-day existence.[46]

The Roman Empire, especially the elite, spent large amounts of money to purchase exotic goods from the other nations brought by the shipping industry. Shipping also provided a forum for guilds where business and social relationships were advanced. In addition, guilds also had a "religious character," often centering "on the patron gods or goddesses of the association."[47] The significant commercial benefits of shipping have led Nelson Kraybill to

---

41. See Boyd, *God at War*, 83–100.

42. Incidentally the numeral "third" is mentioned 28 times in 8:7–9:18. Ford, *Revelation*, 159, suggests a "third" denotes a part of Satan's kingdom is under divine judgment. According to Paulien, *Decoding Revelation's Trumpets*, 369–70, "the number three has divine implications in the ancient world. John parodies this background with a satanic trinity (Rev 12–13; 16:13) whose leader has cast down a third of the stars of heaven (Rev 12:4) and whose kingdom has three parts (16:19). The thirds of the trumpets, therefore, may represent parts of Satan's kingdom which are brought under God's judgments." As hearers later engage the notion of third in Rev 12:3 they could align this numeral with Satanic activity. See Tondstad, *Saving God's Reputation*, 111–12, who asserts that the numeral third is an indicator of satanic agency. He suggests that it is a "qualitative reference" and answers to the question "who." Contra Bock, *Apocalypse of Saint John*, 81, who suggests the concept of one third is to be taken qualitatively and refers to man or human beings.

43. BDAG, 830.

44. Paulien, *Decoding Revelation's Trumpets*, 262–63.

45. See Rev 18:12–13. For a full discussion on the importance of grain and travel see Kraybill, *Imperial Cult and Commerce*, 102–9.

46. Ibid., 107, suggests "200,000 families in Rome received from the government a regular 'dole' of free grain."

47. Ibid., 117.

write: "The imperial government had more interest in the shipping industry than in any other commercial enterprise."[48] The ancient hearers would have understood πλοίων as a symbol of the military, commercial and religious might of the Roman Empire.

The sixth period is introduced by the phrase Καὶ ὁ τέταρτος ἄγγελος. During this period listeners learn that a third of the sun (τὸ τρίτον τοῦ ἡλίου) was struck, a third of the moon (σελήνης), and a third of the stars (τῶν ἀστέρων), so that a third of them turned dark (ἵνα σκοτισθῇ τὸ τρίτον αὐτῶν). Commentators suggest that John was alluding to Exod 10:21; Ezek 32:7-8; Joel 2:10; Matt 24:19; and Mark 13:24-25.[49] While the texts provide the interpreter with clues to meaning, it is doubtful whether ancient listeners would have remembered or indeed known all these verses.

Period six colon five highlighted the symbol of darkness (σκοτισθῇ) with the use of ἵνα. This is the only colon that does not begin with καί. Darkness is generally conveyed as a symbol of destruction and judgement in the Qumran and Second Temple literature and it is likely that ancient listeners would have understood the symbol in this way.[50] More specifically ancient hearers would acknowledge that this judgment is against the Roman Empire.[51]

Conclusion

This article has enlisted a sound map to better understand the compositional features and organic structure of Rev 8:7-12. The sound map has highlighted the central use of καί and various sounds like ῶν and ος. Furthermore, it has highlighted significant words and phrases like τὸ τρίτον τῶν, ὄρος μέγα, ἐβλήθη and other phrases of aural interest. Sounds, words and phrases are clearly seen on the sound map so that the interpreter can clearly see what ancient hearers heard. The cola provide a step-by-step unfolding of

48. Ibid.

49. Osborne, *Revelation*, 355; Smalley, *Revelation to John*, 223; Sweet, *Revelation*, 164, Beale, *Revelation*, 481; Roloff, *Revelation*, 111; Mounce, *Revelation*, 181; and Stefanovic, *Revelation*, 295.

50. See 1QM 13:5-6; 4 *Ezra* 5:4-5; 6.45; 1 *En.* 80:4-8; and *Sib. Or.* 3:801; 5:346-49; Wis 15:1—16:29; 17:1-21; and 18:3-4; Josephus, *Ant.* 2.14.5, 299; and in the New Testament, 2 Cor 6:14-15.

51. So Beale, *Revelation*, 482, and Smalley, *Revelation to John*, 224. Aune, *Revelation 6-16*, 414, suggests that the motif of darkness on the *Yom Yahweh* is developed into the motif of the darkening of the sun or the destruction of the sun, moon and stars in Jewish apocalyptic. If this is so, then the fourth trumpet judgment can be considered to be ushering in the *Yom Yahweh* and reinforces the fact that the trumpets cannot be analysed chronologically.

ideas, concepts and symbols. Once again the interpreter can clearly see how the ancient hearers would have engaged the symbols and ideas in the cola in their cultural register.

Since the book of Revelation has a complex structure at both the micro and macro levels the sound map can assist the interpreter to better understand the organic structure of Rev 8:7–12. The sound map is a valuable interpretive strategy that focuses on the ancient hearing community of faith and how they would have potentially made meaning of the apocalyptic symbols they heard read to them in the churches of Asia Minor. This "aural reading" of the trumpets situates them in the context of the Roman Empire.

Bibliography

Achtemeier, Paul J. "*Omne Verbum Sonat*: The New Testament and the Oral Environment of Late Western Antiquity." *Journal of Biblical Literature* 109 (1990) 3–27.

Aune, David E. "The Prophet Circle of John of Patmos and the Exegesis of Revelation 22:16." *Journal for the Study of the New Testament* 37 (1989) 103–16.

———. *Revelation 1–5*. Word Biblical Commentary 52A. Dallas: Word, 1997.

———. *Revelation 6–16*. Word Biblical Commentary 52B. Nashville: Nelson, 1998.

Barr, D. "The Apocalypse as Oral Enactment." *Interpretation* 40 (1984) 243–56.

Bauckham, Richard. *The Climax of Prophecy: Studies in the Book of Revelation*. Edinburgh: T. & T. Clark, 1993.

Beale. G. K. *The Book of Revelation*. New International Greek Testament Commentary. Grand Rapids: Eerdmans, 1999.

Bock, Emil. *The Apocalypse of Saint John*. Rev. ed. London: Christian Community, 2005.

Boxall, Ian. *The Revelation of Saint John*. Black's New Testament Commentaries. Peabody, MA: Hendrickson, 2006.

Boyd, Gregory A. *God at War: The Bible and Spiritual Conflict*. Downers Grove, IL: InterVarsity, 1997.

Brickle, Jeffrey E. *Aural Design and Coherence in the Prologue of First John*. London: T. &. T. Clark, 2012.

Caird, G. B. *A Commentry on the Revelation of St. John the Divine*. New York: Harper & Row, 1966.

Collins, Adela Yarbro. *Crisis and Catharsis: The Power of the Apocalypse*. Philadelphia: Westminster, 1984.

Charles, R. H. *Revelation*. Vol. 1. International Critical Commentary. Edinburgh: T. &. T. Clark, 1920.

Charlesworth, James H. *The Dead Sea Scrolls, Hebrew, Aramaic, and Greek Texts with English Translations. Damascus Document, War Scroll and Related Documents*. Louisville: Westminster John Knox, 1995.

———, ed. *The Old Testament Pseudepigrapha*. 2 vols. Garden City, NY: Doubleday, 1983–1985.

Danker, Frederick W., ed. *A Greek-English Lexicon of the New Testament and Other Early Christian Literature*. 3rd edition. Chicago: University of Chicago Press, 2000.

Davis, Casey W. *Oral Biblical Criticism: The Influence of the Principles of Orality on the Literary Structure of Paul's Epistle to the Philippians.* Journal for the Study of the New Testament Supplements 172. Sheffield: Sheffield Academic, 1999.

Ford, Josephine Massyngberde. *Revelation.* Anchor Bible 38. Garden City, NY: Doubleday, 1975.

Friesen, S. J. "Satan's Throne, Imperial Cults and the Social Settings of Revelation." *Journal for the Study of the New Testament* 27 (2005) 351–73.

Gamble, Harry. *Books and Readers in the Early Church: A History of Early Christian Texts.* New Haven: Yale University Press, 1995.

Harris, William V. *Ancient Literacy.* Cambridge: Harvard University Press, 1989.

Harvey, John D. "Orality and Its implications for Biblical Studies: Recapturing an Ancient Paradigm." *Journal of the Evangelical Theological Society* 45 (2002) 99–110.

Hoeksema, Herman. *Behold He Cometh: An Exposition of the Book of Revelation.* Grand Rapids: Kregel, 1969.

Josephus. *Jewish Antiquities.* Loeb Classical Library. 9 vols. Translated by H. St. Thackeray. Cambridge: Harvard University Press, 1961.

Kelber, Werner H. *The Oral and Written Gospel: The Hermeneutics of Speaking and Writing in the Synoptic Tradition, Mark, Paul and Q.* Philadelphia: Fortress, 1983.

Kraybill, J. Nelson. *Imperial Cult and Commerce in John's Apocalypse.* Journal for the Study of the New Testament Supplements 132. Sheffield: Sheffield Academic, 1996.

Lee, Margaret Ellen, and Bernard Brandon Scott. *Sound Mapping the New Testament.* Salem, OR: Polebridge, 2009.

Lupieri, Edmondo F. *A Commentary on the Apocalypse of John.* Italian Texts and Studies on Religion and Society. Translated by Maria Poggi Johnson and Adam Kamesar. Grand Rapids: Eerdmans, 1999.

Millard, Alan. *Reading and Writing in the Time of Jesus.* New York: New York University Press, 2000.

Morton, Russell S. *One upon the Throne and the Lamb: A Tradition Historical/Theological Analysis of Revelation 4–5.* Studies in Biblical Literature 110. New York: Lang, 2007.

Mounce, Robert H. *The Book of Revelation.* Revised. New International Commentary on the New Testament. Grand Rapids: Eerdmans, 1998.

Müller, Ulrich B. *Die Offenbarung des Johannes.* Okumenischer Taschenbuch-Kommentar zum Neuen Testament 19. Gutersloh: Gutersloher, 1984.

Naden, Roy. *The Lamb among the Beasts.* Hagerstown, MD: Pacific Press Pub. Association, 1996.

Osborne Grant R. *Revelation.* Baker Exegetical Commentary on the New Testament. Grand Rapids: Baker, 2002.

Pattermore, Stephen. *The People of God in the Apocalypse: Discourse, Structure and Exegesis.* Society for New Testament Studies Monograph Series 128. Cambridge: Cambridge University Press, 2003.

Paulien, Jon. *Decoding Revelation's Trumpets: Literary Allusions and Interpretations of Revelation 8.7–12.* Andrews University Seminary Doctoral Dissertation Series 11. Berrien Springs, MI: Andrews University Press, 1988.

Pliny. *Natural History.* Translation by H. Rackham. 10 vols. Loeb Classical Library. Cambridge: Harvard University Press, 1979–1983.

Roloff, Jürgen. *Revelation*. Translated by John E. Alsup. Continental Commentary. Minneapolis: Fortress, 1993.

Resseguie, James L. *The Revelation of John: A Narrative Commentary*. Grand Rapids: Baker Academic, 2009.

Rhoads, David. "Performance Criticism: An Emerging Methodology in Second Testament Studies—Part II." *Biblical Theology Bulletin* 36 (2006) 1–21.

Shiell, William. *Reading Acts: The Lector and the Early Christian Audience*. Biblical Interpretation Series 70. Boston: Brill Academic, 2004.

Skaggs, Rebecca, and Priscilla C. Benham. *Revelation*. Pentecostal Commentary Series. Dorset, UK: Deo, 2009.

Siew, Antonius King Wai. *The War between the Two Beasts and the Two Witnesses: A Chiastic Reading of Revelation*. Library of New Testament Studies 283. London: T. &. T. Clark, 2005.

Smalley, Stephen S. *The Revelation to John: A Commentary on the Greek Text of the Apocalypse*. London: SPCK, 2005.

Sweet, John. *Revelation*. Westminster Pelican Commentaries. Philadelphia: Westminster, 1979.

Swete, Henry Barclay. *Commentary on Revelation*. Grand Rapids: Kregel, 1977.

Talbert, Charles H. *The Apocalypse: A Reading of the Revelation of John*. Louisville: Westminster John Knox, 1994.

Titrud, Kermit. "The Function of *kai* in the Greek New Testament." In *Linguistics and New Testament Interpretation: Essays on Discourse Analysis*, edited by David Alan Black, et al., 240–70. Nashville: Broadman, 1992.

Tonstad, Sigve. *Saving God's Reputation: The Theological Function of Pistis Iesou in the Cosmic Narratives of the Apocalypse*. Library of New Testament Studies 337. London: T. & T. Clark, 2007.

9

Rhythm, Sound, and Persuasion

Nina E. Livesey

"It doesn't make me happy to hold back the sounds," she began softly, "for if we listen to them carefully they can sometimes tell us things far better than words."

THE SOUNDKEEPER IN NORTON JUSTER'S
THE PHANTOM TOLLBOOTH, 158

Sound affects us. Thunderous sounds startle, while soft and harmonious[1] sounds soothe. Modern scholar of rhetoric Vessela Valiavitcharska remarks that rhythm has the power to carry us away.[2] It insists upon participation, demands assent, and holds our emotions captive. Rhythm lures with the promise of harmony.[3] Harmony, according to Valiavitcharska, is not identical to rhythm. It is instead a sense of concord and is experienced as the

---

1. "Harmony refers to the way sounds are combined." In literary compositions, it refers to word arrangement. Lee and Scott, *Sound Mapping*, 177.

2. Rhetoric and Rhythm in Byzantium, 1. Lee and Scott remark that the author of On the Sublime, "states the obvious fact that melody provides 'a natural instrument of persuasion and pleasure.'" According to the ancient author, the melody of words "casts a spell" on its hearers (39.3). Quoted in Lee and Scott, Sound Mapping, 177.

3. Valiavitcharska, *Rhetoric and Rhythm in Byzantium*, 1.

abandonment of self. According to Valiavitcharska, to submit to rhythm is to blur the boundaries between self and other, to abandon autonomy in exchange for participation in the experience of the other.[4] That sound has these abilities indicates its effectiveness for persuasion.

Valiavitcharska's remarks and observations regarding sound's inherent power and its oftentimes unnoticed force on emotions complements, reinforces and in some cases directly coincides with sound mapping's underlying principles. Valiavitcharska, Margaret E. Lee and Bernard B. Scott all stress that ancients were keenly aware of sound's effects on hearers. Not only is language and grammar based on sound, as Lee and Scott indicate, but so too were ancient rhetorical theories. The notion of the inseparability of content and style, and the awareness that a composition's meaning derives not from semantic meaning alone, grounds the work of all of these sound theorists.

What follows is a brief overview of the place of rhythm among ancient rhetorical theorists, and then examples of how awareness of sound and rhythm—made possible through the use of sound mapping techniques—makes possible a rich and comprehensive rhetorical analysis of ancient compositional units. I conclude by indicating why and how sound mapping techniques are indispensable for rhetorical analyses of ancient compositions.

The Place of Rhythm in Ancient Rhetoric

Ancient rhetoricians from Gorgias[5] in the fifth century BCE to Joseph Rhacendytes in the fourteenth century CE were well aware of the emotional effect and power of oratorical rhythm.[6] In his *Encomium of Helen*, Gorgias argues that Helen of Troy, who abandoned her husband, Menelaos king of Sparta, to marry Paris, the prince of Troy, should be considered innocent of the charge of abandonment.[7] Of the four possible justifications of her actions Gorgias advances—the gods, force, persuasive speech, or love—persuasive speech (λόγος) is the most convincing. Nearly a third of the entire

---

4. Valiavitcharska cites Levinas, "Reality and Its Shadow," 132. Elements of rhythm "*impose themselves on us without our assuming them*"; italics are by Levinas.

5. It is said that due to his exceptional skills in oratory the people of Leontinoi commissioned Gorgias (ca. 485–380 BCE) to lead an envoy to Athens to secure help for their besieged city. Gorgias, *Encomium of Helen* 9.

6. Valiavitcharska, *Rhetoric and Rhythm in Byzantium*, 1. Lee and Scott note that in compositions rhythm "furnishes the character and impact of prose." *Sound Mapping*, 108.

7. Debates on Helen's guilt or innocence were prevalent and date to as early as the myth itself. Gorgias, *Encomium of Helen*, 12.

short work (8–14) concerns the power of speech to persuade. Gorgias remarks that speech is persuasive because it orders (τάξιν) the mind,[8] just as drugs order the body.[9] Gorgias's work is effective not only on account of his argument,[10] but also because of his careful employment of sound features and rhythm. MacDowell remarks, "In sentence after sentence, individual words and longer phrases are set side by side to produce symmetry in grammar and sound."[11] Valiavitcharska notes the rhythm in the parallel and asyndetic (the omission of conjunctions) opening of Gorgias's *Encomium*.[12] Gorgias arranges his topics with attention to the sound quality of words. He employs considerable repetition and he excels in the effective use of antithesis and parallel expressions.

Rhythm plays a crucial role in the highest goal of Cicero's ideal orator, that of "rhetorical transport."[13] According to Cicero, audiences are predisposed by nature to orient themselves to sounds and rhythms,[14] judging orations not only by their content but also by their rhythms and sounds.[15] For Cicero, orators who disregard sound and rhythm in their orations do so at their own peril; they resemble wrestlers untrained in gymnastics.[16] He remarks, "To speak with well-knit rhythm without ideas is folly, to present ideas without order and rhythm in the language is to be speechless."[17] Quintilian echoes the thoughts of Cicero when he states, "For in the first place nothing can penetrate to the emotions that stumbles at the portals of the ear, and secondly man is naturally attracted by harmonious sounds."[18]

Cicero devotes nearly a third of his treatise *Orator* to discussions on the connection between rhythm (a component of style) and content.[19] According to him, an effective orator must consider three things: what to say, in what

---

8. Lee and Scott comment, "sound creates structure, sound trains the ear, and sound balances the importance of signifier and signified." *Sound Mapping*, 80. Sound is also the basis for the primary units of composition, the colon and the period. Ibid., 104.

9 *Encomium of Helen* 14.

10. *Encomium of Helen* 15.

11. See D. M. MacDowell's introduction in Gorgias, *Encomium of Helen*, 18.

12 *Rhetoric and Rhythm in Byzantium*, 65.

13. Ibid., 1. For Cicero, "to prove is the first necessity, to please is to charm, to sway is victory" (*Orat.* 21.69). Translation is by H. M. Hubbell in Cicero, *Orator*, 357.

14 *Orat.* 51.173.

15 *Orat.* 48.162.

16 *Orat.* 68.229.

17. *Orat.* 71.236 in Cicero, *Orator*, 507.

18. *Inst.* 9.4.10. Translation is by H. E. Butler in Quintilian, *The Institutio Oratoria of Quintilian* 3.511. Quoted also in Lee and Scott, *Sound Mapping*, 176.

19. Valiavitcharska, *Rhetoric and Rhythm in Byzantium*, 1.

order, and in what manner and style to say it.[20] Each of the three oratorical styles he outlines—grandiloquent, plain, and in-between—concern matters of content as well as style.[21] For instance, composers of grandiloquent style demonstrate "splendid power of thought and majesty of diction; they were forceful, versatile, copious and grave, trained and equipped to arouse and sway the emotions."[22] They employ rough or harsh style, without regular construction and rounded periods, or a smooth style, consisting of "ordered sentence-structure with a periodic cadence."[23] Elsewhere, Cicero comments that effective orators embellish ideas with figures, rhetorical tropes that require attention to proper arrangement.[24] Yet arrangement regards a consideration of sound and rhythm: the final syllables are to fit with the initial ones, so that the words have an agreeable sound; the symmetry of the words are to produce their own rounded periods. The periods are to have a rhythmical cadence.[25] According to Cicero, due to their inherent balance and symmetry, symmetrical clauses or certain figures of speech, such as rhyme (*homoeoteleuton*), antithesis, and parallelism, are themselves rhythmical.[26]

During the Byzantine era, students learned rhetorical rhythm from the Hermogenic corpus and its commentaries.[27] Yet Byzantine rhetoricians considered that their rhetorical education and practice stretched back to Hellenistic Greece.[28] The Hermogenic corpus consists of Aphthonius' *Progymnasmata*, and the treatises *On Issues*, *On Invention*, *On the Method of Forcefulness*, and *On Types of Styles*. Only *On Issues* and *On Types of Styles*

---

20 *Orat.* 13.43.

21. *Orat.* 5.20, 23.79. Other classical commentators, such as Dionysius of Halicarnassus and Demetrius, also discuss stylistic types. See Lee and Scott, *Sound Mapping*, 114–17.

22. *Orat.* 5.20 in Cicero, Orator, 319.

23. *Orat.* 5.20 in Cicero, Orator, 319.

24 *Orat.* 40.140.

25. *Orat.* 44.149. As Lee and Scott remark, more important than stylistic types was the desired effect. "Certain rhythms and melodies were deemed appropriate for specific social occasions." *Sound Mapping*, 118.

26 *Orat.* 220. As cited in Valiavitcharska, *Rhetoric and Rhythm in Byzantium*, 65.

27 The commentaries of the Hermogenic corpus appear in Walz's editions of *Rhetores Graeci*. The materials for the commentaries were originally the scholia to the Hermogenic corpus and were initially compiled and edited in the sixth century. Other extant commentaries date up to the thirteenth century, such as the commentary of Maximus Planudes. The commentaries are representative of the teaching tradition of the Macedonian and Comnenian periods, in which there was a conscious tendency to classicize. See Valiavitcharska, *Rhetoric and Rhythm in Byzantium*, 34 n.20.

28. Valiavitcharska, *Rhetoric and Rhythm in Byzantium*, 49.

are recognized as authentically by Hermogenes (fl. 161–180 CE).[29] For the Byzantines, "rhythm in prose was generated by clause length, word composition, and closing cadence, and measured out not by a sequence of metra but by individual words with its own length, stress, and contextual relation to other words in the utterance."[30]

The Byzantine understanding of prose rhythm, however, was not fixed but flexible. They considered, as did Cicero, that certain figures of speech, such as rhyme (*homoeoteleuton*), antithesis, and parallelism (symmetrical clauses) had their own inherent rhythm.[31] Byzantine rhetoricians also observed rhythm in "the identical distribution of stresses from clause to clause" (responsion).[32] Parallel ideas can also create a sense of rhythm,[33] as can certain instances of hiatus.[34]

While rhetoricians from the ancient to the Byzantine period were keenly aware of the emotional impact of sound and rhythm for persuasion, modern rhetorical scholars pay scant attention to it. For modern scholars of rhetoric, sound and rhythm are merely forms of embellishment. Sound's integral place in rhetoric has been largely lost. Valiavitcharska attributes the wholesale disparagement of sound and rhythm to various causes. The Enlightenment, she suggests, saw the rupture of "argument from language and of reason from emotion," with subsequent priority given to the former over the latter.[35] In the early twentieth century, there was a split of the National Council of Teachers of English (1911) and the National Association for Academic Teachers of Public Speaking (1914) from the Modern Language Association. These divisions resulted in the field of English incorporating literature, and rhetoric falling under the umbrella of Speech. Speech Communication scholars adopt a scientific methodology for the study of rhetoric, focusing on argumentation, observation, and analysis, and designate a separate field within Speech for production and writing. These ruptures at the institutional level break the Western rhetorical tradition of the unity

---

29 Valiavitcharska, *Rhetoric and Rhythm in Byzantium*, 33–34. For more on discussions of the Byzantine educational process, see Ibid., 90–114.

30 Ibid., 50.

31 Ibid., 65.

32 Ibid., 72.

33 Ibid., 66.

34 Ibid., 52. The Byzantine writers noted that hiatus slows speech and takes "longer to pronounce." They differentiated between internal hiatus (within a word) and external hiatus, which surrounds a phrase or group of words. According to them, words that stand within a hiatus take on a rhythmical quality. Those words within the hiatus take on a "solemn and majestic" pace.

35. Ibid.

between theory and practice. Despite the contributions of I. A. Richards, Kenneth Burke and Chaïm Perelmen, who pay attention to stylistics, twentieth-century rhetorical theorists greatly emphasize "argumentation and reasoning, at the expense of form and style."[36]

Sound Mapping and Rhetorical Analysis

Sound mapping, which brings to light a composition's "acoustic features,"[37] restores the study of ancient compositions to its original emphasis on the inseparability of content/argument and style.[38] Yet by enabling the visualization of sound patterns, sound maps also reveal a composition's *rhetorical* meaning. Distinctive sounds—smooth ones that move a discourse along in a harmonious fashion and harsh ones that disturb it—are affective; they operate on the emotions, a primary factor for decision-making. In that repetition selects sounds for emphasis,"[39] thereby guiding comprehension and shaping "audience expectations,"[40] it is also a function of *logos* (appeal through reason), one of rhetoric's leading tools.[41] Thus, because the rhetoric of sound is already built into ancient compositions, sound mapping is native to rhetorical analysis.

Sound mapping founds the analysis of my 2016 monograph, *Galatians and the Rhetoric of Crisis: Demosthenes, Cicero, Paul*. The book is an exploration into the question of why Paul counseled so strongly against

36. Ibid., 2.

37. According to Lee and Scott, "A sound map is a visual display that exhibits a literary composition's organization by highlighting its acoustic features and in doing so depicts aspects of a composition's sounded character in preparation for analysis." *Sound Mapping*, 168.

38. Lee and Scott discuss sounds' importance for ancient compositions: ancient compositions originated in sounds and are the result of trapping sounds and converting them to graphemes (written symbols). Ibid., 69–70.

These written symbols gain further expression and elaboration in written compositions through a devised system of grammar, which is itself based on sound. "From its inception . . . grammar primarily served to analyze and preserve speech sounds." Citing the work of Robert H. Robins, Lee and Scott report, "The study of grammar started among the Pre-Socrates as part of the wider study of the nature of speech." Ibid., 97.

39. Lee and Scott, *Sound Mapping*, 156–57. According to John Foley, repetition re-signifies meaning each time. Foley, *Immanent Art*, 56–57. See also Ong, *Orality and Literacy*, 40.

40. Lee and Scott, *Sound Mapping*, 79, 142.

41. Galen Rowe lists, for example, the following word figures that involve some type of repetition: *epanalepsis, anaphora, antistrophe, symploche, anadiplosis, prosapodosis, polyptoton, metaclisis, synonymia, diaphora, polysyndeton*, and *homoeoptoton*. See "Style," 129–38.

circumcision and Torah adoption for his gentile Galatian audience.[42] Despite a significant shift, a virtual sea change, in our understanding of Paul—in which he changes from being understood as Christian to a lifelong Jew,[43] retains his allegiance to the God of Israel, and is not against Torah—the reasons adduced for his strong rejection of circumcision and Torah adoption for gentiles remain unpersuasive. Pauline scholars have tended to look either outside his letters to his presumed socio-cultural or theological

---

42. While I focus only on Paul's Letter to the Galatians, his so-called anti-nomistic stance is apparent in his other letters as well (i.e., Rom 4:9-12; Phil 3:2-11).

43. In the mid-twentieth century, Krister Stendahl argued convincingly that Paul never converted to another religion but instead was called by God on a mission to the gentiles. See "Paul among Jews and Gentiles," 8. On this, see the arguments of the following scholars: Stowers, *Rereading of Romans*, 156. Daniel Boyarin writes that Paul "lived and died convinced that he was a Jew living out Judaism." *Radical Jew*, 2. In his book *Paul and the Stoics*, Troels Engberg-Pedersen writes, "Paul did not in any way see his own form of Christ faith as constituting a break with Judaism. On the contrary, in the best sectarian manner he conceived of it as the true apogee of Judaism." *Paul and the Stoics*, 15. L. Michael White notes that Paul "clearly saw himself as a pious Jew who had been called on by God, through Jesus, to take this message to non-Jews." *From Jesus to Christianity*, 145. Arthur Dewey comments that modern views regarding the notion that Paul converted have been influenced by the work of William James, A. D. Nock, and Alan Segal. According to Dewey, these writers rely on modern categories such as emotional experience and are as such inadequate for defining Paul's first-century context and rhetorical situation. "The Masks of Paul," 159-68. In her 2009 monograph, *Paul Was Not a Christian*, Pamela Eisenbaum, a former student of Stendhal, summarizes much of the recent scholarship and outlines several important implications for understanding Paul as a Jew. See *Paul Was Not a Christian*. Mark D. Nanos is at present one of, if not the strongest, proponent of this position. Nanos pushes beyond many of these more general assessments of Paul as a lifelong Jew and argues that Paul was also Torah-observant throughout his life. According to him, Paul wanted non-Jews to observe certain aspects of the Torah. See *Mystery of Romans*, 3-9; Nanos, *Irony of Galatians*, 2-9. For a brief summary of Nanos' position see Zetterholm, *Approaches to Paul*, 147-55.

concerns[44] or to assumptions about his agenda (his good news)[45] rather than to the rhetorical contours of the letter for solutions to this problem.[46]

Through a comparison of the orations of Demosthenes and Cicero, I indicate the degree to which Paul's letter to the Galatians is rhetorical and polemical. I argue that Paul's deep dispute with his opponents—evident in the details of his rhetoric—accounts for his anti-Torah stance. Like Demosthenes and Cicero, who in their Philippic orations railed against their opponents to argue their case, Paul too employed similar tactics, a rhetoric of crisis,[47] to spur his audience to his side. Above all else—above even the good

44. In his *The Irony of Galatians*, Mark Nanos assesses Paul's letter to the Galatians through a socio-rhetorical lens. His assessment of the question of why Paul jettisons circumcision for gentiles, however, lies more on theological than on socio-rhetorical grounds. According to Nanos, Paul was against circumcision, that is, the conversion of gentiles to Jews, because such an action would bring about one group of persons (namely, Jews) and thereby circumscribe or limit God's domain. The creation of one group of Jews compromises God's oneness: God is God of Jews and non-Jews (gentiles) alike. See *Mystery of Romans*, 9–10; Zetterholm, *Approaches to Paul*, 147–55. Nanos' solution, however, fails to convince because Paul does not express the concern that God's oneness would be compromised should gentiles become Jews. Furthermore, Paul does not express a concern about Jewish particularism, implied in this view. That is, whereas Paul indicates a desire to include gentiles under the Judean God—for example through Abraham—it is not because God's body of adherents is felt to be restricted to Jews alone. Finally, and significantly, Nanos' view assumes that Paul is a systematic thinker and had a formulated agenda. Yet all of Paul's letters, with the possible exception of Romans, indicate just the reverse, namely, that Paul addressed local and specific issues. Situations dictate Paul's discussions.

45. Paula Fredriksen gave voice to the influential view that the Jewish Paul faced the question of how to bring gentiles, non-Jews, to the God of Israel as history draws to a close. Paul, Fredriksen argues, was guided by certain prophetic texts of the Hebrew scriptures, such as Isa 2:2–4; Mic 4:1–3; and Zech 8:21–23, which discuss events of the last days, when all nations/gentiles will come to the God of Israel as gentiles, as non-Jews. Paul's apocalyptic vision, founded on these scriptural texts, explains why he counsels against the circumcision of gentiles. See "Judaism, the Circumcision of Gentiles," 244–47; Eisenbaum, *Paul Was not a Christian*, 96–98. The difficulty with this view, however, is that Paul never articulates this as his reason for discouraging the circumcision of gentiles and furthermore he does not slavishly follow scriptural commands or prophetic texts. By contrast, Paul is not bound by scriptural texts and instead freely manipulates them for his own rhetorical purposes.

46. There are, however, some exceptions. Shaye Cohen, for example, observes that Paul's statements in Galatians against Torah are exaggerated and that competition prompted his anti-Torah position. See "Galatians," 332. Observing an abundance of self-contradictions and ad hoc arguments, Heikki Räisänen notes that Paul's arguments on the subject of Torah are polemical. See *Paul and the Law*, 261–62.

47. For an explanation of the origin and aims of this model, see Wooten, *Rhetoric of Crisis*. Generally speaking, the rhetoric of crisis employs four dominant means of persuasion: the creation of a sense of urgency, the formation of a lofty self-characterization, the use of emotive language, and the employment of disjunctive argumentation.

news he promotes—Paul desires to win the Galatians from his competitors, those advocating for circumcision and Torah adoption.[48]

One of the components of the rhetoric of crisis is the development of an authoritative or lofty sense of self, superior to others. In Aristotelian terms, this type of argumentation is called persuasion by moral character or ethos (ἦθος). "The orator persuades by moral character," remarks Aristotle, "when his speech is delivered in such a manner as to render him worthy of confidence."[49] The perception of the development of a fully authoritative self, superior to others, made possible in part through sound mapping techniques, contrasts sharply with the assumption of many Pauline interpreters that Paul in Galatians is apologetically defending his good news.[50] Moreover, the related insight that Paul is entirely strategic in how he argues undermines another and often unacknowledged assumption that Paul's discourse is something other than rhetoric. The comments of J. Louis Martyn provide an example of this view: "Rhetoric . . . can serve the gospel,

---

Authors employ the rhetoric of crisis to encourage swift action toward a specific position (their own) and against an alternative one. The Philippic-cycle orations of Demosthenes and Cicero exemplify this type of rhetoric.

48. Kennedy remarks that "the function of Galatians is to establish Paul's ethos and thus to support his view of the truth of his gospel." *New Testament Interpretation Through Rhetorical Criticism*, 145. I have argued that establishing his ethos is primary. Paul hardly discusses what his gospel might be.

49. *Rhet.* 1.2.4. Translation is by John H. Freese in Aristotle, *The 'Art' of Rhetoric*, 17. Being a person of worth, however and while important, is nevertheless secondary to self-characterizing as worthy. Indeed, the techniques employed to self-characterize as worthy of audience confidence leave room/allow for the orator/author to dissemble. On this, see Yoos, "Revision of the Concept of Ethical Appeal," 41-46.

50. For the ubiquitousness of the view that Paul is on the defensive, see Sumney, "Studying Paul's Opponents," 18.

With his 1979 Commentary on Galatians, Hans Dieter Betz re-inaugurated New Testament rhetorical analysis. Betz termed Galatians an "apologetic letter." Within the Greco-Roman rhetorical framework, the letter fell, according to him, within the forensic species. Betz pictures Paul as a defender of his gospel. *Galatians*, 14-25. Others have followed on Betz's analysis. See Martin, "Apostasy to Paganism," 93. The process of mirror-reading—reading Paul's statements as a mirror of the situation of his opponents—also assumes a passive Paul, someone who for the most part responds to the arguments of others. For a discussion of mirror reading, see Barclay, "Mirror-Reading a Polemical Letter: Galatians as a Test Case," 367-82.

For the view that Paul is not defensive and not apologetic, see Gaventa, "Autobiography as Paradigm," 309-10. According to Jerry Sumney, various studies have made Paul's defensive posture difficult to sustain. See "Studying Paul's Opponents," 18. See also Kennedy who writes, "Paul certainly *could* have written a defense of the charges made against him in Galatia or elsewhere; but one of the most important things to notice about Galatians is that he did not choose to do so." *New Testament Interpretation through Rhetorical Criticism*, 144-45. (Italics are the author's.)

but the gospel itself is not fundamentally a matter of rhetorical persuasion (1:10–12). For the gospel has the effect of placing at issue the nature of argument itself. That is to say, since the gospel is God's own utterance, it is not and can never be subject to ratiocinative[51] criteria that have been developed apart from it."[52]

Paul's authoritative self-characterization begins at the start of Galatians.[53] He opens his letter forcefully, abruptly, and in a confrontational tone.[54] Competition comes into view right from the start. While his anger is noticeable, Paul is nevertheless fully in control of his discourse.[55] The sound map of the first period of Galatians highlights these points.[56] (See the legend below the sound map for an explanation of the various notations employed.)

---

51. "The action or process of reasoning, esp. deductively or by using syllogisms." "ratiocination, n." OED Online. Oxford University Press. http://www.oed.com/view/Entry/158489?redirectedFrom=ratiocination.

52. Martyn, *Galatians*, 22. Thus, according to Martyn, Paul's statements cannot be analyzed rhetorically, nor are they subject to the rules of rational argumentation. Betz, who as mentioned revives rhetorical analysis of New Testament texts, rather paradoxically holds a view similar to Martyn's. Betz maintains that Paul's letter differs from other letters of his time and is instead a "magical letter." By this, he too means that it is not subject to the rules of rhetoric. See *Galatians*, 25. In contrast to Martyn, Tod Penner and Davina Lopez cogently remark, "There is no place outside of rhetoric in Paul's letters." "Rhetorical Approaches," 37. See also the statement by the well-known classist George Kennedy: "The writers of the New Testament had a message to convey and sought to persuade an audience to believe it or to believe it more profoundly. As such they are rhetorical, and their methods can be studied by the discipline of rhetoric." *New Testament Interpretation through Rhetorical Criticism*, 3. Commenting further, Kennedy explains, "Sacred language affects to be outside of time, but the very process of casting it into words casts it into history," 159.

53. Robert Hall remarks, "Paul asserts a powerful ethos as the one chosen by God." "Rhetorical Outline for Galatians," 34. Robert Berchman notes, Gal 1:1 "establishes Paul's view that he is a true apostle. Paul amplifies this fact topically and syllogistically. His rhetorical argument leaves little room for either his opponents in Galatia, or the Galatians themselves, to reject his claims, or as Paul will argue later, to ignore the course of conduct he advocates." "Galatians (1:1–5)," 65. Similarly, Troy Martin comments, "[B]eginning with the prescript and continuing throughout the letter, Paul establishes as a matter of record that he is the authorized representative of the deity. . ." "Apostasy to Paganism," 80.

54. Nanos, *Irony of Galatians*, 32.

55. Ian Elmer notes, there is "no doubt that Paul is a skillful rhetorician who could twist a story to his own ends." "Setting the Record Straight," 32.

56. The English translation is my own.

Galatians 1:1

Galatians 1:1
1.1 Παῦλο<u>ς</u> ἀπόστολο<u>ς</u>
    1.2 <u><u>οὐκ</u></u>   ἀπ'   ἀνθρώπων
    1.3 <u><u>οὐδὲ</u></u>   δι'*   ἀνθρώπου
1.4 ἀλλὰ διὰ* Ἰη<u>σ</u>οῦ Χρι<u>σ</u>τοῦ καὶ θε<u>ο</u>ῦ πατρὸ<u>ς</u># τοῦ* ἐγείραντο<u>ς</u> αὐτὸν ἐκ# νεκρῶν.

1.1 Paul apostle
    1.2 not by humans
    1.3 nor through a human
1.4 but through Jesus anointed and God the father who raised him from the dead.

Dotted-underlining	Repetition of multiple syllables (and phrases)
Single-underlining	Repetition of a single syllable, ending and opening sounds (consonance and anaphora)
Double-underlining	Adversatives
Pound Sign (#)	Dissonance; clash of consonants (hiatus)
Asterisk (*)	Clash of vowels

Period 1 jars its hearers: the brevity of the cola combined with the double adversatives, οὐκ ("not") and οὐδὲ ("and not") (marked in dotted-underline type above; 1.2–3),[57] evoke harshness, and are rhythmic by virtue of their parallel structure.[58] The abrasive opening establishes the tone of the letter and its content provides evidence of conflict.[59] Furthermore, by beginning this letter with a reference to himself and to himself alone, Paul establishes himself as a focal point. *Homoeoteleuton*, or rhyming of the ending ος sound, an aspect of prose rhythm,[60] accentuates the two lexemes of 1.1 and hence emphasize that point.

The abrupt and harsh opening of Galatians becomes even more apparent through a comparison with the opening of 2 Corinthians. This letter begins with the identical words, Παῦλος ἀπόστολος, yet as seen below its tone is quite different.

---

57. See Johan Vos, who argues that the two adversatives in Gal 1:1 are in the form of a twofold *"correctio,"* which underscores Paul's "claim to authority." "Paul's Argumentation in Galatians 1–2," 71.

58 On the rhythmic nature of parallelism, see Valiavitcharska, *Rhetoric and Rhythm in Byzantium*, 65.

59. See, for example, Gal 5:7–12, cutting remarks that occur toward the end of the letter.

60 Valiavitcharska, *Rhetoric and Rhythm in Byzantium*, 65.

2 Cor 1:1

1.1 Παῦλ<u>ος</u> ἀπόστολ<u>ος</u> Χριστ<u>οῦ</u> Ἰησ<u>οῦ</u> διὰ θελήματ<u>ος</u> θε<u>οῦ</u> καὶ Τιμόθε<u>ος</u> ὁ ἀδελφ<u>ὸς</u>

1.2 <u>τῇ</u> ἐκκλησίᾳ τοῦ θεοῦ <u>τῇ</u> οὔσῃ ἐν Κορίνθῳ σὺν <u>τοῖς</u> ἁγίοις πᾶσιν <u>τοῖς</u> οὖσιν ἐν ὅλῃ <u>τῇ</u> Ἀχαΐᾳ,

1.1 Paul apostle of anointed Jesus through the will of God and brother Timothy

1.2 to the gathering of God that is in Corinth together with all the saints who are in the whole of Achaia,[61]

Unlike the opening of Galatians, period 1 of 2 Corinthians is drawn out (the cola are longer) and descriptive. It is characterized by rhyming (indicated by underlining) and hence smooth-flowing sounds. There is nothing particularly abrasive or disruptive about it. Repetition of the articles τῇ and τοῖς harmoniously carry colon 1.2 along. While 2 Corinthians opens with Paul, its focus does not remain with him. Timothy and Paul jointly send the letter (1.1). Indeed, the Paul-Timothy partnership is strengthened by the shared rhyming (*homoeoteleuton*) of their names and positions (Παῦλ<u>ος</u> ἀπόστολ<u>ος</u>, Τιμόθε<u>ος</u> ὁ ἀδελφ<u>ὸς</u>), an instance of prose rhythm which bookend colon 1.1. Like all his other extant epistles, this opening moves on to a greeting of those gathered (1.2) as well as a lengthy thanksgiving (2 Cor 1:3–7),[62] both of which are absent from Galatians.[63] In Galatians, it is as though Paul cannot get to the issue—his displeasure with his opposition—fast enough.

Already in colon 1.1 of Galatians Paul creates a distinction between himself, the divinely commissioned apostle, and others (his opponents; 1.2–3). He constructs this distinction through the double adversatives, which head successive short and parallel cola (1.2–3),[64] and by the coordinating conjunction but (ἀλλὰ), which begins colon 1.4. The placement of adversatives at the start[65] of cola and their duplication in the form of *polyptoton*, the repetition of a word under a different form,[66] emphasize the sense

---

61. Translation is my own.
62. For the fragmentary nature of 2 Corinthians, see Dewey, et al., *Authentic Letters of Paul*.
63. See Doty, *Letters in Primitive Christianity*, 31, 43.
64. Nanos notes that Paul begins "the letter with a polemic sharply contrasting God's authority with that of human agents or agencies." *Irony of Galatians*, 39.
65. On this point, see Lee and Scott, *Sound Mapping*, 156.
66. Rowe, "Style," 132.

of contrariety they convey.[67] Paul also twice repeats the word for human (ἀνθρώπων, ἀνθρώπου; 1.2–3) (marked in dotted-underline type), another instance of *polyptoton* and a second occurrence of alliteration within two successive cola. Repetition of the noun ἄνθρωπος forcefully marks others (his opponents) as being humanly commissioned, leaving Paul uniquely and distinctively divinely commissioned (1.4). Furthermore, Paul emphasizes the contrast between himself and these others through a chiastic (abba) structure.

The period (1.4) ends as aggressively as it begins. The final colon contains distinctive/memorable sound signals,[68] instances of hiatus (marked with an asterisk), and dissonance, a clash of consonants (marked with a pound sign). Like colon 1, colon 4 also has Paul as its referent. Indeed, the repetition of the rhyming ὸς sound in πατρὸς and ἐγείραντος (1.4) echo the rhyming sounds in 1.1 and thus at the auditory level return the hearer to the subject of Paul. On the semantic level, Paul becomes associated with two divine figures, Jesus and God.[69] Elongation and repetition of beginning sounds, found in 1.4, are characteristic of a well-formed period[70] and signal completion.

Paul extends his lofty and aggressively construed self-characterization in a lengthy autobiographical section (Gal 1:10—2:21). In the first four periods of this section, mapped below, Paul furthers the human/divine contrast made at the start, arguing that unlike other humans, or even any other human, God set him apart. While Paul's self-characterizations are exceedingly elevated, exaggerated, as well as highly controlled, such self-portrayals are the norm among ancient biographers and autobiographers. George Lyons explains:

> The major interest of most ancient biographers and autobiographers was not historical reality but human potentiality and idealization. Thus, exaggeration and/or suppression were considered legitimate devices. Ancient biographers and autobiographers seldom began with personal experiences but from existing ideals and literary forms, whether from consciously imitated model works, philosophical presuppositions as to the

---

67. Lyons notes that the "negative and antithetic elaboration" on the notion of apostle is found nowhere else in Paul's extant letters. See *Pauline Biography*, 124.

68. According to Lee and Scott, a consonant clash or hiatus stand apart and "make a stronger impression than aurally nondescript" sounds. *Sound Mapping*, 178.

69. See Betz, *Galatians*, 39. Marcion's copy of Galatians does not include the phrase "and God the Father." Ibid., 39 n.26. See also Jason D. BeDuhn, *The First New Testament: Marcion's Scriptural Canon*, 229.

70. Lee and Scott, *Sound Mapping*, 171.

constituents of virtue, or generally followed rhetorical rules. This partnership of rhetoric and philosophy resulted in a dubious mixture of sincerity and posing, fact and fantasy, truth and fiction, actual and ideal.[71]

While his opponents are not made explicit in these first four periods, they nevertheless influence this unit. Moreover, Paul's competition is very much in evidence in the important propositional section[72] (Gal 1:6–9) that immediately precedes this section. His hyperbolic animosity against his opponents (Gal 1:8–9) within the proposition—a section designed to provide the letter's purpose—suggests that his opponents are integral to the rhetorical situation.[73]

Galatians 1:10–17

1.1 Ἄρτι γὰρ ἀνθρώπους# πείθω ἢ τὸν# θεόν

1.2 ἢ ζητῶ ἀνθρώποις ἀρέσκειν;

1.3 εἰ* ἔτι ἀνθρώποις ἤρεσκον, Χριστοῦ δοῦλος οὐκ ἂν ἤμην.

2.1a Γνωρίζω γὰρ ὑμῖν, ἀδελφοί, τὸ εὐαγγέλιον τὸ εὐαγγελισθὲν ὑπ' ἐμοῦ* ὅτι*

2.1b οὐκ ἔστιν# κατὰ* ἄνθρωπον

2.2 οὐδὲ γὰρ ἐγὼ παρὰ* ἀνθρώπου παρέλαβον αὐτὸ

2.3 οὔτε* ἐδιδάχθην ἀλλὰ δι'* ἀποκαλύψεως Ἰησοῦ Χριστοῦ.

3.1 Ἠκούσατε γὰρ τὴν ἐμὴν ἀναστροφήν ποτε* ἐν# τῷ* Ἰουδαϊσμῷ,

3.2 ὅτι καθ' ὑπερβολὴν ἐδίωκον# τὴν ἐκκλησίαν# τοῦ θεοῦ καὶ* ἐπόρθουν αὐτήν,

3.3 καὶ προέκοπτον ἐν# τῷ* Ἰουδαϊσμῷ* ὑπὲρ# πολλοὺς# συνηλικιώτας ἐν# τῷ γένει μου,

3.4 περισσοτέρως# ζηλωτὴς ὑπάρχων# τῶν# πατρικῶν# μου παραδόσεων.

---

71. Lyons, *Pauline Biography*, 30. For a similar view, see also Misch, *A History of Autobiography in Antiquity*, 1.163, 1.175.

72. See Kennedy, *New Testament Interpretation through Rhetorical Criticism*, 148. The proposition states the letter's purpose and is central for the letter as a whole. Hall, "Rhetorical Outline for Galatians," 35. Betz also understands the purpose of Galatians in ways that parallel Hall and Kennedy. See Galatians, 46; "Literary Composition and Function," 9.

73. The English translation is my own.

Rhythm, Sound, and Persuasion 207

4.1 Ὅτε δὲ* εὐδόκησεν ὁ* ἀφορίσας# με* ἐx# κοιλίας# μητρός# μου

4.2 καὶ καλέσας# διὰ τῆς# χάριτος αὐτοῦ* ἀποκαλύψαι τὸν υἱὸν αὐτοῦ* ἐν ἐμοί,
ἵνα* εὐαγγελίζωμαι* αὐτὸν ἐν# τοῖς ἔθνεσιν,

4.3 εὐθέως οὐ προσανεθέμην# σαρκὶ καὶ* αἵματι

4.4 οὐδὲ* ἀνῆλθον εἰς Ἱεροσόλυμα πρὸς# τοὺς# πρὸ* ἐμοῦ* ἀποστόλους,

4.5 ἀλλ' ἀπῆλθον εἰς Ἀραβίαν, καὶ πάλιν ὑπέστρεψα* εἰς# Δαμασκόν.

1.1 For am I now persuading humans or God?

1.2 Or am I seeking to please humans?

1.3 If I were still pleasing humans, I would not be the anointed's slave.

2.1a For I am making known to you, brothers, the good news proclaimed by me

2.1b is not according to a human.

2.2 For I did not receive it from a human

2.3 nor was I taught it but [I received it] through it a revelation of Jesus, the Anointed.

3.1 For you heard of my earlier life in Judaism,

3.2 that I persecuted to the superlative degree the assembly of God and tried to destroy it.

3.3 and [how] I advanced in Judaism beyond many of my people of the same age,

3.4 for I was extremely zealous for the traditions of the ancestors.

4.1 But when it pleased [God], who separated me from my mother's womb

4.2 and called [me] through his grace to reveal his son in me, so that I might proclaim him among the non-Jews,

4.3 immediately, I did not consult with flesh and blood

4.4 nor did I go into Jerusalem, to those who were apostles before me,

4.5 but I went into Arabia and again I returned to Damascus.

In this next unit of prose, Paul continues with an aggressive and attention-grabbing rhetorical style.[74] Rhetorical questions head the unit (1.1–2).

---

74. Hall refers to Gal 1:10 as the start of the proof section of Galatians and terms the section defined by Gal 1:10—2:21 the narration section. See "Rhetorical Outline for Galatians," 38. According to Kennedy, the proof section of Galatians runs from Gal

Unlike deliberation, questions probe and challenge an audience. Sound signals relay a sense of discomfort and hence reinforce the sense of challenge that the questions are meant to convey. Harsh tones—in evidence by hiatus (marked by asterisks) and consonant clashes (marked by pound signs)—characterize the unit and garner audience attention through disruption. The uneven combination of short and long cola throughout the unit contributes to this sense of disruption, while it also elicits attention.

Additional sound signals contribute to the distinction Paul seeks to draw between himself and others. The five-fold repetition of ἄνθρωπος (1.1–3, 2.1–2; marked in dotted-underline), combined with a series of adversatives (1.3, 2.1–3, 4.3–4; marked in double-underline) strongly reinforce Paul's disassociation from human-like activities and further the divine-human contrast he introduced previously. Paul claims not to be in the business of persuading (1.1) or of pleasing other humans (1.2–3). Clearly, however, he *is* in the business of persuading; thus, he dissembles.[75] Assonance or internal rhyming of ρέσκ (marked in dotted-underline) from the verb "to please" ἀρέσκειν (1.2–3), coupled in two instances with the noun for human, emphasize his "non-participation" in these activities. Rhythm—in the form of parallel words and ideas[76]—also reinforces this notion (1.2–3). The point Paul is arguing here is that unlike others, namely his opponents, God and not humans influences his behavior.

In period 2, Paul emphasizes that the good news he proclaims (εὐαγγέλιον τὸ εὐαγγελισθὲν) is not by him. He builds to his point that the good news is instead through a revelation of Jesus, the Anointed. He does this through the employment of internal rhythm in the form of parallel structure (οὐκ ἔστιν κατὰ ἄνθρωπον, 2.1b and οὐδὲ γὰρ ἐγὼ παρὰ ἀνθρώπου, 2.2) to state what the good news is not, and with a chiastic structure defined by 2.1a/2.1b, 2.2/2.3.

Paul's highly exaggerated self-characterization continues in period 3, in which he provides a highly compressed and selective review of his past.[77]

1:11–5:1. *New Testament Interpretation through Rhetorical Criticism*, 148–50. While Gal 1:10 marks an abrupt transition from 1:9, Betz does not make a section break at this point. Instead he views Gal 1:6–11 as a unit and refers to it as the *exordium* or opening. He reasons that Gal 1:10–11 are transitional verses. *Galatians*, 54.

75. See Betz, who implies that Paul is engaging here with the notion that persuasion (the art of rhetoric) has negative connotations. Whether or not Paul considered that the act of persuasion was unfitting, he nevertheless engages in it. *Galatians*, 54. See also Kennedy, *New Testament Interpretation through Rhetorical Criticism*, 159.

76. Valiavitcharska notes, "The parallel ideas themselves create a sense of rhythm by virtue of their cyclical repetition." *Rhetoric and Rhythm in Byzantinum*, 66.

77. With regard to Gal 1:15 (above period 4), Betz writes, "It is extremely difficult—if not altogether impossible—to extract from Paul's words the facts as they really

The period is characterized by dissonance. As such, it is grating and attention-getting.[78] These early-life experiences have in common an association with Judaism. Indeed, the sound map makes apparent the repetition of the expression ἐν τῷ Ἰουδαϊσμῷ (3.1, .3) and then the allusion to it with the truncated prepositional phrase ἐν τῷ in 3.3 (marked in dotted-underline). Since it is very unlikely that there was a fully formed Judaism at that time,[79] Paul provides a term that serves to summarize an association with certain Jewish regulations,[80] including circumcision. Significantly, the term "Judaism" pertains to Paul's opponents, those advocating for the circumcision of the Galatians. While it is important to note that Paul remains Jewish throughout his life, his use of the term "Judaism" in this context clearly suggests his distancing from the customs and regulations of his past.

Paul supplies two episodes of his past life in "Judaism" (ἐν τῷ Ἰουδαϊσμῷ). In each, he self-characterizes as someone who lived life at the extreme. He begins by raising a damaging[81] episode from his past. Indeed, Paul forcefully draws his audience's attention to his negative past behavior, as seen by the second-person verb Ἠκούσατε, (you have heard) that heads period 3. Rather than minimizing the harm he caused, Paul amplifies it. Paul states that he actively persecuted the assembly of God (καθ' ὑπερβολὴν ἐδίωκον), even attempting to destroy (ἐπόρθουν) it (3.2). The noun ὑπερβολὴν ("exceedingly," or "to the superlative degree") is strong and emotionally evocative. It receives additional emphasis by the repetition of ὑπέρ, meaning "more than" found in the next colon (3.3). One must keep in mind that Paul is depicting/characterizing/interpreting his own past. In other words, he could easily have softened the portrayal. The exegete, then, must ask why he chose to depict his past in the way that he has.

---

happened." *Galatians*, 69. See also Scott, who writes that Paul's is not a neutral telling of his own story. Scott writes, "[H]e tells his story to prove a point to win a debate." *The Real Paul*, 20.

78. Lee and Scott, *Sound Mapping*, 178.

79. This is a controversial subject in New Testament scholarship, and entirely too large a topic to discuss here. In the entire New Testament, the word "Judaism" appears only here and in Gal 1:14. Outside the New Testament, the term is next found in the letters of Ignatius (*Mag.* 8.1; 10.3; *Philad.* 6.1). Paul may have been the first author to employ this term and it is difficult to know precisely what he meant by it. For the non-existence of a religion called Judaism until the fifth century, see especially Boyarin, *Border Lines*, 11.

80. According to Cohen, the Greek term refers to the "distinctive ways and manners, customs and beliefs of the Judean people." "The Letter of Paul to the Galatians," 333. For more on the term "Judaism," see also Betz, *Galatians*, 67 n.105.

81. Lyons remarks that discussions of one's past are typical within ancient autobiographies. *Pauline Biography*, 28, 61.

In the second episode, also "in Judaism," Paul self-portrays as someone not just interested in the traditions of the fathers but very zealous (περισσοτέρως ζηλωτὴς) for them (3.3-4). The comparative adverb περισσοτέρως, translated above as "extremely," heads colon 3.4. Taken together, περισσοτέρως ζηλωτὴς means that Paul self-characterizes his past in the words of one exegete as "a standout example of what it means to be a Jew."[82] The object of Paul's zeal—the traditions of the ancestors—receives special emphasis through rhyme, the repetition of the ending ων and ῶν (underlined above; 3.4), considered a form of rhythm. The two events share in common the portrait of a fiery and fervent individual, even a religious fanatic, who lived life at the extreme. Again, the exegete must ask why Paul chose to depict himself as such and to associate this type of behavior with "Judaism."

As is the case with other ancient autobiographers,[83] Paul's potentially damaging self-disclosures[84] serve rather than harm the favorable ethos he builds.[85] That is, Paul deploys these aspects of his past life to bring about an overall positive evaluation of his present-self. At the same time, his past association with "Judaism" furthers a negative evaluation of his present opponents.

It is the Ὅτε δὲ ("But when") that heads period 4, that makes apparent Paul's rhetorical purpose. With it, he brings about a dramatic shift in time and situation. At a certain yet undisclosed time, God became the active agent in Paul's life (4.2), even as God was latently present from the beginning (4.1). The harsh repetitive κ sound as seen in ἐκ κοιλίας (4.1), καὶ and καλέσας that heads 4.2 emphasize this divine activity. An instance of prose rhythm, in the form of external hiatus (the presence of hiatus on each side of a group of words), sets off Paul's revelation or divine insight as significant (italicized in 4.2). The dramatic shift in situation, initiated also by the Ὅτε δὲ (4.1), distinguishes Paul from his former human self in "Judaism" to someone God controls. Paul is now not like his humanly-driven opponents, but instead directed by God. In his present state, he is distinct from his

---

82. See Scott, *Real Paul*, 20. Similarly, according to Betz, Paul was saying that he was "an ardent observer of Torah." *Galatians*, 68. For a similar view regarding how to understand the meaning of being zealous, see Reumann, *Philippians*, 514.

83. I indicate how Demosthenes and Cicero self-portray in ways that parallel Paul. They too raise issues that are potentially damaging to their otherwise lofty and positively construed self-characterizations. Like Paul, they put potentially damaging details of their life to positive use. *Galatians and the Rhetoric of Crisis*, 53–67.

84. On this point, see Lyons, *Pauline Biography*, 30.

85. According to Lyons, Paul is "fully at home in antiquity to the extent that they [his autobiographical statements] are not purely informative personal histories but serve other motives." *Pauline Biography*, 66.

opponents. Paul's self-characterization of his past serves in support of his present self-portrayal.

Thus, aided in large measure by sound mapping, this rhetorical analysis of two units of Paul's letter to the Galatians indicates that Paul is every bit as rhetorical as other ancient writers. Paul showcases his compositional skills and self-characterizes as authoritative, aggressive and confrontational and wholly in control of his discourse. In the first unit, the map brings to light Paul's emphasis on himself and the sharp hierarchical distinctions he develops between himself and others. In the second unit, sound mapping reveals a high degree of dissonance and thus discord, which supports his aggressive self-portrayal. Beyond that, the map serves to make prominent under-observed aspects of Paul's rhetoric, such as the way he accentuates his extreme past behaviors and his unrelenting contrast between himself and others. Paul's dispute with his competition suggests that it, and not the good news to which he briefly alludes, is the dominant issue driving these compositional units.

Conclusions

In her thorough and convincing study, Valiavitcharska aptly indicates the longstanding awareness and interest in prose rhythm for persuasion. While the focus of her inquiry is Byzantine educational practices and is based on the Hermogenic corpus and its later commentaries, she clarifies that Byzantines traced their tradition to the Hellenistic era and that students learned to observe rhythm using classical texts. The sound maps above make apparent aspects of prose rhythm, such as rhyme, parallelism and hiatus, which ancient authors employed and discussed. Furthermore, the sound maps, as I indicate above, make apparent additional authorial tools, such as the structure of units and the repetitive opening and closing sounds. These tools pertain to sound, yet they affect hearers and shape meaning. The tools function rhetorically for persuasion. Thus, bringing notice to them significantly helps to strengthen my case for Paul's extensive deployment of persuasion by ἦθος.

Ancient rhetorical theorists were fully aware that persuasion involved much more than cogent argumentation. It required catching an audience's ears and once there, penetrating hearts and minds. The many and various rhetorical tools they developed—largely focused on different forms of repetitive sounds—aimed to do just that. By emphasizing semantic meaning over style, modern rhetorical theorists forego a significant part of a composition's meaning. With its emphasis on the sound features of ancient compositions, sound mapping provides an important avenue by which modern rhetorical analysts can once again access meaning that inheres in a composition's style. At the same time, it returns rhetorical analysis of ancient compositions to its original emphasis on not just argumentation/reason but also on style/form. Rhythm works altogether naturally with sound mapping and adds further evidence of the use and deployment of sound, now in the form of movement.

Because sound mapping deals with how compositions were initially woven together, employing the technique brings the interpreter closer to the composer. Just as brush strokes, overall design and color considerations provide insight into an artist's use of artistic tools to impart meaning—the rhetoric of the painting—so too does the observation of the tools of sound aid the literary interpreter to better understand the author's arguments, the rhetoric of the composition.

Bibliography

Aristotle. *The 'Art' of Rhetoric*. Translated by John Henry Freese. Loeb Classical Library. Cambridge: Harvard University Press, 1991.

Barclay, John M. G. "Mirror-Reading a Polemical Letter: Galatians as a Test Case." In *The Galatians Debate*, edited by Mark D. Nanos, 367–82. Peabody, MA: Hendrickson, 2002.

BeDuhn, Jason David. *The First New Testament: Marcion's Scriptural Canon*. Salem OR: Polebridge, 2013.

Berchman, Robert M. "Galatians (1:1–5): Paul and Greco-Roman Rhetoric." In *The Galatians Debate*, edited by Mark D. Nanos, 60–72. Peabody MA: Hendrickson, 2002.

Betz, Hans Dieter. *Galatians: A Commentary on Paul's Letter to the Churches in Galatia*. Hermeneia. Philadelphia: Fortress, 1979.

———. "The Literary Composition and Function of Paul's Letter to the Galatians." In *The Galatians Debate*, edited by Mark D. Nanos, 3–28. Peabody, MA: Hendrickson, 2002.

Boyarin, Daniel. *Border Lines: The Partition of Judaeo-Christianity*. Divinations: Rereading Late Ancient Religion. Philadelphia: University of Pennsylvania Press, 2004.

———. *A Radical Jew: Paul and the Politics of Identity*. Berkeley: University of California Press, 1994.

Cicero. *Orator*. In *Cicero: Brutus, Orator*, 307–507. Translated by H. M. Hubbell. Loeb Classical Library. Cambridge: Harvard University Press, 1939.

Cohen, Shaye J. D. "The Letter of Paul to the Galatians." In *The Jewish Annotated New Testament*, edited by Amy-Jill Levine and Marc Zvi Brettler, 332–44. New York: Oxford University Press, 2011.

Dewey, Arthur J. "The Masks of Paul." *Forum* 7.2 (2004) 159–75.

Dewey, Arthur J., et al. *The Authentic Letters of Paul: A New Reading of Paul's Rhetoric and Meaning*. Salem, OR: Polebridge, 2010.

Doty, William G. *Letters in Primitive Christianity.* 1973. Reprint, Eugene, OR: Wipf & Stock, 2014.
Eisenbaum, Pamela. *Paul Was not a Christian: The Original Message of a Misunderstood Apostle.* New York: HarperOne, 2009.
Elmer, Ian J. "Setting the Record Straight. Paul's *Narratio* (Gal 1:12—2:14) as a Response to the Galatian Conflict." In *Religious Conflict from Early Christianity to the Rise of Islam,* edited by Wendy Mayer and Bronwen Neil, 21–37. Arbeiten zur Kirchengeschichte 121. Berlin: de Gruyter, 2013.
Engberg-Pedersen, Troels. *Paul and the Stoics.* Louisville: Westminster John Knox, 2000.
Fredriksen, Paula. "Judaism, the Circumcision of Gentiles, and Apocalyptic Hope: Another Look at Galatians 1 and 2." In *The Galatians Debate,* edited by Mark D. Nanos, 235–60. Peabody, MA: Hendrickson, 2002.
Gorgias. *Encomium of Helen.* Translated by D. M. MacDowell. London: Bristol Classical, 2009.
Hall, Robert G. "The Rhetorical Outline for Galatians: A Reconsideration." In *The Galatians Debate,* edited by Mark D. Nanos, 29–38. Peabody, MA: Hendrickson, 2002.
Kennedy, George A. *New Testament Interpretation through Rhetorical Criticism.* Chapel Hill: University of North Carolina Press, 1984.
Lee, Margaret Ellen, and Bernard Brandon Scott. *Sound Mapping the New Testament.* Salem, OR: Polebridge, 2009.
Levinas, Emmanuel. "Reality and Its Shadow." In *The Levinas Reader,* edited by Seán Hand, 129–43. Oxford: Oxford University Press, 1989.
Levine, Amy-Jill, and Marc Zvi Brettler, eds. *The Jewish Annotated New Testament.* Oxford: Oxford University Press, 2011.
Livesey, Nina E. *Galatians and the Rhetoric of Crisis: Demosthenes, Cicero, Paul.* Salem, OR: Polebridge, 2016.
Lyons, George. *Pauline Biography: Toward a New Understanding.* Atlanta: Scholars, 1985.
Martin, Troy. "Apostasy to Paganism." In *The Galatians Debate,* edited by Mark D. Nanos, 73–94. Peabody, MA: Hendrickson, 2002.
Martyn, J. Louis. *Galatians.* Anchor Bible 33A. New York: Doubleday, 1997.
Misch, George. *A History of Autobiography in Antiquity.* 2 vols. Translated by E. W. Dickes. London: Routledge & Kegan Paul, 1950.
Nanos, Mark D., ed. *The Galatians Debate.* Peabody, MA: Hendrickson, 2002.
———. *The Irony of Galatians: Paul's Letter in First-Century Context.* Minneapolis: Fortress, 2002.
———. *The Mystery of Romans: The Jewish Context of Paul's Letter.* Minneapolis: Fortress, 1996.
Penner, Todd, and Lopez, Davina C. "Rhetorical Approaches: Introducing the Art of Persuasion in Paul and Pauline Studies." In *Studying Paul's Letters: Contemporary Perspectives and Methods,* edited by Joseph A. Marchal, 33–52. Minneapolis: Fortress, 2012.
Quintilian. *The Institutio Oratoria of Quintilian* Translated by H. E. Butler. 4 vols. Loeb Classical Library. Cambridge: Harvard University Press, 1986.
Räisänen, Heikki. *Paul and the Law.* Wissenschaftliche Untersuchungen zum Neuen Testament 29. Tübingen: Mohr/Siebeck, 1983.

Reumann, John. *Philippians*. Anchor Bible 33B. New Haven: Yale University Press, 2008.

Rowe, Galen O. "Style." In *Handbook of Classical Rhetoric in the Hellenistic Period 330 B.C.-A.D. 400*, edited by Stanley E. Porter, 121–57. Leiden: Brill, 2001.

Scott, Bernard Brandon. *The Real Paul: Recovering His Radical Challenge*. Salem, OR: Polebridge, 2015.

Stendahl, Krister. "Paul among Jews and Gentiles." In *Paul among Jews and Gentiles and Other Essays*, 1–77. Philadelphia: Fortress, 1976.

Stowers, Stanley K. *A Rereading of Romans: Justice, Jews and Gentiles*. New Haven: Yale University Press, 1994.

Sumney, Jerry. "Studying Paul's Opponents: Advantages and Challenges." In *Paul and His Opponents*, edited by Stanley E. Porter, 7–58. Pauline Studies 2. Leiden: Brill, 2005.

Valiavitcharska, Vessela. *Rhetoric and Rhythm in Byzantium: The Sound of Persuasion*. Cambridge: Cambridge University Press, 2013.

Vos, Johan S. "Paul's Argumentation in Galatians 1–2." In *The Galatians Debate*, edited by Mark D. Nanos, 169–80. Peabody MA: Hendrickson, 2002.

White, L. Michael. *From Jesus to Christianity*. New York: HarperOne, 2004.

Wooten, Cecil W. *Cicero's Philippics and Their Demosthenic Model: The Rhetoric of Crisis*. Chapel Hill: University of North Carolina Press, 1983.

Yoos, George E. "A Revision of the Concept of Ethical Appeal." *Philosophy & Rhetoric* 12 (1979) 41–58.

Zetterholm, Magnus. *Approaches to Paul: A Student's Guide to Recent Scholarship*. Minneapolis: Fortress, 2009.

10

The New Testament Soundscape and the Puzzle of Mark 16:8

Thomas E. Boomershine

Introduction

The development of sound mapping is a foundational step in the reevaluation of the sensorium or sensory matrix of biblical scholarship and our perception of the sensorium of the biblical tradition as sound.[1] Sound mapping seeks to develop a system of graphic representation of the sounds of biblical compositions. It is analogous to the highly developed system of writing and publishing musical compositions in printed scores that can then serve as the source for performances of those compositions.

The purpose of this essay is to set sound mapping in the context of the larger question of the sensory perception of biblical compositions then and now. The proposal is that there is a fundamental discontinuity between the predominantly visual sensory system of contemporary biblical study and the predominantly auditory sensory system of the biblical world. A dimension of that discontinuity is the difference between the auditory and visual sensory systems of the human brain. When biblical scholarship is evaluated in this context, the implication is that biblical scholarship has been based on a systemic misperception of the Bible as texts read by silent readers rather than as compositions performed for audiences.

---

1. Lee and Scott, *Sound Mapping*.

The puzzle of the ending of Mark's gospel presents a telling case study. The mapping and analysis of the story's sound reveals a concentration of highly sophisticated compositional techniques. When Mark 16:8 is experienced and analyzed as a composition of sound rather than as a text of visual signs, it makes sense as the intended ending of the gospel. While Mark 16:8 is a very small sample, the possibility emerges that the entire corpus of New Testament literature needs to be reassessed as compositions of sound for which sound mapping is a foundational step.

The Discontinuity between Ancient and Modern Biblical Sensoria

The sensorium of contemporary biblical scholarship and the sensorium of the Bible and ancient media are inextricably linked.[2] The presuppositions about the media world of the Bible shape the ways in which the "texts" are perceived and interpreted now and in their original context. The sensorium of current biblical scholarship is predominantly a sensorium of sight. The biblical texts are examined by looking at them. It is normal to walk the office corridors of biblical scholars and hear nothing behind those doors. And the classrooms of biblical scholars rarely echo with the sounds of biblical compositions while reference to and discussion of the texts is omnipresent. To the degree that biblical scholarship has as its goal the interpretation of the Bible in its original historical context, the implicit justification for this sensory system of sight is that it corresponds to the sensorium of the biblical world. The presupposition is that biblical authors were writing texts that were read by individual readers, usually in silence. The terms "texts," "authors," and "readers" are ubiquitous in the commentaries, monographs, and journals of biblical scholarship and they refer to this underlying concept of the Bible and ancient media. Exegesis is based on the reimagined experience of readers of texts. The underlying and largely unexamined assumption is that there is essential continuity between the sensorium of the Bible in its original context and the sensorium of twenty-first century biblical scholarship.

The problem is that recent research into the media culture of antiquity has revealed that this assumption is false. The sensorium of the literature of the ancient world was predominantly a sensory world of sound.[3] Classic stories such as the Iliad were memorized and performed in all night orgies

---

2. For a comprehensive exposition of the concept of "the sensorium," the sensorium of the Word of God, and "Word as Sound," see Ong, *Presence of the Word*, 1–175.

3. Ibid.

of sound and wine. Literary works were read aloud for groups of listeners. The receivers of ancient literature were usually audiences rather than individual readers. Furthermore, in those instances of individuals reading manuscripts, they usually read aloud.

The recognition of the centrality of sound is in part an inference from the preponderance of evidence that most people in the ancient world were illiterate.[4] Current estimates are that the rates of illiteracy in the various regions of the ancient near east in the biblical periods were 85–95 percent. The probability is that there were increasing rates of literacy in the millennium from 1000 BCE to 100 CE during which most of the works of biblical literature were composed. But while literacy rates undoubtedly increased, the overall rate remained very low. By the end of the first century CE, it was still the case that most people couldn't read. The literary compositions of this period were composed and performed for predominantly illiterate audiences.

During this period in which the compositions of the Bible were produced, literate culture gradually expanded from a small, elite culture of scribes to a much wider network of writing and reading that in turn generated the characteristic institutions of literate culture: military and economic empires, libraries, schools, and bookstores. The primary centers of literacy—Egypt, Babylonia, Greece, Rome—were also the centers of political and economic power.[5] All of these institutions appeared during this period of the gradual ascendency of literacy. But that wider communication network of the literate, including literate slaves, was a predominantly elite group of the classes of power and their coteries.[6] The communication of the products of the literate class to the illiterate majority took place by performances.

In the current discussion about "orality" and "literacy" there has been an extensive critique of the so-called "Great Divide" theory and the focus on orality as a distinctive system of cultural communication. This theory has called attention to the major differences between "oral culture" and "literate culture" and has emphasized the radical character of this transition. Rather than conceiving this transition as a "seamless" and natural transition, as was characteristic of form criticism, this body of research has emphasized both the psychological and sociological differences between the two cultures and their communication systems.[7] The critique of this theory has identified

---

4. Harris, *Ancient Literacy*. For rates of literacy, see 13.

5. Innis, *Empire and Communication*. This study of the correlation between the development of literacy and the emergence of the empires of western civilization introduced the study of media technology and communication culture.

6. Carr, *Writing on the Tablet of the Heart*, 287–88.

7. Kelber, *Oral and the Written Gospel*; also see Kelber, *Imprints, Voiceprints, &*

the various ways in which individuals and institutions have integrated these two communication systems and have formed multi-faceted syntheses of orality and literacy.

There are, therefore, major areas of ambiguity that remain in the assessment of orality and literacy in the ancient world. How extensive was the spread of literacy in the biblical period and specifically in the first century CE? What was the role of memory in ancient performance of manuscripts? When did the oral proclamation of New Testament manuscripts in worship begin and to what degree did that require memorization? How available were manuscripts of the gospels for public and private reading? How extensive was the practice of silent reading? How much of a gospel was performed at any particular gathering in the various periods of the gospel tradition? These are specific dimensions of the larger cultural and technological ambiguities of our ever-evolving understanding of the relationship between orality and literacy.

There is, however, one area in which there is no ambiguity: sound. Since 85 to 95 percent of persons were illiterate, the only way in which the vast majority of persons could experience biblical compositions was by hearing them performed as members of an audience. Individual reading was relatively unusual because of the limited availability of manuscripts. And when individuals read manuscripts alone, they usually read aloud. Silent reading was rare and anomalous.[8] Some three hundred years after the composition of the New Testament and the further development of literate culture in the Roman world, Augustine wrote about the strange behavior of his beloved mentor, Ambrose, who read in silence, with "his voice and his tongue . . . at rest":

> But when he was reading, his eye glided over the pages, and his heart searched out the sense, but his voice and tongue were at rest. Ofttimes when we had come (for no man was forbidden to enter, nor was it his wont that any who came should be announced to him), we saw him thus reading to himself, and never otherwise; and having long sat silent (for who durst intrude on one so intent?) we were fain to depart, conjecturing that in the small interval which he obtained, free from the din of others'

Footprints of Memory.

8. See Slusser, "Silent Reading," for evidence of individual instances of silent reading. See also Knox, "Silent Reading." In his article, "Oral Fixation and New Testament Studies?" Larry Hurtado has argued that there was a very extensive literary culture and a greater prevalence of private and even silent reading. For a more extensive exposition of literacy in early Christianity, see Hurtado, "A Bookish Religion," in *Destroyer of the Gods*.

business, for the recruiting of his mind, he was loath to be taken off; and perchance he dreaded lest if the author he read should deliver any thing obscurely, some attentive or perplexed hearer should desire him to expound it, or to discuss some of the harder questions; so that his time being thus spent, he could not turn over so many volumes as he desired; although the preserving of his voice (which a very little speaking would weaken) might be the truer reason for his reading to himself. But with what intent soever he did it, certainly in such a man it was good.[9]

The questions raised for Augustine's readers by this practice of Ambrose were not only about his unusual way of reading but also concerned the assessment of his character. Such was the prevalence of reading aloud at the beginning of the fifth century with persons as highly literate as Augustine and his audience.

Therefore, whether biblical compositions such as Mark's gospel were told from memory with no manuscript or read from a manuscript, the compositions of the New Testament were experienced as sound. As Gamble has observed about ancient texts:

> The text was an inscription of the spoken word. Because authors wrote or dictated with an ear to the words and assumed that what they wrote would be audibly read, they wrote for the ear more than the eye. As a result, no ancient text is now read as it was intended to be unless it [is] also heard, that is, read aloud.[10]

That is, the sensory registers that were activated by the performance of biblical compositions were predominantly auditory throughout the period from 1000 BCE to 500 CE.[11] Auditory address was the intention of ancient authors.

Furthermore, a predominantly oral sensorium continued to be the dominant character of the Bible until the advent of the printing of vernacular translations, the extension of silent reading in the eighteenth to nineteenth centuries, and the advent of historical criticism. Thus, for example, the King James translation in the early seventeenth century was structured

9. Augustine, *Confessions* 6.3.
10. Gamble, *Books and Readers*, 204.
11. There were also visual dimensions to the experience of ancient audiences. The visual field of the early audiences focused on the face and the gestures of the performer, but also included the setting of the performance. In those early stages of the tradition, the settings were predominantly small groups in homes. As the tradition developed, the settings became larger and more elaborate culminating in the performances in great cathedrals. The visual elements of the sensory data of the New Testament, however, were by no means as well defined for the original audiences as the auditory.

220 Sound Matters

for public readings in churches, as was implemented by the initial publication of a series of large pulpit Bibles.[12]

The implication of this realization about the media world of antiquity is that there is a foundational discontinuity between the sensorium of the Bible and the sensorium of contemporary biblical scholarship. The problem with the assumption of continuity between these two media worlds is that we as biblical scholars are deceived into thinking that we have experienced the Bible in its original medium when we read the "text" with our eyes only. If the biblical documents were compositions and recordings of sound, the sensory vibrations of the compositions are only experienced when they are heard.

Sensory Systems of the Human Brain

We now know that the auditory and visual perceptual systems of the human brain are located in separate and distinct places.[13] A brief summary of the scientific exploration of human sensory systems will help to specify the differences between the sensory processing of sight and sound.

The perception and processing of sound begins as a disturbance in the air. The path of a particle can be described as a wave. The waves of a particle can range from high to low frequencies. The speed of sound in air is about 1,100 feet per second. The sound waves enter the outer ear. The sound strikes the eardrum and the eardrum moves in and out, starting movements in a set of tiny bones, the ossicles, in the middle ear. The three bones of the middle ear are the malleus (hammer), the incus (anvil) and the stapes (the stirrup). They are the smallest bones in the human body; the stapes, for example, weighs four ten-thousandths of an ounce. Their function is to transmit the sound waves from air to liquid. They work like a chain of levers that transmit the air vibrations in the outer ear to the fluids in the inner ear.

The equipment of the tiny inner ear is packed into a fluid-filled snail-shaped shell, the cochlea. It is half an inch across at its base and rises only a quarter of an inch into the temporal bones of the skull. The cochlear duct is coiled a full two and three-fourths turns in the shell that holds the organ of Corti. Inside the cochlea are two ramps, an upper scala vestibuli and a lower scala tympani, both of which contain perilymph, a water-and-salt solution

---

12. For a discussion of the predominance of oral reading in the late medieval period and "the reader" in the seventeenth-century fiction of Henry Fielding, see Boomershine, "Audience Asides," 84–88.

13. For diagrams of the visual and auditory centers of the human brain, see Wilentz, *Senses of Man*, 23, 182, 273. Also see Brynie, *Brain Sense*, 225–30.

very much like cerebrospinal fluid. The fluid in the cochlear duct contains endolymph, more viscous than the perilymph in the scala and differing in salt content. Three membranes lie between the three chambers within the cochlea. The fluid in the organ of Corti vibrates the basilar membrane that is lined with 16,000 to 24,000 tiny hair cells, each of which registers specific vibrations in the spectrum of sound frequencies.

Nerve fibers from both the inner and outer ear hair cells assemble to form the spiral ganglion of the organ of Corti, the beginning of the auditory branch of the eighth cranial nerve. The auditory nerve enters the medulla and spreads via the geniculate body of the thalamus to the auditory cortex of the temporal lobe of the cerebrum. This chain of nerve cells follows a devious path from the cochlea to the auditory cortex. At the end, the vibrations of sound are processed in the temporal lobe of the cerebrum. These complex pathways are duplicated in each ear.

The perception of sound is made possible by this highly complex system of transmission of the vibrations of air to the vibrations of the fluids in the inner ear. Significant dimensions of this sensory system are still essentially a mystery and are the object of ongoing research. The distinctive character of this sensory system is the detection of vibrations and resonance.

Vision is the best understood of the senses. The sensory perception of light begins in the retina. It is composed of three parallel layers of nerve cells that are arranged in alternating rows of axons and dendrites. The first layer in the front of the eye is primarily ganglion cells, the second layer is horizontal, bipolar and amacrine cells, and the third layer at the back of the retina is 120 million light-sensitive neurons—photoreceptors, cones and rods. Cones detect color and work best in bright light. Rods work best in dim light. Cones and rods operate at different speeds, rods being slower than cones. Individual cones and rods have highly specific receptive fields and detect single, minute points of light. The signals from the rods and cones travel to the front of the eye to the ganglion cells that are responsible for the transmission of most of the signals to the brain via more than a million optic nerve fibers.

Most of the impulses from the retina travel through the optic nerve to the lateral geniculate nucleus (LGN) that lies in the thalamus. The LGN is organized in six layers of cells, each with specific functions and inputs from only one eye. The signals from the LGN end up on the two sides of the occipital lobe in the primary visual cortex, called the striate cortex or V1. Thirty different visual processing regions have been identified in the brain, most of which draw on data from the V1.

Recent research shows that visual processing also happens in areas outside the neurons of the brain's outer layer of the cortex. Visual sensory impulses are processed in the brain in multiple places that can operate independently. For example, there is a specific center in the frontal cortex that lights up at the sight of a baby's face.[14] Most of the brain's cells are glial cells, between one and five trillion cells, that support the neurons of the two hemispheres of the brain. The processing of visual stimuli is highly diversified and even creates new tracks and connections when there has been damage to particular cells.[15]

This brief summary of the sensory systems of the human brain makes it clear that the sensory systems of the eye and the ear, of visual and auditory stimuli, are different and distinct. While the two systems also interact with each other at various intersections in the brain, the auditory and visual systems of the human brain are highly differentiated: different sensory registers, different optic and auditory nerve tracks, and different auditory and visual cortex centers in the brain. Each system perceives distinct sensory impulses, transmits that data in distinctive ways through millions of cells, and processes those sensory impulses in distinct centers of the amazingly complex human brain.

Implications for Biblical Scholarship

Hearing and seeing are different systems of perception and knowledge. One way of conceiving the biblical tradition is as a set of sensory stimuli. When the gospel of Mark, for example, is heard, we literally perceive a different set of sensory stimuli than if we read it in silence. The analogy of music is helpful in describing this difference. Reading Exodus or Mark in silence is like reading the manuscript of Beethoven's Ninth Symphony and never hearing the music. We are like the deaf Beethoven who was present at the first performance of his greatest work but heard nothing.

The difference is that Beethoven wanted to hear the music whereas we have made a communal decision to read the texts in silence. If biblical compositions are read in silence, they are a different set of sensory stimuli than what the original composers/authors assembled and intended for their audiences. The assumption of the "composers" of the biblical books was that every receiver would perceive the compositions with their ears in

---

14. Brynie, *Brain Sense*, 114. The baby face center in the front of the brain just above the eyes responds instantly (100 milliseconds) and instinctively to an infant's face but not to more mature faces.

15. Ibid., 110–15. For a more extensive treatment, see Geldard, *The Human Senses*, 18–153.

interaction with a performer. Their compositions were always for "those who have ears to hear."

It is important to acknowledge that I do not know the actual practice of biblical scholars in the privacy of their own studies. It may be that many read the texts aloud as common practice. There is a growing number of instances of the phrase, "readers and hearers" in New Testament monographs and commentaries. For example, Robert Stein in his article on Mark's ending has the following footnote to his earlier article cited in the note below: "When we speak of Mark's 'readers,' we should not envision a group of 'readers' silently reading Mark's original scroll or codex but a group of *hearers* listening to Mark's text being read to them."[16] However, the ubiquitous reference in New Testament scholarship to "the reader" implies the imagined picture of an individual looking at a text and remains the dominant framework for the reconstruction of the meaning of the Bible in its original historical context. Furthermore, my hunch is that most New Testament scholars study the texts in silence and that few have performed them for an audience.

I will state this issue as provocatively as I can. If the Bible was originally composed in a sensorium of sound, the Bible is not perceived when the Bible is read now as a "text" (in silence with our eyes). If we as biblical interpreters only read the Bible as a "text" and claim to interpret the Bible in its original historical context, we are engaged in misrepresentation and a kind of fraud. Our studies claim to be an investigation of the original documents. But our studies are actually an analysis of a different set of sensory data than was originally structured and intended by the composers of the biblical compositions. As a result of this discontinuity, many of our conclusions about the meanings of biblical "texts" in their original contexts are, so to speak, wrong-headed. We have used the wrong parts of our heads to perceive the "texts."

If we want to perceive and interpret the compositions of the Bible in their original historical context, it is necessary for our sensory system to correspond with the sensorium in and for which they were composed. This would be in contrast to our present situation in which we have read back our sensory system of silent reading into the ancient world. This book addresses the foundational problem: how can we perceive and study the Bible in its original sensory medium—sound?

---

16. Stein, "Ending," 86 n.31. For the article, see Stein, "Is Our Reading the Bible the Same as the Original Audience's Hearing It? A Case Study of the Gospel of Mark." Stein's answer is "no" to the question identified in the title. The article is an excellent delineation and documentation of the predominant practice of reading aloud both to audiences and to oneself in antiquity.

The Colon Hypothesis and Sound Mapping

Rather than continuing to make assertions, however, it might be more inviting to approach this reorientation as an hypothesis, just as Frank Scheppers has done in his monumental treatise, *The Colon Hypothesis*. On the basis of a systematic study of the extant works of Lysias and four of Plato's dialogues, Scheppers concludes that the hypothesis that the colon was the basic unit of composition in that tradition is confirmed by three patterns of usage: word order, discourse segmentation, and discourse coherence.[17] If the Bible was originally composed as sounds to be performed for audiences, what difference would it make if we began to listen to the compositions with our auditory sensors rather than reading the texts with our visual sensors? What difference would listening make?

The foundation on which the development of performance criticism is being constructed is the ubiquity of sound as the dominant sensorium of ancient literature. Sound mapping is an integral dimension of that foundation. Cascade Books's Biblical Performance Criticism Series edited by David Rhoads has now reached sixteen volumes. The publication in 2017 of *The Dictionary of the Bible and Ancient Media* is another milestone in the gathering of knowledge about the communication culture of the ancient world.[18] The dictionary provides a detailed summary of the multi-faceted media research into the Bible and ancient media during the past 200 years and, in particular, since the establishment of the Bible in ancient and modern media group in 1983. And, while not always explicitly identified as such, the description of the Bible and ancient media in these works is an explication of a communication culture of sound.

The problem that has not been adequately addressed, however, is the discontinuity between the current visual sensorium of biblical scholarship and the predominantly sound sensorium of the media world of antiquity. If the Bible has been misperceived as a "text," what have appeared to be puzzles in a predominantly visual sensorium might be perceived differently if those puzzles were approached in an auditory sensorium. That is, the Bible has been misperceived. Dimensions of a reorientation toward an auditory sensorium would include:

1. empirical analysis of New Testament compositions as units of sound rather than as units of text,

2. comparison of the units of sound in particular New Testament compositions with the sound characteristics of the other compositions

---

17. Scheppers, *Colon Hypothesis*.
18. Thatcher et al., eds., *Dictionary of the Bible and Ancient Media*.

recorded in the New Testament and the broader compendium of compositions in classical Greek,

3. identification of the dynamics of interaction with listening audiences rather than the perceptions and responses of readers, and
4. specific decisions about representation of the compositions in a sound map.

Such a reexamination of a traditional puzzle would constitute a test case of the difference listening might make.

The Puzzle: Mark 16:8 and the Intended Ending of the Gospel

The ending of the gospel of Mark is one of the most vexing puzzles of the New Testament. D. E. Nineham has called it, "the greatest of all literary mysteries,"[19] and James R. Edwards has named it "the gravest textual problem in the NT."[20] The great majority of extant Markan manuscripts end with the story of Jesus' appearances to the disciples and his ascension (Mark 16:9-20). That ending has been included in the most authoritative editions of the Greek and English texts, designated as "The Longer Ending of Mark." A significant group of scholars, most notably William Farmer, has argued that 16:9-20 is the original ending.[21] A cornerstone of the empirical evidence against 16:9-20 is that the best manuscripts (Codex Vaticanus and Codex Sinaiticus) end at 16:8. The majority of Markan scholars now consider 16:8 as the original ending of the best Markan manuscripts.

There remains, however, significant division on whether 16:8 is the intended ending of the gospel. Adela Yarbro Collins concludes that 16:8 continues the emphasis throughout the gospel on "wonder" in response to "the manifestation of heavenly power" and was the intended ending.[22] Joel Marcus in his Anchor Bible commentary tries to make sense of the ending at 16:8, but concludes: "there is not enough evidence to say definitely whether Mark intended his work to end at 16:8."[23] In a thorough and carefully nuanced article, Robert Stein finds that 16:8 is the "best preserved" ending but argues that it is not the intended ending. The two strongest arguments that

19. Nineham, *Gospel of St. Mark*, 439.
20. Edwards, *Gospel according to Mark*, 439.
21. Farmer, *Last Twelve Verses of Mark*.
22. Collins, *Mark*, 801.
23. Marcus, *Mark 8-16*, 1096.

he finds for this conclusion are, first, that the prophecies in 14:28 and 16:7 about Jesus' meeting the disciples in Galilee create an expectation for "the intended readers" that is unfulfilled. Second, modern attempts to find 16:8 as a meaningful ending[24] "lose sight of the Christological purpose of Mark in his gospel and in this passage."[25]

The conclusion of Clayton Croy's book, *The Mutilation of Mark's Gospel*, is that the original ending was lost, probably as the result of the original codex losing the sheet that included both the lost beginning and the lost ending.[26] In Croy's appendix listing the conclusions of generations of Markan scholars, beginning with J. J. Griesbach (1789–90), eighty-six scholars agree that 16:8 was not the intended ending and seventy-seven agree that the original ending was somehow lost.[27] Croy has called the ending at 16:8 "a gaping wound" and judiciously explicates eight major arguments against 16:8 as the original intended ending.[28]

To state the problem of Mark's ending in terms of sensory perception, when 16:8 is evaluated as a text ending the gospel, it looks strange. Here is the UBS Greek text of Mark's resurrection narrative:

> Καὶ διαγενομένου τοῦ σαββάτου Μαρία ἡ Μαγδαληνὴ καὶ Μαρία ἡ [τοῦ Ἰακώβου καὶ Σαλώμη ἠγόρασαν ἀρώματα ἵνα ἐλθοῦσαι ἀλείψωσιν αὐτόν. καὶ λίαν πρωΐ τῇ μιᾷ τῶν σαββάτων ἔρχονται ἐπὶ τὸ μνημεῖον ἀνατείλαντος τοῦ ἡλίου. καὶ ἔλεγον πρὸς ἑαυτάς, Τίς ἀποκυλίσει ἡμῖν τὸν λίθον ἐκ τῆς θύρας τοῦ μνημείου; καὶ ἀναβλέψασαι θεωροῦσιν ὅτι ἀποκεκύλισται ὁ λίθος. ἦν γὰρ μέγας σφόδρα. καὶ εἰσελθοῦσαι εἰς τὸ μνημεῖον εἶδον νεανίσκον καθήμενον ἐν τοῖς δεξιοῖς περιβεβλημένον στολὴν λευκήν, καὶ ἐξεθαμβήθησαν. ὁ δὲ λέγει αὐταῖς, Μὴ ἐκθαμβεῖσθε. Ἰησοῦν ζητεῖτε τὸν Ναζαρηνὸν τὸν ἐσταυρωμένον. ἠγέρθη, οὐκ ἔστιν ὧδε. ἴδε ὁ τόπος ὅπου ἔθηκαν αὐτόν. ἀλλὰ ὑπάγετε εἴπατε τοῖς μαθηταῖς αὐτοῦ καὶ τῷ Πέτρῳ ὅτι Προάγει ὑμᾶς εἰς τὴν Γαλιλαίαν. ἐκεῖ αὐτὸν ὄψεσθε, καθὼς εἶπεν ὑμῖν. καὶ ἐξελθοῦσαι ἔφυγον ἀπὸ τοῦ Μνημείου, εἶχεν γὰρ αὐτὰς τρόμος καὶ ἔκστασις, καὶ οὐδενὶ οὐδὲν εἶπαν, ἐφοβοῦντο γάρ.

The most natural response to the reading of this ending is a series of questions that are imagined as the responses of ancient and modern readers.

---

24. Some of the scholars who argue that Mark 16:8 is the intended ending include Petersen, "When Is the End Not the End?" 153; Best, *Mark*, 132; Lincoln, "The Promise and the Failure: Mark 16:7, 8," 283– 300; Tolbert, *Sowing the Gospel*, 297-99; Danove, *End of Mark's Story*, 221-22.

25. Stein, "The Ending of Mark," 97-98.

26. Croy, *The Mutilation of Mark's Gospel*.

27. Ibid., 174-77.

28. Ibid., 47-64.

So what happened? Did the women tell the disciples? If not, how did the resurrection story get told? Did Jesus meet the disciples in Galilee? These questions then lead to others. Why did the author end the story like this? Is this really appropriate for a story that claims to be good news for the entire world? That is, when read as a text, the ending naturally leads to the questions of a critical reader. It is a puzzle and, to many readers, an unacceptable ending. What difference would it make if the ending was originally heard by audiences in interaction with a storyteller or reader? How did Mark 16:8 sound?[29]

I have engaged the issue of Mark 16:8 as the intended ending of the gospel for many years. This body of work has included my dissertation, *Mark, the Storyteller*, two major articles in the *Journal of Biblical Literature*, several essays in collections, and a major monograph, *The Messiah of Peace*.[30] The purpose of this essay is to focus on the evidence that emerges from the study of Mark as sound. The other factors in the assessment of the meaning and impact of Mark 16:8 in the broader perspective of Mark's story performed as a whole for ancient audiences will not be addressed here.

The Characteristics of the Sound of Mark 16:8

This volume of essays has been generated by the publication of *Sound Mapping the New Testament* and is edited by the co-author of that book, Margaret Ellen Lee. Lee and co-author, Bernard Brandon Scott, have based their proposal of sound mapping on the works of the grammarians of the classical and Hellenistic periods, especially Dionysius of Halicarnassus, Demetrius, and Aristotle. Their survey concludes: "Greek authors crafted their works with their auditory impact in mind at every level of construction."[31] The basic units of sound composition that can be identified in Hellenistic Greek literature are the syllable, the colon, and the period. The identification of these basic units of composition in Mark 16:8 will be a goal of this analysis of the sound of Mark 16:8.

A principal dialogue partner in this research is Frank Scheppers, the author of *The Colon Hypothesis: Word Order, Discourse Segmentation,*

---

29. For a performance of Mark's passion and resurrection narrative in Greek and in English, listen to (and see) my recording at http://messiahofpeace.com. In Scheppers's essay in this volume, he refers to this recording several times. It is significant that he finds a strong correlation between his analysis of the cola of Mark 15 and the colometric segmentation implied in the performance.

30. See the bibliography for a listing of my earlier engagement with the controversy regarding Mark's ending.

31. Lee and Scott, *Sound Mapping*, 121.

and Discourse Coherence in Ancient Greek, who also has a major essay in this volume. Scheppers's work has sought to identify the patterns of sound composition in classical Greek literature and argues that the colon rather than the period is the most consistent and verifiable unit of composition in this literary corpus.[32] Scheppers has found the period to be a more ambiguous guide to discourse segmentation than the colon. His subtitle names the patterns of sound that are characteristic signs of the colon. Scheppers's identification of the colon is related to the "discourse analytical approach" of Wallace Chafe and a group of related linguists who have concluded that the basic unit of discourse analysis is best conceived as the "intonation unit."[33] In Scheppers's work, the colon and the intonation unit are virtual synonyms. Chafe and Scheppers also have adopted a similar practice as Lee and Scott of transcribing texts, often in Chafe's case of spontaneous conversations, with every discourse unit on a separate line.

Word Order and Colon Segmentation

An important starting point for Scheppers's work is the recognition of the correlation between word order and colon segmentation. As he states in his contribution to this volume, "Word order played a relatively important part in my own work on classical Greek, in that it offered me clear, formal and objective evidence that 'grounded' the research empirically."[34] This empirical basis was connected with Wackernagel's Law, as originally conceived, "enclitics tend toward the second position of the clause/sentence."[35] This "law" meant that the presence of particles in a postpositive position (P2) was an objective indication of a new colon. Particles that tend to occur in the postpositive position (P2) include particles such as γάρ, δὲ, οὖν, indefinite pronouns, adjectives and adverbs, and personal pronouns. A further related rule is that a number of 'introductive' particles (such as καί) take first position (P1) within the colon. Prepositives are words that, in Scheppers's terms, "cling to" the words that follow them while postpositives cling to the words that precede them.

---

32. Scheppers, "Discourse Segmentation," 137. The period was Aristotle's literary unit of choice and is adopted by Lee and Scott as the next higher unit of composition above the colon. Scheppers found the period to be an ambiguous unit of composition and focused on the colon as the basic intonation unit.

33. Scheppers, *Colon Hypothesis*, 18–19.

34. Scheppers, "Discourse Segmentation," 140.

35. Scheppers, *Colon Hypothesis*, 4.

As Scheppers notes in his essay in this book, these rules, which are highly reliable criteria for colon segmentation in classical Greek, are less so in New Testament Greek.[36] Particles are less frequent and non-emphatic pronouns do not occur as consistently in the P2 position. But, as is evident in the sound map of Mark 15, with these relatively minor qualifications, the basic rules are operative in New Testament Greek. The recognition of this pattern in Scheppers's analysis of classical Greek is important for the study of New Testament Greek because it establishes the presence of this pattern in the much larger corpus of classical Greek literature.

When Mark 16:8 is analyzed in this comprehensive context, the pattern of word order can be readily identified. There is an ABAB alternation between prepositive καί and postpositive γάρ particles: καὶ ἐξελθοῦσαι/ εἶχεν γάρ/καὶ οὐδενὶ/ἐφοβοῦντο γάρ (a literal translation: And going out/ had seized them for/said nothing/they were afraid for). The identification of this pattern makes it possible to reconstruct the colon boundaries in this composition. There are four cola with clearly marked boundaries. When each of these intonation units is placed on a separate line, the sound map of Mark 16:8 is as follows:

> καὶ ἐξελθοῦσαι ἔφυγον ἀπὸ τοῦ μνημείου
> εἶχεν γὰρ αὐτὰς τρόμος καὶ ἔκστασι
> καὶ οὐδενὶ οὐδὲν εἶπαν
> ἐφοβοῦντο γάρ

> So they went out and fled from the tomb
> For terror and amazement had seized them
> And they said nothing to anyone
> For they were afraid (NRSV)

The striking feature of this sound map is the cluster of four short cola that are progressively shorter. As can be seen, it looks very different than the following UBS/Nestle–Aland Greek text:

> καὶ ἐξελθοῦσαι ἔφυγον ἀπὸ τοῦ μνημείου, εἶχεν γὰρ αὐτὰς τρόμος καὶ ἔκστασις· καὶ οὐδενὶ οὐδὲν εἶπαν· ἐφοβοῦντο γάρ.

> So they went out and fled from the tomb, for terror and amazement had seized them; and they said nothing to anyone, for they were afraid. (NRSV)

The UBS punctuation and textual arrangement is based on a grammatical analysis. The editors of the various Nestle/Aland and UBS Greek texts punctuate and arrange this text as a sentence with clauses, rather than

---

36. Scheppers, "Discourse Segmentation," 141.

as cola. They punctuate 16:8 as one sentence with a comma, two half stops and a concluding full stop.

However, a function of punctuation related to sound can be to indicate the length and quality of the pauses between grammatical units: a comma indicates a short pause/catch breath; a half stop in a Greek text (usually transcribed as a semicolon in English texts) indicates a longer pause/half breath; a full stop/period indicates a major pause/full breath. As presently punctuated, the UBS Greek text above would be recited with a catch breath and two short pauses prior to the concluding full breath and full stop. In the context of the conclusion that 16:8 is four short cola, what is the quality and length of the pauses between the four cola? How should 16:8 be punctuated?

Short Cola in Mark

The composer of Mark used short cola as a basic technique of composition, particularly in the creation of climactic endings. The climactic effect is often the result of a short colon following a longer colon. The climactic ending can also be heightened in its intensity by a cluster of short cola and, in the case of 16:8, a crescendo of increasingly shorter cola.

The composer consistently uses short cola in emotionally charged endings. Most of these moments are either climaxes in the stories of Jesus' conflicts with various opponents or the stories of wrong responses by Jesus' disciples.

The following are climactic short endings prior to the passion narrative:

Rejection at Nazareth	καὶ ἐθαύμαζεν διὰ τὴν ἀπιστίαν αὐτῶν And he was amazed at their unbelief	6:6
Cursing of the fig tree	καὶ ἤκουον οἱ μαθηταὶ αὐτου And his disciples heard it	11:14
Parable of the wicked tenants	καὶ ἀφέντες αὐτὸν ἀπῆλθον And they left him and went away	12:12
Paying taxes to Caesar	καὶ ἐξεθαύμαζον ἐπ'αὐτῷ And they were utterly amazed at him	12:17

With the exception of the cursing of the fig tree, each of these short cola is the climax of a conflict story and the cursing of the fig tree is the surprising and emotionally charged prelude to the prophetic demonstration in the temple that leads to Jesus' death.

The New Testament Soundscape 231

The frequency of highly charged and climactic short endings increases in the passion narrative:

Judas' betrayal	καὶ ἐζήτει πῶς αὐτὸν εὐκαίρως παραδοῖ	14:11
	And he looked for the best way to betray him	
Prophecy of flight and denial	ὡσαύτως δὲ καὶ πάντες ἔλεγον	14:31
	And they all said the same thing	
Arrest and flight	καὶ ἀφέντες αὐτὸν ἔφυγον πάντες	14:50
	And forsaking him they all fled	
Sanhedrin trial	καὶ οἱ ὑπηρέται ῥαπίσμασιν αὐτὸν ἔλαβον	14:65
	And the guards took him away beating him	
Peter's denial	καὶ ἐπιβαλὼν ἔκλαιεν	14:72
	And beating himself he wept	
Mocking by Romans	καὶ ἐξάγουσιν αὐτὸν ἵνα σταυρώσωσιν αὐτόν	15:20
	And they led him out to crucify him	
Mocking by Judeans	καὶ οἱ συνεσταυρωμένοι σὺν αὐτῷ ὠνείδιζον αὐτόν	15:32
	And those crucified with him taunted him	
Death of Jesus	ὁ δὲ Ἰησοῦς ἀφεὶς φωνὴν μεγάλην ἐξέπνευσεν	15:37
	And giving a loud cry he breathed his last	

All of these endings are emotionally intense moments in the story. Two of these endings, the beating by the Sanhedrin's guards and the mocking by the Roman soldiers, are the climax of stories of the humiliation of Jesus. Judas' betrayal, the prophecy of flight and denial, the flight of the disciples as the climax of the arrest, and Peter's denial are climactic endings of the stories of the responses of Jesus' disciples. The climactic ending of the story of Jesus' death is a response to the mockery by the Judean passersby, the chief priests and scribes, and the "insurrectionists" crucified with him. The shortest of these climactic cola is the three-word/eight syllable ending of the story of Peter's denial.

Thus, the final colon in the best manuscripts of Mark, ἐφοβοῦντο γάρ (for they were afraid), is the shortest of the climactic cola in the gospel. As can be seen in the sound map above, the segmentation of the cola in 16:8 shows that there is a four step shortening in successive cola: 6, 6, 4, 2 words and 14, 11, 8 and 5 syllables. The proposition that this pattern in the usage of short cola is accidental or unintentional is highly unlikely. This technique of composition and performance occurs throughout the gospel and is used only in highly climactic and emotionally charged moments in the larger story. The ending at 16:8 uses this technique of sound composition in a climactic manner.

This pattern is also a guide in estimating the length of the pauses and the punctuation between these four climactic cola. The lengths of the cola are an indication of their tempo: longer cola are faster and shorter cola are slower. This slowing of the tempo at the end is then a clue to the length of the pauses between cola. The pauses become longer and participate in the gradual retard with each successive colon, the longest being the pause between the report that the women said nothing to anyone and the performer's explanation that they were afraid. This in turn leads to the conclusion that the best punctuation would be four full stops.

Audience Address

As noted above, the alternation between the prepositive καί cola and the postpositive γάρ cola marks the four cola in 16:8:

καὶ ἐξελθοῦσαι ἔφυγον ἀπὸ τοῦ μνημείου (prepositive)
εἶχεν γὰρ αὐτὰς τρόμος καὶ ἔκστασι (postpositive)
καὶ οὐδενὶ οὐδὲν εἶπαν (prepositive)
ἐφοβοῦντο γάρ (postpositive)

This alternation is also an objective sign of the change of tone in the address to the audience that concludes the gospel. The alternation between the description of the surprising actions of the women in fleeing and saying nothing and the audience asides explaining their actions by the performer of the story creates this dynamic.

The storyteller reports something that is surprising or puzzling in a straightforward indicative to the audience. The more shocking or surprising this initial report is the more the audience is hooked into wondering. In effect, the audience is invited to ask: "Why?" or "What?" The γάρ colon that follows this provocation is an aside in which the performer changes tone and explains the apparent anomaly to the audience. In performance, this is often accompanied by a gesture of leaning into the audience that establishes a higher level of connection or intimacy between the storyteller and the audience. The gesture may be a direct looking at the audience, a knowing smile or a hand to one side of the mouth. And the change of tone can be a lower volume or a lower vocal pitch. It creates a moment of inside information that indirectly says, "Now let me tell you the inside story."

In 16:8, the initial indicative is the surprising report that the women fled. The question that this report raises is, "Why did they flee?" The aside to the audience explains that they had been seized by "trauma" and "ecstasy." The second report that they said nothing to anyone is even more surprising in light of the angel's command to "go, tell. . ." The audience aside explains that they were "afraid."

This pattern of audience address is present throughout the gospel.[37] For example, the explanation of why the woman snuck up behind Jesus and touched his garment is, "For she said, 'If I can touch his garment, I will be made well'" (5:27–28). Earlier in the resurrection story, the aside to the audience explains the reason that the women were so surprised at finding the stone rolled back: "For it was a big stone!"(16:4).[38] When heard in the context of the earlier instances of this pattern, 16:8 is the only instance in the gospel in which this pattern of provocation/explanation occurs twice in succession. That is, there is a climactic concentration of this technique of sound composition in 16:8. In the ending of the gospel, the performer of the gospel, whether a storyteller or a lector, turns to the audience twice and addresses them.

Furthermore, this ending is another instance of a distinctive Markan way of audience provocation. The typical function of audience asides is to explain a puzzle or surprise in the previous cola. The explanation brings closure to the audience's questions. For example, in the story of Jairus' daughter (5:22–24, 35–43), the storyteller reports that the "little girl" (ταλιθά) got up and started walking around the room. In order to resolve the audience's ambiguity about whether the little girl was an infant, the storyteller explains that she was twelve years old. Most of the audience asides introduced by γάρ listed above have this function.

However, in two earlier instances, the explanations are themselves enigmatic and raise more questions than they answer. The most graphic of these provocative explanations is the ending of the story of Jesus walking on the water (6:45–52). The surprise needing explanation is the disciples' utter amazement at seeing Jesus walking on the water. The aside is: "For they didn't understand about the loaves, but their hearts were hardened." This

---

37 Audience asides introduced by γάρ that explain confusing or surprising events reported in the previous colon are: 1:16, 22; 2:15; 3:21; 5:8, 28, 42; 6:17, 18, 20, 31, 48; 9:6, 34; 10:22; 11:13; 14:2, 40, 56; 15:10; 16:4. For an analysis of the two asides (7:3–4; 15:21) that have been misperceived as "narrative comments" and as clues to the identity of Mark's audience, see Boomershine, "Audience Asides."

38. The major recent translations of Mark have eliminated this climactic audience aside and made it a subordinate clause earlier in an indicative sentence, e.g., "When they looked up, they saw that the stone, which was very large, had already been rolled back" (NRSV). For a more extensive discussion of these translation issues, see Boomershine, *Messiah of Peace*, 333–37.

explanation provokes further questions. What didn't the disciples understand about the loaves? How are the disciples like hard-hearted Pharoah?

The second instance is the plot of the chief priests and scribes that begins the passion narrative:

> Now the feast of Passover and unleavened bread was the next day. And the chief priests and the scribes were seeking how to arrest him by treachery and kill him. For they had been saying, "Not during the feast, lest there be a riot of the people (14:1-2).

The surprise that demands explanation is that the authorities were taking criminal steps to kill Jesus on that day: "Why the sudden urgency?" The explanation is that they had to arrest him "today" because they had ruled out an arrest during the feast that begins "the next day."[39] But this raises more questions: "Will they abandon their plot if they cannot arrest him today? What is Jesus doing today?" The second question is answered by the story of the anointing at Bethany, with its implication that Jesus didn't go into the city on that Wednesday: "On that day Jesus was in Bethany . . ."(14:3).

Thus, the supremely provocative ending at 16:8 is a climactic instance of a pattern in Markan storytelling that also occurs frequently in the parables of Jesus and in Israelite storytelling.[40] The widespread conviction among Markan scholars that 16:8 is an unintended ending is itself a sign that Mark's provocation continues to work.

Sonic Echoes

A basic technique in the composition of sound is repetition. In contrast to text that does not disappear when perceived, sound immediately begins to deteriorate or disappear. For example, a note struck on the piano, even if the key is held down or maintained by the damper pedal, will instantly begin to decline in volume and will disappear in a few seconds. With the voice, the disappearance of the sound is almost instantaneous unless the sound

---

39. The NRSV mistakenly translates this phrase, as "It was two days before . . ." (NIV—"two days away"). Just as μετὰ τρεῖς ἡμέρας means "on the third day" and counts "today" as the first day, so also here the meaning in 14:2 is "on the second day." Counting "today" as the first day, "the second day" is "tomorrow/the next day." For a further discussion of the evidence supporting "the next day" as the meaning of the phrase in the context of the plot of the chief priests, see *Messiah of Peace*, 37–44.

40. For a more extensive exploration of this characteristic pattern in Mark, in the storytelling traditions of Israel and in Jesus' parables, see Boomershine, *Messiah of Peace*, 342–44.

is produced in a highly resonant room, in which case it may resonate for a second or two.

But regardless of the resonance of the space, the only way to return to a sound is to repeat it. Repetition is a basic technique of musical composition. A typical structure is the sonata. It has an ABA structure in which there is the statement of a theme (A), a variation or complementary theme (B), and a restatement of the original theme (A). Another type of composition is a theme with variations. In this form, the basic theme is repeated with variations either in the theme itself or more frequently in various harmonies and tempos that surround the theme. In popular music, including contemporary Christian music, a musical motif or theme may be sung or played over and over again, sometimes ten to twenty times.

The primary function of repetition in sound compositions is the reinforcement of the audience's memory. In biblical stories, repetition of key words and phrases from earlier episodes shapes the memory context in which the current story is heard. In addition to the associations of content, repetitions will sometimes have a similar tone that evokes the emotional atmosphere of the earlier story. A graphic example of this is Peter's remembering Jesus' prophecy of his denial "before the cock crows twice." The repetition sets Peter's denial in the context of the audience's memory of Peter's vehement vow to die with Jesus rather than to deny him.

The impact of these repetitions is often subtle and may only be perceived in hearing the story. One of the classic instances of misperception of biblical compositions is the so-called doublet. A doublet is a repetition of words that are perceived as redundant. The doublet is often seen as a sign of the merging of two disparate sources. The identification of doublets has been one of the primary clues to the analysis of tradition history in biblical scholarship. But it is often also a misperception that is the result of examining the text with the eyes rather than listening to the story with the ears.

When biblical compositions are heard, repetitions are experienced as sonic echoes that make connections between elements of the composition. A frequent pattern of New Testament composition is the repetition of individual words, metaphors, and portions from the written traditions of the Old Testament, either as quotations or as allusions. The most frequent pattern, however, is the repetition and development of sound motifs from earlier episodes in the individual composition.

In Mark 16:8 there are four prominent sonic echoes: the tomb, flight, said nothing to anyone, and fear. Discussing them in their order of occurrence, the first is the tomb. The tomb is a structural element in the resurrection story. The women "went out to the tomb" (ἔρχονται ἐπὶ τὸ μνημεῖον), "enter into the tomb" (εἰσελθοῦσαι εἰς τὸ μνημεῖον), and "going out they fled from the tomb" (ἐξελθοῦσαι ἔφυγον ἀπὸ τοῦ μνημείου). This sonic echo continues the theme established in the burial story: "and he laid him in a tomb that had been carved out of the rock and rolled a stone over the door of the tomb" (καὶ ἔθηκεν αὐτὸν ἐν μνημείῳ ὃ ἦν λελατομημένον ἐκ πέτρας, καὶ προσεκύλισεν λίθον ἐπὶ τὴν θύραν τοῦ μνημείου). The echo is a kind of tolling bell in the story that evokes the grief associated with Jesus' death and burial. It also establishes the place of the story and the repetition invites the listeners to see the tomb in their imagination.

The women's seeing a young man "clothed in a white robe" and their flight from the tomb is a sonic echo of the flight of the disciples and the linen-clothed young man that concludes the arrest story (14:50–52). In the following sound map, the intonation unit beginning καὶ νεανίσκος is mapped as a period with three cola:[41]

καὶ ἀφέντες αὐτὸν ἔφυγον πάντες.
καὶ νεανίσκος τις συνηκολούθει αὐτῷ
    περιβεβλημένος σινδόνα ἐπὶ γυμνοῦ,
    καὶ κρατοῦσιν αὐτόν.
ὁ δὲ καταλιπὼν τὴν σινδόνα γυμνὸς ἔφυγεν.

And forsaking him, they all fled.
And there was a young man following him
    wearing a linen cloth over his nakedness,
    and they seize him.
But leaving the linen cloth, he fled naked.

The sound of the word ἔφυγον ("they fled") resonates with the memories of the disciples' fear of being arrested, tried, and executed with Jesus. It also resonates with their failure to keep their promise that they would die with him. The flight of the naked young man carries the vibes of shame associated with forsaking Jesus. The women have been commissioned to announce the resurrection and this word is the first clue in the story that they will fail to fulfill the commission they have been given.

The next surprise in the story is the report that they told no one anything: καὶ οὐδενὶ οὐδὲν εἶπαν. The sonic echoes connected with these words are the earlier soundings of various forms of the verb λέγω, "to say, tell." The most immediate is the command of the young man: ἀλλὰ ὑπάγετε εἴπατε

---

41. For a full outline of the possible units of sound in Mark's Gospel including the relationship between "cola" and "periods," see Appendix 2, "A Sound Map of Mark's Passion-Resurrection Narrative," in Boomershine, *Messiah of Peace*, 368–86.

τοῖς μαθηταῖς αὐτοῦ καὶ τῷ Πέτρῳ ("but go, tell his disciples and Peter" (16:7)) Saying nothing is an explicit and immediate contradiction of the young man's command.[42]

The earlier instances of this sonic theme are Jesus' admonitions to the leper and the disciples to say nothing. The most fully resonant with 16:8 of these earlier commands is Jesus' stern command to the leper: Ὅρα μηδενὶ μηδὲν εἴπῃς ("See that you tell no one anything" (1:44)). The only differences between Jesus' charge to the leper and the report of the women's silence are the forms of the negative particles and the endings of the verb: μηδενὶ μηδὲν εἴπῃς /οὐδενὶ οὐδὲν εἶπαν ("tell no one anything"/"they told no one anything"). The irony, perhaps with a touch of ironic humor, is that both of these responses indicate explicit disobedience of earlier commands and a reversal of audience expectations. Jesus commands the leper to tell no one anything and he proclaims it everywhere; the women are commanded to "tell" the news to the disciples and they tell no one anything.

Jesus' admonition to the disciples to say nothing about him immediately follows Peter's declaration, "You are the Messiah": καὶ ἐπετίμησεν αὐτοῖς ἵνα μηδενὶ λέγωσιν περὶ αὐτοῦ ("and he strongly commanded them to say nothing about him") The actual words in the messianic confession are more explicitly a sonic echo of the command to the leper (μηδενί) than the report of the women's silence. But the report of the women's silence is definitely sonically linked with the messianic confession.

The primary impact of these sonic echoes with earlier moments in the story is the irony of the women's silence. The leper is commanded to say nothing but instead proclaims the news and the disciples are commanded to say nothing about him being the Messiah. The reason for Jesus' effort to maintain secrecy in relation to his messianic identity has been fully clarified by the high priest's immediate charge of blasphemy in response to Jesus' messianic confession. But now in the wake of the resurrection, they are commanded to tell the story and they tell no one anything.

The sonic echoes of the women's fear in the earlier stories of the gospel are the most highly developed sonic theme that resonates with the words of 16:8, specifically the ending: ἐφοβοῦντο γάρ ("For they were afraid"). Various forms of the verb occur eleven times prior to the ending. In the

---

42. The NRSV translation of the command, "tell," which has been continued from the King James translation, is not the same sound as the women's response ("they said"). This is an example of the translators' failure to listen to the sounds of the Greek composition and to maintain as many of the sonic echoes as possible in translation. It would be equally congruent with the meaning of the original Greek to translate the young man's command as: "Go, say to his disciples and Peter . . ." The other sonically connected possibility would be to translate the women's response as, "And they told no one anything." I like the last best.

early parts of the gospel prior to the messianic confession and the passion-resurrection prophecies, the verb is primarily used to describe the responses of persons to Jesus' powerful deeds:

The disciples' fear at the calming of the sea	ἐφοβήθησαν φόβον μέγαν feared a great fear	4:41
The Gerasenes' response to the demoniac clothed and in his right mind	καὶ ἐφοβήθησαν and they were afraid	5:15
The bleeding woman's response to her healing	ἡ δὲ γυνὴ φοβηθεῖσα καὶ τρέμουσα and the woman afraid and trembling	5:33
Jesus' response to the disciples' terror	θαρσεῖτε, ἐγώ εἰμι· μὴ φοβεῖσθε Take heart. I am. Don't be afraid.	6:50

The same word, ἐφοβοῦντο, occurs twice in the stories of Jesus' passion/resurrection prophecies. In response to the second passion-resurrection prophecy, the disciples "were afraid to ask him" (καὶ ἐφοβοῦντο αὐτὸν ἐπερωτῆσαι-9:32). And just prior to the third prophecy, Jesus walks ahead of them and they are amazed, and "those who followed were afraid" (οἱ δὲ ἀκολουθοῦντες ἐφοβοῦντο-10:32). The last three instances of this verb name the responses of the chief priests and the scribes to Jesus' actions and teaching in the temple. After Jesus' prophetic demonstration in the temple, they wanted to arrest him but they "feared" him because of the crowd's enthusiastic response to his demonstration and teaching (11:18). In the stories of their questioning Jesus' authority and in response to his parable of the wicked tenants, the chief priests and the scribes "feared" the crowd (11.32; 12:12).

When analyzed as sonic echoes, therefore, the associations of this theme are first with Jesus' power and authority and second with the prophecies and conflicts that led to his death. That is, the sonic echoes of this climactic word prior to the ending are associated with the words and events connected with his authority and his death. For Mark's listeners, therefore, death is the answer to the implicit question of why the women were afraid.

In the context of these sonic echoes, the women's flight, silence, and fear are fully understandable. Mark 16:8 resonates with the sounds of the earlier stories that lead up to Jesus' death and resurrection. The principal theme around which these earlier themes coalesce in 16:8 is the commissioning of the women by the divine messenger and not Jesus' appearance.

This theme is the focus of the addresses to the audience that conclude the gospel. The last words, the climactic short cola, are neither descriptions of what happened with Jesus' death and resurrection nor statements of the promise of his appearance in Galilee. They are explanations of the women's flight and silence that are addressed to the audience. In Mark's provocative manner, however, those explanations of the women's flight and fearful silence raise as many questions as they answer. At the end of the story, the performer turns to the audience and addresses them directly. In the provocative silences that are the climax of the story, therefore, hang the questions: how will I/we respond to the news of the resurrection? Will I/we flee? Will I/we be silent and say nothing to anyone? Will I/we be afraid?

The other three gospels end with the same theme of the commissioning of Jesus' followers. In Matthew and Luke, Jesus commissions the disciples. In Matthew, the great commission takes place on a Galilean mountain (28:16–20). In Luke, the commission to be Jesus' witnesses to all the nations is located in Jerusalem (24:36–49). In John, Jesus addresses the commission to feed his lambs and sheep to Peter by the sea of Galilee (21:15–19).

Conclusions about Mark 16:8

The principal conclusion of this case study is that, when Mark 16:8 is perceived and analyzed as sound, it is a climactic and intended ending. The sounds of the ending are a climactic use of techniques of composition that are present throughout the gospel. The analysis of those techniques of composition and the actual sound of the words reveals a high degree of sophistication in the art of oral storytelling. In light of this attention to sonic detail, it is impossible to imagine that such a pervasive use of composition techniques of sound in the formation of the cola, the dynamic address to the audience, and the sonic echoing of major thematic elements was accidental or in some way unintended.

Thus, the following sonic structures can be identified in Mark 16:8.

Word order and segmentation of intonation units

The word order follows the patterns of colon demarcation in Greek compositions of classical and archaic as well as Koine Greek of the New Testament period. The alternation of postpositive and prepositive word order is a clear indication that 16:8 is structured as four cola. The intonation units of Mark's ending are segmented in a manner that occurs throughout the composition.

Climactic shortening of cola

The four cola are progressively shorter (6, 6, 4, 2 words; 14, 11, 8, 5 syllables) and, therefore, slower. In musical terms, it is a long retard. The cola build to a climax of sound and silence. This usage of short cola in climactic positions occurs frequently in earlier moments in the gospel composition, most notably in the ending of Peter's denial. 16:8 is a climactic instance of this pervasive technique of composition in the whole story.

A Crescendo of Lengthening Pauses

The alternation between reports of the women's surprising actions and audience asides that give an inside explanation of the women's emotions creates a crescendo of pauses between successive cola that are progressively longer. Those pauses give the performer time to turn to the audience for the asides and give the audience time to ponder both the women's response and their own response to the commission and the fear of death associated with it. The composer of Mark uses earlier pauses like those in 16:8 prior to enigmatic audience asides that explain puzzling elements in a provocative manner that raises more questions (e.g., the ending of the walking on the water story in 6:52).

Sonic Echoes

The sonic echoes of the words naming the women's actions and internal responses link the women's flight and silence with central themes of the gospel story as a whole. In musical terminology, the sonic echoes are the climactic endings of *leitmotifs*, as in Wagnerian operas, that link elements of the longer story. Prominent themes in the sonic echoes are the women's presence at the death and burial, the injunctions to silence and the maintenance of the messianic secret, the flight of the disciples, and being afraid.

The hypothesis that listening to Mark 16:8 might make a difference in the perception and evaluation of its credibility as an ending is confirmed. Listening to Mark's ending creates a perception of the story that makes sense as an ending. When Mark's composition has not been processed through auditory perceptual systems, it has been for many readers a puzzle that does not make sense as an ending. The implication is that Mark's ending has been misperceived as a result of the discontinuity between the auditory sensory data of the original composition and the visual sensory data of the silent reading of Mark's text.

Implications

The identification of the discontinuity between the silent reading of New Testament texts and the original character of the New Testament as compositions of sound has broader implications.

The Importance of Sound Mapping

Sound mapping lays a foundation for the study of New Testament compositions as sound. The implication of the difference between the auditory and visual sensory systems is that auditory perception is a necessary first step in scholarly methodology. Furthermore, the creation of a sound map requires a disciplined attention to the sounds of New Testament compositions that brings a degree of objectivity to the otherwise highly subjective voicing of the compositions.

Sound mapping also has major implications for the editing of New Testament compositions. The presentation of the Greek text and of the various vernacular translations as sound maps would more adequately represent the sound of the stories in a printed manuscript. Such reediting would include a re-examination of the punctuation of the texts as intonation units. The need for sound mapping of the New Testament carries with it the implication that the entire corpus of biblical literature needs to be reassessed and reedited as compositions of sound rather than as texts.

The Practice of New Testament Scholarship

The customary scholarly practice of silent reading needs to be modified as the dominant sensory perception of the Greek compositions that comprise the New Testament. A higher degree of congruence between the original sensory character of the Greek compositions and contemporary perception and analysis of the compositions as sound would lead to a more accurate and compelling interpretation of the New Testament in its original context. Performance criticism emerges from the current methodological mess as a central methodology for the study of the New Testament. The need for this reorientation of scholarly practice applies equally to the study of the Old Testament. The discontinuity between the sensorium of the ancient world and the sensorium of contemporary scholarship and the radical difference between auditory and visual perception justifies the description of this reorientation of biblical scholarship as a paradigm shift.

The Pedagogy of the New Testament

Teaching the New Testament as performance literature is a natural extension of this reorientation from sight to sound as the sensory matrix of learning and teaching. This new pedagogy is based on the performance of the compositions by both faculty and students. Among other benefits, it is more interesting and engaging for students.

The Liturgical Performance of Biblical Literature

The Bible is probably the most widely performed literature in the world, as happens every Sunday in millions of churches around the world.[43] However, in contrast to the performance of the Hebrew/Aramaic scriptures in synagogues and of the Quran in mosques, biblical performance in churches has largely lost contact with its ancient performance traditions. The present practice of liturgical proclamation has mirrored the assumption that the Bible is a disembodied text intended to be read in silence. The emotionally detached and monotone performance of the Bible in Christian liturgy has become a rote recital of texts characterized by poor preparation and audience boredom. Attention to the Bible as sound would contribute to the revitalization of the performance of the Scriptures in Christian worship.

Bibliography

Ackerman, Diane. *A Natural History of the Senses.* New York: Random House, 1990.

Augustine *The Confessions of Saint Augustine.* Translated by E. B. Pusey. Gutenberg Project. https://www.gutenberg.org/files/3296/3296-h/3296-h.htm#link2H_4_0006.

Best, Ernest. *Mark: The Gospel as Story.* Studies of the New Testament and Its World. Edinburgh: T. & T. Clark, 1983.

Boomershine, Thomas E. "Audience Address and Purpose in the Performance of Mark." In *Mark as Story: Retrospect and Prospect,* edited by Kelly R. Iverson and Christopher W. Skinner, 115–44. Resources for Biblical Study 65. Atlanta: SBL, 2011.

———. "Audience Asides and the Audiences of Mark: The Difference Performance Makes." In *From Text to Performance: Narrative and Performance Criticism in Dialogue and Debate,* edited by Kelly R. Iverson, 80–96. Biblical Performance Criticism Series 10. Eugene, OR: Cascade Books, 2014.

---

43. A current estimate is that there are approximately thirty-seven million churches in the world. This number does not include all of the house churches. The performance of the Bible happens in virtually all of those churches every Sunday; see https://www.quora.com/How-many-Christian-churches-are-there-in-the-world.

———. "Mark 16:8 and the Apostolic Commission." *Journal of Biblical Literature* 100 (1981) 225–39.
———. "Mark, the Storyteller: A Rhetorical-Critical Investigation of Mark's Passion and Resurrection Narrative." PhD diss., Columbia University: New York, 1974.
———. "The Medium and Message of John: Audience Address and Audience Identity in the Fourth Gospel." In *The Fourth Gospel in First-Century Media Culture*, edited by Anthony LeDonne and Tom Thatcher, 92–120. Library of New Testament Studies 426. London: T. & T. Clark, 2011.
———. "Peter's Denial as Polemic or Confession: The Implications of Media Criticism for Biblical Hermeneutics." *Semeia* 39 (1987) 47–68.
Boomershine, Thomas E., and Gilbert L. Bartholomew. "The Narrative Technique of Mark 16:8." *Journal of Biblical Literature* 100 (1981) 213–23.
Brynie, Faith Hickman. *Brain Sense: The Science of the Senses and How We Process the World around Us*. New York: Amacom, 2009.
Danove, Paul L. *The End of Mark's Story: A Methodological Study*. Biblical Interpretation Series 3. Leiden: Brill, 1993.
Edwards, James R. *The Gospel according to Mark*. Pillar New Testament Commentary. Grand Rapids: Eerdmans, 2002.
Farmer, William R. *The Last Twelve Verses of Mark*. Society of New Testament Studies Monograph Series 25. Cambridge: Cambridge University Press, 1974.
Gamble, Harry Y. *Books and Readers in the Early Church: A History of Early Christian Texts*. New Haven: Yale University Press. 1995.
Geldard, Frank A. *The Human Senses*. 2nd ed. New York: Wiley, 1972.
Hurtado, Larry W. *Destroyer of the Gods: Early Christian Distinctiveness in the Roman World*. Waco, TX: Baylor University Press, 2016.
———. "Oral Fixation and New Testament Studies? 'Orality,' 'Performance' and Reading Texts in Early Christianity." *New Testament Studies* 60 (2014) 321–40.
Kelber, Werner H. *The Oral and the Written Gospel: The Hermeneutics of Speaking and Writing in the Synoptic Tradition, Mark, Paul, and Q*. Philadelphia: Fortress, 1983.
———. *Imprints, Voiceprints, and Footprints of Memory: Collected Essays of Werner H. Kelber*. Resources for Biblical Study 74. Atlanta: Society of Biblical Literature, 2013.
Knox, B. W. "Silent Reading in Antiquity." *Greek, Roman and Byzantine Studies* 9 (1968) 421–35.
Lee, Margaret Ellen, and Bernard Brandon Scott. *Sound Mapping the New Testament*. Salem, OR: Polebridge. 2009.
Lincoln, Andrew T. "The Promise and the Failure: Mark 16:7, 8." *Journal of Biblical Literature* 108 (1989) 283–300.
Ludel, Jacqueline. *Introduction to Sensory Processes*. San Francisco: Freeman, 1978.
Nineham, D. E., *The Gospel of St. Mark*. Baltimore: Penguin, 1963.
Ong, Walter. *The Presence of the Word*. New Haven: Yale University Press, 1967.
Petersen, Norman R. "When Is the End not the End? Literary Reflections on the Ending of Mark's Narrative." *Interpretation* 34 (1980) 151–66.
Rhoads, David. "Performance Criticism: An Emerging Methodology in Second Testament Studies—Part I." *Biblical Theology Bulletin* 36 (2006) 118–33.
———. "Performance Criticism: An Emerging Methodology in Second Testament Studies—Part II." *Biblical Theology Bulletin* 36 (2006) 164–84.

Rhoads, David, and Joanna Dewey. "Performance Criticism: A Paradigm Shift in New Testament Studies." In *From Text to Performance: Narrative and Performance Criticisms in Dialogue and Debate*, edited by Kelly R. Iverson, 1–26. Biblical Performance Criticism Series 10. Eugene, OR: Cascade Books, 2014.

Scheppers, Frank. *The Colon Hypothesis: Word Order, Discourse Segmentation and Discourse Coherence in Ancient Greek*. Brussels: VUBPress, 2011.

———. "Discourse Segmentation, Discourse Structure and Sound Mapping, including an analysis of Mark 15." In *Sound Matters: New Testament Studies in Sound Mapping*, edited by Margaret E. Lee. Biblical Performance Criticism Series 16. Eugene, OR: Cascade Books, 2018.

Slusser, Michael. "Reading Silently in Antiquity." *Journal of Biblical Literature* 111 (1992) 499.

Stein, Robert H. "The Ending of Mark." *Bulletin for Biblical Research* 18.1 (2008) 79–98.

———. "Is Our Reading the Bible the Same as the Original Audience's Hearing It? A Case Study of the Gospel of Mark." *Journal of the Evangelical Theological Society* 46 (2003) 63–78.

Tolbert, Mary Ann. *Sowing the Gospel: Mark's World in Literary-Historical Perspective*. Minneapolis: Fortress, 1989.

Wilentz, Joan Steen. *The Senses of Man*. New York: Crowell, 1968.

Author Index

Ancient Authors

Aphthonius, 196
Aristotle, 17, 23, 137, 144, 201, 227, 228
Augustine, 218, 219

Cicero, 124, 129, 195, 196, 197, 198, 200, 201, 210

Demetrius, 23, 123, 196, 227
Demosthenes, 137, 198, 200, 201, 210
Dionysius of Halicarnassus, 16, 18, 23, 74, 75, 97, 185, 196, 227

Empedocles, 137
Epaphroditus, 91, 111
Euripides, 130

Gorgias, 194, 195

Hermogenes, 197
Homer, 1, 78

Ignatius, 209

Josephus, 189

Lysias, 21, 136, 137, 147, 224

Petrounias, 85, 86, 88, 118
Philo, 78, 79
Plato, 21, 78–79, 139, 224

Quintilian, 124, 195

Modern Authors

Achtemeier, Paul J., 180
Aland, Barbara, 42, 46, 53, 114, 115, 187, 229
Allen, W. Sidney, 87, 88, 89, 90, 138
Attridge, Harold W., 77
Aune, David E., 179, 180, 182, 185, 187, 189

Bakker, Engbert, 133, 149
Barclay, John M. G., 201
Barr, David, 179
Bartholomew, Adam Gilbert, 15
Bauer, David R., 9
Bauer, Walter, 61, 77, 78, 188
Beale, Gregory K., 80, 187, 189
BeDuhn, Jason David, 205
Benham, Priscilla C., 179
Berchman, Robert M., 202
Best, Ernest, 226
Betz, Hans Dieter, 95, 107, 201, 202, 205, 206, 208, 209, 210
Bewernick, Hanne, 77
Bigand, Emmanuel, 76
Black, Stephanie, 148
Blass, Friedrich, 61, 93
Bock, Emil, 188
Boomershine, Thomas E., 4, 5–6, 11, 13–14, 15, 16, 19, 22, 24, 69, 145, 149, 154, 160, 167, 168, 220, 227, 233, 234, 236
Botha, Pieter J. J., 69
Boxall, Ian, 189
Boyarin, Daniel, 199, 209

Author Index

Boyd, Gregory A., 188
Brandt, Jo-Ann, 127
Brickle, Jeffrey E., 3, 4, 11, 12, 14, 16, 70, 72, 73, 75, 77, 80, 181
Brucker, Ralph, 94, 100, 101, 102, 104, 106, 107, 110, 113
Brynie, Faith Hickman, 220, 222
Bubenik, V., 88
Burke, Kenneth, 198
Burridge, Richard A., 136
Butler, H. E., 195, 213
Butler, Shane, 80

Caird, G. B., 187
Campbell, Constantine R., 15, 16
Caragounis, Chrys C., 4, 16, 72–73, 74, 87, 106
Carruthers, Mary, 77
Chafe, Wallace, 22, 133, 140, 142, 145, 170, 228
Charles, R. H., 179, 180
Chidester, David, 69
Christidis, A. F., 86, 87
Ciampa, Roy E., 29, 32
Clay, Jenny Strauss, 80
Cohen, Shaye J. D., 200, 209
Collins, Adela Yarbro, 176, 179, 186, 225
Collins, Raymond F., 30, 34, 35, 38,
Couper-Kuhlen, Elizabeth, 146
Cranfield, C. E. B., 143, 167, 169
Croy, Clayton, 226
Culpepper, R. Allen, 167

Danker, Fredrick W., 188
Danove, Paul L., 226
Davis, Casey Wayne, 20, 181
de Waal, Kayle B., 5, 11, 12–13, 16, 24, 69
Dean, Margaret E., 9
   see also Lee, Margaret E.
Debrunner, Albert, 61, 93
Decker, Rodney J., 148, 158
Devine, A. M., 87, 90, 94, 138
Dewey, Arthur J., 199, 204
Dodd, C. H., 43, 65
Doty, William G., 204
Dover, K. J., 140

Drettas, G., 88, 94
Dykes, Jason, 76

Eckman, Barbara, 106
Edwards, James R., 225
Eisenbaum, Pamela, 199, 200
Ellingworth, Paul, 77
Elmer, Ian J., 202
Engberg-Pedersen, Troels, 199
Evans, Craig A., 147

Farmer, William R., 225
Fee, Gordon D., 28, 33, 34, 105, 106, 107
Fielding, Henry, 220
Fitzmyer, Joseph A., 46, 47, 63
Foley, John Miles, 10, 198
Ford, Josephine Massyngberde, 188
Fraenkel, Eduard, 21, 140
Fredriksen, Paula, 167, 200
Freese, John Henry, 201
Friesen, S. J., 182
Funk, Robert W., 61

Gamble, Harry Y., 179, 219
Gaventa, Beverly Roberts, 201
Geldard, Frank A., 222
Gnilka, Joachim, 102, 110
Griesbach, J. J., 226
Goldstein, D. M., 23
Gurd, Sean A., 97

Hall, Robert G., 202, 206, 207
Harris, William V., 179, 217
Harvey, John D., 180
Hays, Richard B., 80
Hoeksema, Herman, 180
Hoekstra, Marieke, 139
Hofius, Otfried, 105, 106, 107
Holloway, Paul A., 91, 94, 95, 96, 99, 103, 106, 114
Holmes, Michael W., 149, 156
Horrocks, Geoffrey, 86, 87, 88, 89, 93
Hort, Fenton John Anthony, 149, 164, 167
Hubbell, H. M., 195
Hultgren, Arland J., 43, 57
Hurtado, Larry W., 120, 134, 218

Author Index

Innis, Harold, 217
Iverson, Kelly R., 120

James, William, 199
Janse, Mark, 135, 136, 141
Jeal, Roy R., 80
Jefferson, Gail, 139
Jeremias, Joachim, 105, 106, 107
Johnson, Luke Timothy, 79
Joseph, B. D., 87, 88, 89
Jülicher, Adolf, 57
Juster, Norton, 193

Kazazis, J. N., 92
Keith, Chris, 2, 69
Kelber, Werner H., 1, 182
Kennedy George A., 201, 202, 206, 207, 208
Kennel, Gunter, 106
Kleist, James A., 20
Knox, B. W., 218
Köstenberger, Andreas J., 136
Kraybill, J. Nelson, 188
Kyrtatas, D. J., 87

Lamb, William R. S., 169
Lampe, Peter, 29
Lane, William L., 77
Lausberg, Heinrich, 122
Lee, Margaret E., 2, 4, 9, 11, 15, 17, 19, 23, 27, 40, 42, 44, 57, 67, 69, 75, 76, 84, 86, 92, 94, 96, 98, 121, 123, 124, 125, 126, 127, 129, 131, 134, 138, 149, 156, 171, 180, 181, 184, 185, 193, 194, 195, 196, 198, 204, 205, 209, 215, 227, 228
Levinas, Emmanuel, 194
Lincoln, Andrew T., 226
Lindemann, Andreas, 32
Livesey, Nina E., 5, 198, 201, 210
Lohmeyer, Ernst, 90, 94, 101, 105, 114
Lopez, Davina C., 202
Lord, Albert Bates, 1
Lupieri, Edmundo F., 185
Lyons, George, 205, 206, 209, 210

MacDowell, D. M., 195
MacEachren, Alan M., 76

Mackie, Scott D., 79
Maier, Paul L., 136
Malikouti-Drachman, A., 86, 90
Marcus, Joel, 225
Marshal, I. Howard, 47
Marshall, M. H. B., 140, 141
Martin, Troy, 201, 202
Martyn, J. Louis, 201, 202
Matthews, Victor H., 127
McAdams, Stephen, 76
Melion, Walter S., 80
Millard, Alan, 179
Minchin, Elizabeth, 80
Misch, George A., 206
Morton, Russell S., 180
Mounce, Robert H., 179, 190
Müller, Ulrich B., 90, 179

Naden, Roy, 180
Nanos, Mark D., 199, 200, 202, 204
Nässelqvist, Dan, 4–5, 11, 14, 15, 16, 17, 18, 19, 24, 69, 120, 121, 122, 123, 124, 125, 126, 128, 129, 130, 134, 140, 145
Nestle, Eberhard, 42, 46, 53, 114, 115, 149, 156, 167, 187, 229
Nikiforidou, K., 85, 86, 87, 88
Nineham, D. E., 225
Nock, A. D., 199

O'Brien, Peter T., 94, 95, 101, 103, 104, 106, 110, 111, 112, 114
Oestreich, Bernard, 4, 111
Ong, Walter J., 1, 198, 216
Osborne, Grant R., 180, 187, 189

Parry, Milman, 1
Pattermore, Stephen, 179
Paulien, Jon, 186, 187, 188
Pearson, Brook W. R., 19
Pederson, Sigfred, 110
Penner, Tod, 202
Perelmen, Chaïm, 198
Person, Raymond F., Jr., 2, 69
Petersen, Norman R., 226
Planudes, Maximus, 196
Plummer, Alfred A., 43
Porter, Stanley E., 19, 135, 136, 148

Author Index

Powell, Mark Allen, 9
Purves, Alex, 80

Räisänen, Heikki, 200
Rehkopf, Friedrich, 93
Resseguie, James L., 186
Reumann, John, 210
Rhoads, David, 185, 224
Richards, I. A., 198
Rico, Christophe, 136
Robbins, Vernon K., 80
Robins, Robert H., 198
Robinson, James M., 47
Roloff, Jürgen, 189
Rosner, Brian S., 29, 32
Rowe, Galen O., 198, 204
Runge, Steven E., 148
Russell, D. A., 128
Ryan, Sean Michael, 12

Sacks, Harvey, 139
Schenck, Kenneth, 79
Scheppers, Frank, 5, 20–23, 24, 42, 137, 139, 144, 224, 227, 228, 229
Schnabel, Eckhard J., 29, 37
Schuchard, Bruce G., 70
Scott, Bernard Brandon, 2, 3, 4, 8, 9, 11, 15, 17, 19, 23, 27, 40, 42, 44, 57, 61, 66, 67, 69, 75, 76, 84, 86, 92, 94, 96, 98, 121, 123, 124, 125, 126, 127, 129, 131, 134, 138, 149, 156, 171, 180, 181, 184, 185, 193, 194, 195, 196, 198, 204, 205, 209, 210, 215, 227, 228
Seal, David, 92
Segal, Alan, 199
Selby, Gary S., 80
Shiell, William, 180
Shiner, Whitney, 69
Sicoli, Mark A., 146
Siew, Antonius King Wai, 182
Silva, Moisés, 20
Skaggs, Rebecca, 179
Slings, Siem R., 133, 134, 137
Slocum, Terry A., 76
Slusser, Michael, 218
Smalley, Stephen S., 180, 186, 187, 189
Squire, Michael, 70, 77, 80

Stanley, Christopher D., 12
Stein, Robert H., 223, 225, 226
Stendahl, Krister, 199
Stephens, L. D., 87, 90, 94, 138
Stirewalt, M. Luther, 87
Stowers, Stanley K., 199
Sumney, Jerry, 201
Sweet, John, 180, 182, 187, 189
Swete, Henry Barclay, 180

Talbert, Charles H., 180
Tannehill, Robert C., 65
Tannen, Deborah, 135, 139
Taylor, Ann, 141
Taylor, D. R. Fraser, 76
Thatcher, Tom, 1, 80, 224
Thiselton, Anthony C., 28
Thompson, James W., 77, 78
Thrall, Margaret E., 146, 147
Titrud, Kermit, 185, 186
Tolbert, Mary Ann, 226
Tonstad, Sigve, 188
Tsagalis, Christos, 80

Vahrenhorst, Martin, 115
Valiavitcharska, Vessela, 193–97, 203, 208, 211
Vatri, Alessandro, 135
Vines, Michael E., 136
Voelz, James W., 147, 148
Vos, Johan S., 203

Wackernagel, Jacob, 21, 141, 228
Walter, Nikolaus, 91, 114
Walton, Steve, 136
Walz, Christian, 196
Webb, Ruth, 80
Weiss, Johannes, 37
Welborn, L. L., 32, 37
Westcott, Brooke Foss, 149, 164, 167
White, Adam G., 3, 28
White, L. Michael, 199
Wick, Peter, 99, 100, 115
Wilentz, Joan Steen, 220
Winter, Bruce W., 32
Wojtkowiak, Heiko, 91, 102, 110, 111
Wooten, Cecil W., 200
Yoos, George E., 201

Zerubavel, Eviatar, 76
Zerwick, Maximilian, 52

Zetterholm, Magnus, 199, 200

Scripture Index

Exodus
10:21	189
16:2	58
16:7	58
16:8	58
25:40	78

Numbers
13:1—14:38	78

Deuteronomy
6:5	50
9:23	78

Psalms
1:3	187
11:6	186
18:13	186
52:8	187
80:8–11	186
80:14–16	186
92:12–13	187

Isaiah
2:2–4	200
2:13	187
10:16–20	186
29:1–6	186
29:14	30, 31
30:30	186
44:3–4	187

Jeremiah
11:16–17	186
21:12–14	186
51:25	187
51:41–42	186

Ezekiel
5:1–4	186
13:11–13	186
15:6–7	186, 187
20:47–48	187
32:7–8	189
39:1–6	186

Joel
1:19–20	186, 187
2:10	189

Amos
1:4	186
7:4	186

Micah
4:1–3	200

Zechariah
8:21–23	200
11:1	187

Scripture Index

Matthew

5–7	9, 21, 136–37
9:20	48
13:17	47
13:24–30	43
13:36–43	43
19:16	48
24:19	189
27:26	156
27:50	166
28:16–20	239

Mark

1	167
1:16	233
1:22	233
1:44	237
2:15	233
3:1–27	148
3:21	233
4:13–20	43
4:41	238
5:8	233
5:15	238
5:22–24	233
5:27–28	233
5:28	233
5:33	238
5:35–41	148
5:35–43	233
5:42	233
6:6	230
6:17	233
6:18	233
6:20	233
6:31	233
6:45–52	233
6:48	233
6:50	238
6:52	240
7:3–4	233
8	150
8:1–13	148
9:6	233
9:32	238
9:34	233
10:22	233
10:32	238
11:13	233
11:14	230
11:18	238
11:28	151
11:32	238
12:1–5	148
12:12	230, 238
12:17	230
12:28b–32	50
12:30–31	50
12:38	50
13:24–25	189
14–15	170
14:1	170
14:1–2	234
14:1—16:8	4, 5, 13, 15, 22, 227
14:2	233, 234
14:3	234
14:12	170
14:11	231
14:28	226
14:31	231
14:32–41	148
14:40	233
14:50	231
14:50–52	236
14:53–72	148
14:56	233
14:65	231
14:72	231
15	133, 149–73, 227, 229
15:1	149, 150–51, 159
15:1–24	150, 171
15:2a	150
15:2–5	151–53
15:6–7	151, 152, 153–54
15:8	142, 154
15:8–15	143, 154–56
15:10	233
15:11–24	136
15:16	156, 172
15:16–17	158
15:16–24	142, 156, 157–59, 165
15:17–19	141–42
15:20	231
15:21	171, 233
15:23–24	158

Scripture Index

15:24	142	10:2–12	46
15:25a	150	10:2–16	45–46
15:25	159	10:13	46
15:25–32	159–60	10:13–15	46
15:25–41	171	10:16	46
15:32	231	10:17–24	46–47
15:33a	150	10:24	47
15:33	160	10:25	49–50, 53, 54
15:33–34	160	10:25–37	44, 47–48
15:34a	150, 165	10:26–29	50–52
15:34	167	10:28	56
15:34–36	162–65	10:30	48, 52–53, 54
15:34–39	161–69	10:31	54
15:36	152, 155	10:31–32	53–54
15:37	138, 231	10:32–35	55–56
15:37–39	165–69	10:33	54–55
15:39	138	10:33–35	43, 52–56
15:40	149	10:36–37	56
15:40–41	161, 169–70, 173	10:38–42	48–49
15:42a	150	11:1	45, 50
15:42	150	11:31	48
15:42–45	172	11:32	48
15:42–47	170	13:30	48
15:42–48	171	15	44, 58
15:46–47	171	15:1	62, 64, 67
16:1	150, 170	15:1–2	58, 64
16:1–8	148, 226	15:1–3	64
16:3–4	147	15:1—16:31	66
16:4	233	15:3–7	58–59
16:7	226, 237	15:5	60, 61
16:8	6, 215, 216, 225, 226, 227, 229, 230, 231, 232, 233, 234, 235, 237, 238, 239, 240	15:6	61
		15:7	61
		15:8–10	59
		15:9	60, 61
16:9–20	225	15:11–32	60

Luke

		15:23	61
		15:24	58, 60, 61
2:11	45	15:25–32	60–62
2:25	48	16:1	64, 65
6:5	45	16:1–8	62
7:13	45	16:1–16	44, 64
7:29	52	16:8a–16	64
7:35	52	16:8b–13	65
8:11–15	43	16:8b–16	65
9:51–53	44	16:9–16	63–65
9:51—19:27	44, 45	16:14	64
10:1	44–45, 46	16:31	65
10:1–42	43, 49	17:1	65

Luke (continued)

19:28	44
18:14	52
23:50	48
24:13	48
24:36-49	239

John

1-4	14, 120
1:1-5	123
1:3	14
1:3-4	121, 122, 123, 131
1:4	14
1:4-5	123
1:7	129
1:11	129
1:13	129
1:18	129
1:26b-27	129
1:45 b-c	129
1:47-51	125
1:48c-d	129
1:50	130, 131
1:50b-c	129
2:19	129
2:19b-c	129
3:17	129
3:21	129
3:26d-e	129
3:36	129
4:9	128
4:28	127
4:29	127, 128, 131
21:15-19	239

Romans

4:9-12	199

1 Corinthians

1-4	27, 28
1:18	28, 29-30
1:18-24	35
1:18-25	28
1:18-31	27, 28
1:19	30
1:20	31-32
1:21	32-33
1:22-24	33-35
1:25	35
1:26-29	36-37
1:26-31	28, 36-38
1:27-28	27, 28
1:30-31	38
2:1-5	28
2:5	28
3:18	37

2 Corinthians

1:1	204-06
1:3-7	204
6:14-15	189

Galatians

1:1	202, 203
1:1-5	202
1:6-9	206
1:6-11	208
1:8-9	206
1:9	208
1:10	207, 208
1:10-11	208
1:10-12	202
1:10-17	206-11
1:10—2:21	205, 207
1:11—5:1	207-08
1:14	209
1:15	208
3:1	115

Philippians

1:1-2	90
1:3-11	90
1:11-20	90
1:15-17	97
1:18	97
1:21-26	90
1:22—2:18	91
1:23	95
1:25-26	91, 95
1:26	90, 91, 92, 114

1:27	90, 91, 92, 93–96, 98, 116
1:27–30	91, 93–96, 102
1:27—2:16	91, 114
1:27—2:18	4, 91
1:28	97–98
1:29–30	98–100
1:30	91
2:1	91, 101–02
2:1–4	91, 101–04
2:1–11	91
2:2	102–03
2:3–4	103–04
2:4–5	91
2:5–7b	106
2:5–11	105–07
2:6–11	105
2:9–11	99
2:12	91, 116
2:12–13	108–11
2:12–18	91, 102, 108–15, 116
2:14–16b	112–14
2:16	91, 96, 114
2:16b	91
2:16–17	92
2:16–18	92
2:17	91, 114
2:17–18	91, 92, 95, 114–15, 116
2:19	91
2:20–21	91
2:25	111
2:30	91
3:1	91
3:2–11	199
3:8	85
3:17	100
4:1	91
4:4	91
4:10	91

Hebrews

1:1	77
1:2	78
1:3	78
3:1—4:16	78
4:1–11	77
8	78
8:5	78, 79
11:1	78
12:5	79
12:8	79
12:11	79

1 John

1:1–4	70–72
1:3	73

Revelation

1:3	180
8:1—11:19	180
8:7–12	179, 180, 183–85, 189, 190
8:7—9:18	188
12–13	188
12:3	188
12:4	188
16:13	188
16:19	188
18:12–13	188

www.ingramcontent.com/pod-product-compliance
Lightning Source LLC
Chambersburg PA
CBHW030823230426
43667CB00008B/1349